THE CAMBRIDGE COMPANION TO
ORTHODOX CHRISTIAN THEOLOGY

Orthodox Christian theology is often presented as the direct inheritor of the doctrine and tradition of the early Church. But continuity with the past is only part of the truth; it would be false to conclude that the eastern section of the Christian Church is in any way static. Orthodoxy, building on its patristic foundations, has blossomed in the modern period. This volume focuses on the way Orthodox theological tradition is understood and lived today. It explores the Orthodox understanding of what theology is: an expression of the Church's life of prayer, both corporate and personal, from which it can never be separated.

Besides discussing aspects of doctrine, the book portrays the main figures, themes and developments that have shaped Orthodox thought. There is particular focus on the Russian and Greek traditions, as well as the dynamic but less well-known Antiochian tradition and the Orthodox presence in the West.

Mary B. Cunningham is a lecturer in theology at the University of Nottingham. Her publications include *Faith in the Byzantine World* (2002).

Elizabeth Theokritoff is an independent scholar and translator, with particular interests in liturgical theology and theology of creation. She has lectured and led workshops widely and published numerous articles.

CAMBRIDGE COMPANIONS TO RELIGION
A series of companions to major topics and key figures in theology and religious studies. Each volume contains specially commissioned chapters by international scholars which provide an accessible and stimulating introduction to the subject for new readers and non-specialists.

Other titles in the series

THE CAMBRIDGE COMPANION TO CHRISTIAN DOCTRINE
edited by Colin Gunton (1997)
ISBN 0 521 47118 4 hardback   ISBN 0 521 47695 X paperback

THE CAMBRIDGE COMPANION TO BIBLICAL INTERPRETATION
edited by John Barton (1998)
ISBN 0 521 48144 9 hardback   ISBN 0 521 48593 2 paperback

THE CAMBRIDGE COMPANION TO DIETRICH BONHOEFFER
edited by John de Gruchy (1999)
ISBN 0 521 58258 X hardback   ISBN 0 521 58781 6 paperback

THE CAMBRIDGE COMPANION TO KARL BARTH
edited by John Webster (2000)
ISBN 0 521 58476 0 hardback   ISBN 0 521 58560 0 paperback

THE CAMBRIDGE COMPANION TO CHRISTIAN ETHICS
edited by Robin Gill (2001)
ISBN 0 521 77070 X hardback   ISBN 0 521 77918 9 paperback

THE CAMBRIDGE COMPANION TO JESUS
edited by Markus Bockmuehl (2001)
ISBN 0 521 79261 4 hardback   ISBN 0 521 79678 4 paperback

THE CAMBRIDGE COMPANION TO FEMINIST THEOLOGY
edited by Susan Frank Parsons (2002)
ISBN 0 521 66327 X hardback   ISBN 0 521 66380 6 paperback

THE CAMBRIDGE COMPANION TO MARTIN LUTHER
edited by Donald K. McKim (2003)
ISBN 0 521 81648 3 hardback   ISBN 0 521 01673 8 paperback

THE CAMBRIDGE COMPANION TO ST PAUL
edited by James D. G. Dunn (2003)
ISBN 0 521 78155 8 hardback   ISBN 0 521 78694 0 paperback

THE CAMBRIDGE COMPANION TO POSTMODERN THEOLOGY
edited by Kevin J. Vanhoozer (2003)
ISBN 0 521 79062 X hardback   ISBN 0 521 79395 5 paperback

THE CAMBRIDGE COMPANION TO JOHN CALVIN
edited by Donald K. McKim (2004)
ISBN 0 521 81647 5 hardback   ISBN 0 521 01672 X paperback

THE CAMBRIDGE COMPANION TO HANS URS VON BALTHASAR
edited by Edward T. Oakes, SJ and David Moss (2004)
ISBN 0 521 81467 7 hardback   ISBN 0 521 89147 7 paperback

THE CAMBRIDGE COMPANION TO REFORMATION THEOLOGY
edited by David Bagchi and David Steinmetz (2004)
ISBN 0 521 77224 9 hardback   ISBN 0 521 77662 7 paperback

Continued

THE CAMBRIDGE COMPANION TO AMERICAN JUDAISM
edited by Dana Evan Kaplan (2005)
ISBN 0 521 82204 1 hardback   ISBN 0 521 52951 4 paperback

THE CAMBRIDGE COMPANION TO KARL RAHNER
edited by Declan Marmion and Mary E. Hines (2005)
ISBN 0 521 83288 8 hardback   ISBN 0 521 54045 3 paperback

THE CAMBRIDGE COMPANION TO FRIEDRICH SCHLEIERMACHER
edited by Jacqueline Mariña (2005)
ISBN 0 521 81448 0 hardback   ISBN 0 521 89137 X paperback

THE CAMBRIDGE COMPANION TO THE GOSPELS
edited by Stephen C. Barton (2006)
ISBN 0 521 80766 2 hardback   ISBN 0 521 00261 3 paperback

THE CAMBRIDGE COMPANION TO THE QUR'AN
edited by Jane Dammen McAuliffe (2006)
ISBN 0 521 83160 1 hardback   ISBN 0 521 53934 X paperback

THE CAMBRIDGE COMPANION TO JONATHAN EDWARDS
edited by Stephen J. Stein (2007)
ISBN 0 521 85290 0 hardback   ISBN 0 521 61805 3 paperback

THE CAMBRIDGE COMPANION TO EVANGELICAL THEOLOGY
edited by Timothy Larsen and Daniel J. Trier (2007)
ISBN 0 521 84698 6 hardback   ISBN 0 521 60974 7 paperback

CAMBRIDGE COMPANION TO MODERN JEWISH PHILOSOPHY
edited by Michael L. Morgan and Peter Eli Gordon (2007)
ISBN 0 521 81312 3 hardback   ISBN 0 521 01255 4 paperback

THE CAMBRIDGE COMPANION TO THE TALMUD AND RABBINIC LITERATURE
edited by Charlotte E. Fonrobert and Martin S. Jaffee (2007)
ISBN 0 521 84390 1 hardback   ISBN 0 521 60508 3 paperback

THE CAMBRIDGE COMPANION TO LIBERATION THEOLOGY, SECOND EDITION
edited by Christopher Rowland (2007)
ISBN 9780521868839 hardback   ISBN 9780521688932 paperback

THE CAMBRIDGE COMPANION TO THE JESUITS
edited by Thomas Worcester (2008)
ISBN 9780521857314 hardback   ISBN 9780521673969 paperback

THE CAMBRIDGE COMPANION TO CLASSICAL ISLAMIC THEOLOGY
edited by Tim Winter (2008)
ISBN 9780521780582 hardback   ISBN 9780521785495 paperback

THE CAMBRIDGE COMPANION TO PURITANISM
edited by John Coffey and Paul Lim (2008)
ISBN 9780521860888 hardback   ISBN 9780521678001 paperback

Forthcoming

THE CAMBRIDGE COMPANION TO PAUL TILLICH
edited by Russell Re Manning

THE CAMBRIDGE COMPANION TO THE VIRGIN MARY
edited by Sarah Boss

THE CAMBRIDGE COMPANION TO ANCIENT CHRISTIANITY
edited by Rebecca Lyman

THE CAMBRIDGE COMPANION TO

ORTHODOX CHRISTIAN THEOLOGY

Edited by Mary B. Cunningham and
Elizabeth Theokritoff

CAMBRIDGE
UNIVERSITY PRESS

CAMBRIDGE UNIVERSITY PRESS
Cambridge, New York, Melbourne, Madrid, Cape Town, Singapore, São Paulo,
Delhi, Dubai, Tokyo

Cambridge University Press
The Edinburgh Building, Cambridge CB2 8RU, UK

Published in the United States of America by Cambridge University Press, New York

www.cambridge.org
Information on this title: www.cambridge.org/9780521683388

First published 2008
Third printing 2010

Printed in the United Kingdom at the University Press, Cambridge

A catalogue record for this publication is available from the British Library

ISBN 978-0-521-86484-8 hardback
ISBN 978-0-521-68338-8 paperback

This volume is dedicated to the memory of Nicolas and Militza Zernov, without whose labours such a book might never have been commissioned – or would certainly have looked very different.

May their memory be eternal!

Contents

Notes on contributors

Dr Nicolas Abou Mrad is Assistant Professor of Biblical Studies at Saint John of Damascus Faculty of Theology, University of Balamand (Lebanon), and Lecturer at various non-Orthodox theological schools in Lebanon. He is author of various articles and reviews in biblical theology and literature.

The Rt Revd Dr Hilarion Alfeyev holds doctorates from Oxford and Paris. He is currently the Moscow Patriarchate's Bishop of Austria and Representative to the European Institutions. He has published widely in the areas of Byzantine and Syriac patristics, Church history, dogmatic theology and contemporary theological, moral and social issues. His writings in English include *St Symeon the New Theologian and Orthodox Tradition* (2000), *The Spiritual World of Isaac the Syrian* (2000), *The Mystery of Faith. An Introduction to the Teaching and Spirituality of the Orthodox Church* (2002) and *Orthodox Witness Today* (2006).

The Very Revd Boris Bobrinskoy has served as Dean and Professor of Dogmatic Theology at St Sergius Institute of Orthodox Theology in Paris. A pupil of Georges Florovsky and Nicolas Afanasiev, he has published numerous studies on the theology of the Trinity and the Holy Spirit, the Church, and the Eucharist. Translations of his writings include *The Mystery of the Trinity: Trinitarian Experience and Vision in the Biblical and Patristic Tradition*, trans. A. P. Gythiel (1999) and *The Mystery of the Church* (2005).

Dr Peter Bouteneff is Associate Professor in Theology at St Vladimir's Seminary, New York, having served for five years as Executive Secretary for Faith and Order at the World Council of Churches. He has written extensively on Orthodox relations with other churches, as well as on patristic and dogmatic themes. Recent publications include *Sweeter than Honey: Orthodox Thinking on Dogma and Truth* (2006) and *Beginnings: Ancient Christian Readings of the Biblical Creation Narratives* (2008).

Dr Augustine Casiday is Lecturer in Historical Theology and Director of the Monastic Studies Programme at the University of Wales, Lampeter. He is author of *Tradition and Theology in St John Cassian* (2007), has translated works by Evagrius Ponticus and St Mark the Monk, and co-edited (with Andrew Louth) *Byzantine Orthodoxies* (2006) and Volume II of *The Cambridge History of Christianity*.

The Revd Dr John Chryssavgis has taught at universities in Sydney, Australia, and Boston, USA. A deacon of the Greek Orthodox Archdiocese in America, he has written and lectured widely, and currently serves as theological advisor to the

Ecumenical Patriarchate on environmental issues. His writings include *Soul Mending: The Art of Spiritual Direction* (2000) and *In the Heart of the Desert: The Spirituality of the Desert Fathers and Mothers* (2002).

Dr Mary B. Cunningham is Lecturer in the Department of Theology at the University of Nottingham, where she teaches Eastern and Western Church history and patristics. She has published numerous articles on Byzantine homiletics, spirituality and early Church history. Her books include (with P. Allen) *Preacher and Audience: Studies in Early Christian and Byzantine Homiletics* (1998) and *Faith in the Byzantine World* (2002).

Mariamna Fortounatto studied icon painting under Leonide Ouspensky in Paris. For many years she taught icon painting at a school organised at the Russian Orthodox Cathedral in London, as well as teaching students individually and advising former students of Professor Ouspensky. She has lectured widely in a freelance capacity on the history, theology and meaning of icons at ecumenical gatherings, extra-mural departments of universities and theological colleges. Publications include 'The icon' in *The Cambridge Encyclopaedia of Russia and the Soviet Union* (Cambridge University Press, 1981).

Sister Nonna Verna Harrison, an Orthodox nun and theologian, is currently Assistant Professor of Church History at Saint Paul School of Theology in Kansas City, Missouri. Her writings include *Grace and Human Freedom according to St Gregory of Nyssa* (1992) and *St Basil the Great on the Human Condition* (2005), as well as scholarly articles in the fields of patristics and Orthodox theology.

The Very Revd Dr John A. Jillions is Assistant Professor of Theology at the Sheptytsky Institute of Eastern Christian Studies at Saint Paul University in Ottawa, Canada, and Dean of Annunciation Orthodox Cathedral in Ottawa. He was founding Principal of the Institute for Orthodox Christian Studies in Cambridge, England, and has served as a priest in the USA, Australia, Greece and England. He contributed chapters to *Orthodox and Wesleyan Spirituality* (2007) and *Evangelicalism and the Orthodox Church* (2001).

The Very Revd Leonid Kishkovsky is Director of External Affairs for the Orthodox Church in America and Editor of its Church-wide publication, *The Orthodox Church*. He has written and lectured widely on Orthodoxy in America and the Church in Eastern Europe. His published writings include 'Reflections on American Orthodoxy' in *Orthodox Christians in North America: 1794–1994* (1995) and 'Patriarch Tikhon: a vision of Orthodox mission in the New World' in *The Legacy of St. Vladimir: Byzantium–Russia–America* (1990). His addresses and editorials are available on www.oca.org.

The Very Revd Archimandrite Ephrem Lash lectured in theology at the University of Newcastle (1979–85) and is widely known as a translator, with a particular interest in liturgical and scriptural translation. Much of his work is available on his web-site, www.anastasis.org.uk. His writings include *Kontakia: On the Life of Christ. St Romanos the Melodist* (1995). He was also the principal translator of *The Divine Liturgy of our Father among the Saints John Chrysostom* (1995).

The Revd Andrew Louth is Professor of Patristic and Byzantine Studies at the University of Durham, having previously taught patristics at the University of Oxford and Byzantine history at the University of London (Goldsmith's College). His writings include *Maximus the Confessor* (1996), *St John Damascene. Tradition and Originality in Byzantine Theology* (2002) and *The Origins of the Christian Mystical Tradition from Plato to Denys* (1981).

Dr Aristotle Papanikolaou is Associate Professor of Theology in the Department of Theology and Co-Director of the Orthodox Christian Studies Program at Fordham University, New York. He also serves on the Social and Moral Issues Commission for the Standing Conference of the Canonical Orthodox Bishops in America. Recent publications include 'Byzantium, orthodoxy and democracy' in *Journal of the American Academy of Religion* 71.1 (March 2003), 75–98, and *Being with God: Trinity, Apophaticism, and Divine–Human Communion* (2006).

Dr Athanasios N. Papathanasiou teaches science of religion and missiology at the State Ecclesiastical Academy in Athens, and is Editor-in-Chief of the theological quarterly *Synaxi*. His publications include 'Missionary experience and academic quest. The research situation in Greece' in *European Traditions in the Study of Religion in Africa*, ed. Frieder Ludwig and Afe Adogame (2004); *Religion, Ideology and Science* (2004) and *Future, the Background of History: Essays on Church Mission in an Age of Globalization* (2005).

The Revd Dr Michael Plekon is Professor in the Department of Sociology/Anthropology and the Program in Religion and Culture, Baruch College of the City University of New York. He has published extensively on Kierkegaard's theology and social criticism, and on the lives and writings of theologians of the Russian emigration in Paris and the USA. Recent books include *Living Icons: Persons of Faith in the Eastern Church* (2002) and (with Sarah Hinlicky) *Discerning the Signs of the Times: The Theological Vision of Elisabeth Behr-Sigel* (2002).

The Revd Dr Matthew Steenberg is Professor of Theology and Head of Theology and Religious Studies at Trinity and All Saints College, Leeds, having previously taught patristics at Greyfriars, University of Oxford. He has published numerous articles on themes in patristics and Church history. His monograph *Irenaeus on Creation* will be published soon, and a critical translation and commentary on Irenaeus is also forthcoming. Matthew Steenberg also maintains a web-site dedicated to Orthodox patristic study at www.monachos.net.

The Revd Dr Theodore G. Stylianopoulos is Archbishop Iakovos Professor of Orthodox Theology and New Testament at Holy Cross Greek Orthodox School of Theology in Brookline, Massachusetts. He has written many articles and a number of books, including *The New Testament: An Orthodox Perspective* (1997) and *The Spirit of Truth: Ecumenical Perspectives on the Holy Spirit* (1985).

Dr Elizabeth Theokritoff is an independent scholar and theological translator. She has lectured at Holy Cross Greek Orthodox Theological School in Brookline, Massachusetts, and the Institute for Orthodox Christian Studies in Cambridge, and written widely on liturgical theology and Christian ecology. She has contributed chapters to S. T. Kimbrough (ed.), *Orthodox and Wesleyan Scriptural Understanding and Practice* (2005), and Lukas Vischer (ed.), *Witnessing in the Midst of a Suffering Creation* (2007).

Preface

Gone are the days when an occasional intrepid traveller would venture to Eastern Europe or the Levant and return with colourful tales of the beliefs and practices of the natives. Several Orthodox countries now belong to the European Union; there is an extensive body of Orthodox literature, both original and translated, available in Western languages; Orthodox theologians are to be found at many major Western universities. Yet the Orthodox theological tradition as a whole remains surprisingly little known. One could easily get the impression that the Christian East belongs to the realm of history.

The present volume aims to tell a different story. Building on its patristic foundations, Orthodox theology has blossomed in the modern period. This is true also of the still less well-known Oriental Orthodox (non-Chalcedonian) traditions, which fall outside the scope of this volume. These ancient Churches, with their very diverse histories and traditions, deserve a volume to themselves and cannot adequately be treated as an appendix to Chalcedonian Orthodoxy.

One can also not speak about Orthodox theology without referring to the Church Fathers; and even where the patristic background is shared by Christians of East and West, it cannot be assumed that the Fathers are read in the same way. Nevertheless, the predominant focus of this book will be on the Orthodox theological tradition as it is understood and lived today. Some basics of historical as well as geographical background are given in the introductory chapter. Following this overview, the book is divided into two parts. The first covers various aspects of doctrine, while the second introduces some of the main figures, themes and movements of ideas that have helped to shape Orthodox theology as it exists today. We have defined 'theology' broadly, so as to include aspects of doctrine that would more strictly be classed as cosmology, anthropology or ecclesiology. We also include areas that today would be categorised as 'spirituality'; this reflects a conviction that Orthodox theology cannot be separated from the Christian's effort to live the truth. On the other hand, it should be pointed out that 'Orthodox theology' is not synonymous with 'Eastern Christian thought'. The fascinating area of Russian religious philosophy therefore falls outside the proper scope of this volume, even though there will be several references to its influence.

It is our hope that this book will not only be informative about the specifics of Orthodox teaching, but also – and very importantly – convey the Orthodox understanding of what theology is: not an academic discipline or a set of philosophical propositions, but an expression of the Christian life of prayer, both corporate and personal, from which it can never be separated. We have tried to convey this approach to theology through the sequence of chapters. Part I begins with two chapters relating to the sources of theology, affirming the inextricable connection of scripture, tradition and the Church, especially the Church as worshipping community. Christian theology will always be grounded in scripture, but the starting point for understanding scripture is its use and interpretation in liturgy. Chapters 3–6 cover fundamental doctrinal themes: the Holy Trinity; the created order in relation to its Creator; the theological understanding of the human being as a creature in God's image; the doctrine of Christ and the understanding of salvation in Christ. The next four chapters (7–10) can be seen as dealing with sub-themes of Christology, exploring the implications of the Incarnation and the salvation brought thereby. We have placed 'eschatology' immediately after 'Christ and salvation' in order to emphasise that eschatology does not concern only the 'last things' in a chronological sense: the Church is interested in the 'last things' because it lives in the time inaugurated with the coming of the 'last Adam'. This 'inaugurated eschatology' is glimpsed in the Church, the body of Christ on earth (Ch. 8); and it is expressed in the icon, which reveals the transformation of human beings and the entire creation in the light of Christ's Incarnation (Ch. 9). The same eschatological vision informs the 'spiritual way' (Ch. 10), the practical path by which humans appropriate salvation as the divine image in each of us is restored to the likeness of God.

The second part of the book tries to give more of the context of Orthodox Christian theology and witness today. Inevitably, it is a collection of samplings with certain overlaps and it is far from comprehensive. Yet, disparate though these chapters are, they share a common theme: theology comes out of the experience of the Church. It may be the experience of the Church through the ages as it appropriates the work of the councils and Church Fathers (Ch. 11), or the experience of local Churches and communities as they bring the resources of Christian tradition to bear on particular historical circumstances. It may be the testimony of people of

1at this raises for both Orthodox and Western Christians form the subject
f the final chapter.

We have endeavoured to touch on a broad range of subjects and, as a
:sult, treatment of important ideas is often tantalisingly brief. It is a
1atter of particular regret that there is no space to explore aspects of
pplied theology': approaches to ethical issues, engagement with
:ience, questions of Church and society. Several of the chapters do,
owever, contain enough references to this aspect of Orthodox thinking
) make clear its importance; and the select bibliography includes some
1rther reading on this subject.

Our practice in transliterating Greek, Russian and Serbian names gen-
rally follows accepted conventions so as to distract the reader as little as
ossible. Thus, we have followed the general practice among patristic scho-
1rs of latinising Greek names such as Evagrius or Maximus the Confessor.
Vith more modern figures, however, we try to give a phonetic translitera-
10n of the name, unless it is widely used in English in another form (thus
Jikodimos of the Holy Mountain, but Florovsky rather than Florovskii).

As Archimandrite Ephrem Lash points out in his chapter, the Ortho-
ox Churches accept the Septuagint, or the Greek translation of the
lebrew Old Testament, as their scripture. We have therefore cited
'salms according to the numbers employed in the Septuagint, with the
lebrew numbers appended in brackets. In order to avoid confusion, we
ave used the names of Old Testament books familiar to readers from
nglish translations of the Hebrew, such as 1–2 Samuel and 1–2 Kings
1stead of 1–4 Reigns; again, however, we have added the Greek names
f books at the first citation of each.

We have endeavoured to include definitions of terms that might be
1nfamiliar. If a term is not defined when it is introduced, the reader's
irst recourse should be to the Glossary. Failing that, the Index may turn
ip passages where the term is explained more fully.

In the matter of 'inclusive language', we should clarify that many
)rthodox authors, writing in English, are accustomed to using 'man' in
1n inclusive sense: this is equivalent to the Greek word 'anthropos', a
vord which, depending on its gender, may refer to human beings of both
exes. There are contexts in which one can just as well speak of humans
ingly ('the human person'), or as a plurality ('humans') or as a collective
humanity'). But none of the circumlocutions for 'man' fully conveys
hat sense, so important to Orthodox anthropology, of humankind personi-
ied as one unified creature – the one who falls in Adam, says 'yes' to God
1 the Virgin Mary and is raised from the dead in Christ.

holiness, whose theological insights are shaped by 'wh
seen' (cf. 1 Jn 1.1). We had planned to include a chapte
Orthodox theology, but unfortunately this proved im
there is a lesson here in the hiddenness of holiness, it:
trumpet its own contributions.

It is because of the Orthodox emphasis on the cor
theology that we have decided not to single out a
figures to be the subject of separate chapters. This migh
trating for the reader; but it avoids creating the impr
schools of theological thinking. As the doctrinal chapte
Orthodox instinct is to focus on a synthesis rather tl
strands of thought. For more systematic introducti
figures mentioned in this book, we would refer the rea
as *The Historical Dictionary of the Orthodox Church*,[1] 1
tionary of Eastern Christianity[2] or *The Blackwell Com
Christianity*.[3]

Part II does introduce some of the main theological f
the background of broader movements of which they
movements may be obviously international in scope, su
ery of the Church Fathers in which many Orthodox ar
tians have been engaged (Ch. 12), or the revival ir
thought (Ch. 13) which has done much to define the 1
in the West. In other cases, we have focused for the sa
on a particular local Church (Greece, Antioch, Russi
has been made precisely because their story is of more t
Greek theology is increasingly known in the West, and h
in the Balkans, where many theologians are Greek-educ
see mutual influences and convergence of interests betw
the Russian émigré and Greek traditions; this is illust
study of the very topical theme of personhood. The ch
reminds us that the challenge of living and bearing witne
a non-Christian society – an unwelcome novelty to We
has been the experience of many of the ancient East
most of their existence.

We conclude with two chapters suggesting some of t
Orthodox theology may take in the twenty-first century.
Russia, home to most of the world's Orthodox Christian
crucible for debate of quite novel questions about the pl
in modern society and the meaning of theology today.
presence in the West is also of increasing importanc

It only remains to express our gratitude to all who have worked with us on this volume. This includes above all our contributors for their painstaking work and gracious patience throughout the editing process, as well as Dr Katharina Brett of Cambridge University Press, for suggesting the project and for her unfailing, helpful guidance. We would also like to thank Dr Peter Gilbert for compiling the index, Dr George Theokritoff for his help with the map, and many others who have contributed help and support in a variety of ways, including Drs David and Mary Ford, Zaga Gavrilović, Dr Tamara Grdzelidze, Dr Valerie Karras, and Dr Michel Nseir.

Despite the efforts of so many, this volume is not without its limitations, for which we take full responsibility. It is our hope, however, that the reader will be able to look beyond them and so discover some of the riches of the Orthodox Christian tradition.

Notes

1. M. Prokurat (ed.), *The Historical Dictionary of the Orthodox Church* (Lanham, MD, and London: Scarecrow Publishers, 1996).
2. K. Parry, D. J. Melling, D. Brady, S. H. Griffith and J. F. Healey (eds.), *The Blackwell Dictionary of Eastern Christianity* (Oxford: Blackwell Publishing, 1999).
3. K. Parry (ed.), *The Blackwell Companion to Eastern Christianity* (Oxford: Blackwell Publishing, 2007).

A chronology of the Eastern Churches

(All dates are AD (*anno domini*) or CE (Christian era))

c. 64–313	Persecution of Christians by Roman emperors and governors
2nd–3rd century	Gnostic and heterodox sects challenge orthodoxy
c. 130–200	St Irenaeus of Lyons
c. 185–254	Origen of Alexandria
c. 251–356	St Anthony of Egypt, founder of monasticism
c. 296–373	St Athanasius the Great
c. 300	Armenia adopts Christianity (first Christian state)
312	Conversion of Emperor Constantine I
313	Edict of Milan ends persecution of the Church
325	First ecumenical council at Nicaea formulates Creed in opposition to Arianism
c. 350	Church of Georgia founded
329/30–89/90	St Gregory of Nazianzus, also known as 'the Theologian'
c. 330–79	St Basil the Great
c. 330–95	St Gregory of Nyssa
346–99	Evagrius of Pontus, teacher of asceticism and prayer
c. 347–407	St John Chrysostom
c. 350	Church of Georgia founded
381	Second ecumenical council, Constantinople, completes formulation of Nicene Creed
late 300s	Macarian Homilies
c. 400 – after 446	Diadochus of Photike, ascetic theologian
431	Third ecumenical council, Ephesus, counters Nestorianism: rejected by Assyrian Church of the East (sometimes called 'Nestorian')
451	Fourth ecumenical council, Chalcedon, counters 'Monophysitism': rejected by all 'non-Chalcedonian' Churches
476	Last Western Roman emperor deposed by Ostrogothic general, Odoacer
c. 500	writings of (ps-)Dionysius the Areopagite
537	Church of Hagia Sophia (Constantinople) rebuilt by Justinian

553	Fifth ecumenical council, Constantinople, affirms unity of Christ's person; recognition of five patriarchal sees; Constantinople given second place after Rome
555	Death of Romanos the Melodist, hymnographer
c. 570–649	St John Climacus, Abbot of Sinai, author of *The Ladder of Divine Ascent*
c. 580–662	St Maximus the Confessor
589	*Filioque* added to Creed in Spain at the Third Council of Toledo
630s	Rise of Islam; Muslim conquests of Damascus (635), Jerusalem (638), Alexandria (642)
c. 650–5 – 750	St John of Damascus: hymnographer, theologian, defender of the icons
676	St Isaac the Syrian, spiritual teacher, appointed Bishop of Nineveh
680–1	Sixth ecumenical council, Constantinople, affirms two wills of Christ
692	Quinisext Council 'in Trullo': canons on sacred art
730–87; 815–43	Iconoclasm
759–826	St Theodore of Stoudios: hymnographer, theologian, defender of the icons
787	Seventh ecumenical council, Nicaea, affirms theology of images
843	Restoration of the icons by Empress Theodora
858–67, 878–86	St Photius, as Patriarch of Constantinople
863	Baptism of the Bulgars
864–85	Missionary work of Sts Cyril and Methodius among Slavs
917	Patriarchate of Bulgaria established
949–1022	St Symeon the New Theologian: abbot, theologian, poet
963–4	Great Laura monastery founded on Mt Athos
988	Baptism of Rus': Prince Vladimir of Kiev
1027–1107	Peter of Damascus, monastic theologian
1054	'Great Schism': anathemas exchanged between Rome and Constantinople
1095–9	First Crusade: Crusaders occupy Jerusalem and Antioch and install Latin hierarchs
1204	Constantinople sacked by Fourth Crusade
1204–61	Latin rule in Constantinople
1237	Tartar invasion of Russia
1255–65 – 1337	St Gregory of Sinai, Hesychast, teacher of the Jesus Prayer
1274	Council of Lyons: failed attempt at reunion between Constantinople and Rome
c. 1296–1359	St Gregory Palamas, Archbishop of Thessaloniki, defender of the Hesychasts

c. 1314–92	St Sergius of Radonezh, founder of Holy Trinity monastery near Moscow
c. 1322–90	St Nicolas Cabasilas, lay theologian, Hesychast
1340–96	St Stephen of Perm, scholar and missionary to the Zyrians
1341, 1347, 1351	Councils in Constantinople uphold Gregory Palamas's teaching
1346	Patriarchate of Peć (Serbia) established by St Sava
1380	Battle of Kulikovo: Russian prince St Dimitri Donskoi defeats Tartars
1389	Battle of Kosovo: Serbian prince St Lazar defeated by Turks
1433–1508	St Nil Sorsky, Hesychast, 'Non-Possessor'
1438–9	Council of Florence–Ferrara: official end of schism between Rome and Eastern Churches (but overturned in 1484)
1439–40 – 1515	St Joseph of Volokolamsk, abbot, 'Possessor'
1448	Autocephaly of Church of Russia
1453	Constantinople falls to Turks
1459	Serbia falls to Turks
1517	Ottoman Turks occupy Syria and Egypt
1572–1638	Cyril Loukaris, author of Calvinist-leaning 'Confession'
1573–81	Lutheran scholars in correspondence with Patriarch Jeremias II
1589	First Patriarch of Russia elected
1596	Union of Brest: creation of uniate church in Ukraine; establishment of lay 'brotherhoods' in Kiev to defend Orthodoxy
1597–1646	Peter Mogila, Westernising metropolitan of Kiev
1625–72	Various 'Orthodox confessions'
1652	Liturgical reforms of Patriarch Nikon of Moscow: 'Old Believer' schism
1721	Moscow Patriarchate abolished by Peter the Great
1722–94	St Paisius Velichkovsky, translator of the *Philokalia* into Slavonic (1793)
1724	Schism in Antioch: 'Melkites' unite with Rome
1749–1809	St Nikodimos of the Holy Mountain: publication of the *Philokalia* and the *Rudder*
1759–1833	St Seraphim of Sarov, monk, spiritual father
1794	Russian mission to Alaska: St Herman
1821	Greece liberated from Ottoman empire
1840s	'Slavophile' movement in Russia; Alexei Khomiakov, 1804–60
1850s	Ottoman massacres in Syria prompt emigration of Christians
1853–1900	Vladimir Soloviev, religious philosopher
1861	Russian mission to Japan: St Nicholas (Kasatkin) of Tokyo

late 19th century	Greek/Arab/Russian parishes established in Australia, North America
1871–1944	Sergius Bulgakov, economist, speculative theologian, ecumenist
1882–1937	Pavel Florensky, theologian, scientist
1891–1909	Uniate parishes in USA brought into Orthodox Church by Archpriest Alexis Toth
1893–1979	Georges Florovsky, patristic theologian, Church historian
1899	Meletius Al-Doumani elected Patriarch of Antioch; Arab hierarchy restored in Antioch
1917	Russian Church Council: Patriarchate of Moscow restored
1926	Founding of St Sergius Institute of Orthodox Theology, Paris
1938	Founding of St Vladimir's Seminary, New York
1942	Founding of Orthodox Youth Movement, Patriarchate of Antioch
1946	Orthodox Church of Uganda received into Patriarchate of Alexandria
1953	Founding of Syndesmos (World Fellowship of Orthodox Youth)
1960s	Theological revival in Greece; monastic revival on Mt Athos
1964–5	Meeting between Patriarch Athenagoras of Constantinople and Pope Paul VI of Rome; formal lifting of anathemas of 1054.
1970	Russian Metropolia in North America granted autocephaly by Moscow as Orthodox Church in America
1982	Orthodox Church of Ghana received into Patriarchate of Alexandria
1989	Eastern Orthodox – Oriental Orthodox Dialogue issues agreed statement
1992	Church of Albania revived: Archbishop Anastasios (Yannoulatos) elected primate

Abbreviations

ANF	A. Roberts and J. Donaldson (eds.), Ante-Nicene Fathers, The Writings of the Fathers Down to A.D. 325, 10 vols., rev. edn A. Cleveland Coxe (Peabody, MA: Hendrickson Publishers, Inc., 1995). Also available at: www.ccel.org
c.	*circa*; about
CSCO	Corpus Scriptorum Christianorum Orientalium (series)
CUA	Catholic University of America
CWS	Classics of Western Spirituality (series)
GCS	Die griechischen christlichen Schriftsteller der ersten drei Jahrhunderte, Leipzig: J. C. Hinrichs 1897– (a series)
GOTR	*Greek Orthodox Theological Review*
JTS, n.s.	*Journal of Theological Studies*, new series
LXX	Septuagint (The Greek Old Testament)
MECC	Middle East Council of Churches
MJO	Mouvement de la Jeunesse Orthodoxe
NPNF	Philip Schaff, Henry Wace *et al.* (eds.), Nicene and Post-Nicene Fathers, A Select Library of the Christian Church, Series 1–2, 13 and 14 vols., repr. Peabody, MA: Hendrickson Publishers, Inc., 1995. Also available online at: www.ccel.org
NRSV	New Revised Standard Version, *The Holy Bible*
PG	Patrologia Graeca
PL	Patrologia Latina
RSV	Revised Standard Version, *The Holy Bible*
SC	Sources Chrétiennes (series)
sed.	Latin *sedit*, 'sat' or 'held office'
SPCK	Society for the Promotion of Christian Knowledge
SVS	St Vladimir's Seminary, Crestwood, NY
SVTQ	*St Vladimir's Theological Quarterly*
WCC	World Council of Churches

Map of the Eastern Orthodox Churches

Who are the Orthodox Christians?
A historical introduction

MARY B. CUNNINGHAM
and ELIZABETH THEOKRITOFF

The Orthodox Church consists historically of the local Churches of the Eastern Roman empire, including Constantinople, Alexandria, Antioch and Jerusalem, as well as the Churches that came into being as a result of their missions. During the first millennium of Christianity, this communion included the Church of Rome. It is important to remember that the Orthodox and Roman Catholic Churches, as well as Rome's Protestant offshoots, all share a common ancestry in the one, universal Christian communion of the early centuries.

The Christian mission, as it is described by Luke in Acts and in Paul's Epistles, spread rapidly through the territories of the Roman empire. Orthodox tradition holds that it spread beyond the Roman world even in the apostolic period, with St Thomas travelling as far as southern India, converting many people along the way. Most of the more distant missions, such as Georgia, Armenia and Ethiopia, however, were probably achieved in the fourth or fifth centuries after the Roman empire had finally adopted Christianity as its state religion, following the conversion of Constantine I. By this time, the Church, which had earlier been an illegal, minority organisation within a predominantly pagan society, was slowly becoming the dominant force in shaping government laws and social traditions. The Roman empire, consisting of its Eastern and Western halves, became a fully Christian state: it was believed to be sanctioned by God, with its emperors or kings fulfilling special duties as God's representatives in the secular realm.

It is important at the beginning of any discussion of the Christian Church to ask what in fact this body represents. Was Jesus Christ's vision of the Church, when he told his disciples to go forth and baptise in the name of the Father, Son and Holy Spirit (Mt 28:19), the same as that of a believer of later centuries? The Eastern Orthodox response would be that the Church was then, and remains now, above all a eucharistic community. Because all participate in the one bread of the Eucharist, the Church is one body (cf. 1 Cor 10:16–17): it is not simply a collection of individuals united to Jesus. A body needs a structure, and this is provided by a threefold hierarchy of bishops, presbyters or priests, and deacons. Such a structure appears to have been in place by the beginning of the second century.

In the Orthodox understanding, the Church has always existed as 'Churches' in the plural, as in the Christian East today. This is a source of confusion to many Western Christians for whom 'a Church' means a denomination, confessionally defined. In ancient and Orthodox usage, a Church is defined by geography, referring originally to a community gathered around a bishop. In the third to fourth centuries, dioceses were grouped into metropolitan areas; the metropolitan bishop was first among equals, charged with preserving unity. In the fifth century, these areas in turn were organised into the five Churches of Rome, Constantinople, Antioch, Alexandria and Jerusalem – the so-called pentarchy – and their bishops later came to be known as patriarchs. Rome enjoyed a recognised primacy among the local Churches, although the understanding of this primacy varied over the centuries and developed very differently in Rome and in the East.

DEFINING CHRISTIAN FAITH

Controversies concerning fundamental issues of faith and doctrine arose at a very early period. Orthodox Christianity developed its apologetic and dogmatic defence of the faith in response to an atmosphere of sophisticated intellectual debate, especially in the first eight centuries after Christ. In the late first and second centuries, diverse views concerning God's relationship with creation, cosmology and authority within the Church prompted a more formal definition of 'orthodoxy', led by bishops such as St Irenaeus of Lyons. The affirmations of this period on creation, scripture and the Church provide the foundations for all later discussions of doctrine and discipline within the Christian Church.

The first three centuries of Christianity were dominated not only by internal intellectual challenges, but also by persecution at the hands of a pagan, largely hostile, state. Persecution was in fact sporadic and varied in its force region by region, but this did not prevent it from having a profound effect on the Christian community. Martyrs, venerated for their steadfast faith, remain important members of the 'communion of saints' until the present day. In the early fourth century, the persecution of Christians ended after the Edict of Milan in AD 313. Although Constantine's personal conversion to the new religion may have been slow, the effects on the position of the Church were dramatic. The court historian Eusebius chronicled these developments, also articulating the role of the Christian emperor as one who 'by bringing those whom he rules on earth to the only begotten and saving Word, renders them fit subjects for his Kingdom'.[1]

The Christianisation of the Roman empire took place slowly. Nevertheless, the process, once started, was unstoppable; it was characterised by the gradual introduction of laws such as the ban on commerce and official business on Sundays, the building of churches and other Christian monuments, imperial supervision of ecclesiastical councils to settle doctrinal disputes and, on occasion, state enforcement of doctrinal decisions, whether orthodox or heterodox. By the reign of Justinian (AD 527–65), the Church had become fully integrated into imperial life. Court ceremonial included elaborate liturgical celebrations based in the Great Church of Hagia Sophia with the emperor playing a prominent, although always non-clerical, role. This nicely illustrates the Byzantine doctrine of 'symphony': Church and state were seen as aspects of one organism, the Christian empire, each with its own proper sphere. Many in East and West today would have reservations about this way of thinking. We should recognise, however, that it builds on the belief that the incarnation of God has saved *all* that is human: culture and polity too can be 'baptised'.[2]

Trinitarian and christological doctrine was defined in the universal Church with the help of the ecumenical councils, which are recognised in the East as beginning with the first council of Nicaea in AD 325 and finishing with the seventh in 787. The councils were called in response to continuing controversy concerning the nature of the Trinity and, from the beginning of the fifth century, the manner in which two natures come together in the person of Christ. As the term 'ecumenical' or 'universal' indicates, these councils included representatives from both Eastern and Western Churches. Tragically, substantial parts of the Church were unable to agree with the decisions of various ecumenical councils. Thus, the Church of the East (now known as 'Assyrian'), based in Mesopotamia, refused to accept the decisions of the third ecumenical council at Ephesus (431) and has thus remained out of communion with mainstream Christianity ever since. A substantial part of the Alexandrian and Syrian Churches could not accept the formula 'in two natures' adopted at the fourth council at Chalcedon (451), and broke away to form the 'monophysite' or 'miaphysite' Churches, now usually called 'Oriental Orthodox'. This group is represented today by the Coptic, Ethiopian and Armenian Churches, the Syrian or 'Jacobite' Church of Antioch, and the Syrian Church of India. The Eastern (i.e. Chalcedonian) and Oriental

Orthodox Churches have actually remained remarkably close in theology and ethos, and today there is widespread recognition that their differences are terminological rather than substantive.

The schism over Chalcedon greatly diminished the Churches of Alexandria and Antioch. After the Arab conquests in the first half of the seventh century, these territories were lost to the empire; for most of the ancient Christian world, the brief interlude of Christian empire was over. Antioch continued to show theological vitality, mainly in the form of Christian apologetics countering Islamic teachings, but Constantinople was now the undisputed centre of Eastern Christianity.

DIVISION BETWEEN EAST AND WEST

The estrangement between the Eastern and Western Churches culminated in the mutual excommunications of AD 1054, but it is difficult to pinpoint exactly when this process began. As early as the third and fourth centuries of Christian history, a cultural divide is perceptible between the Latin-speaking territories of Italy and points west, and the largely Greek-speaking Eastern Mediterranean. Later Roman emperors, beginning with Diocletian, in fact divided the empire into two halves for more effective governance. In AD 476, the Ostragothic general Odoacer deposed the last Western Roman emperor and the resulting power vacuum gave the Roman Church a political prestige which it retains to the present day. But the 'fall' of the West was not mirrored in the East, where the Roman empire continued until 1453.

Although tensions between East and West were developing in the course of the fifth and sixth centuries, it is in the middle of the seventh century that a real rupture between the Roman pope and the ecumenical patriarch in Constantinople took place. The arrest of Pope Martin in 653 by the Byzantine emperor, followed by his trial and condemnation ostensibly for treason but in reality for his opposition to Monothelite doctrine, represents a low point in East–West Church relations. Tension increased in the ninth and tenth centuries with the dispute between East and West over the *filioque*, the controversial addition to the Nicene-Constantinopolitan Creed which has implications for the status of both Son and Spirit in the Trinity. The excommunications of 1054 thus represent a stage in a process of growing distrust between the Eastern and Western Churches; at the time it was probably believed that the schism would soon be healed. But then came the Crusades. The indigenous Christian population found themselves second-class citizens in the Crusader states of Antioch and Jerusalem, and the establishment of

Latin patriarchs in those cities sent an unambiguous message: Rome no longer recognised the local Churches. Many historians in fact view the sack of Constantinople by the Latins in 1204, in the course of the Fourth Crusade, as the seal of division between Rome and Constantinople. This invasion, followed by over sixty years of Latin occupation, inspired a continuing distrust of the West on the part of Orthodox Christians. Two major attempts at reunion with Rome (the Council of Lyons in 1274 and that of Florence–Ferrara in 1438–9) ultimately failed because of this tension, along with diverging views not only on the *filioque*, but also on Western doctrine concerning purgatory and disciplinary matters such as the use of leavened or unleavened bread in the Eucharist.

BYZANTINE MISSIONS

Another aspect of Byzantine religious policy with far-reaching implications was the missionary activity that took place in Slavic and Balkan territories from about the middle of the ninth century onwards. Photius, patriarch of Constantinople (AD 858–67, 878–86), was responsible for initiating these missions and for deciding to translate scripture and liturgical books into Slavonic with the help of two brothers, Sts Cyril (Constantine) and Methodius. Although the first mission to Moravia failed, subsequent efforts among the Bulgars, Serbs, and finally the Rus', who were in this period based in the region around Kiev, succeeded in converting these Slavic nations to Christianity within the Byzantine sphere of influence. Tensions between Latin and Greek missionaries working in the same areas added to the growing distrust between Eastern and Western Christendom. The results of these missions can still be observed in the configuration of Orthodox and Roman Catholic populations today: Russia, Ukraine, Romania, Bulgaria and Serbia remain largely Orthodox, whereas Poland and Hungary possess a majority of Roman Catholics. In the thirteenth century, Constantinople recognised the Churches of both Serbia and Bulgaria as self-governing – an acknowledgement of the new reality of dealing with territories outside the administrative framework of the empire. While the West moved increasingly towards a centralised structure, in the East a new community of local Churches began to counterbalance the dominance of the imperial city.

THEOLOGICAL DEVELOPMENTS AND THE CONTRIBUTION OF MONASTICISM

Theological developments between approximately the seventh and the fifteenth centuries were complex and cannot be treated in detail here.[3] It is important to note that the seventh council of Nicaea (AD 787), which defended the theology of images against Iconoclasm, was the last episcopal gathering to be universally recognised as an ecumenical council. Further local councils did of course take place. However, the definition of Orthodox doctrine was in its essentials complete by the end of the eighth century, with further statements offering refinements rather than addressing fundamental doctrinal issues.

This does not mean that theology stagnated, but it was principally in the monastic milieu that its vitality was preserved. Notable is the figure of St Symeon the New Theologian, who flourished in a Constantinopolitan monastery in the early eleventh century and left an indelible mark on Orthodox Christianity with his experience of the divine light. Personal spiritual experience is fundamental to this theology, and to the elaborate science of spiritual life developed by monastic writers. A resurgence of monastic life, evidenced in the foundation of new houses throughout the Byzantine empire, helped to drive the Orthodox vision of theology as a living encounter with God. Of particular significance was the foundation in the tenth century of the first monasteries on Mt Athos: the Holy Mountain brought together monks from various parts of the Christian world, including, at least at the beginning, Latins.

The monastic revival culminated in the theological contributions of St Gregory Palamas (c. 1296–1359). While on Mount Athos, Gregory became immersed in the Hesychast tradition of contemplative prayer. His experience of divine light through prayer led him to develop the ancient distinction between the essence and energies of God: whereas the divine essence remains unknowable, the uncreated energies permeate all things. This affirmation of a holistic theology, which maintains the presence of God throughout creation and the ability of human beings to experience him, has its foundation in Chalcedonian theology.

Hesychasm inspired a spiritual and cultural renewal whose influence spread far beyond the walls of the monasteries. The 'Hesychast International', as it has been called, centred on Paroria in Bulgaria, where St Gregory of Sinai had settled, and on Mount Athos. St Sava, founder of Hilandar monastery and founding archbishop of the Serbian Church, is emblematic of this movement in his international vision and his rooted-ness in spiritual values even while skilfully managing affairs of Church and state. Something of the spirit of this revival can be glimpsed in the churches and monasteries of Peć (in modern Kosovo) – although some of these monuments have tragically been destroyed since the Kosovo Force (KFOR) occupation of the region. Bulgarians and Serbs were responsible for the dissemination of this spiritual revival through Romania and

Russia, where the same spirit inspired the monastic founder St Sergius of Radonezh and the missionary St Stephen of Perm.

THE CHURCH IN THE OTTOMAN EMPIRE

The last flowering of Byzantine culture and spiritual life was short-lived. Most of Serbia was reduced to vassalage after defeat by the Turks at the battle of Kosovo in 1389. Bulgaria fell to the Turks in 1396, and the fall of the imperial capital in 1453 completed the loss to Muslim rule of the ancient heartlands of Christianity. As had been true in the Middle East for some centuries, so now in Asia Minor and the Balkans the Church's main focus became survival.

The conquering Turks recognised no distinction between religion and nation: the Christians were therefore treated as a subject people with the Patriarch of Constantinople as its 'ethnarch'. This enabled Constantinople to claim an authority over all the other Churches within the empire, which in practice entrenched Greek domination of other local Churches, including the other ancient patriarchates.

Five centuries of Turkish domination have left a mark on the Greek and Balkan peoples that is still evident today. The subject Christians enjoyed freedom of worship and a measure of tolerance most of the time, but at the price of being second-class citizens. The poll-tax, the child levy and humiliating social restrictions kept up a relentless pressure, resulting in a steady haemorrhage of conversions; public attempts to revitalise and strengthen the faith of the Christian population were liable to end in death. Yet the demoralised state of hierarchy and the general low level of education did not prevent the appearance of many who would be revered as 'new martyrs' – often people who had converted to Islam, in some cases as children, and then recanted.

THE CHURCH IN RUSSIA

The Russian Church alone remained free of the Turkish yoke, a circumstance which led some Russian churchmen to see it as the 'Third Rome'. The fall of Constantinople was widely viewed as divine retribution for the compromise of Orthodox faith at the council of Florence–Ferrara (1438–9), in a futile attempt to gain Western assistance against the Turks. When the head of the Russian Church, the Greek Metropolitan Isidore of Kiev, returned home after signing the act of union, he was summarily arrested. In due course, the Russians elected their own Metropolitan of Moscow to lead the Church, without the assent of

Constantinople. So began Russia's de facto autonomy from Constantinople, although a patriarchate was established, with the blessing of the Patriarchate of Constantinople, only in 1589. It should be made clear that this was a matter of order, not a split in the Church. Russia would go on to play an important role as protector of the Christians in the Ottoman empire.

Russia at this time was beginning to emerge from its own period of servitude to the Tartars. A key figure in the resurgence of ecclesial and cultural life was St Sergius of Radonezh, a Hesychast monk who also gave advice and moral support to the Prince of Moscow. Sergius's dedication of his monastery to the Holy Trinity (Sergiev Posad or Zagorsk) would be seen as a sermon in action, a call to unity in love.[4]

The controversies in the Russian Church generally concerned church life and ritual rather than theology; but one fifteenth-century controversy had important implications for the place of the Church in society. The 'Possessors', whose protagonist was Joseph of Volokolamsk, stood for a Church with influence in society, deferential to the Tsar's authority and possessing the means to organise practical works of charity. Nil Sorsky and the 'Non-Possessors' stood for simplicity, prayer and inner freedom. Given the climate of the times throughout Europe, Joseph's enthusiasm for the coercion of heretics is less remarkable than Nil's advocacy of religious toleration. The party of the 'Possessors' achieved dominance, but both men were canonised.

By contrast, Patriarch Nikon's reforms, begun in 1652, led to a schism that persists to this day, the tragic consequence of a preoccupation with ritual (on both sides) and an obsession with uniformity. Nikon's heavy-handed attempts to bring liturgical practice into line with contemporary Greek usage provoked a violent backlash. The 'Old Believer' schism exemplifies a recurring pattern: schisms in Orthodox Christianity typically reflect conservative rather than reforming tendencies.

Nikon was also a vehement proponent of the superiority of spiritual power over secular authority, but the tide of history was against him. Inspired by Protestant models of Church–state relations in Western Europe, Peter the Great abolished the patriarchate (1721), ignoring the protests of the other Orthodox patriarchs; it was replaced with a 'holy synod'. The Church effectively became a department of state. Despite repeated attempts on the part of the Church to extricate itself, this anomalous arrangement, with its stultifying effect on the hierarchy and church structures, was to continue until 1917. This synodal period was also characterised by a marked Westernisation in approaches to theology, iconography and church singing. Nevertheless, the body of the Church was able to show some remarkable signs of life, especially in the nineteenth century – a subject to which we will return.

ORTHODOXY AND THE WEST

The fall of Constantinople put an end to plans for union with Rome in exchange for Western support against the Turks, but it did not end contact with the West. Christians from the Ottoman empire seeking higher education had little alternative but to turn to the Roman Catholic (or later Protestant) schools of the West. In 1581, Pope Gregory XIII obliged by founding the College of St Athanasius in Rome, with the purpose of converting Orthodox young men and sending them home to promote union with Rome. Lacking the resources and education to give adequate pastoral care, hierarchs and clergy in Greece and the Levant frequently welcomed Jesuit missionaries as preachers and confessors; presumably they were unaware that the Jesuits were making many secret converts.[5] The success of Jesuit tactics became apparent in 1724, when one such convert became Patriarch of Antioch and led a section of his Church into union with Rome (the group now known as 'Melkites'). As a result, Christians in the Ottoman empire came to regard Rome with much the same suspicion as did the Orthodox in other parts of Europe, where 'unions' had been established among Orthodox who found themselves under Roman Catholic rulers (Unions of Brest-Litovsk (1596) in Ukraine and Alba Iulia (1698) in Transylvania). In the former case especially, the Union accepted by the hierarchy met with vigorous opposition from a substantial group of laity.

The turmoil of the Reformation and Counter-Reformation in the West affected the Orthodox world indirectly but drastically. In their argument with Rome, the Reformers had an understandable interest in trying to enlist the support of the rest of the ancient Churches for their interpretation of authentic Christianity. In 1573 a group of Lutheran scholars from Tübingen sent Patriarch Jeremias II a copy of the Augsburg Confession, to which he responded with a detailed critique affirming the Orthodox understanding; amicable correspondence continued for some years until it became clear that there would be no meeting of minds. Later hierarchs, however, would find themselves swept into the vortex of Western arguments. The most famous instance is Patriarch Cyril Loukaris of Constantinople. Cyril's work in Poland in the immediate aftermath of the Union of Brest-Litovsk had left him with considerable sympathy with the Protestants; his 1629 'Confession' was strongly influenced by Calvinism. With the aid of the Catholic powers of France and Austria, Loukaris was deposed and murdered. The 'Confession' was subsequently condemned by six councils in succession. But this was not the last attempt to adapt for the defence of Orthodoxy the ill-assorted toolbox of Western theology. Peter Mogila, Metropolitan of Kiev (1632–47), took the opposite approach from Loukaris; hoping to use Rome's own weapons to counteract Rome's influence, he drew directly and un-critically on Roman Catholic manuals. After judicious removal of some of the most egregious Latinisms, Mogila's *Confession* was approved by the council of Jassy in 1642. Mogila's Latinising theology and adoption of Jesuit educational models proved tremendously influential, and came to dominate theological education also in Russia. The rash of 'Orthodox confessions' culminated in that of Patriarch Dositheus, approved by the council of Jerusalem in 1672; Dositheus too resorts to a Latin framework, despite his mistrust of Roman influence.

RETURN TO THE SOURCES

Characteristic of these 'Confessions' is 'a marked inferiority complex towards the formularies of the Counter-Reformation',[6] a complex that has bedevilled Orthodox theology into the twentieth century. The history of modern Orthodox theology is the story of a prolonged and erratic progress towards rediscovering an authentic voice: a process of learning to use Western thought and research as a tool, not a straitjacket, and acquiring the confidence to draw on Eastern resources to avoid Western impasses.

Despite the apparently parlous state of the entire Church, a spiritual and theological revival began in the eighteenth century. It came from the traditional source, the monastic tradition, in creative engagement with the spirit of the age. The intellectual and political ferment of eighteenth-century Western Europe had reverberations in Ottoman territory too, in the so-called 'Greek Enlightenment'. For some, this meant adopting the ideas and rehearsing the arguments of the Western 'Enlightenment', as their predecessors had done with the Western Reformation. For others, however, the new ideas coming from the West provided an impetus to look more deeply into their own tradition. Church-men were prominent in both parties: but none can match the lasting influence of a representative of the latter tendency, St Nikodimos of the Holy Mountain,[7] best known today for his collection of spiritual and ascetic writings entitled the *Philokalia*. This was soon translated into Slavonic by Paisius Velichkovsky, who had fled from the sterile scholasticism of the Kiev Academy to learn the spiritual life on the

Holy Mountain. In this way, its influence spread to Russia and to Moldavia, where Paisius spent the latter part of his life.

The effects of this spiritual renewal were felt first in Russia, where the nineteenth century saw a blossoming of monastic life and particularly of the institution of spiritual fatherhood. St Seraphim of Sarov and the Elders of the Optina monastery are the best-known examples. This revitalisation at the heart of church life produced no immediate transformation, but it strengthened the Church for the firestorm that was to come. The witness of contemplative prayer, and the 'golden chain' of spiritual fatherhood or motherhood exercised by people of holiness, would prove vital in preserving Christian faith when church structures were wiped out or rendered powerless.

The long-term theological importance of this spiritual rejuvenation was enormous, for it succeeded in bridging the gap between the church tradition and the religious revival of the intelligentsia.[8] That revival began as a movement of religious philosophy rather than of theology, but its legacy was to be fundamental to the theology of the Russian emigration and, through it, to the entire Orthodox world today.

The Russian intelligentsia of the nineteenth century were profoundly influenced by Western and especially German philosophy, and some engaged with these influences in a creative way. Key figures include Alexei Khomiakov (1804–60), an early representative of the 'Slavophile' movement which was convinced of the unique vocation of Russia as an Orthodox culture. It is to him that we owe the notion of 'sobornost' (unity in freedom, the unity of an interdependent living body), which was to become such an important concept for Orthodox theology and beyond. It has profound implications for both the Church and human society, and continues to be seen as a vital corrective to the equation of 'freedom' with individualism. We see here the roots of the interest in social thought characteristic of the Russian emigration, and now re-emerging within Russia itself.[9]

Wholeness and unity are leitmotifs of nineteenth-century Russian thought. Often this takes a more mystical turn, as in the thought of the highly influential Vladimir Soloviev (1853–1900). Influenced by Boehme's mysticism and Schelling's 'panentheism', Soloviev saw a primordial 'Godmanhood' as key to the union of God with his creation. But he further attempted to express the unity of all things in terms of 'Sophia', or divine Wisdom personified; his speculations on this mysterious figure took him well beyond the traditional bounds of Orthodox theology. His thinking on the subject was developed in various ways by Pavel Florensky and Sergius Bulgakov, among others. 'Sophiology' in the narrow sense remains very much a fringe interest. Yet the vision that it strives to express, of the oneness of created being and the ultimate union of creation with God, has become one of the hallmarks of modern Orthodox theology.

Even though the rediscovery of Orthodox tradition had begun with Greek scholars such as Nikodimos, it was slow to bear fruit in Greece. Where Russia had its Slavophiles, Greece had only Philhellenes. Despite a few dissenting voices, the emergent Greek nation preferred to define itself according to what 'enlightened Europe' valued, namely, its pre-Christian Classical past. The position of the Church in the Greek state was established with an eye on Protestant models, and theology was envisaged as an academic discipline. Not until the 1960s would Greek theology experience its own renaissance.

THE CHANGING FACE OF THE ORTHODOX WORLD

The Ottoman conquest had concentrated the 'Byzantine commonwealth' of diverse peoples and nations into the 'Rum millet' led by the Greek patriarch. So it was not entirely surprising that, as the various peoples gained liberation, they should seek 'independence' also from the ecclesiastical authorities in Constantinople. If Constantinople itself had been liberated, history might have been different. But what actually happened in the wake of the Greek war of independence (1821) was the establishment of national Churches in the new nation states. These included ancient patriarchates that had been suppressed (Serbia, Bulgaria), but also new independent Churches (Greece, Romania, Albania). The establishment of self-governing Churches in sovereign territories can be seen as a natural evolution of early Christian practice (thus Georgia and Armenia had their own Churches from an early date), but the definition of a local Church in ethnic or nationalistic terms clearly is not. This issue arose late in the nineteenth century when Bulgarian bishops sought to establish jurisdiction over their compatriots regardless of locality: the attempt was formally condemned as 'phyletism' or nationalism. The condemnation of the Bulgarian attempt established an important point of principle, but failed to go to the root of the problem. Ecclesiastical separatism is sometimes motivated by naked nationalism; but it is often a reaction to ethnic and cultural bias within a local Church.

As the Churches in the Balkans were emerging from Turkish domination, new Churches were growing up outside Europe. The revival in Russian Church life had led to a revival in mission, both in the Russian Far East and in China, Japan and Korea. Drawing on the tradition of Sts Cyril and Methodius, the Russian missionaries attached great importance to use of the vernacular and the formation of a truly indigenous Church.

Notable among the Russian missions was Alaska. Significant numbers were evangelised by the gentle monk Herman and the energetic polymath John Veniaminov (later Metropolitan Innocent of Moscow). Orthodox clergy were a strong voice in defence of the native peoples against abuses by the Russian trading companies, and later by the American authorities. Despite aggressive Protestant proselytism following the sale of the territory to the United States, a substantial Orthodox population remains.

In the 1870s, the Russian missionary diocese in North America moved from Alaska to San Francisco to serve growing numbers of Orthodox emigrants across the continent. For some fifty years, the Orthodox Church in North America approximated to a model of canonical order: most parishes recognised the Russian bishop, who made strenuous efforts to find suitable clergy and bishops to serve the pastoral needs of the various ethnic groups. But increasing numbers of Greek communities were making their own arrangements; in 1921 Ecumenical Patriarch Meletios (Metaxakis) brought them under his jurisdiction, and in the chaos following the Russian revolution many other ethnic communities made similar moves back to their original mother Churches.

The political upheavals of the twentieth century have resulted in a significant Orthodox 'diaspora' in Western Europe as well as the Americas and Australia. This unsatisfactory term is used to denote communities started by groups of migrant Orthodox rather than by missions; nevertheless, most of these communities are now well established and include many indigenous Westerners, despite a disinclination to proselytise among other Christians. Orthodox emigration to Western Europe presents new problems of church order: it would run counter to Orthodox ecclesiological sensibilities to establish another autocephalous Church within what is historically the territory of Rome. Most communities are still under the jurisdiction of their original mother Churches; but in several places there is close cooperation at episcopal level and a real desire to work towards functioning as a local Church.[10]

The ancient Churches of the Middle East continue to decline in numbers, due both to emigration and to proselytism by other Christian groups. The picture is not uniform, however. The vitality of the Church of Antioch in Lebanon and Syria contrasts with the Patriarchate of Jerusalem, where the Palestinian Orthodox population has suffered drastic attrition: the overwhelming pressures that they share with their

Muslim compatriots are often compounded by inadequate pastoral care on the part of the Greek hierarchy.[11] Alexandria, on the other hand, has been given a new lease of life by the emergence of new Churches in sub-Saharan Africa, notably Uganda, Ghana and Kenya. The origins of these communities go back to the African independent Churches founded in the 1920s and 1930s in an effort to reclaim an ancient Christian tradition not associated with colonial rule.

CONVERGENCE AND RENEWAL

The Russian revolution was the decisive event for modern Orthodoxy, ushering in a new 'age of martyrs' for most of the Orthodox Church. Furthermore, the emigration following the revolution meant that the heirs to the intellectual ferment of the nineteenth century were largely scattered abroad. Many Russians fled to the Baltic states, Yugoslavia and Bulgaria. But the centre of the emigration was Paris, where the St Sergius Institute of Orthodox Theology (founded 1926) and the Russian YMCA Press would remain key centres for the dissemination of Orthodox theological thought.

Many émigrés came to see a providential meaning in the catastrophe that had engulfed their country; indeed, this resulted in an unprecedented mutual encounter between Orthodoxy and the West. Through the ecumenical efforts of the émigrés, Western Christians were able to hear for the first time the voices of highly articulate and thoughtful Orthodox theologians from various traditions.

Adversarial encounters between Orthodoxy and the West in earlier centuries had led to superficial attempts to 'package' Orthodoxy in Western terms. This new encounter, however, elicited a more creative response: an awareness of the need first to 'possess what is "one's own" in order to benefit from what is "the other's"'.[12] This set in train a profound rediscovery of the Orthodox tradition which included recognising where it was present in the Christian West. The logic of the Russian émigrés' understanding of the Church and its mission required a rediscovery of the universality of Orthodoxy across national cultural boundaries, but it was ecumenical contacts that allowed this to happen. Through the good offices of the enormously influential Russian Student Christian Movement, the YMCA was able to set up organisations of specifically Orthodox character in the Balkans, so as to promote spiritual renewal without raising suspicions of proselytism. The period between the two world wars saw a welter of meetings and conferences bringing together youth and theologians from Greece, the Balkans and the Russian emigration. These included the 1936 conference of Orthodox theologians in Athens, which agreed on the task of freeing Orthodox theology from scholastic influences and reconnecting with the Church Fathers.

Within ten years, however, almost the whole of Orthodox Europe had fallen to Communism. Yet, remarkably, this did not altogether derail the project of theological renewal. That project is well exemplified in one of the great theologians of the twentieth century, Fr Dumitru Stăniloae (1900–93), whose continued teaching and writing transformed the character of theology in Romania. Having studied in Athens and Paris in the 1920s, Stăniloae was profoundly influenced by the theology of the Russian emigration, and had a keen sense of Romania's place as meeting-point of the Greek and Slav worlds. Serbia followed a somewhat different path: the dominant figure was Iustin Popović (1894–1979), a pioneer of patristic scholarship and spiritual renewal who reached out to the Greek and Russian traditions but was deeply suspicious of Ecumenism. A similar orientation can be seen in some of his prominent disciples such as Bishop Atanasije Jevtić and Bishop Amfilohije Radović, patristic scholars trained in Athens and closely involved with the current revival in Greek theology.

Communities outside Eastern Europe have acquired an increasingly prominent role in world Orthodoxy. In 1942, a chance encounter with Russian émigré theological writings inspired a group of young Orthodox Lebanese and Syrians to found the Orthodox Youth Movement, which was to make Antioch one of the foremost heirs to the Paris renewal. Paris itself continues to be an important theological centre: the tradition of the émigré thinkers has been carried on by such figures as Elisabeth Behr-Sigel, Fr Cyrille Argenti, Olivier Clément and Fr Boris Bobrinskoy, and by a younger generation of theologians from Russian, Greek and French backgrounds. In Britain, the spirit of the renewal had been represented since the 1920s mainly through the Fellowship of St Alban and St Sergius and its leaders such as Nicolas and Militza Zernov and Nadejda Gorodetzky. It gained momentum after the Second World War through the ministry of Metropolitan Anthony (Bloom) at the head of the Russian diocese, and Archimandrite Sophrony (Sakharov), whose unconventional monastery in Essex is both a meeting place for pilgrims from all over the world and a strong presence in the Anglo-Greek community. The Orthodox presence in Britain includes such internationally known theologians as Metropolitan Kallistos Ware, who during his years as lecturer at Oxford supervised large numbers of graduate students from around the world. The journals *Sobornost* and, more recently, *Sourozh* (1980–2006) have been an important source of theological writing in

English, along with *St Vladimir's Theological Quarterly* and the *Greek Orthodox Theological Review* in America.

In 1948, Fr Georges Florovsky and other leading theologians from Paris left for America, to be followed shortly by Alexander Schmemann and John Meyendorff. All of these figures were to have a great impact on Orthodoxy in North America, and especially on St Vladimir's Seminary in New York (founded 1938). The seminary's publishing house has become the leading source of Orthodox books in English, many of which have subsequently been translated into the languages of other Orthodox countries.

Even during the Communist period, contacts and interchange among Orthodox Christians continued on the level of theological education. The World Council of Churches, too, provided valuable opportunities for representatives of the various Orthodox Churches to meet. It was also instrumental in re-establishing contact between the Eastern Orthodox and Oriental Orthodox Churches, leading in the 1960s to an official Dialogue. The sense of de facto unity between the two families of Churches is strong, and indeed Oriental Orthodox such as Metropolitan Paulos Mar Gregorios, Abba Matta el-Meskin or Vigen Guroian are important figures for contemporary Eastern Orthodox theology.

Perhaps the most vital instrument of contact and renewal has been the Orthodox youth fellowship Syndesmos, founded in Paris in 1953. Syndesmos has formed generations of hierarchs and lay leaders with a profound sense of shared responsibility for the Church, and first-hand experience of the unity of Orthodoxy across national and cultural borders. Its early leaders included John Meyendorff, later Dean of St Vladimir's Seminary; Georges Khodr, now Metropolitan of Mount Lebanon; and ecumenical theologian Nikos Nissiotis. Syndesmos broke new ground in 1961 by establishing an inter-Orthodox missionary centre; its first director, Anastasios Yannoulatos, is now Archbishop of Tirana, where he has presided over the dramatic rebirth of the Albanian Church following the fall of Communism.

A remarkable aspect of Orthodox renewal in the later twentieth century has been the resurgence of monasticism. Mount Athos, widely given up for dead in the 1960s, now has some 1,600 monks, many highly educated; several of the monasteries are quite international in composition.[13] A similar renewal can be seen in men's and women's monasticism throughout the Orthodox world. Monasticism has traditionally been a prime source of authentic theology, understood as 'praying in truth';[14] now we once again see the monastic experience re-invigorating theological life. The teaching of St Silouan of Mount Athos has reached a global audience through his disciple Fr Sophrony, while architects of the Athonite revival such as Archimandrite Vasileios of Iviron and Archimandrite Aimilianos of Simonopetra have been greatly influential in Greece and beyond. This is not an influence readily discernible from footnotes or bibliographies. But many Orthodox who write about theology today have been marked by their encounters with people of holiness who know at first hand the realities that doctrines seek to describe.[15]

The fall of Communism in Eastern Europe has had an impact on the Orthodox world comparable to that of its advent. Suddenly, almost all Orthodox are faced with the same challenges, those of an increasingly globalised world dominated by an economic ideology. Some Churches find themselves ill prepared for the rapid changes in society; the advent of foreign missionaries of assorted denominations only fuels suspicion of 'the West' and hinders constructive exchange. On the other hand, many more theologians from Orthodox countries are now studying and indeed teaching abroad, greatly increasing the opportunities for contact both among Orthodox and between Orthodox and Christians of Western traditions. The accession of several Orthodox countries to the European Union gives new opportunities for inter-Orthodox discussion of contemporary challenges, as well as increasing the visibility in Western Europe of Orthodox traditions. There is hope that Orthodox theological thinking will continue to develop in dialogue with the West, and that the process will increasingly be reciprocal.

Further reading

Binns, J., *An Introduction to the Christian Orthodox Churches*, Cambridge: Cambridge University Press, 2002.

Herrin, J., *The Formation of Christendom*, Oxford: Basil Blackwell, 1987.

McGuckin, J., *The Orthodox Church*, Oxford: Blackwell Publishing, 2008.

Meyendorff, J., *The Orthodox Church: Its Past and Its Role in the World Today*, trans. J. Chapin, London: Darton, Longman and Todd, 1962.

  Rome, Constantinople, Moscow: Historical and Theological Studies, Crestwood, NY: SVS Press, 1996.

Papadakis, A., with Meyendorff, J., *The Christian East and the Rise of the Papacy*, Crestwood, NY: SVS Press, 1994.

Parry, K. (ed.), *The Blackwell Companion to Eastern Christianity*, Oxford: Blackwell Publishing, 2007.

Ware, T., *The Orthodox Church New Edition*, London: Penguin Books, 1993.

Notes

1. Eusebius of Caesarea, *Oration on the Tricennalia of Constantine* II.2.
2. See further J. McGuckin, 'The legacy of the thirteenth Apostle', *SVTQ* 47:3–4 (2003), 251–88.

3. See A. Casiday, 'Church Fathers and the shaping of Orthodox theology', below.
4. N. Zernov, *The Russians and Their Church* (Crestwood, NY: SVS Press, 3rd edn, 1978), pp. 36–41, 51.
5. See K. T. Ware (new Metropolitan of Diokleia), 'Orthodox and Catholics in the seventeenth century: schism or intercommunion?' in D. Baker (ed.), *Schism, Heresy and Religious Protest* (Cambridge: Cambridge University Press, 1972), pp. 259–76.
6. J. Meyendorff, *The Orthodox Church: Its Past and Its Role in the World Today* (London: Darton, Longman and Todd, 1962), p. 95.
7. See A. Louth, 'The patristic revival and its protagonists' and A. N. Papathanasiou, 'Some key themes and figures in Greek theological thought', below.
8. J. Meyendorff, *Rome, Constantinople, Moscow: Historical and Theological Studies* (Crestwood, NY: SVS Press, 1996), p. 180.
9. See L. Kishkovsky, 'Russian theology after totalitarianism', below.
10. See M. Sollogoub, 'Orthodox Christians in Western Europe move towards a local Church', *Sourozh* 92 (May 2003), 8–32.
11. See further T. Pulcini, 'Tensions between the hierarchy and the laity of the Jerusalem patriarchate: historical perspectives on the present situation', *SVTQ* 36.3 (1992), 273–98.
12. Basil Zenkovsky, quoted in H. Bos, 'Orthodox youth and Orthodox culture: the genesis of Syndesmos, 1923–1953', available on www.syndesmos.org.
13. See further G. Speake, *Mount Athos. Renewal in Paradise* (New Haven and London: Yale University Press, 2002).
14. Cf. Evagrius, *Chapters on Prayer* 60.
15. See further A. Golitzin, 'Spirituality: Eastern Christian' in *Encyclopedia of Monasticism*, vol. II (Chicago: Fitzroy Dearborn, 2000).

Part I

Doctrine and Tradition

1 Scripture and tradition in the Church

THEODORE G. STYLIANOPOULOS

From an Orthodox perspective, scripture, tradition and Church are viewed as a comprehensive unity with interdependent parts. Scripture finds its centre in the mystery of the eternal Christ, veiled in the Old Testament and revealed in the New. Tradition in its theological substance is defined by the gospel, the sum of scripture's saving message – namely, the good news of God's saving work in Christ and the Spirit by which the powers of sin and death are overcome and the life of the new creation is inaugurated, moving towards the eschatological glorification of the whole cosmos. The Church itself, the ongoing living community of God's people, far from being a mere historical appendage, is the body of Christ and the temple of the Holy Spirit, constitutive of revelation. As such, the Church forms the very ground from which scripture and tradition emerge and together, in turn, make up a coherent source of revelation, the supreme norm for the life of the Church.

THE NATURE OF SCRIPTURE

To know the nature of the Bible is to acquire insights into its origins, contents, character, purpose and saving value. In terms of divine inspiration, the primary author of scripture is God himself. Scripture represents God's 'oracles' or sacred words (*logia theou*, Romans 3:2). St Justin Martyr (around AD 150) cited many of the Old Testament texts (the New Testament had not yet fully been established) with the words 'God speaks' or 'God says' as the immediate speech of God. The later Church Fathers continued this tradition and viewed the entire corpus of scripture, Old and New Testaments, as directly inspired by God and disclosing God's express will. On that basis, because God is the main actor both behind and in the Bible, the Orthodox tradition advocates the supreme authority and primacy of scripture. The Bible constitutes the record of divine revelation and forms the measuring standard for the faith and practice of the Church.

The official evidence for the authority and primacy of scripture is its canonisation as a sacred corpus in the Church's tradition over the first four centuries of church life.

What is the essential content and purpose of the Bible viewed theologically? If the Bible is God's word, what does God wish to communicate through scripture? Three aspects define the substance of the Bible. First is the narration of the great deeds or 'wonders' of God (*megaleia theou*, Acts 2:11), ranging from the act of creation to the outpouring of the Spirit at Pentecost. These great acts of God form the bedrock of revelation on which everything else depends. A second aspect is the disclosure of the will of God recorded in the form of commands, theological truths, moral teachings and spiritual wisdom concerning God and salvation. At this level of teaching and guidance the Bible offers innumerable instructions and admonitions about a way of life that pleases God and leads to salvation. The third and deepest aspect of the Bible is personal encounter and communion with God. At this level, knowledge *about* God leads to immediate knowledge *of* God in his loving presence and power, through prayerful reading and worshipful hearing of God's word. The overarching purpose of scripture is not the mere conveyance of religious knowledge but rather the personal self-disclosure of and intimate communion with the mystery of God. Scripture is never an end in itself but a sacred road map pointing to a spiritual world; what the Church Fathers called 'true realities' (*ta pragmata*), at the heart of which is the mystery of Christ and new life in him.

But is not the Bible written in human words – Hebrew, Aramaic and Greek? How can it be speech from God and the word of God? The biblical authors themselves never seem to have considered the human factor in the composition of the Bible. Likewise some early Christian theologians, such as Athenagoras (second century), and very likely many ordinary believers, held a rather mechanistic view of inspiration. They believed that God whispered directly in the human author's ear just as the author's hand recorded God's exact words. In that case, the Bible would amount to a kind of enormous computer printout of the mind of God. Every word would have to be taken literally and absolutely; one would be committed to the literal historicity of all events in the Old Testament and the literal truth of all religious and moral instructions in the entire Bible. Such an approach to the scriptures creates a set of impossible intellectual and moral problems pertaining to biblical texts that speak about, for example, hatred and curses for enemies, the killing of children, human slavery, subservience of women to men and, of course, a literal seven-day creation.

In contrast to that approach, the preeminent Church Fathers of the fourth century – Athanasius, Basil the Great, Gregory the Theologian, Gregory of Nyssa and John Chrysostom – perceived an intrinsic human element behind the genesis of the Bible. The Bible is the word of God in human words.[1] Without diminishing the divine inspiration of scripture in its saving message, those Fathers acknowledged that God's revelation inescapably involved human beings with intellectual and spiritual limitations. They assumed a dynamic view of inspiration that allows for the contingency of human understanding. Not every verse of the Bible is to be taken literally. To speak of scripture as the 'word' of God pertains not necessarily to every word of the Bible, but to the Bible's saving message and to those of its passages and verses that communicate its saving message in various degrees of clarity. For example, the Bible in places appears to teach straight predestination (Jn 12:39–40; Mk 4:11–12; Rom 8:29). John Chrysostom called such instances 'idioms' of scripture which must not be taken at face value; otherwise ideas unworthy of God would accrue,[2] presenting him as an arbitrary and cruel tyrant. Again, in Revelation 20:2–4 we read about the expectation of a millennial Kingdom upon Christ's glorious return. But the major ancient interpreters from Origen to Gregory of Nyssa either entirely ignored this book or interpreted it symbolically. The Church eventually condemned the teaching of a literal millennium as a heresy. Furthermore, numerous texts of the Bible present women as being subservient to men. But Gregory the Theologian, when consulted by Emperor Theodosius on marriage and divorce, strongly argued by his interpretation of the underlying message of scripture that the same rights ought to be equally accorded to both men and women.[3] These are but a few examples showing that the 'mind' (*phronema*) of the major Fathers with respect to biblical interpretation held a flexible view of the Bible as a divine and human book.

A paradigm for understanding the nature of scripture in its divine and human aspects is the Incarnation. Christ is the incarnate divine Word (Logos) who, by becoming human, experienced the whole range of human attributes and emotions such as physical growth, hunger, pain, joy, anger, sorrow and true death, apart from sin (Hebr 4:15; 5:7). By analogy, though not to be pressed too far, the Bible is an incarnation of God's saving will embodied in human categories of language and expressions which are not necessarily inerrant in every detail but only in the underlying saving message. Scripture constitutes the *image* of truth or *record* of revelation in human words and not the *original direct revelation* behind the reported biblical events and narratives.[4] The Bible is true and trustworthy in its theological and ethical teachings but not always inerrant in its specific historical and geographic data. Moreover, even theological and ethical passages must be assessed in the light of the Bible's governing purpose and saving message. John Chrysostom viewed scripture as God's humble accommodation (*synkatabasis*) to humanity out of love.[5] The whole Bible is, to use another metaphor, a lowly manger of human concepts and language signifying the divine treasure of the mystery of the eternal Christ. In the end it is the Church, inspired by the same Spirit that moved the biblical authors, which has the final discernment and normative interpretation about what is historical and cultural and what is theological and binding in the scriptures.

Thus another definitive aspect of scripture is its ecclesial character. St Irenaeus of Lyons in the late second century argued powerfully that scripture belonged exclusively to the Church. Those outside of the Church had no right to it. Modern scholarship has corroborated the fact that the historical origins of the Bible, in both Israel and the Church, lie primarily in the respective communal memories and traditions celebrated in acts of worship and handed down by word of mouth over generations. For example, the Pentateuch and the Gospels largely incorporate oral traditions and interpretations first transmitted orally and eventually committed to writing. Justin Martyr referred to the Gospels as the 'memoirs' of the apostles. In the case of the apostle Paul, we have the composition of individual letters by a specific and known author. He too, however, lived, worked and wrote within the broad stream of the Jewish and Christian traditions. In fact part of Paul's distinct concern was firm adherence to developing Christian traditions (Rom 6:17; 1 Cor 11:2; 15:3; 2 Thess 2:15; 3:6). The force of tradition behind the formation of the Bible is so enormous that scholars have mused whether the slogan 'the Bible alone' (*sola scriptura*) ought to be replaced with the slogan 'tradition alone' (*sola traditio*). But in fact, neither slogan is true because scripture and tradition are mutually interdependent.

That the Church is the foundational reality behind both scripture and tradition is abundantly evident. Memories and traditions neither arise nor endure without a community. When God called Abraham, God intended to create a community. When God summoned Moses to liberate Israel from Egypt, his goal was to establish a covenant people based on the gift of the Mosaic law. When Christ commissioned Paul on the Damascus road, he charged him to preach the gospel to the Gentiles, calling them to join the one body of Christ, the Church. Divine revelation neither occurs in a vacuum nor is primarily addressed to individuals. God's word establishes and nurtures community. It is through community that God seeks to fulfil his purposes in history. In their mutual interdependence, scripture, tradition and Church cannot be played off against each other.

Those Christians who follow the Protestant Reformation rightly claim that the gospel is supreme. They draw, however, the debatable inference that the gospel itself established the Church and/or that the gospel stands above the Church and its tradition. The Orthodox view is different. In the Orthodox perspective, what established the Church was not the gospel as such, but the original acts of revelation experienced by specific men and women drawn together by the Spirit to form the early Church. The gospel as a saving message has intrinsic power but no voice of its own. There could be no gospel apart from Mary Magdalene, Peter, James, Paul, Barnabas and the others who proclaimed the good news. The opponents of Jesus, who put him to death as a religious and political troublemaker, were not about to advance his cause in the world. The ones who did proclaim him were the apostles and others who experienced the decisive acts of revelation and were thrust forward by the outpouring of God's Spirit. The gospel was never a disembodied, floating message that could exist or act apart from the Church in which it is lived and to which it leads. Moreover, empowering and increasing the Church, the gospel from earliest times was seen as tradition, indeed the heart of the apostolic tradition as St Paul declares, using the explicit language of *paradosis* or tradition (1 Cor 15:1–11).[6]

Nevertheless, the Church does not possess the Bible in such a way that it can do whatever it pleases with it, for example through virtual neglect or excessive allegorisation. That view would compromise the interdependence of scripture and Church. In its canonical status, scripture occupies the primacy among the Church's traditions. The gospel informs and empowers the soul of the Church. The Bible as the supreme record of revelation is the indisputable norm of the Church's faith and practice. The scriptures thereby bear God's authority and challenge the Church, making it accountable to the revealed will of God. The neglect of the Bible and the silencing of its prophetic witness are inimical to the Church's evangelical vibrancy and sense of mission in the world. Nothing in the Church must therefore contradict the teaching and spirit of the Bible. Everything in the Church must be in harmony with the scriptural witness.[7] The Church in every generation is called to maintain the primacy and centrality of the Bible in its life, always attentive, repentant and obedient to God's word.

THE USES OF SCRIPTURE IN THE CHURCH'S TRADITION

Scripture becomes truly scripture, a sacred text bearing a saving message, as it is used and applied in the life of faith. The Bible has always functioned in multiple ways for the building up of God's people, such as in worship, preaching, education, mission, personal devotions, daily life and theology. Where people enjoyed neither literacy nor access to costly editions of the Bible, God's word reached them through liturgical recitation, hymnology, iconographic depiction and the ministries of preaching and teaching. Space does not allow here extended examination of any of those aspects. Nonetheless, it is helpful to comment briefly on the various uses of scripture, their mutual connections and distinctive elements, as part of the role and function of scripture in the Church's living tradition guided by the Holy Spirit. Scripture becomes the living word of God insofar as it is believed, embraced, applied and enjoyed in communal and personal life.

The Church's central use of the Bible is *liturgical*, that is, in the context of worship where biblical events are remembered and enacted (*anamnesis*) in close connection with selected scriptural readings, preaching and teaching. Scripture and worship share strong connections in language and content. From ancient times, ritual has functioned as the context for the solemn recitation and celebration of God's great acts of salvation, while the descriptive content and language of ritual is incorporated in the composition of the texts of the Bible. Further, the use of the Bible in worship meant that the contents and language of scripture would saturate the developing liturgical traditions. The corpus of Orthodox liturgical texts today is astonishing in its scriptural witness and scripturally based theological richness. The distinctive element of the liturgical usage of scripture is its solemn recitation to the gathered assembly in the spirit of prayer and invocation of God's presence. In this context of worship, the chanted or recited word of God becomes actualised as God's living word, stirring hearts and transforming lives. However, the empowering experience of God's living word in worship can occur only to the degree that worshippers themselves are attentive and receptive to God's holy presence and word.

The *homiletical* use of scripture, namely preaching, is closely but not exclusively bound to worship. Of course worship can strengthen the impact of the homily, just as the inspired homily can enliven worship. The distinctive aspect of the homily lies in its evangelical meaning and spirit. The eucharistic liturgy finds its focus in the last supper. In parallel, the homily finds its integrity in the gospel, the *kerygma* or heralding of

God's message of salvation. Just as the gospel proclaims the death and resurrection of Christ, so also the eucharistic service enacts the gospel
through solemn sacramental action. The gospel does not merely *tell*
about salvation; it *is* the power of God for salvation (Rom 1:16). God's
word carries with it God's power. Preaching reaches theological and spiritual integrity to the degree that it concentrates on God's saving activity in
Christ, proclaims its blessings and invites hearers to respond with gratitude and obedience. Its efficacy is in part connected to the evangelical
life and spirit of the homilist as an agent of the Spirit.

The *catechetical* use of scripture has its own distinctive aim, namely,
instruction. The homily often carries catechetical elements just as
catechesis ought to manifest evangelical aspects. The specific functions
of each complement the other. They also differ in that the one stirs up
faith by heralding God's word and the other nurtures the life of faith
through teaching. In the Bible, the ministry of teaching and training is a
divinely commanded ministry. For their part, the Church Fathers wrote
not only doctrinal works but also catechetical commentaries and homilies
for the education and pastoral nurture of the faithful and the catechumens
prior to baptism. According to the Church Fathers, Christ himself is the
supreme instructor (*paidagogos*), while the Bible is the textbook for
Christian 'training' (*paideia*). Inasmuch as scripture and theology involve
knowledge and wisdom, the ministry of biblical teaching is of enormous
importance.

The *devotional* use of the Bible marks one of the richest traditions that
Christianity derived from Judaism. The prayerful reading of the scriptures
became a major part of the early monastic tradition.[8] For example, in Athanasius's *Life of St Anthony*, three pillars are said to define monastic life in
this order: Christ, scripture and *ascesis* (the monastic discipline).[9] But the
Church Fathers urged the regular reading of the Bible by all Christians. To
read the Bible is, according to Chrysostom, to open the gates of heaven.
Through prayerful scriptural reading, Chrysostom taught, hearts respon-
sive to God's word are transformed from clay to gold.[10] One partakes of
the mystery of Christ, 'eating' the bread of God's word, as one partakes
of the same mystery of Christ by consuming the bread of the Eucharist.
The distinctive context for the meditative reading of scripture is that of
concentrated prayerfulness. Times of prayer and scriptural reading
become times of personal revelation through encounter with God's
living word. In worship this happens as a corporate experience, whereas
in devotional reading it is intimately personal. In both ways, through his
word, God spiritually intervenes, speaks, convicts, forgives, illuminates,
renews and lifts up the believer into the company of the saints and the

angels. True worship and biblical reading mutually enhance each other. Together with instruction, the liturgical and devotional uses of scripture transform receptive men and women into 'living Bibles' (*empsychoi bibloi*) embodying the scriptural witness in their daily lives.

Another crucial use of the Bible is *theological* or *doctrinal*. Doctrine has to do with normative principles and teachings that define the dogmatic framework of the faith critical to the unity of the Church. In the patristic tradition, St Irenaeus was the first great defender of the faith against those who claimed to have an authentic secret tradition.[11] His primary line of defence was to invoke the Church's 'rule of faith', grounded in the apostolic tradition and the apostolic interpretation of the Old Testament heritage. The 'rule of faith' was not some vague theological awareness but a doctrinal sense of clarity pertaining to foundational beliefs. Examples are that God the Father is the sole true God and Creator of the universe; that the Old Testament is holy scripture; that the Son of God truly took on flesh, died a true death, and rose from the dead in a transformed body, and that the human body and all of creation are intrinsically good and redeemable. All of these major teachings, often disputed by heretical teachers, defined the content of the Church's doctrinal sensibilities in the heat of controversy. The theological interpretation of scripture continued in subsequent centuries, especially during the great christological and trinitarian debates. Those debates centred on the interpretation of biblical texts and ended with the formulation of the Nicene-Constantinopolitan Creed. In scope and content the Creed is but an official theological manifesto, a normative doctrinal framework of the faith, based on the Bible and summing up the Church's binding teaching pertaining to God and salvation. Both the Creed and the theological tradition behind it constitute the substance of the Church's theology. In biblical interpretation, the appeal to the Church Fathers or to the 'mind' of the Church is essentially an appeal to the authority of the Church's normative doctrinal tradition pertaining to core issues of the faith. It is not intended to restrict scholarship and creativity. A rigid traditionalism based on scripture ought not to be replaced by a rigid traditionalism based on the Church Fathers and an inflexible view of tradition that would preclude use of critical non-biblical words such as *homoousios* ('of one substance') in the Creed.[12]

The *scholarly* use of scripture is not a modern development. It has important precedents particularly in Origen, Irenaeus, Athanasius, the three Cappadocians, Didymus the Blind, Theodore of Mopsuestia, Cyril of Alexandria and others. The Church Fathers were notable scholars of the Bible in their own right. Although the focus of their study of the Bible was the pastoral edification of God's people, the patristic tradition also demonstrates rich intellectual curiosity in pursuing biblical and theological knowledge for the sake of truth. The Fathers used contemporary methodologies derived from the Greek and Jewish traditions, properly qualified by theological criteria, to explore the depths of scripture. Convinced of the universal significance of the truth of scripture and the universal mission of the Church, they did not shrink from engaging the contemporary intellectual world philosophically and philologically. A striking example is Gregory of Nazianzus, also known as 'the Theologian' (fourth century). In the struggle between the Church and Emperor Julian's failed rejuvenation of paganism, the emperor tried in vain to prohibit the use of the Hellenic heritage by Christians. Gregory loudly protested that no one was about to cut him off from the intellectual discourse (*logos*) of his culture.[13]

Today Orthodox theologians who concentrate on biblical studies engage in the whole array of critical methodologies and discussions in international biblical scholarship. Orthodox biblical scholarship, not without creative tensions, has been established in Orthodox seminaries and universities as a field with its own integrity, but with a close eye on the patristic exegetical tradition.[14] In view of certain radical developments in liberal biblical studies, Orthodox scholars are aware that they must not repeat the mistakes of their Western colleagues.[15] Suffice it here to say that scholarship has a wholly positive purpose, namely, to explore the wealth of scripture and offer its riches to the Church and to the world. Scholarship in the Church, as in the case of the great Fathers, has a guiding role in the explication of texts and analysis of theological issues for the sake of clear teaching and the spiritual health of the Church's life. Orthodox biblical scholarship finds its true patristic character when it is integrated with all the above uses of scripture in the context of the Church's life, where the biblical message is enacted and actualised by the indwelling of Christ and the Holy Spirit. The Orthodox define the essence of tradition as the communal experience of salvation itself, the living and continuous presence of the Holy Spirit in the Church's ongoing life. The ultimate goal of all the above uses of scripture, including the scholarly use, is to let the scriptures speak afresh with God's explosive and transforming word.

THE INTERPRETATION OF SCRIPTURE

The study of scripture is best accomplished with love for the Bible and accompanied by spiritual interests in harmony with its nature and message. But 'the word of God is not fettered' (2 Tim 2:9). Countless women and men throughout the centuries have read the scriptures for comfort and direction without concern for formal matters of interpretation. Indeed most people, even preachers, usually read and interpret the Bible by means of free association within the community they live in and the body of knowledge they possess at any given time. Nevertheless, the issue of interpretation is critical to the integrity of biblical truth and the unity and soundness of the Church. Because Christians have been divided over the interpretation of scripture, it is all the more important to acknowledge the necessity of careful reflection on the principles and presuppositions of interpretation as part of the ecumenical dialogue and the pursuit of unity in obedience to Jesus' prayer (Jn 17:20–1). Of course, here is not the place for an analysis of 'hermeneutics', the art and science of biblical interpretation.[16] What follows, leaving aside debatable points, is a bare sketch of how the Church Fathers approached scripture and how contemporary Orthodox scholars have discussed this task.

It is important first to note that the Orthodox approach to scripture is not determined by commitment to any particular methodology or ideological bent. Rather the chief concern is how to be faithful to the revelatory witness of scripture, and its authentic application in the life of the Church, in harmony with the scripture's own purpose, nature and saving message. The approach of the Church Fathers combined both spiritual dispositions and interpretative principles. The spiritual dispositions included love of God, love of his word, faith, true repentance, prayer, cleansing of the heart, a life of evangelical virtue and a ceaseless striving after perfection in the image and likeness of Christ. Those aspects were viewed as absolutely necessary presuppositions for a personal encounter with God and communion with him, the essence of biblical study. Without such dispositions, St Symeon the New Theologian taught, the Bible in its spiritual treasures remains a closed book even to its most erudite scholars.

The interpretative principles that can be gleaned from the patristic exegetical heritage may be summed up as follows: (1) acknowledgement of the authority, primacy and unity of the scriptures according to God's inspiration and providence; (2) the centrality of the mystery of Christ as the decisive criterion of interpretation; (3) harmonious interdependence between scripture, tradition and church; (4) seamless coherence of theology, spirituality and daily life; (5) the importance of the 'rule of faith' and the accompanying theological tradition in interpretation; (6) creative use of available methodologies with emphasis on spirit rather than letter; (7) attention to the contextual intent of scripture interpreted in the light of its governing purpose (*skopos*) and narrative coherence (*akolouthia*); (8) full accessibility of the scriptures to the faithful and use of scripture for their pastoral benefit; and (9) the role of the ongoing living tradition as normative interpretative agent ultimately expressed through church councils and their reception by the whole Church.

Orthodox scholars in modern times have shown unwavering commitment to the above guidelines. The challenge has been how to reclaim the patristic heritage effectively in the context of modern culture in order to advance the mission of the Church. Georges Florovsky, perhaps the foremost Orthodox theologian of the twentieth century, raised the issue in a 1936 proposal for a 'Neo-patristic synthesis'.[17] Florovsky's proposal was essentially a plea for moving beyond rigid traditionalism to a more creative theology in the encounter with modern realities. What was needed, according to Florovsky, was to follow the 'mind' (*phronema*) of the Church Fathers rather than slavishly to quote them. The 'mind' of the Fathers was for him an integration of spirituality and scholarship anchored in the fullness of the gospel and the life of the Church, yet permitting self-criticism and creativity.[18] Florovsky did not take up the specifics of the hermeneutical task but wrote valuable theological essays on biblical topics expounding dynamic views of scripture, revelation, inspiration, interpretation, tradition and the Church.[19]

Some forty years later, John Romanides advocated a striking theological and biblical hermeneutic based on the model of the charismatic saint.[20] He defined the saint as one who has already achieved deification (*theosis*) in the present life. According to Romanides, only such living deified saints, who have experienced the spiritual realities to which the scriptures testify, can function as unerring agents of biblical interpretation and all other theological discourse besides. In later decades, John Breck has placed the emphasis not on individual saints but on the charisma of spiritual vision (*theoria*) itself. For him, *theoria* manifests the attribute of receptivity and spiritual perception of God's saving presence, the essence of the witness of scripture, supremely experienced in worship.[21] Breck finds modern historical methodology virtually useless, but the use of allegory, typology and chiasmus valuable, in that regard. Rather than looking to modern biblical scholarship, according to Breck, the true meaning and saving significance of the Bible can be apprehended only within the 'closed hermeneutical circle' of scripture and tradition in the life of the Church.[22] Savas Agourides and his student Petros Vassiliadis have found the key in worship itself, particularly the eucharistic liturgy. Here is the living tradition of truth where the narrated events and verities of scripture are celebrated and actualised. For Vassiliadis, the 'eucharistic criterion' is 'perhaps the only criterion' crucial to the approach to the Bible by the Orthodox: 'the way they know, receive, and interpret the Bible; the way they are inspired and nourished by the Bible'.[23]

Additional paradigms open a wider horizon. John Panagopoulos laid out a form of an ecclesial model grounded in the Church Fathers but taking modern biblical studies quite seriously.[24] He named his proposal 'christological, biblical, and ecclesial'. Its cornerstone is the classic mystery of the human and divine natures of Christ. On that christological basis, according to Panagopoulos, one and the same biblical text ought to be approached both historically and theologically. Historically the text must be entirely accessible to honest critical study according to the standards of historical and literary criticism. Theologically the text ought to lead the interpreter beyond the diverse results of exegesis to the unified transcendent reality of scripture's spiritual world signified by the text. That mystical reality, when scripture is read and taught, is actualised in both the practice and worship of the Church, 'the living Bible of Christ', which is identical to scripture in function and witness, manifesting the same mystery of Christ. More recently, John McGuckin has offered another form of ecclesial paradigm.[25] Calling it an 'ecclesial reading' of scripture, in tune with the collective 'song' of the Church's living tradition, he lays it out as a reliable option over against the 'chaos' of modern biblical studies. McGuckin explicates this 'ecclesial reading' in terms of three principles. The 'principle of consonance' marks a spiritual and moral connection between contemporary and ancient interpreters achieved by mutual communion in the Spirit. The 'principle of authority' leads to required respect for the apostolic heritage, expressed particularly in the rule of faith, as guide to interpretation. The 'principle of utility' applies to the usefulness of the study of the Bible for the actual life of the Church, namely, the pastoral nurture of God's people through preaching, a primary patristic concern.

The above Orthodox scholars are deeply committed to the Orthodox tradition of faith and learning. While they come at the hermeneutical task from various angles, they share a theological outlook that is built on common foundations: the centrality of the Church and its traditions; the unquestioned authority of the scriptures; profound respect for the Church Fathers; the inseparability of spiritual life and academic work; high concern for doctrinal truth; and disquiet over the disruptive impact of modern biblical studies. To proceed further, several things are necessary. The first is to establish a tradition of constructive scholarly conversation towards a commonly defined Orthodox hermeneutic. Another is to recognise that, despite the radicals and revisionists in modern biblical studies, there are many more biblical scholars, committed believers, and people of the Church who take very seriously the authority of scripture and the classic Christian tradition, and strive mightily to speak a word from God to the Church and the world today. In the face of secularism and pluralism, scholars from diverse backgrounds who share such commitments have every reason and responsibility to work together and learn from each other in obedience and witness to Christ. Still another need is for Orthodox hermeneutical proposals to refer far more specifically to the actual exegetical issues arising from the biblical texts themselves; and this should be done in conversation with Western colleagues who have wrestled with the same or related exegetical issues.[26] Orthodox scholars have much to learn as they also have much to teach.

Further reading

Breck, J., *Scripture in Tradition: The Bible and its Interpretation in the Orthodox Church*, Crestwood, NY: SVS Press, 2001.

Florovsky, G., *Collected Works of Church History*, vol. I: *Bible, Church, Tradition: An Eastern Orthodox View*, Belmont, MA: Nordland Publishing Co., 1972.

Collected Works of Church History, vol. IV: *Aspects of Church History*, Belmont, MA: Nordland Publishing Co., 1975.

Hopko, T., 'The Bible in the Orthodox Church', *SVTQ* 14 (1970), 66–99.

McGuckin, J., 'Patterns of biblical exegesis in the Cappadocian Fathers: Basil the Great, Gregory the Theologian, and Gregory of Nyssa' in S. T. Kimbrough, Jr (ed.), *Orthodox and Wesleyan Scriptural Understanding and Practice*, Crestwood, NY: SVS Press, 2005, pp. 37–54.

'Recent biblical hermeneutics in patristic perspective: the tradition of Orthodoxy', in T. G. Stylianopoulos (ed.), *Sacred Text and Interpretation: Perspectives in Orthodox Biblical Studies, Papers in Honor of Professor Savas Agourides*, Brookline, MA: Holy Cross Orthodox Press, 2006, pp. 293–324.

Pelikan, J., *Christianity and Classical Culture: The Metamorphosis of Natural Theology in the Christian Encounter with Hellenism*, New Haven and London: Yale University Press, 1993.

Stylianopoulos, T., *The New Testament: An Orthodox Perspective, Scripture, Tradition, Hermeneutics*, Brookline, MA: Holy Cross Orthodox Press, 1997.

'Orthodox biblical interpretation', in J. H. Hayes (ed.), *Dictionary of Biblical Interpretation*, Nashville, TN: Abingdon Press, 1999, pp. 227–30.

Vassiliadis, P., 'Canon and authority of scripture: an Orthodox hermeneutical perspective', in S. T. Kimbrough, Jr (ed.), *Orthodox and Wesleyan Scriptural Understanding and Practice*, Crestwood, NY: SVS Press, 2005, pp. 21–35.

Young, F. M., *Biblical Exegesis and the Formation of Christian Culture*, Cambridge: Cambridge University Press, 1997.

Notes

1. G. Florovsky, *Collected Works of Church History*, vol. I *Bible, Church, Tradition: An Eastern Orthodox View* (Belmont, MA: Nordland Publishing Co., 1972), pp. 17–21.
2. John Chrysostom, *Homily 16 on Romans* (Rom 9:20–1).
3. John A. McGuckin, 'Patterns of biblical exegesis in the Cappadocian Fathers: Basil the Great, Gregory the Theologian, and Gregory of Nyssa',

in S. T. Kimbrough, Jr (ed.), *Orthodox and Wesleyan Scriptural Understanding and Practice* (Crestwood, NY: SVS Press, 2005), pp. 41–3.

4. Florovsky, 'The Catholicity of the Church', in *Collected Works*, I, p. 48.

5. See R. C. Hill, 'St. John Chrysostom and the Incarnation of the Word in scripture', *Compass Theological Review* 14.1 (1980), 34–8; cf. Hill, 'St. John Chrysostom's teaching on inspiration in "Six Homilies on Isaiah"', *Vigiliae Christianae* 22 (1968), 20–6.

6. In the RSV translation, 'I *delivered* ... what I also *received*' (verse 3).

7. T. Hopko, 'The Bible in the Orthodox Church', *SVTQ* 14 (1970), 66–7.

8. D. Burton-Christie, *The Word in the Desert: Scripture and the Quest for Holiness in Early Christian Monasticism* (Oxford and New York: Oxford University Press, 1993).

9. Athanasius, *The Life of St Anthony*, 5, 7.

10. John Chrysostom, *Homilies on John*, 1.5.

11. See J. Behr, *Formation of Christian Theology*, vol. I: *The Way to Nicaea* (Crestwood, NY: SVS Press, 2001), pp. 111–33.

12. See J. Pelikan, *The Vindication of Tradition* (New Haven: Yale University Press, 1984).

13. F. M. Young, *Biblical Exegesis and the Formation of Christian Culture* (Cambridge: Cambridge University Press, 1997), pp. 73–4.

14. See T. G. Stylianopoulos (ed.), *Sacred Text and Interpretation: Perspectives in Orthodox Biblical Studies, Essays in Honor of Professor Savas Agourides* (Brookline, MA: Holy Cross Orthodox Press, 2006).

15. Such as demythologisation of scripture, rejection of the historical reliability of the Gospels, separating the Jesus of history from the Christ of the Church, and programmatic hermeneutical suspicion regarding the truth of the theological and moral witness of the Bible.

16. See further, Stylianopoulos, *The New Testament*.

17. G. Florovsky, *Collected Works of Church History*, vol. IV: *Aspects of Church History* (Belmont, MA: Nordland Publishing Co., 1975), pp. 22–5.

18. An example of self-criticism and creativity in the late patristic tradition is St Symeon the New Theologian. See Theodore Stylianopoulos, 'Holy Scripture, interpretation, and spiritual cognition in St Simeon the New Theologian', in Kimbrough (ed.), *Orthodox and Wesleyan*, pp. 55–71.

19. Most of these essays are compiled in his book *Bible, Church, Tradition*.

20. See Stylianopoulos, *The New Testament*, pp. 175–85.

21. J. Breck, *The Power of the Word in the Worshiping Church* (Crestwood, NY: SVS Press, 1986) and *Scripture in Tradition: The Bible and Its Interpretation in the Orthodox Church* (Crestwood, NY: SVS Press, 2001).

22. *Scripture in Tradition*, p. 10.

23. Vassiliadis, 'Canon and authority of scripture: an Orthodox hermeneutical perspective', in Kimbrough (ed.), *Orthodox and Wesleyan*, p. 27.

24. J. Panagopoulos, *Introduction to the New Testament* (Athens: Akritas, 1994), in Greek, pp. 430–59.

25. 'Recent biblical hermeneutics in patristic perspective: the tradition of Orthodoxy', in Theodore Stylianopoulos (ed.), *Sacred Text and Interpretation*, pp. 306–19.

26. My own hermeneutical concern and proposal expressed in Stylianopoulos, *The New Testament*.

2 Biblical interpretation in worship

ARCHIMANDRITE EPHREM LASH

The Orthodox understanding of scripture is based on two important principles of interpretation. In the first place, as the First Epistle to Timothy puts it, 'All scripture is inspired by God and is useful for teaching' (2 Tim 3:16). Secondly, holy scripture, both Old and New Testaments, forms one divine revelation. The Fathers of the Church and the writers of its hymns and prayers believed that the whole Bible spoke directly of Christ. This is what our Lord implies in Luke 24:44, 'Everything written about me in the law of Moses and in the prophets and psalms must be fulfilled.'[1] Holy scripture, therefore, is central to the worship of the Orthodox Church. Its text is chanted and proclaimed, but its words are also woven into the fabric of the Church's prayers and hymns, many of which are in fact little more than mosaics of biblical words and phrases. The Eucharistic Prayer of the Liturgy of St Basil contains over one hundred direct quotations and allusions to the biblical text.[2] Many other prayers are similarly constructed. Here is the prayer which introduces the Lord's Prayer in the Liturgy of St Basil:

> *Our God, the God who saves* [Ps 67 (68):21], teach us to thank you
> worthily for all the benefits, *which you have done* and do *for*
> *us* [Tob 12:6]. Do you, our God receive these gifts and *cleanse us from*
> *every defilement of flesh and spirit* [2 Cor 7:1], and teach us *to*
> *accomplish holiness in fear of you* [2 Cor 7:1], so that, receiving a part
> of your holy gifts with *the witness of a pure conscience* [cf. 2 Cor 1:12;
> 1 Tim 3:9], we may be made one with the holy body and blood of your
> Christ. And when we have received them worthily may we have
> *Christ dwelling in our hearts* [Eph 3:17], and become *a temple of your*
> *Holy Spirit* [1 Cor 6:19]. *Yes, our God* [Rev 16:7], make none of us
> *guilty* of these your dread and heavenly Mysteries, nor *weak* in soul
> and body through partaking of them *unworthily* [1 Cor 11:27, 30]; but
> grant us, until our last breath, to receive our part of your holy things as
> provision for the journey of eternal life, for an acceptable defence

before the dread *judgement seat of your Christ* [2 Cor 5:10]; so that
we too, with all the Saints, who have been well-pleasing to you since
time began, may become partakers of your eternal good things, *which
you have prepared*, Lord, *for those who love you* [1 Cor 2:9].

The hymn writers employ the same technique, as this hymn by
St Germanos, the eighth-century Patriarch of Constantinople, for the
feast of the Nativity, illustrates:

Come, let us rejoice in the Lord [Ps 94 (95):1], as we tell of the
present mystery. The *middle wall of partition* [Eph 2:14] has been
destroyed; the *sword of flame* turns back, *the Cherubim* withdraw from
the tree of life [Gen 3:24]; and I partake of *the delight of Paradise*, from
which I was cast out through *disobedience* [Rom 5:19]. For the
unchangeable *Image of the Father* [2 Cor 4:4; Col 1:15], the *Imprint*
[Hebr 1:3] of his eternity, takes *the form of a slave* [Phil 2:6], coming forth
from a Mother who did not know wedlock, not undergoing change; for
what he was he has remained: *true God* [Jn 17:3]; and what he was not he
has taken up, becoming man through love for humankind. To him let us
cry out, 'O God, born from a Virgin, have mercy on us.'

THE ORTHODOX BIBLE

The text of both the Old and the New Testaments is the Greek, as it
has been received by the Church. The precision is important because there
are numerous differences, some of them significant, between modern,
critical editions of the Greek Bible and the text enshrined in the liturgical
books of the Church. Moreover, there are passages where the differences
between the Greek and the Hebrew are theologically significant; others
where the Greek adds to the Hebrew. For example, the praise of the ant
in Proverbs, chapter 6, is followed in the Septuagint by the praise of the
bee, which is not in the Hebrew: 'Or go to the bee and learn what a
worker she is and how serious the work that she does; which kings and
private individuals make use of for health; she is desired and held glorious
by all; and though she is weak in her strength, she has become outstanding
by honouring wisdom.' It may not be irrelevant that the ant, in Greek, is
male, but the bee female.

The Orthodox Old Testament includes those books described by Protestants as 'Apocrypha' and by Roman Catholics as 'Deuterocanonical'.[3]
The latest edition of *The Old Testament According to the Septuagint*
published in Athens is based on the edition of Alfred Rahlfs, but also

takes into account that published by the Church of Greece in 1997, edited on the basis of the liturgical text by P. Bratsiotes. The text of the New Testament is in general what scholars call 'the Byzantine text'. The text of both Testaments is in effect the revision made in the late third century by St Lucian of Antioch, largely to 'improve' the Greek style of the original.

Whole Bibles in a single volume are not normally used in Orthodox worship; rather the necessary texts are found in three separate books: Psalter, Gospels and Apostle (including Acts). The passages used as liturgical readings at Vespers and Matins, which were sometimes collected as the *Prophetologion*, are nowadays to be found in the relevant volumes of the liturgical texts. Under monastic influence, Orthodox liturgy from the sixth century has been enriched with an extraordinary treasury of liturgical poetry which is collected in some fifteen volumes, covering the whole liturgical year. The *Paraklitiki*, or *Oktoechos*, contains the hymns for the eight-week cycle of services throughout the year; the *Triodion*, those for the Lenten period; the *Pentecostarion*, those for the period from Pascha to Pentecost; and the twelve volumes of the *Menaia*, those for the fixed feasts of the months of the year. Abbot Gregorios of the monastery of Docheiariou on Mt Athos likes to remind his monks, 'If you want to learn Orthodox theology, you will find it in the service books of the Church.'

THE PSALTER

The Psalms are the backbone of the daily round of offices, and, after the Gospels, are the most familiar part of scripture to Orthodox Christians.

The Psalter is divided into twenty main sections, known as *kathismata* (or 'sittings'), each of which is subdivided into three sections, or *staseis*. The number of psalms in a *kathisma* is not fixed, because there is no tradition of subdividing the longer psalms, such as we find in the Roman tradition. The numbering of the psalms follows that of the Septuagint, which, from Psalm 10 to Psalm 146, is one behind the Hebrew used in most English Bibles.

In theory, and in many monasteries, all 150 psalms are read in order – *lectio continua* – each week. In Lent the whole Psalter is read twice each week. The reading of the Psalter is suspended during the last three days of Holy Week and in Easter Week.

The arrangement of the psalms is essentially monastic in origin, though the use of Psalm 118 (119) at Sunday Matins and of Psalm 140 (141) at Vespers was also found in the 'sung', or 'cathedral', office. St John Chrysostom attests the use of Psalm 140 (141) at Vespers in his commentary on the Psalter. Most of the psalms for the hours have been chosen as appropriate to the time of day.

The total number of psalms read or chanted during an ordinary week is in theory around 400. Psalm 50 (51) is recited four times each day.

Psalm 118 (119) occupies a special place, and is recited daily. On Saturdays and Sundays the last verse of the psalm is followed by a set of short hymns, each preceded by verse 12, 'Blessed are you, Lord, teach me your statutes'. On Sundays the theme of these hymns is the resurrection. On Saturdays the theme is death, with an emphasis on humanity's being made in God's image and on the hope of Paradise. Psalm 118 (119) is also used at funerals and at some memorial services. On Holy Saturday, when the Church liturgically re-enacts the burial of Christ, it is chanted in front of the *Epitaphios*, or winding sheet, an icon of the dead Christ, each verse being followed by a short hymn of lamentation.

THE GOSPELS

The book of the Gospels is itself an object of particular reverence, as an icon of Christ himself. It is frequently bound in metal and often richly adorned. Traditionally the front cover is decorated with an icon of the Crucifixion and the back with one of the Descent into Hades. Its place is in the centre of the Holy Table. It is censed before the reading of the Gospel and accompanied by lights when carried in procession. As the chief teacher and evangelist of his flock, a bishop is ordained before the proclamation of the Gospel, and no one below the rank of deacon may proclaim the Gospel liturgically.

The four Gospels are read almost in their entirety during the year in a virtual *lectio continua*. This begins with the Gospel according to John from Pascha to Pentecost and continues with the Gospels according to Matthew, Luke and Mark until the Sunday before Palm Sunday. Naturally the major feasts have special Gospel readings in the Divine Liturgy.

On Sundays, major feasts and during Holy Week there are also Gospel readings at Matins. The cycle of the eleven Sunday Gospels of the Resurrection begins on the Sunday after Pascha and continues until the fifth Sunday of Lent. In the ninth century the Emperor Leo the Wise wrote a set of eleven hymns for these Gospels. They are poetic meditations on the biblical text. The tenth reflects on John 21:1–14:

> After your descent into Hades and your Resurrection from the dead,
> your disciples, O Christ, losing heart most probably at your
> separation from them, turned back to their work: and once again

there were boats and nets and a catch nowhere. But you appeared as
Master of all things, O Saviour, and ordered them to cast their nets
on the right hand side: and at once the word was deed, and there was a
great multitude of fish, and a strange supper ready on land. Your
disciples partook of it then; make us also worthy to enjoy it now in
spirit, O Lover of humankind.

Leo detects in the Gospel a suggestion that the disciples, despite
Christ's having appeared to them after his resurrection, have 'gone back
to square one'. Peter's 'I'm going fishing' takes us back to the beginning,
to the lakeside, the boats and the fishing nets, from which Jesus had
called them to be 'fishers of men'. Leo also sees an allusion to the Eucharist
in the meal by the lake, for though in the text Jesus invites the disciples
to 'come and breakfast', he speaks of a 'strange supper' and prays that we
too may be found worthy to partake of it.

A particular feature of the Sundays before Lent and those between Pascha
and Pentecost is that the hymns for those Sundays are inspired by the Gospel
reading appointed for the Liturgy. The following hymn for the Sunday of the
Prodigal Son (Luke 15) is also used in the rite of monastic profession: 'Make
haste and open to me your *fatherly embrace* [verse 20]. Like the *Prodigal* [13]
I have *squandered my whole livelihood* [13], turning away from the inexhaustible wealth of your mercy. Do not now despise my beggared heart, for
to you, Lord, with compunction I cry, "*I have sinned* [18]. Save me!"'

On the second Sunday before Lent, the Gospel is the description of
the Last Judgement in Matthew 25. The *kontakion* for the day is one of
St Romanos's finest poems, the opening stanza of which is also inspired
by Daniel 7:

When you *come* upon the earth, O God, *in glory* [Mt 25:31],
And the whole universe trembles,
While *a river of fire flows* before the seat of judgement,
And *books are opened* and all secrets are disclosed [Dan 7:10; Rev
    20:12],
Then deliver me from *the unquenchable fire* [Mt 3:12; Mk 9:43]
And count me worthy to *stand at your right hand* [Mt 25:33],
Judge most *just* [2 Tim 4:8].[4]

The weeks after Pascha are marked by the great Gospels linked to
baptism and enlightenment in the Gospel according to John: the pool of
Bethesda (ch. 5), the Samaritan woman (ch. 4) and the man born blind
(ch. 9). The hymns for the following week continue the celebration of
the event commemorated on the Sunday.

THE APOSTLE

The readings from the Acts and Epistles follow a similar arrangement to that of the Gospels. Acts is read in order, though with many omissions, from the Sunday of Pascha to Pentecost Sunday. From the Monday after Pentecost the Epistles are read in New Testament order, with the exception of Hebrews, which is read in Lent.

The Apocalypse, or Revelation, is never read liturgically, no doubt because its canonical status was disputed in the East at least until the late fourth century.

THE OLD TESTAMENT

Whereas the four Gospels are read each year almost in their entirety together with a considerable amount of the Acts and Epistles, outside Lent the Old Testament is little used liturgically.[5] The surviving homilies of the Fathers suggest that something similar may have been the case quite early in the history of the Church. St John Chrysostom commented in detail on the Gospels of Matthew and John, on Acts and on the Epistles of Paul, including Hebrews, but his only surviving extended Old Testament series of homilies is that on Genesis, which were begun, significantly, at the beginning of Lent to a crowded church of enthusiastic people.

In present practice Genesis, Isaiah (Isaias) and Proverbs are read daily during the six weeks of Lent. In Holy Week they are replaced by readings from Exodus, Ezekiel and Job. The readings from the first three cover a fair amount of the text, but those for Holy Week can only scratch the surface. In the Septuagint the final verses of Job are read on Good Friday at Vespers, because they include some extra verses 'from the Syriac' which refer to his 'rising again'.

Festal readings

Outside Lent, readings from the Old Testament are used at Vespers on major feasts. The regular pattern is for there to be three readings, except for the three great feasts of the Lord, Nativity, Theophany and Pascha, which have retained their ancient vigils, consisting of Vespers followed by the Liturgy of St Basil. All three are provided with a rich selection of readings from the Old Testament, followed by readings from the books of the Apostle and the Gospel. The first reading is always the opening of Genesis (1:1–12). For the Nativity there follow seven further Old Testament readings, for Theophany twelve and for Pascha fourteen.[6]

A study of the choice of readings throws valuable light on the meaning of the feasts and the typological use of the Old Testament. One of the most striking things about the readings from the Old Testament is the freedom with which the Church takes the text. Readings from the wisdom literature are frequently, to use the modern idiom, 'cut and paste jobs', and it is sometimes impossible to give a more precise reference than 'selection'.

The Nativity

The readings for the Nativity include the well-known passages from Isaiah 7, 9 and 11 and Micah (Michaias) 4 on Bethlehem. In the Septuagint the first title of the Child is 'Angel of Great Counsel' (Is 9:6), which is not in the Hebrew. The other passages are taken from the prophecy of Balaam in Numbers 24, Daniel 2 and Baruch 3.[7] In Numbers 24:17 the Septuagint has an important difference from the Hebrew. Where the Hebrew has 'A star shall come out of Jacob, and a sceptre shall rise out of Israel', the Greek has 'A star shall come out of Jacob, and a man shall rise out of Israel', a clear reference to an individual. This passage lies behind the story of the magi, who came from the East, the land of Balaam, and the Star in Matthew 1. The passage from Daniel describes the 'stone not cut by human hand', which destroys the great statue in Nabuchodonosor's dream, and which is understood as prophesying the Incarnation. Moreover, the image of the mountain from which the stone was cut is frequently applied to the Mother of God, as in this Sunday hymn in Tone 4: 'A *Stone not cut by human hand* [Dan 2:34] was cut from you, O Virgin, unhewn *mountain*: Christ, *the head of the corner* [Is 28:16, Ps 117 (118):22, Mt 21:42, Acts 4:11, 1 Pet 2:7], who joined together the natures that were parted; and so with joy, Mother of God, we magnify you'.

The passage from Baruch contains the sentence 'He appeared on earth and went about among men.' In the original the reference is to Wisdom, but in the patristic tradition it is one of the key texts on the Incarnation, and occurs frequently in the Fathers and the liturgical texts.[8]

Theophany

The readings for Theophany fall into two groups, in each of which, to use the Hebrew classification, the passages are taken from Torah (Genesis and Exodus), Former Prophets (Jesus son of Navi, Judges and 1 and 2 Kings (3 and 4 Reigns)) and Latter Prophets (Isaiah). Naturally there are a number of passages about the Jordan. Others contain references to miracles involving water: Moses' rescue by Pharaoh's daughter from the Nile, the crossing of the Red Sea, the waters of Mara, the fleece in the story of Gideon, Elijah (Elias) and the prophets of Baal. Of the passages from Isaiah, the first speaks of washing as a sign of repentance and forgiveness and the second speaks of God 'comforting his people' – with an echo of Isaiah 40, which itself is taken as prophetic of John the Baptist – and 'leading them through springs of water'.

Pascha

An early eleventh-century *Euchologion* from Constantinople includes a description of the paschal baptismal rite of the Great Church. From this it is clear that most of the fifteen readings would have been read in the Church while the patriarch was performing the baptisms in the baptistery. A rubric states that, after the Entrance at Vespers when the second reader begins 'Be enlightened, be enlightened' – that is Isaiah 60, the second of the present fifteen readings – 'the patriarch enters the vestry of the great baptistery'. After the baptisms, as the singers chant, 'As many of you as have been baptised into Christ have put on Christ', he anoints the newly baptised with the holy *myron* and then 'makes the entrance with them and begins the Liturgy'. The other readings include the story of the Passover (Ex 12), the crossing of the Red Sea and the song of Moses (Ex 13–15), and the last Passover before entering the promised land (Josh (Jesus son of Navi) 5). There are stories of only sons saved, or brought back from death, in Genesis 22 and 1 and 2 Kings. The whole book of Jonah, who is taken by Jesus himself as a type of his resurrection, is read, together with two passages taken as prophetic of the resurrection, Zephaniah (Sophonias) 3:8, 'Wait upon me for the day of my resurrection' (LXX), and Isaiah 63:11, 'Where is he who brought the shepherd of the sheep out of the earth?'[9] Translations dependent on the Hebrew, including the Vulgate, have 'sea' here rather than 'earth'. Other prophecies are relevant to baptism: the 'garment of salvation', the gift of 'the Spirit of the Lord' in Isaiah 61, and the promise of the New Covenant in Jeremiah 38. The final reading is the story of the three youths from Daniel 3, together with their song, which, as well as being a type of baptism, forms a triumphant conclusion to the readings just before the return of the patriarch to the church with the newly baptised for the paschal Liturgy. In the pagan world of the early Church, the story of the three youths who refuse the idolatrous worship of Nabuchodonosor's golden idol would have been particularly apposite.

The 'Ascension'

For the feast of the 'Ascension'[10] two passages from Isaiah and one from Zachariah are chosen. Isaiah 2 speaks of the 'mountain of the Lord', that from Zacharias 14 of the Lord 'standing on the mount of

Olives' (cf. Acts 1:12). Isaiah 63:1 contains the passage beginning 'Who is this who comes from Edom, the scarlet of his garments from Bosor?', a text that is quoted in a hymn at Vespers, which gives 'from the flesh' as the etymology of 'from Bosor'. This is wrong, but may be why the passage was chosen for this feast, one of whose main themes is that the Lord was taken up 'in the flesh', 'in his humanity'. The principal hymn for the feast cites 1 Timothy 3:16, with allusions to Luke 24:49, 50, 52: 'You *were taken up in glory*, Christ our God, giving *joy* to your disciples by the *promise* of the Holy Spirit, when through *the blessing* they had been assured that you are the Son of God, the Redeemer of the world.'

Pentecost

The readings for Pentecost are concerned with the gift of the Spirit. The first, from Numbers 11, tells how the Lord puts on the seventy elders some of Moses' spirit, and ends: 'and who would not give that all the Lord's people were prophets, whenever the Lord should put his Spirit upon them?' The second, from Joel 3, which St Peter quotes in his Pentecost sermon in Acts 2, contains the words, 'After this I shall pour out my spirit on all flesh.' The third, from Ezekiel 36, contains God's promise: 'And I will give you a new heart, and will put a new spirit in you' (Ezek 36:26).

The Transfiguration

'Why Moses and Elijah?' is a question people sometimes ask about the story of the Transfiguration. The Old Testament readings for the feast supply the explanation. Both Moses and Elijah were recipients of personal theophanies. In Exodus 24 Moses is called by God to ascend Mt Sinai. God's glory comes down upon the mount and Moses enters the cloud where he remains for forty days and forty nights. In Exodus 33 and 34 Moses asks to see God, but is told that no one can see the 'face of God' and live. God does though allow him to see his 'back': 'The Lord passed before his face, and proclaimed, "The Lord, the Lord, God compassionate and merciful, slow to anger, and full of mercy and true". And Moses quickly bowed to the earth, and worshipped the Lord.' In the story of Elijah at Horeb in 1 Kings 19 it is not said that Elijah saw anything, but the clause 'And behold, the Lord will pass by' evidently recalls the words in Exodus 34: 'And while my glory passes by I will put you in a cleft of the rock.' Elijah's reaction to the 'sound of the light breeze' is similar to that of Moses in Exodus: 'he wrapped his face in his mantle and went out and stood by the cave'.

The universal exaltation of the precious Cross

The first two readings contain Old Testament prefigurings of the Cross. The first, from Exodus 15, recounts how Moses made the bitter waters at Mara sweet, and therefore drinkable, by throwing into them a piece of wood, shown to him by God. At baptism the priest plunges the Cross into the font so that it may become water of salvation. In the second, from Isaiah 60, the prophet says to Jerusalem, 'The glory of Lebanon shall come to you, with cypress, pine, and cedar, to glorify my holy place; and I will make the place of my feet glorious.' Traditionally the Cross was made from these three woods. The Cross is also seen as God's footstool, and other texts about the Cross quote or refer to Psalm 98 (99):5: 'Exalt the Lord our God, and bow down before his footstool; for he is holy.' The third reading, from Proverbs 3, is a praise of Wisdom, chosen because the closing verse identifies Wisdom with the 'Tree of Life' – that is, the Cross: 'She is a tree of life to all who lay hold of her, and for those who lean hard upon her, as upon the Lord, she is safety.' If Adam lost Paradise and with it the Tree of Life, the Good Thief by means of a Tree is the first to re-enter it (Lk 23:43). The hymns for the feast assemble a remarkable collection of Old Testament passages that are taken as types of the Cross. Jacob forms a cross with his hands when he blesses Joseph's sons (Gen 48:17–19). Moses makes a cross over the Red Sea as he divides it to let the Israelites pass over and completes the cross by closing the waters over Pharaoh's army (Ex 14). He forms a cross as he stretches out his arms as Israel battles against Amalek (Ex 17:8–16). Even the piece of wood by which the prophet Elisha (Elissaios) makes the lost axe head float (2 Kings 6:4–7) is taken as a type of the Cross.

The saints

The readings for the feasts of saints follow a fairly clear pattern. Where possible they have specific relevance to the saint; where there is none, readings appropriate to the category of saint are chosen.

On feasts of the Mother of God the first two readings, from Genesis 28 and Ezekiel, present two of the most frequent types applied to her in the liturgical texts, that of the Ladder seen by Jacob at Bethel that unites heaven and earth and on which[11] the Lord was standing, and that of the Shut Gate of the new temple in Ezekiel 44, through which only the Prince may pass. A hymn from Matins in Tone 1 combines a number of these images of the Mother of God: 'Hail source of grace, hail *ladder* and *gate of heaven*, hail *lampstand* and *golden jar*, and *unhewn mountain*, who bore for the world Christ the Giver of life.'

Another, from the feast of the Dormition, sees Mary as the Ark of the Covenant and its furnishings: 'Your Offspring, O Virgin, has truly made you dwell in the *Holy of Holies* as shining *Lampstand* of the immaterial Fire, golden *Censer* of the divine Coal, *Jar* and *Rod* and *Tablet* written by God, holy *Ark* and *Table* of the Bread of Life.'[12]

Mary is the Ark of the Covenant because the Ark contained the Tables of the Law, on which were inscribed by God the Ten Words, and, in both Greek and Hebrew, which use the letters of the alphabet as numbers, 'ten' is represented by the letter 'I', which is the first letter of the name 'Jesus'. The other images underline Mary's role in the Incarnation as the one who carried God in her womb.

One of the most frequently met types of the Mother of God is the Burning Bush (Ex 3:1–6). God is in the bush, but the bush does not burn; God is in Mary's womb, but she is not consumed by the fire of the godhead. St John of Damascus puts it thus in the first Ode of his poetic canon for Christmas:

Clearly prefigured by the bush unburned
A hallowed womb has borne in it the Word,
God mingled with a mortal form, who now
Frees Eve's unhappy womb from bitter curse
Of old. Him now we mortals glorify.

Mary is the mountain of God because, as the psalm says, it is 'the mountain on which God was pleased to dwell'. In Exodus the 'glory of the Lord' appears in the cloud which covers Mt Sinai and the Tent of Witness, just as the incarnate Lord dwells in Mary the Mother of God. She is 'Paradise' and 'Eve's deliverance' because the Tree of Life made his dwelling in her, and her obedience (Lk 1:38) reversed Eve's disobedience (Gen 3:13). The phrase 'great treasured vessel of the inhabited world', which again recalls Mary's role as Mother of God, is not from scripture, but is a quotation from St Cyril of Alexandria.

The third reading, from Proverbs 9, about Wisdom building her house, may not, at first sight, appear to have any clear reference to the Mother of God. However, the Fathers frequently identify Wisdom with the Logos and so Wisdom's house is the body of the Mother of God. Thus St Athanasius links this passage with Proverbs 8:22 and John 1:14. He writes, 'It is clear that Wisdom's house is our body, which he assumed when he became man.' In the fifth book of the *Apostolic Constitutions*, Proverbs 9:1 is listed between Proverbs 8:22 and Isaiah 11:1 as a prophecy of the Incarnation.

The feast of the Angels on 8 November has readings from Joshua, Judges and Daniel, which recount Old Testament 'angelophanies'. Four of the six feasts of St John the Baptist have readings. Those for his Nativity include the stories of the births of Isaac and Samson to previously barren women. Samson also would, like John, be a Nazirite.[13] The third reading is from Isaiah 40, which is taken in the Gospels as prophetic of John: 'A voice of one crying out in the desert: "Prepare the way of the Lord, make straight his paths"' (Mk 1:3). This reading is also used for his other feasts, but the first two are replaced by Malachi 3 – 'See, I am sending out my messenger, and he will prepare a road before me' – and a text made up of selected verses from Wisdom 4 and 5, which is suitable for a martyr: 'A just man who dies will condemn the ungodly who are alive . . . We reckoned his life folly and his end dishonour. How has he been numbered among the children of God and his lot with the Saints?' It is therefore also used on the feast of St George. None of these three readings is taken unaltered from scripture, but all include other verses suitable to the feast.

The readings for the feasts of the Fathers of the seven councils of the undivided Church include Genesis 14, because the number of Abraham's servants, 318, corresponds to the traditional number of Fathers at the first council of Nicaea (AD 325), though not to the 630 at Chalcedon. The number is also symbolic, since in Greek it would be written TIH; that is, the Cross (T) and the first two letters of the name Jesus (IH). The liturgical celebration of the councils seems to be peculiar to Orthodoxy.

The readings for the feast of St Constantine from 1 Kings, Solomon's prayer at the dedication of the temple, and Isaiah 60 and 61 are clearly chosen in order to present him as the new Solomon and founder of Constantinople, the New Jerusalem. In Russian use, the same readings are used for St Vladimir of Kiev.

Modern offices

Some more recent offices are less traditional in their choice of readings. The readings from Joel in the Russian office for St John of Kronstadt seem to be a call to repentance following the events of 1917. In the new service which the late Fr Gerasimos composed for the feast of the Protecting Veil of the Mother of God, when the Church of Greece moved it to 28 October as a celebration of national deliverance in the 1940s, he replaced the readings from Genesis and Proverbs with ones from Numbers 9 and Exodus 40, which describe the protecting cloud over the Tabernacle. In his office for the Environment on 1 September, he had no precedents to follow and felt free to make his own choice of suitable passages from the Prophets. He retained the reading from Leviticus in the traditional office for the new church year on 1 September, but replaced the other two with passages from Isaiah 63–4 – a prayer that God will have mercy on humanity, fashioned in his image from clay, but which has turned from the right path – and Jeremiah 2: 'And I led you to Carmel to eat its fruits and its good things; and you went in and you defiled my land and made my inheritance an abomination.'

CONCLUSION

The second council of Nicaea in 787 decreed the following in its second Canon: 'Every one who is raised to the rank of the episcopate shall know the Psalter by heart, so that from it he may admonish and instruct all the clergy who are subject to him.' The majority of those who composed the Church's services were monastics whose daily reading was the Bible, much of which they would have known by heart, and this formed the raw material from which they worked. This makes Orthodox liturgy profoundly scriptural. As a Methodist minister remarked after attending the Vesperal Liturgy at Christmas, 'I have never attended such a scriptural service in my life.'

The hymn-writers did not have to search for types and images; 'wood,' or 'tree', immediately suggested the Cross; vessels or buildings containing something precious, the womb of the Mother of God. For the Fathers and hymn-writers, all the words of scripture spoke of Christ, the Word incarnate, and they have bequeathed to the Church an extraordinary wealth of theology and spirituality, which is a constant reminder that Christianity is not a religion of a book, but of a living Word.

Further reading

Barrois, G., *Scripture Readings in Orthodox Worship*, Crestwood, NY: SVS Press, 1977.

Cunningham, M., 'The meeting of the old and the new: the typology of Mary the Theotokos in Byzantine homilies and hymns', in R. N. Swanson (ed.), *The Church and Mary*, Studies in Church History 39, Woodbridge and Rochester: Boydell Press, 2004, pp. 52–62.

Hopko, T., 'The Transfiguration Liturgy in the Orthodox Church' in S. T. Kimbrough Jr (ed.), *Orthodox and Wesleyan Scriptural Understanding and Practice*, Crestwood, NY: SVS Press, 2005, pp. 305–20.

Lash, Archimandrite E., 'Mary in Eastern Church literature' in A. Stacpoole, OSB (ed.), *Mary in Doctrine and Devotion*, Dublin: Columba Press, 1990, pp. 58–80.

'Search the scriptures: a sermon preached before the University of Cambridge', *Sourozh* 64 (May 1996), 1–11.

www.anastasis.org.uk (contains English translations of many Orthodox liturgical texts, including some quoted in this chapter; some are copiously annotated).

Theokritoff, E., 'The poet as expositor in the golden age of Byzantine hymnography and in the experience of the Church' in S. T. Kimbrough Jr (ed.), *Orthodox and Wesleyan Scriptural Understanding and Practice*, Crestwood, NY: SVS Press, 2005, pp. 259–75.

Notes

1. Cf. Lk 24:25–7.
2. A fully annotated translation may be found on the internet at: www.anastasis.org.uk/basil_liturgy.htm. Full translations of the hymns cited below may also be found at this web-site.
3. See E. Lash, 'The canon of scripture in the Orthodox Church' in P. S. Alexander and J.-D. Kaestli (eds.), *The Canon of Scripture in Jewish and Christian Tradition* (Lausanne: Editions du Zèbre, 2007), pp. 217–32.
4. St Romanos the Melode, *Kontakia on the Life of Christ*, p. 221.
5. Before the Reformation the English forms of names of Old Testament persons were the Greek, which had passed, via Latin, into English. The present forms, such as 'Elijah' and 'Jeremiah', are not Hebrew, but pseudo-Hebrew, and seem to have been coined in the sixteenth century. The older forms were used by Roman Catholics until the middle of the twentieth century. The same is true of the names of the biblical books.
6. Modern Greek use has, most unfortunately, reduced the readings for Pascha to three, removing both the readings from Exodus on the original Pascha and those on the crossing of the Red Sea, retaining only those from Genesis 1, the book of Jonas and the Song of the Three Youths.
7. Baruch was considered to be part of Jeremiah (Jeremias) and therefore part of canonical scripture.
8. Modern versions of Baruch, therefore, have a feminine pronoun. The Greek is in fact ambiguous, since the subject of 'appeared' could grammatically be 'God', which is how the Fathers, including St Jerome, understood it. The traditional reading therefore passed into the Vulgate and the Latin tradition.
9. The liturgical text, which follows the Lucianic revision, differs from the standard Septuagint, which has 'he remembered everlasting days, the one who brought up from the earth the shepherd of the sheep'.
10. In both Greek and Slavonic the name of the feast is 'Assumption'. All the biblical texts refer to the Lord's being 'taken up', not to his 'ascending'. Cf. Mk 16:19; Lk 24:50–1; Acts 1:9, 11, 22; 1 Tim 3:16.
11. The Greek Septuagint states that God was 'leaning on the ladder', whereas the Hebrew is usually understood to mean that God 'stood by' Jacob.
12. Cf. Ex 16:32–4; 25; 30:1–10; 31:18; Lev 16:12–13; Num 17:16–26. A very traditional list of types of the Mother of God, all of which are christologically orientated.
13. For the details of the Nazirite vow, see Numbers 6:1–22. It included abstention from alcohol and from cutting the hair.

3 God in Trinity

BORIS BOBRINSKOY

THE DIVINE TRINITY

The mystery of the living God is that of the Tri-Unity. This, which unites the Three and the One in a single aspect and in a unique formulation but which also recalls the mystery of the Three and of the One, is beyond all conceptions of multiplicity and plurality. It is appropriate to cite here the celebrated passage by St Gregory of Nazianzus (known as 'the Theologian') in order to introduce Orthodox trinitarian theology:

> No sooner do I conceive of the One than I am illumined by the splendour of the Three; no sooner do I distinguish them than I am carried back to the One. When I think of any One of the Three I think of him as the whole, and my eyes are filled, and the greater part of what I am thinking escapes me. I cannot grasp the greatness of that One so as to attribute a greater greatness to the rest. When I contemplate the Three together, I see but one torch, and cannot divide or measure out the undivided Light.[1]

The whole trinitarian economy, that is, the joint and particular action of the divine Hypostases in this world, cannot be separated from the revelation and adoration of the Holy Trinity. This trinitarian revelation, which the prophets foretold, is realised by and in Christ in whom the fullness of the divine nature resides and in whom the Father and the Holy Spirit also remain in fullness. It was finally transmitted by and in the Spirit at Pentecost, inspiring and giving perpetual vigour to the sacramental and liturgical life of the Church.

When speaking of the trinitarian economy across the stages of the old covenant, the revelation of the New Testament, and the life of the Church, we must be careful not to slip into the current, widely accepted view that the Father acted in the old covenant, the Son brought about redemption, and the Holy Spirit gives life to the Church. In reality, these three 'stages' or 'epochs' of the history of salvation are all characterised by the common action of the three divine persons: (1) the Spirit inspired the prophets: as the Saviour would say in his turn, 'You search the scriptures … it is they that testify on my behalf' (Jn 5:39); (2) it is in obedience and union with the Father and the Spirit that Jesus accomplishes his work of salvation; (3) in the time of the Church, the Spirit brings us into conformity with Christ and renders us adoptive children of the Father.

THE SHAPING OF TRINITARIAN DOCTRINE AND LANGUAGE

Patristic writings, in continuity with the New Testament, reflect the Church's faith in Jesus Christ, dead and risen. It is from the core of a christological approach that the trinitarian vision of the apostolic Fathers and their successors unfolds. Likewise, the Spirit is known by his advent at Pentecost and by his permanent indwelling of the Church. He is the Giver of new life, that is, the life in Christ, and of prophetic and charismatic gifts (cf. Acts and 1 Cor) in the context of an eschatological inauguration of messianic times in the sacramental 'today' of the Church. Thus, instead of providing reflections *about* the Spirit, the Fathers share with us their experience *of* the Spirit in the Church. Christocentrism and belief in the power of the Holy Spirit do not diminish the early Fathers' fundamental theocentrism: they emphasise that it is God the Father who is the Principle of divine activity in the world and who manifests himself in his incarnate Son and in his life-giving Spirit.

Until about the fourth century, the Fathers of the Church sought above all to examine trinitarian action in the world. The apologetic works of St Irenaeus of Lyons stand out especially here, as he strongly emphasised the joint action of the three persons of the Trinity: the Father plans and gives commands, the Son performs and creates, while the Spirit nourishes and increases, and, by degrees, man ascends towards the Perfect One.[2] All three act simultaneously, but each acts in his own particular way.

It was with a spirit of reverential fear that the Fathers were then compelled to defend the divinity of the Son at the council of Nicaea in AD 325. They sought to remind Christians that Christ's coming into the world was a true manifestation of the eternal God and that his Incarnation opened the way to the fullness of salvation and of deification: '[God] was made man', said St Athanasius, following St Irenaeus, 'that we might be made God'.[3] But such insistence on the eternal unity of the Father and the Son risked compromising or minimising the uniqueness, or irreducible specificity, of each of the divine persons. The Cappadocian Fathers worked in the course of the fourth century to formulate a theological language and to establish the meaning of precise terms that would permit Christians on

one hand to distinguish the unity of the Three in essence, or shared substance, and, on the other, to express the mystery of each of the three
persons by using the philosophical term 'hypostasis'. This term settled
the trinitarian debate more conclusively than did the term 'person',
which had been introduced by Tertullian in the early third century, by
emphasising the unfathomable depth of personal being of each member
of the Trinity.[4]

The language of theology, in which the Church gives an account of
its faith, hope and knowledge of the trinitarian God, reflects the position
of the Church and of theology at the frontier between God and the
world. This language is 'capable of God' (*capax Dei*), yet at the same
time always inadequate. Language itself must undergo a baptism of fire;
it must die to human wisdom and be reborn in 'God's folly' (1 Cor 1:25).

THE TRINITY IN WORSHIP AND SACRAMENTS

Immersed as they are in the ecclesial and sacramental experience of
the trinitarian mystery, the Fathers and teachers of the Church have also
tried through the ages to formulate this mystery in rational and conceptual
language. They have defended it against trinitarian heresies by means of
conciliar formulations, and they have expounded it in theological and dogmatic treatises – not without fear and reticence about approaching
unfathomable depths with a human language which is always inadequate.
But they have also celebrated it in song, in the totality of the Church's
liturgy and hymnography. All language that speaks about God in the
third person entails the mortal risk of objectifying him or of speaking of
him merely in conceptual language: theological language must be 'doxological', issuing out of and returning to prayer.

The primary source of trinitarian doctrine is scripture. Orthodox
Christians therefore recognise the importance of studying the Bible and
being 'nourished' thereby, as they perpetually rediscover the sacramental
sense of the Word of God. And scripture is both interpreted and experienced, or relived, in the liturgical life of the Church. Liturgical and
sacramental theology thus constitute jointly an essential guide for understanding the Holy Trinity and for entering into communion with it.
Fr Alexander Schmemann demonstrates in his *Introduction to Liturgical
Theology* that one may truly speak of liturgical theology, thus introducing
a new concept into scholarship.[5] He speaks firstly of the sanctification of
time by the liturgical cycles of the day, week and year, showing that each
of these divisions of time reveals the mystery of Christ and, in consequence, that of the Holy Trinity. Sacramental remembrance, carried out

in the presence of the Holy Spirit, reminds Christians of the events of the past – and of the future.

In distinction from the liturgical cycles, the sacraments or mysteries of the Church break the closed and repetitive cycle of created temporality and introduce the faithful into the here and now of the redemptive sacrifice. Believers commune with this sacrifice both as contemporaries of the earthly life of Christ and as recipients of his heavenly intercession as he, the High Priest, intercedes for them at the right hand of the heavenly Father.

In the Orthodox understanding, it is not possible to comprehend the nature of liturgical action without constant reference to the trinitarian mystery into which worship introduces the Christian. All worship is an ecclesial, and personal, celebration addressed to the Father, through Christ, in the Holy Spirit. Christian worship also expresses the gift of knowledge and of the new life that comes from the Father, through Christ, in the Holy Spirit. St Basil of Caesarea (d. 379) expresses this concept in the following words: 'The way to divine knowledge ascends from one Spirit through the one Son to the one Father. Likewise, natural goodness, inherent holiness and royal dignity reaches from the Father through the Only-Begotten to the Spirit.'[6]

One image of the Trinity that appears frequently in Byzantine hymnography is that of illumination by the trinitarian Light. The Midnight Office of Sunday contains eight canons addressed to the Holy Trinity. One stanza reads as follows: 'Only source of Lordship beyond understanding, and single triple source of Godhead, now count me worthy of your radiance that shines with threefold light, that I may sing your praise, who are praised without ceasing by the mouths of Angels with thrice-holy hymns.'[7] We are here at the very heart of the liturgical inspiration of Byzantine Orthodoxy. Trinitarian mysticism is expressed in Christian worship in a comprehensive celebration of the Holy Trinity. At the same time, the divine persons do not lose their specificity in the common praise. The presence and the personal character of the Father, the Son and the Holy Spirit are stated forcefully and clearly. We may call this the christological–pneumatological dimension of worship.

On the other hand, it is the person and the mystery of Christ, the incarnate Word, and Son of Mary exalted at the right hand of the Father in the power of the Holy Spirit that allows us to define and clarify the specificity of Christian worship. The mystery of Christ represents the basis of Christian worship in its origin, nature and final goal. In its origin and nature, because the very life of Christ is 'liturgical': it is praise, intercession and perfect, unceasing communion with the Father. It is Jesus who leads to perfection humankind's relationship with the Father – a relationship of adoration, of praise, of thanksgiving, of knowledge, of communion, of love and of obedience. The final goal of Christian worship is christological because it actualises the living, active and sanctifying presence of Christ in the ecclesial community and in the world. Worship places the Church in a state of expectancy that is at once impatient and confident, steering it away from a desire to possess or become settled in the world.

Christian worship is also pneumatological. The proper function of the third person is actually to *be* the ability to praise and adore. It is the Holy Spirit who instils the desire for God in the faithful, who tears them away from their earthly ties, turning them towards the Lord Jesus, and thereby showing them the Father. Everything is given by the Holy Spirit; he is also the 'divine milieu', that is, the place of sanctification. There are certain defining moments of the hypostatic revelation of the Spirit: for example, in the 'farewell discourse' of Christ, the letters of the churches in the Apocalypse, and the 'sighing of the Spirit' in the Pauline epistles. The tension in the life of the Church as it awaits the heavenly City is possible through the action of the Spirit, who places it in a permanent *epiclesis* ('calling down').

It is the proper function of the Spirit, then, to be not the object of witness, but the power and the act of witnessing. But the revelation of the gospel also includes a reciprocal testimony in which it is the Lord Jesus who speaks to us of the other Comforter and reveals him to us. It is thus possible for Christians to bear witness to the presence of the Spirit in the Church and to his work of sanctification in the saints. Ecclesial worship clearly makes manifest this reciprocity of service of the incarnate Word and of the divine Spirit. The Holy Spirit permeates and gives life to liturgical language, validating theological language and upholding Christians' spiritual experience. Christian worship is thus worship in Spirit and in truth (Jn 4:23–4) and Christians may therefore become 'pneumatophores' or bearers of the Spirit. They can become transparent and obedient to the Spirit, transformed to the point of attaining the full stature of Christ (Eph 4:13), the form of Christ both abased and exalted (Phil 2:6–11).

If it is true that Christian worship integrates the faithful into the great movement of prayer, through the earthly and heavenly intercession of Jesus the High Priest, it must be added that the Holy Spirit is the sole content of Christ's *epiclesis*. All of Christian worship thus constitutes an unceasing *epiclesis* that culminates in a permanent Pentecost, that is, in the continuous presence of the Spirit in the Church.

The heavenly Father, on the other hand, represents the ultimate recipient of Christian prayer. He is the One to whom Jesus as High Priest

(Jn 14:16; Heb 7:25; 1 Jn 2:1) and the Spirit Comforter (Rom 8:26; Gal 4:6) intercede simultaneously, and to whom the whole Christ, the Head and the Body, raises up its prayer. In return, it is from him, the Father of Lights, that every perfect gift flows (cf. Jn 1:17): this includes sanctification, every blessing, and the gift of new life in the Church. In addition to this, the Lord's Prayer and the Divine Liturgy lead Christians into a relationship of intimacy with the Father, giving them the boldness to call on him as 'Abba' or 'Father'. This allows them to move, by an endeavour that is constantly renewed, from fear to love, from death and judgement to life, from the position of servant to that of friend and of son, or, in brief, to a state of fullness of life and of glory. The Lord's Prayer may thus not be recited except when one is inspired by the Spirit. This is why, in the Divine Liturgy, it is placed after the eucharistic *epiclesis*.

The relationship to the Father that is expressed in worship safeguards a fundamental Christian reality, which is typical of Orthodox spirituality: a sense of divine transcendence, of the mystery of the One who 'dwells in an unapproachable light, whom no man has ever seen or can see' (1 Tim 6:16). This tension or antinomy between filial intimacy and the unbridgeable abyss of the person of the Father is beneficial for the Church and for its worship. Creation and its crowning aspect, the human being, are, in this manner, marked irreducibly by a fundamental imbalance. Grace is present at the very core of the created being's nature, as its ultimate meaning (the Logos), and as its principle of life (the Spirit); also present is the abyss of non-being above which are held the divine, creative and loving Hands of the Father.

Although liturgical prayer may thus be addressed to the Father in specific instances, as in the eucharistic prayer 'Our Father', this is strictly limited. God the Father is not commemorated on his own in a liturgical context, nor are any liturgical feasts dedicated specifically to him. In addition, there can be no icons of the Father, in the strict sense of the term. Orthodox theology is very strict in its prohibition of representing the Father (and the Holy Spirit) in anthropomorphic form. We find instead typological forms of his manifestation, such as the three angels of the Hospitality of Abraham (Gen 18), or the right hand of the Father in the early iconography of the Resurrection or the Ascension.

THE DIVINITY OF THE HOLY SPIRIT

The defence of the divinity of the Son in the course of the fourth century necessarily led the Fathers to confess the divinity of the Holy Spirit and to recall his action in creation, in the life of the Church, and in the personal sanctification of the faithful. The Son and the Holy Spirit, in their joint activity in the world, were visualised by Irenaeus and other early Fathers in an economic sense as 'the two Hands of the Father'.[8] It was at the second ecumenical council at Constantinople (AD 381) that, following the work of the Cappadocian Fathers with regard to the divinity of the Holy Spirit, the Church affirmed that he should be 'worshipped and glorified with the Father and the Son'. At the same time the feast of Pentecost developed into a celebration especially of the descent of the Holy Spirit on the apostles in the 'upper room', the eucharistic *epicleses* invoking the Spirit were added to the Divine Liturgy, and the chrismation with oil after baptism, as the 'gift and seal' of the Holy Spirit, came into practice.

The role and presence of the Holy Spirit are prominent in the contemporary understanding of the Orthodox Church. St Seraphim of Sarov reminds us forcefully that the goal of Christian life is the acquisition of the Holy Spirit.[9] But it is important to trace the development of this tradition from the origins of Christianity to the present day. Along with the major contributions of St Maximus the Confessor and St John of Damascus on this subject, it is necessary to recall the importance of St Gregory Palamas's theological vision. The latter was a defender of the spiritual tradition of Hesychasm in the final period of Byzantine history. The apostles' vision of uncreated divine Light on Mt Tabor constituted the scriptural and christological foundation for his doctrine of the distinction, without division or confusion, between the inaccessible divine essence and the divine energies, which are uncreated but in which humans may participate. Thus, Gregory understands the Fathers' traditional doctrine on salvation in Christ and in the Holy Spirit as meaning deification, that is, participation and communion in the divine life. The current distinction between negative or 'apophatic' theology, which stresses the inadequacy of reason and human language to discern the divine mysteries, and positive or 'cataphatic' theology, which validates the usage of this language and which receives affirmation from a doxological perspective, here takes on its full meaning.

Unlike the scholastic notion of the divine attributes, which deals with them under the rubric of one God (*de Deo uno*), Orthodox tradition, represented by St Gregory Palamas, states that the divine energies are completely trinitarian: all of them issue from the Father and rest in fullness on the Son through the Holy Spirit. Gregory introduces a useful theological distinction which in fact finds a certain congruence with biblical pneumatology. As a trinitarian hypostasis, the Holy Spirit proceeds from the Father alone and rests eternally on the Son, but at the same time he is activated by an energy that belongs to the Holy Trinity as a whole, illumining and sanctifying the world. This distinction is valuable because it underlines the utter human inability to discern the mystery of the Spirit, on the levels both of the eternal trinitarian life (trinitarian doctrine) and of trinitarian grace (trinitarian economy), which affects the human being in his most profoundly inward state.

This distinction between the Spirit as hypostasis and the Spirit as trinitarian gift allows us to say that the Spirit comes into the world as a gift of trinitarian grace, at once sent by the Father and the Son and giving himself so as to be creation's communion with the trinitarian life. This frees us from a tendency to depersonalise the Spirit, such as we see in the scholastic notion of sanctifying grace. The Holy Spirit always acts in person, helping Christians to become persons in the image of the only Son and making each of them uniquely a child of the Father, since they are bearers of the same Spirit. It is in this manner that Augustine's statement that 'God is deeper within me than my most intimate self' ('Deus meus interior intimo meo') is realised.[10] What Augustine said in relation to God is what Orthodox Christians would say above all when pronouncing the names of the divine persons, in particular the Spirit, since we do not know when we pray whether it is we who pray in the Spirit (Rom 8:15) or the Spirit who prays in us (Gal 4:6).

THE FILIOQUE QUESTION

This brings us to the controversy over the *filioque*, the Western addition to the Nicene–Constantinopolitan Creed stating that the Holy Spirit 'proceeds from the Father and the Son'. As an Orthodox theologian, I consider the Augustinian and Thomist doctrines on the *filioque* to be incomplete, rather than erroneous or heretical. The intuitions of the patristic and Byzantine tradition, extending from the Cappadocian Fathers to Gregory of Cyprus and culminating in the creative work of St Gregory Palamas, allow us effectively to enlarge and deepen the approach to the mystery of the procession of the Holy Spirit within its proper theological framework, in which Augustinian theology may perhaps find its place.

Firstly, the notion of a double procession of the Holy Spirit from the Father and from the Son is less questionable in St Augustine than it is in the rationalist theological scheme that considers *first* the eternal generation of the Son without mentioning the Spirit, and then, *only in the second place*, the procession of the Holy Spirit. The Cappadocian Fathers remind us, and this is taken up again by St John of Damascus, that the generation of the Son and procession of the Holy Spirit operate *simultaneously*. One should not therefore discuss the generation of the Son without addressing *at the same time* the procession of the Holy Spirit, and vice versa.

Thus, contemplation and theological discussion of the trinitarian mystery should always have a ternary character, appropriate to the mystery of the Tri-Unity. In other words, one should never consider the relation of two divine hypostases without speaking at the same time of the third hypostasis, in such a way that each divine hypostasis eternally unites in himself the two others. Binary language (in other words, first Father and Son, then, in a following section, Father, Son *and* Spirit) betrays and contradicts the equality of theological language with regard to the trinitarian mystery. Because of the complete reciprocal inherence of the divine hypostases, the Son and the Spirit are each in the other. The Spirit rests on the Son; he is in the Son insofar as is also the fullness of the Father's love. St Gregory of Cyprus introduces an idea that is implicit in the previous patristic tradition when he says that the Spirit represents the eternal, intra-trinitarian manifestation of the Son, pouring forth eternally from him.[11]

It is appropriate here to mention the contributions of several twentieth-century Orthodox theologians on the subject of the procession of the Holy Spirit and its place in the long-standing schism between East and West. Vladimir Lossky underlines the importance of the Orthodox position, showing that a correct trinitarian doctrine necessarily requires that both salvation and the mystery of the Church, as Body and Bride of Christ, should have their beginning in what he calls the 'economy' of the Holy Spirit; this 'economy' is linked to the economy of the Son in the history of salvation.[12] Fr Georges Florovsky, on the other hand, argues against distinguishing between the two economies since, as he states, the Son and the Spirit act jointly in the trinitarian economy of salvation as 'the two Hands of the Father'.[13]

Following these theologians, the question of the *filioque* has been treated by Bishop Cassian Bezobrazoff, Fr John Meyendorff and Serge Verkhovsky.[14] In addition, we should mention the writings of Fr Florovsky's disciple, John Zizioulas, Metropolitan of Pergamon.[15] He underlines the constitutive role of the Holy Spirit in the mysteries of the Incarnation, redemption and Christ's presence in the Church, in what we might term a 'pneumatological christology'. On the other hand, it would not be illegitimate to describe the Orthodox understanding of the Spirit as 'christological pneumatology', since the Holy Spirit does nothing apart from resting on Christ, while at the same time being eternally in his divine person, both during Christ's life on earth and sub-sequently in his Church, insofar as it is his Body and his Bride. It is appropriate to mention here Fr Nicolas Afanasiev's important work with regard to what he calls 'eucharistic ecclesiology'.[16] The question is taken up again by such scholars as Paul Evdokimov,[17] Nikos Nissiotis[18] and Olivier Clément,[19] all of whom add significant insights to the debate.

As Lossky forcefully reminds us, the problem of the *filioque* is not one of secondary importance in the history of Byzantine controversies. What we say about the trinitarian God has repercussions in the life of the Church and in the spiritual development of human beings, since both are in the image of trinitarian life. Ultimately, it is the experience of the Spirit through the sacramental and liturgical life of the Church that opens the heart's understanding to a true theological and spiritual vision of the Trinity in all its fullness and truth. It is in this spirit and perspective that ecumenical dialogue between the Churches of East and West should be established, with respect and reciprocity, since both are led by the same Spirit of unity and love.

TRINITARIAN NAMES AND THE LANGUAGE OF GENDER

The tradition of the Church confesses unanimously the trinitarian God: Father, Son and Holy Spirit. We know, on the basis of Old Testament, Judaeo-Christian and Syrian traditions, that the Spirit is a bearer of feminine and even maternal characteristics, but it is impossible to define further the mystery of the third person who has not assumed a human existence and who is in his divine being beyond any gender determination. In the recent common declaration by the International Commission of Theological Dialogue between the Anglican Communion and the Orthodox Church, mention has been made of the use of masculine and feminine categories in theological language. 'God is beyond gender and sexuality', the document affirms.[20] The terms 'Father' and 'Son', applied to the first and the second persons of the Trinity, 'are in no way analogical, metaphorical or symbolical, but are iconic'.

The 'masculinity' of the proper names of the Father and of the Son belongs to the immutable trinitarian revelation of the New Testament. Jesus reveals to His disciples the name of God as Father and, to the great scandal of the Jews, shows himself to be the Only-Begotten Son. He is not only 'Son of God', but also 'Son of Man', according to the messianic meaning of this title; he is furthermore 'Son of Mary' as he submits himself to all the prescriptions of the mosaic law concerning the birth of a first-born male infant.

Moreover, the Old Testament revelation of God as the Bridegroom and Husband of his chosen people finds its fulfilment in the nuptial relationship of Jesus to his Church. This nuptial relationship is continued in the relationship of the presiding bishop to his Church, or of the priest to his community.

Even so, neither the Father nor the Son is imprisoned within the categories of fallen sexuality. St Paul reminds us that there is no male or female in Christ (Gal 3:28). This statement implies that the spiritual life of each human soul may be expressed by the rich spiritual symbolism of his or her nuptial relationship to Christ, the divine Bridegroom. In fact, the Fathers remind us that each believer, whether male or female, exercises a personal priesthood in the offering of spiritual gifts on the altar of his or her own heart.

THE TRINITARIAN BEING OF THE CHURCH

From its origins, the Church is an epiphany of the divine will for salvation, life and eternal communion. If God is Trinity, then man, created in his image and likeness, is not only an individual, but also a trinitarian communion. 'It is not good for the man to be alone' – these words in Genesis 2:18 do not merely concern a human couple in paradise; they express a reality inherent to human beings who are by nature and vocation beings of communion. We find here the roots of an ecclesiology that will fulfil this anthropology. To speak of a Church that is grounded in the image of the Holy Trinity signifies that the Latter, who is itself the perfect and eternal conciliarity, created a dynamic image, open to likeness with its prototype; an image that creates, establishes and receives humanity and the world into the circle of the trinitarian life. It is thus not enough to speak of the Church as a 'trinitarian communion'; one must also see in the Church the living and personal relationship with the trinitarian persons.

It is important for this ontology of the Church to remind us that the Church is the house of the Father: 'In my Father's house there are many dwelling places' (Jn 14:2). This is the house to which the prodigal son returned and where, as a place of relationship and of intimacy, the Spirit and the Son cry 'Abba, Father!' We have seen already, in relation to St Irenaeus of Lyons, the statement that the Church finds its primary and ultimate truth in its relationship with the Father: 'Christ, having recapitulated everything in himself, will return everything to the Father and then God will be all in all.' The beginning and the end are thus reunited in the mystery of the Father.

The Church of the Father is also of course the Church of the Son. And here we have all the Pauline images, such as house, dwelling-place and temple. The Church is the sanctified Body of which Christ is Head; it is bride, virgin and mother, for whom Christ is Bridegroom. In the Old Testament, it is the people of Israel who figured in this nuptial relationship with the divine Bridegroom; later, the Church became the Bride, sanctified by his precious blood, and representing the place of his Word and of his loyalty.

Finally, the Church is the Church of the Holy Spirit. This is a dimension that is currently being rediscovered, as we saw above. It is by the Holy Spirit that the Church offers life, truth and holiness. And it is by the Spirit – from the resurrection of Christ – that the Church attains victory in the saints and in the repentant sinners.

Thus, to speak of the Church as trinitarian communion is to understand that the mystery of the Church is the same mystery as that of the Trinity, namely, a mystery of love. Trinitarian love is thus the onto-logical, primordial event which establishes and creates the Church in its being and which determines its structures and institutions. The Church is conciliar according to the image of the trinitarian conciliarity which is active within it. Just as the three hypostases of the Holy Trinity are not divided by the divine nature, since each possesses it entirely and alive, similarly with the nature of the Church, the body of Christ is not divided by the multiplicity of Churches. However, just as the divine persons may be counted, as St Basil puts it, so may the Churches be numbered and there is a hierarchy among them. It is for this reason that the thirty-fifth Apostolic Canon establishes the synodal organisation of the ecclesiastical provinces, in order 'that the Father, Son and Holy Spirit may be glorified', as part of the very order of ecclesial life.[21] The organisation of the Church itself, the establishment of the just exercise of ministry, and the acceptance of primacy in the Church, are to the glory of the Holy Trinity.

The connection between the Trinity and the institutions of the Church applies also in the ecclesial life of the Christian community and in the personal consciences of the faithful. People grow and gain understanding both from the richness of the spiritual tradition and from the theological heritage to which they are heirs. They constantly find new meaning in the life in Christ; they are constantly rediscovering the richness of the tradition of the prayer of the heart and the invocation of the name of Jesus. Christians are conscious of the action of the Holy Spirit in Christian life and the need to acquire the treasure of his presence. They seek strength and courage to be witnesses in the Spirit to Christ's death and resurrection. This life in Christ, which is in, by and for the Spirit, represents the programme of Christian life, as well as of all social and political activity. It is to this that the Russian philosopher N. Fedoroff refers when he states 'Our social programme is the Trinity'; in other words, the Church should be concerned not only with the lives of individuals and their salvation, but also with the great human family whose vocation is to discover its trinitarian identity by means of the Church.

Further reading

Behr, J., *The Way to Nicaea, Formation of Christian Theology*, vol. I, Crestwood, NY: SVS Press, 2001.

Bobrinskoy, B., *The Compassion of the Father*, trans. A. P. Gythiel, Crestwood, NY: SVS Press, 2003.

The Mystery of the Trinity. Trinitarian Experience and Vision in the Biblical and Patristic Tradition, trans. A. P. Gythiel, Crestwood, NY: SVS Press, 1999.

Hanson, R. P. C., *The Search for the Christian Doctrine of God. The Arian Controversy, 318–381*, Edinburgh: T. & T. Clark, 1988.

Kelly, J. N. D., *Early Christian Doctrines*, London: A. & C. Black, 5th rev. edn, 1977.

Lossky, V., *The Mystical Theology of the Eastern Church*, London: James Clarke & Co., 1957; repr. Crestwood, NY: SVS Press, 1998.

The Vision of God, trans. A. Morehouse, London: Faith Press, 1963.

Meyendorff, J., *Byzantine Theology. Historical Trends and Doctrinal Themes*, London and Oxford: Mowbrays, 1974.

Prestige, G. L., *God in Patristic Thought*, London: Heinemann, 1936; repr. London: SPCK, 1952.

Vischer, L. (ed.), *Spirit of God, Spirit of Christ. Ecumenical Reflections on the Filioque Controversy*, Geneva: World Council of Churches, 1981.

Notes

Parts of this chapter are adapted from the larger work, B. Bobrinskoy, *The Mystery of the Trinity. Trinitarian Experience and Vision in the Biblical and Patristic Tradition*, trans. A. P. Gythiel (Crestwood, NY: SVS Press, 1999). Permission to use this work has been granted by St Vladimir's Seminary Press, www.svspress.com.

1. Gregory of Nazianzus, *Oration 40, On Holy Baptism* 41.
2. Irenaeus of Lyons, *Against Heresies* IV.38.3.
3. Athanasius of Alexandria, *On the Incarnation* 54; cf. Irenaeus of Lyons, *Against Heresies* IV.38.4.
4. See A. Casiday, 'Church Fathers and the shaping of Orthodox theology', below.
5. A. Schmemann, *Introduction to Liturgical Theology* (Leighton Buzzard: The Faith Press, and Crestwood, NY: SVS Press, 1966; 2nd edn 1975).
6. Basil of Caesarea, *On the Holy Spirit* 47.
7. Metrophanes, *Canon to the Trinity*, Ode 1, Tone 3. Translated by Archimandrite Ephrem Lash at www.anastasis.org.uk.
8. Irenaeus of Lyons, *Against Heresies* IV, preface 4.

9. *Conversation with Motovilov*, in Valentine Zander, *St Seraphim of Sarov* (London: SPCK, 1975), pp. 83–99.
10. See Augustine of Hippo, *Confessions* VII.10.
11. PG 142, cols. 240–85. For further discussion, see Bobrinskoy, *The Mystery of the Trinity*, pp. 298–301.
12. V. Lossky, *The Mystical Theology of the Eastern Church* (London: James Clarke & Co., 1957; repr. Crestwood, NY: SVS Press, 1998), pp. 156–73.
13. G. Florovsky, 'Christ and his Church' in *L'Eglise et les églises. Neuf siècles de douloureuse séparation entre l'orient et l'occident. Etudes et travaux sur l'unité chrétienne offerts à Dom Lambert Beauduin*, vol. II (Chevetogne: Editions de Chevetogne, 1955), pp. 159–70, esp. 168–70.
14. See studies by these theologians in a special issue of *Russie et Chrétienté* 3–4 (1950); also J. Meyendorff, *Byzantine Theology. Historical Trends and Doctrinal Themes* (London and Oxford: Mowbrays, 1974), pp. 91–4.
15. J. D. Zizioulas, Metropolitan of Pergamon, 'Apostolic continuity and Orthodox theology: towards a synthesis of two perspectives', *SVTQ* 19.2 (1975), 75–108.
16. N. Afanasiev, *The Church of the Holy Spirit*, trans. V. Permiakov, ed. M. Plekon (Notre Dame, IN: University of Notre Dame Press, 2007).
17. P. Evdokimov, *L'Esprit Saint dans la tradition orthodoxe* (Paris: Editions du Cerf, 1969).
18. N. Nissiotis, 'Pneumatologie orthodoxe', in *Le Saint Esprit* (Geneva: Labor et Fides, 1963), pp. 85–106.
19. O. Clément, 'A propos du *filioque*', *Le Messager Orthodoxe* 7–8 (1958), 9–32.
20. *Anglican–Orthodox Dialogue: The Dublin Agreed Statement (1984)* (London: SPCK, 1984; repr. Crestwood, NY: SVS Press, 1997).
21. Apostolic Canon 35.

4 Creator and creation

ELIZABETH THEOKRITOFF

According to the Christian understanding, the universe is God's creation. God does not simply give form to pre-existent matter, like Plato's demiurge; he invents the material world, bringing it into being out of nothing. This doctrine speaks of both the *fragility* of creation, in that it has no necessary existence, and its *firm foundation* in that it exists by God's choice. It is less a theory of origins than a doctrine of relationship between the universe and God. In the striking image attributed to Metropolitan Filaret of Moscow in the nineteenth century, 'All things are balanced upon the creative word of God as on an adamantine bridge: above them is the abyss of the divine infinitude, below them the abyss of their own nothingness.'[1]

This doctrine of creation *ex nihilo* leaves many questions to be explored. How does God exercise his will in creating and sustaining the world? What is the 'point of contact' between the uncreated and his creation? How can God be present in a universe that is by definition other than himself? What is God's intention for his handiwork, and what role does the human being play in his purposes? We will look first at some patristic approaches to these questions, and then at ways in which patristic insights are developed in modern Orthodox thought.

CREATION AND INCARNATION

In the second century, the Church was challenged by the dualist cosmology of Gnostic sects who held that Christ and his Father were not responsible for the created world, and that salvation consisted in transcending material creation. It is in response to this teaching that Irenaeus sets out the basis for Christian cosmology.

Irenaeus rejects outright the Gnostics' shadowy world of semi-created intermediaries. God himself is the maker of all things by his Word and Wisdom (Irenaeus identifies divine 'Wisdom' with the Holy Spirit); and God's will is the substance of all that exists.[2] He drives this point home by emphasising the continuity between the work of the Word in creation and in his incarnate life: Christ 'came unto his own' (Jn 1:11) in that he is truly the Creator of the world, invisibly containing all creation and inherent in all creation.[3]

The affirmation that the Creator is also the Saviour has clear eschatological implications. As later Fathers will repeatedly affirm, it is the *fashion* of this world that will pass away (1 Cor 7:31); its substance and essence will not be annihilated but renewed, because God is faithful.[4]

No less seminal is Irenaeus's appeal to the Eucharist as the paradigm for God at work in creation from beginning to end. How, he expostulates, can the Gnostics believe that the Lord gives us his Body and Blood through 'eucharisted' bread and wine, if they do not accept that the very growth of corn and grapes is equally his handiwork?[5] And looking forward, we can be confident that our bodies will rise from the dead, precisely because the grain of wheat itself has fallen to earth and died, and been raised and received the life-giving Word of God.[6] Irenaeus lays the firm foundation for the sacramental cosmology still characteristic of Orthodox Christianity – a vision of a world created at God's hand for incorruption and union with him.

Athanasius inherits Irenaeus's vision of the Word of God at work in the universe; but much of his energy was spent on dealing with problems left by Origen. Origen's failure to distinguish clearly between *generation from* God the Father and *creation by* him allowed the Arians to claim that the Son was some sort of superior creature: was not the Father the origin of both? Athanasius responded by making a clear distinction between the *essence* of God and his *will*. The generation of the Son belongs to the divine essence. Creation, on the other hand, is the product of God's will, his freedom, a truly new reality which has no essential affinity with God.[7]

Athanasius's sharp distinction between Creator and creation might seem to create a problem. If the world has no essential affinity with God, and if the Creator Word is not God's instrument but the uncreated God himself, where then is the point of contact between God and the world? How can we affirm that he is present in it? Athanasius gives a very clear answer, but one that requires the acceptance of a paradox. God in his *essence* has no affinity with the world, but by his *powers* the Word pervades the whole universe. Without this distinction, which we see refined over the next millennium in the Eastern Church, cosmology risks oscillating between pantheism and some sort of deism.

CREATION AS HARMONY AND UNITY

If the 'powers' of God pervade creation, then we would expect the created world itself to be constantly making him manifest and drawing us to him; and this is a recurrent theme in the Cappadocian Fathers. A sustained example is Basil's *Hexaemeron*, a set of sermons on the six days of creation celebrating the variety and dynamism of a world where the Creator has 'left everywhere visible memorials of His wonders'.[8]

The Cappadocians use the Platonist language of their day; and the modern reader, to whom this language is alien, can easily mistake their Platonic starting point for their conclusion. They do speak in terms of a divide between the intelligible and the sensible, and even of an 'affinity' between intelligible creatures and the Godhead. But the main thrust of their thinking is the way these inequalities are evened out in the Christian doctrine of creation. After creating the intelligible world, says Gregory the Theologian, God creates the material world – to show that he can just as easily bring into existence a nature utterly alien to himself. The tangible no less than the intelligible manifests the grandeur of the creator Word and proclaims his mighty works.[9] So we are left wondering whether the 'affinity' really counts for much. Gregory of Nyssa draws the logical conclusion as to the truly fundamental division: in comparison with the exalted nature of God, all created things are inferior to the same degree.[10] The 'unity in universal sympathy' which Basil perceives in the world[11] is more clearly defined as *unity in createdness*. It is for the sake of the whole creation that man the microcosm receives the divine inbreathing, so that nothing in creation should be deprived of a share in communion with God.[12] This sense of solidarity in createdness has remained a leitmotif of Eastern Christian theology.

Up to this point, the sources of Christian cosmological doctrine are essentially the same for East and West. Thereafter, however, Western cosmology is dominated up to modern times by Augustine and his spiritual heirs; many contemporary writers would see in this legacy a narrowing of the early Church's cosmic vision. In the East, by contrast, the development of that cosmic vision is only beginning at the turn of the fifth century.

The enigmatic figure of (Ps-)Dionysius the Areopagite influenced both East and West, but in rather different ways. Vladimir Lossky maintains that in the East, the tradition of (Ps-)Dionysius marks a triumph over Platonic hellenism; whereas in the West, (Ps-)Dionysius's work became a vehicle for Neoplatonic influences.[13] (Ps-)Dionysius takes up the Neoplatonist idea of the scale of being; but he turns it into a structure of *theophany*, revelation of God. Its purpose is to allow each creature to reflect the divine glory in its own unique way, according to its analogy with its Creator.[14] (Ps-)Dionysius's cosmic vision may be too spiritualised for modern tastes; but he does envisage a structure in which vastly incommensurate elements – angelic, human, animate and inanimate – are all held together and function as a coherent whole, focused on their Creator. And it is a cosmos shot through with the radiance of divinity. God is at once totally other, totally beyond everything that is, and 'in everything by the ecstatic power inseparable from himself'.[15] This is the vision that will be developed in the supreme cosmological synthesis of St Maximus the Confessor.

GOD PRESENT IN CREATION: MAXIMUS AND PALAMAS

Maximus the Confessor remains to this day the single most important figure in Orthodox cosmological thought. Using the traditional ideas of divine 'conceptions' or 'predeterminations' and of *logos* in creation, he explores in unprecedented depth and detail the meaning of creation in, through and for the Word (Logos) of the Father. Maximus's doctrine of the *logoi* of things (their 'words', rationales, intelligible principles) can in no way be reduced to a static world of Platonic forms. The *logoi* of things express the creative will of God, according to which each thing comes into being at the appropriate time; but they equally express God's presence within each entity, his providence for it and its ultimate goal. The *logoi* of all things are united in the Logos, and through them the one Logos is wholly present in the infinite variety of creatures. Maximus breaks definitively with Origen in giving full value to both the multiplicity of things and their dynamism: movement, change and becoming are not the result of a fall but part of God's intention. Stability and rest in God is the goal of all things, not their beginning.

All things are to be brought into unity in Christ, by the power of the Holy Spirit: and in this process, a key role has been appointed to the human being. By being himself focused on God, man was to heal the divisions within the created order and unite it with its Creator. But man failed to be centred on God and thus became a force for division instead of unity. This is how Maximus understands the cosmic effects of the Fall: it is not the shattering of a golden age, but a failure to take creation forward to its appointed goal.

There is an amazing boldness in the paradox of distinction and unity that Maximus has bequeathed to Orthodox cosmology. There is no confusion between Creator and creature. Each created thing has its own reality, its own unique manner of reflecting God's glory; and yet he can say that 'properly speaking, God is everything'[16] – since there is no being apart from God. In this vision which encompasses the whole arc of created existence, it can be seen that the process of deification is inseparable from the work of creation. Having their being in God, all things can be fulfilled only when he is all in all.

Maximus speaks of deification as 'being identical with God' – but he makes it clear that this is an identity in every respect *apart from essence*. It is this traditional distinction that makes it possible to express the fullness of God's immanence without lapsing into pantheism. A distinction between divine *essence* (what God is in himself) and divine *energies* or powers (God interacting with creatures) goes back through the Cappadocians and Athanasius to Clement of Alexandria and Philo; but it is only in the fourteenth century with St Gregory Palamas that it receives systematic and detailed formulation. Palamas's principal concern is not cosmology, but human experience of God. But since we are physical creatures, the two cannot be separated. If our bodily eyes can see God as light, as Palamas maintains, then the spiritual potentiality of matter is nothing short of awesome; and God is present in creation in the strongest possible sense. Like Maximus and the rest of his patristic predecessors, Palamas resolutely holds together the paradox: God is the nature of all things, and he transcends every nature. He remains wholly within himself, and dwells wholly within us.[17] But Palamas illuminates the paradox by exploring the real 'distinction in unity' between the essence and the energies of God. Between the utterly transcendent Creator and creatures there is a link, and the link is God himself in action.

So Palamas gives us the conceptual framework to affirm God wholly immanent in his creation without any pantheistic confusion; but the significance of his contribution goes beyond that. To quote Lossky, Palamas's theology 'crowns a long tradition of struggle to surpass the Platonic dualism of the perceptible and intelligible, sense and intellect, matter and spirit'.[18] Here the idea of *unity in createdness* is taken to its logical conclusion, triumphing over any notion of a 'kinship' with God enjoyed by the intelligible realm but not the material.

SOPHIOLOGY AND ITS LEGACY

The created order became a focus of theological interest in modern times as a result of the 'sophiological' speculations of the nineteenth and early twentieth centuries. This movement is associated especially with the names of Vladimir Soloviev, Pavel Florensky and Sergei Bulgakov. It can be seen as a reaction against post-Enlightenment rationalism, against a dualism that opposes faith and reason, spiritual and empirical; and indeed it drew inspiration from Western reactions to those tendencies, such as the mysticism of Jacob Boehme and Schelling's notions of 'panentheism' and 'world soul'. The 'pan-unity' which these thinkers were seeking to recover raised anew questions of God's relationship to the world, and here they invoke the figure of 'Sophia', the divine Wisdom. As the 'ideal personality of the world', Sophia seems also to be in ontological continuity with the divine essence; this comes dangerously close to suggesting a fourth hypostasis of the Holy Trinity. For many Orthodox theologians, the suspicion remains that sophiological thought is in many ways closer to Gnosticism and Origenism than to Orthodox Christianity. It does not seem truly to take seriously the reality of a universe created out of nothing, a wholly new existence radically 'other' than God. Sophiological thought certainly draws on the Church Fathers, but to a degree it also unravels the Fathers' synthesis, revisiting Gnostic and Neoplatonic systems of intermediaries between the divine and the created.

Sophiology has influenced Orthodox cosmological thinking in a peculiar way. The more extravagant speculations about the figure of Sophia have almost no following among Orthodox theologians; but the underlying longing to reclaim a vision of cosmic unity, of a world shot through with God's presence, has defined the agenda for modern thought. Long before 'eco-theology' became fashionable, Florensky and Bulgakov had responded to the challenge facing Christian cosmology in a scientific and increasingly technological age. It is a challenge taken up by theologians who react strongly against Sophiology, as well as by those such as Paul Evdokimov and (especially) Olivier Clément who are not afraid to use some of its daring images.

THE DYNAMISM OF THE WORLD: BUILDING ON MAXIMUS

It was the achievement of Orthodox patristic theologians of the twentieth century to reveal in the Church Fathers that vision of cosmic unity and divine presence that Sophiology was looking for, but without blurring the distinction between Creator and creation or introducing new intermediaries. Starting with Georges Florovsky and Vladimir Lossky, modern Orthodox theologians have done much to elucidate the Eastern Fathers' doctrine of creation. They reveal Eastern patristic cosmology as a largely untapped resource, clearly distinguishing it both from medieval Western doctrines (e.g. the created intermediaries of Eriugena) and from the philosophies whose terminology the Greek-speaking Fathers use so freely.

Modern theologians are concerned to show how the Fathers' grounding of creation in God's *will*, not his *essence*, safeguards the 'splendid newness of creation' as a reality truly distinct from its Creator.[19] It is increasingly emphasised that the notion of *logoi* in creation by no means ties us to a belief in the fixity of forms such as the Fathers themselves held; indeed, the *logoi* provide a promising way of thinking about an evolving universe.[20] They are 'fixed' in the sense that they are expressions of God's will which is not fickle. But they are far from static: they give created being its dynamism, precisely because they include what Florovsky calls the 'beckoning goal' of creation. Here we come to the paradoxical essence of createdness: it is a condition defined at once by being *other than* the Creator and by being *in relation to* him. The truth of creation, its 'transcendental entelechy', lies outside its own substance; so the movement most 'natural' to it, in the sense of 'proper', is to go beyond its own nature. The tension between the *nature* of creation and its *goal* leaves 'room for creation, construction . . . reconstruction – not only in the sense of recovering, but also in the sense of generating what is new'.[21]

CREATION, SALVATION AND TRANSFIGURATION

The goal and purpose of creation is fundamental to its being, and therefore central to Christian cosmology. The universe is not created static: it is created to go somewhere. 'The economy of God', writes Dumitru Stăniloae, 'consists in the deification of the created world, something which, as a consequence of sin, implies also its salvation.'[22]

The pivotal event in the salvation of the cosmos is the Incarnation of Christ. The Word through whom all things were made becomes part of his own creation, and, as Paul Evdokimov says, this event 'has introduced the whole of nature into the work of salvation'.[23] From the human point of view, the coming of Christ undoes the Fall and restores the human race to its intended path; but this fall–redemption arc must be seen as a subsection of the greater arc stretching from creation to deification. The Incarnation is not primarily a remedy for something gone wrong; it inaugurates the union between God and his creation for which all things were created.

The cosmic dimension of salvation is clearly expressed in Orthodox worship. The rejoicing of all creation at Christ's birth, the sanctification of water at his baptism, the darkening of the sun at the crucifixion as 'all things suffer with the Creator of all' – these are not mere literary devices. They signal the intimate connection between the work of creation and the work of bringing what is created into union with God in Christ. This is not to say that the Incarnation can be reduced to a cosmic process. The personal Incarnation of the Word as Son of the Virgin is a unique event, of a different order from divine immanence in the world. Yet it is a unique event that crowns and discloses what John Chryssavgis calls a 'normative spiritual movement'.[24] The personal presence of the Word fulfils the energetic presence of God without which things would not exist, and restores their proper directedness – their movement towards the goal defined in the 'word' of their creation. That goal is a glorious transfiguration, to which Christ's transfiguration provides a pointer.[25]

There is a prudent reticence about trying to define what a transfigured cosmos might actually be like; but all affirm that we look to a transformation of the actual cosmos, not its replacement. As Evdokimov points out, heaven and earth do not simply prefigure the 'new heaven and new earth'; they are the actual substrate of that future transformation.[26] The beginnings of this transformation can actually be glimpsed in the presence of holiness. The person conformed to Christ, whose love of God spills over to embrace all creatures, starts to realise around himself or herself the intended relationship between humans and the rest of creation. Stories of saints enjoying the cooperation of dangerous animals and even of the elements continue up to our own day, and are seen as an important testimony to the intended relationship among all creatures. It is in this light that miracles in general are seen: they are not a matter of overpowering the laws of nature, but rather 'exceptional anticipations of the eschatological state', 'revealing to nature a window that opens out onto its own most appropriate goal'.[27]

HUMANITY'S PLACE IN CREATION

It is no coincidence that the transfiguration of the cosmos is associated with the sanctified human person. The cosmos is our nature; we are its hypostasis, its conscious existence in relationship with God. In Clément's graphic image, our bodily existence is 'simply the form which the person, our "living soul", impresses on the universal "dust"'.[28] While affirming strongly that the human being and the cosmos as a whole are ontologically inseparable and interdependent, many Orthodox writers use the unfashionable language of the world existing 'for man'. The world serves man's temporal existence, so that he in turn can take it forward to eternal existence, to salvation and deification. It is in this sense that the world is said to be saved through man, not man through the world.

John Meyendorff has described the Orthodox view as 'a theocentric anthropology and an anthropocentric cosmology'.[29] This characterisation is true in its intended sense, but misleading nonetheless. Today, 'anthropocentrism' usually implies a human self-centredness altogether incompatible with a 'theocentric anthropology'. It would be less confusing, therefore, to speak of a theocentric cosmology in which human mediation has been given a pivotal role.

The human role in bringing creation to its fulfilment has been explored in great depth by Dumitru Stăniloae. He employs the patristic images of man as *microcosm* or world in miniature, and the world as *macro-anthropos*, man writ large, destined through man to attain its eternal purpose in communion with the personal God.[30] Following Maximus, he develops this theme in relation to God's *logoi*. The rationality of the world is a gift of God to man; man is to use and explore it so as to return it as his gift to God. In this way, the *logoi* of things become a *dia-logue* with our neighbour, and between us and God. It is quite clear that the purpose served is not our own, but God's; and that the work requires a process of synergy between the human spirit and the Holy Spirit. Even so, Stăniloae exudes a confidence in human 'work' and 'mastery' which is hard to share today.

Some of the questions raised by Stăniloae's anthropocentric language are addressed by John Zizioulas, writing some decades later and usually in an ecumenical milieu. In his detailed and systematic explanation of why 'nature needs man', he starts from St Athanasius's account of why creation requires salvation: instability and decay are *natural* to the created order precisely because it is created out of nothing. It must be understood that this in no way disparages the material world – it is simply a realistic description of the state in which all material creatures find themselves. But it means that creation has to *transcend itself* in order to survive. And this movement is possible only through man – precisely because he is 'also an animal' by nature, but in addition has the drive to be free of the laws of nature because he is a person in the image of God.[31] Man is thus called to be 'priest of creation' – a metaphor of which Zizioulas is perhaps the foremost exponent – in that he takes creation into his hands and offers it to God, thus bringing it into communion with God.

This sort of language can be misleading. If man is the necessary link between Creator and creation, one might ask, what becomes of divine immanence in the world? The emphasis on man's essential role as a bond of unity makes sense only if the 'movement', the *directedness*, of creation is central to our understanding. This allows us to make a distinction between the very being of the world which depends directly on God's creative and sustaining energies, and its ultimate goal which he wills to accomplish through the human. *Both* are manifestations of divine grace; Lossky points out that any 'pure nature', separate from the grace implicit in creation, would be a 'philosophical fiction'. But, as he clarifies, there are two levels on which the divine energies function. They are constantly active in all creation as determining causes, 'as the constant willing of God by which all being is created and preserved'. And in the Church, they are also given to humans by the Holy Spirit 'as the grace in which created beings are called to union with God' so that the entire universe may 'become the Church of Christ'.[32] The vital point, which Orthodox writers always have in mind but sometimes fail to explain, is that the latter function is necessarily grounded in the former. Man's role is not to turn a God-forsaken world into its opposite, but to allow it to become what it is. In the words of physicist and theologian Alexei Nesteruk, 'the process of giving the universe its existence in the hypostasis of the human being is deeply rooted in the universe as itself hypostatically inherent ("prior" to human beings) in the logos of God'.[33]

While this is a matter of basic agreement among Orthodox theologians, they differ widely in their enthusiasm for God's presence in the cosmos 'prior' to man. Zizioulas, with his frequent warnings about 'paganism', is at one end of the spectrum. Contrast the 'panentheist' affirmation of Kallistos Ware that 'nature is sacred . . . The entire cosmos is one vast burning bush, permeated by the fire of the divine power and glory.'[34]

Clearly related to the meaning of man as 'link' between creation and Creator is the question of how humans perform this task – a question of obvious practical importance. Many writers speak of 'humanising' or 'personalising' the world, but these terms have a variety of meanings. For Stăniloae, it often seems alarmingly close – despite all his caveats – to ideas of progress and development. Zizioulas shows much more awareness of the chequered history of human 'transformation' of nature, drawing a sharp distinction between developing nature to serve our own interests, and the development of which 'nature itself stands in need . . . *in order to fulfil its own being*'[35] (his emphasis); but it is unclear what this means in practice. Clément's idea of 'personalising' is a much more *cooperative* activity: the point is not to stamp everything with the mark of our own species, but to 'encourage [nature's] secret surge of praise'.[36]

The emphasis on 'use' and 'development' in speaking of humans' role in the world invites the question: what about the vastly greater part of creation that is beyond humans' reach? Nesteruk proposes an understanding of our role that does take the scale of the cosmos seriously. By speaking of 'hypostasising' the universe, he makes clear that the process has to do with the human's *quality* as 'hypostasis of the cosmos' more than with our activity. It is not a matter of shaping things into a human product, but of bringing them into a conscious relationship with God. And we do this through our understanding: our capacity to hold together the intelligible universe with the visible, to understand its meaning and to apprehend it 'in its connection and unity with the primordial ground of the Logos'.[37]

The logic of this is that, if the world exists 'for humanity', it is no less true that humanity exists for the sake of the universe. In this vein, it has been pointed out that the idea of the 'logoi of things' combined with that of man as 'cosmic unifier' is closely related to some variants of the anthropic principle.[38] But, to quote Nesteruk again, 'humanity is not just a purpose of creation (this would be suggested by the Strong Anthropic Principle); it can be understood only in the context of the promise of God for its salvation . . . as the mediating agency that is supposed to bring the whole universe through its knowledge to the new creation'.[39]

AN ECCLESIAL COSMOLOGY

The images that we use for the cosmos are important. We have seen over recent centuries the effects of a mechanistic model, followed by efforts to redress the balance by introducing more organic metaphors.

The images that have predominated in Orthodox thought are essentially ecclesial. The Orthodox understanding has been variously described as sacramental cosmology, eucharistic cosmology or cosmic liturgy, but the common factor is summed up in Maximus's words, 'the world is a church'.[40] It is physical space and matter structured so as to glorify God; and it is the place where the stuff of creation is brought into union with Christ. An ecclesial and sacramental cosmology obviously provides the context for the image of humanity as 'priest of creation'; and it also points to worship, rather than work or technology, as the best model for how we fulfil our role.

According to a hymn for the feast of Christ's baptism, he has been 'made manifest in Jordan to sanctify the waters' – to restore its sacramental potential. This is a recurring theme particularly in Evdokimov and Clément: Christ's presence on earth has rendered all creation 'secretly sacramental', allowing it to become 'a conductor of divine grace, the vehicle of divine energies'.[41] When the Church blesses and sanctifies creation, therefore, it is essentially making manifest what Christ has already accomplished.

'Creation as sacrament' might seem a diminution of the grandeur of the universe if one thinks of a sacrament as *merely* a material pointer to something beyond. A sacramental understanding of cosmology demands a cosmological understanding of the sacraments. As Alexander Schmemann insists repeatedly, consecration does not create a discrete class of sacred matter: it refers matter back to its original and ultimate meaning.[42] There is thus a continuity between the 'natural' qualities of matter and its sacramentality, since both equally manifest God's intention for it and his energies at work within it. This continuity can be clearly seen in Orthodox worship. In any sacrament, the Holy Spirit is invoked to sanctify matter and make it a source of new life; yet his personal coming at Pentecost is celebrated by filling the church with green branches, a reminder of his work as giver and sustainer of all life.

The Eucharist, the centre of sacramental life, is the supreme example of the world transformed into Christ. This idea goes back to Irenaeus, as we have seen. But our increasingly sophisticated understanding of the nature of matter and the interconnectedness of the universe allows ever deeper insights into its significance. Clément speaks of the Eucharist as a 'dot of matter brought into the incandescence of the glorious Body', from which 'the fire spreads even to the rocks and the stars whose substance is present in the bread and wine, gradually pervading with eternity the heart of things'.[43]

The 'organic' way in which the saving effects of the Incarnation are spread throughout the universe points to creation in its very being as a 'cosmic liturgy'. This phrase does not express only the human responsibility of 'offering up' the cosmos in thanksgiving; it refers also to the 'ontological praise' built into the nature of created things – that praise from all creatures evoked so eloquently in the psalms. When Orthodox refer to humanity as 'priest' of the cosmic liturgy, they speak out of a tradition in which a priest cannot celebrate alone. There has to be some congregation, which in a 'cosmic liturgy' can only be the totality of creatures. As Archimandrite Vasileios of Iviron expresses it, the 'words' of all created things concelebrate with the incarnate Word.[44]

LIVING IN GOD'S CREATION: AN ORTHODOX ETHOS

The practical implications of cosmology – the way we behave towards other creatures – is today a matter of increasing concern in light of the gathering environmental crisis. It is widely recognised that the Eastern Christian tradition has something to contribute here. Even those who speak of 'Christianity' as largely to blame for the crisis often note in passing that they are talking largely about the later Western tradition. The Orthodox response, typically expressed in terms of ethos and way of life rather than ethical principles, has been given high visibility by the present Patriarch of Constantinople, Bartholomew, and his predecessor Patriarch Demetrius. It has been worked out in some theological depth by Metropolitan John Zizioulas, Metropolitan Kallistos Ware, Bishop Basil Osborne and John Chryssavgis, among others.

The Orthodox approach to creation is often described as a eucharistic and ascetic ethos. If the rationality and 'usefulness' of the world are seen as a manifestation of God's will, then the proper understanding of it requires more than information and technical skill; it requires drawing closer to God, through sacramental life and ascetic struggle. We have spoken already about the eucharistic approach. Asceticism looms large because it is in essence a struggle to free ourselves from a relationship with the world that is predatory and addictive; this liberation enables us to approach God through creation. And thus we turn back to the created world with new insight, perceiving its essential 'words'.

These are the 'words' which we are called on to fulfil. When, therefore, Orthodox use language such as 'harmonising our life with the life of the universe', this is no pantheistic cosmicism: it is a recognition that 'the life of the universe' is nothing other than the Holy Spirit at work, bringing creation to fulfilment in Christ. At the heart of the Orthodox ethos lies the doctrine of creation, of our own createdness. This doctrine means that 'we have no real choice, if we wish to pursue our own true end, but to live in harmony with the Logos – and the *logoi* – of creation as well'.[45]

Further reading

Chryssavgis, J., *Beyond the Shattered Image*, Minneapolis, MN: Light and Life, 1999.
Clément, O., *On Human Being: A Spiritual Anthropology*, London: New City, 2000.
Constas, N. P., 'Commentary on the patriarchal message on the Day of the Protection of the Environment', *GOTR* 35.3 (1990), 179–94.
Florensky, P., *The Pillar and Ground of the Truth*, trans. B. Jakim, Princeton: Princeton University Press, 1997, esp. 'Letter Nine: Creation'.
Florovsky, G., *Collected Works of Church History*, vol. III, *Creation and Redemption*, Belmont, MA: Nordland Publishing Co., 1976.
Knight, Christopher C., *The God of Nature*, Minneapolis, MN: Fortress Press, 2007.
Meyendorff, J., 'Creation in the history of Orthodox theology', *SVTQ* 27 (1983), 27–37.
Nesteruk, A., *Light from the East: Theology, Science and the Eastern Orthodox Tradition*, Minneapolis, MN: Fortress Press, 2003.
(Osborne), B., Bishop of Sergievo, 'Beauty in the Divine and in nature', *Sourozh* 70 (November 1997), 28–37.
Pelikan, J., *Christianity and Classical Culture: The Metamorphosis of Natural Theology in the Christian Encounter with Hellenism*, New Haven and London: Yale University Press, 1993.

Notes

1. See G. Florovsky, *Collected Works of Church History*, vol. III, *Creation and Redemption*, (Belmont, MA: Nordland Publishing Co., 1976), p. 45; translation adapted.

2. Irenaeus of Lyons, *Against Heresies* II.30.9.
3. Irenaeus of Lyons, *Against Heresies* V.18.3.
4. Irenaeus of Lyons, *Against Heresies* V.36.1.
5. Irenaeus of Lyons, *Against Heresies* IV.18.4.
6. Irenaeus of Lyons, *Against Heresies* V.2.2–3.
7. Athanasius of Alexandria, *Against the Arians* 1.20.
8. Basil of Caesarea, *Hexaemeron* 8.8.
9. Gregory of Nazianzus, Oration 38, *On Theophany* 10–11.
10. Gregory of Nyssa, *Great Catechism* 27.
11. Basil of Caesarea, *Hexaemeron* 2.2.
12. Gregory of Nyssa, *Great Catechism* 6.
13. V. Lossky, *The Vision of God*, trans. A. Morehouse (London: Faith Press, 1963), pp. 104–5.
14. See A. Louth, *Denys the Areopagite* (Wilton, CT: Morehouse-Barlow, 1989), pp. 84–5, 105–9.
15. (Ps-)Dionysius, *On the Divine Names* 4.13.
16. Maximus the Confessor, *Ambigua*, PG 91, col. 1257A.
17. Gregory Palamas, *Triads* 1.3.23.
18. Lossky, *Vision of God*, p. 132.
19. V. Lossky, *Orthodox Theology: An Introduction*, trans. I. and I. Kesarcodi-Warson (Crestwood, NY: SVS Press, 1978), p. 57.
20. See A. Louth, 'The cosmic vision of Saint Maximus the Confessor' in P. Clayton and A. Peacocke (eds.), *In Whom We Live and Move and Have Our Being: Panentheistic Reflections on God's Presence in a Scientific World* (Grand Rapids and Cambridge: Eerdmans, 2004), p. 189.
21. Florovsky, *Collected Works*, vol. III, pp. 67, 62, 73.
22. D. Stăniloae, *The Experience of God. Orthodox Dogmatic Theology*, vol. II, trans. I. Ionita and R. Barringer (Brookline, MA: Holy Cross Orthodox Press, 2000), p. 1.
23. P. Evdokimov, 'Nature', *Scottish Journal of Theology* 18 (March, 1965), 11.
24. J. Chyssavgis, *Beyond the Shattered Image* (Minneapolis, MN: Light and Life Publishing, 1999), p. 54.
25. See Archimandrite Aimilianos, 'The experience of the transfiguration in the life of the Athonite monk' in A. Golitzin, *The Living Witness of the Holy Mountain* (South Canaan, PA: St Tikhon's Press, 1996), p. 200.
26. Evdokimov, 'Nature', 7.
27. Stăniloae, *The Experience of God*, II, p. 61.
28. O. Clément, *On Human Being: A Spiritual Anthropology* (London: New City, 2000), p. 109.
29. J. Meyendorff, 'Creation in the history of Orthodox theology', *SVTQ* 27 (1983), 34.
30. Stăniloae, *The Experience of God*, I, pp. 4–6.
31. J. D. Zizioulas, Metropolitan of Pergamon, 'Preserving God's creation' (Part 3), *Sourozh* 41 (1990), 35.
32. V. Lossky, *The Mystical Theology of the Eastern Church* (London: James Clarke and Co., 1957; repr. Crestwood, NY: SVS Press, 1998), pp. 101, 113.
33. A. Nesteruk, *Light from the East: Theology, Science and the Eastern Orthodox Tradition* (Minneapolis, MN: Fortress Press, 2003), pp. 236–7.

34. K. Ware (Bishop of Diokleia), *Through the Creation to the Creator* (London: Friends of the Centre, 1997), p. 9.
35. J. D. Zizioulas, Metropolitan of Pergamon, 'Proprietors or priests of creation?' (keynote address, Baltic Symposium, June 2003); www.rsesymposia.org/symposium_v, p. 9.
36. Clément, *On Human Being*, p. 35.
37. A. Nesteruk, 'The universe as hypostatic inherence in the Logos of God' in Clayton and Peacocke (eds.), *In Whom We Live*, p. 175.
38. See Louth, 'Cosmic vision' in Clayton and Peacocke (eds.), *In Whom We Live*, p. 195.
39. Nesteruk, *Light from the East*, p. 230.
40. Maximus the Confessor, *The Church's Mystagogy* 3.
41. See Evdokimov, 'Nature', 16–17.
42. See A. Schmemann, *The Eucharist* (Crestwood, NY: SVS Press, 1987), p. 61.
43. Clément, *On Human Being*, p. 116.
44. Archimandrite Vasileios of Iviron, *'The Light of Christ Shines upon All' Through All the Saints* (Montreal: Alexander Press, 2001), pp. 23–4.
45. Bishop Basil (Osborne) of Sergievo, 'Towards the millennium: the transfiguration of the world and humanity in Christ', *Sourozh* 72 (May 1998), 28–39.

5 The human person as image and likeness of God

NONNA VERNA HARRISON

Who am I? What does it mean that I am human? Everybody asks these searching questions, but what is the Orthodox Church's answer? Orthodox reflection on what it is to be human begins with Genesis 1:26, 'Then God said, "Let us make man in our image, after our likeness".' Theological anthropology, that is the study of humanity in the presence of God, begins by asking what it is about each human person that manifests the divine image and likeness. First of all, the Fathers usually distinguish between the image and likeness. The image names those Godlike characteristics with which we began, such as rationality, free choice, perception and the capacity to develop an excellent character. These characteristics form the foundation of our human existence. By choosing to use them wisely, we can then acquire the divine likeness, namely perception of and communion with God, actualisation of all the virtues, and eternal life. Though the two concepts are inseparable, the image is static and the likeness is dynamic: we can become more and more like God over time.

Theological anthropology begins from the first three chapters of Genesis. People today wonder what the historical value of these stories is, given that science tells us another narrative about human origins. Yet when Orthodox theologians have read Genesis 1–3 they have looked for answers to questions about humanity here and now, not about our ancient ancestors. These biblical stories tell us who we are in relationship to God and the natural world around us. By depicting Paradise they tell us what our life is supposed to have been like and what we can hope to become; by depicting the Fall they tell us where we went wrong and what our life has in fact become. Adam represents every human person. St Gregory of Nazianzus or 'Theologian' (fourth century), St Symeon the New Theologian (eleventh century) and St Silouan the Athonite (twentieth century) all identified themselves with Adam and repented before God. In the end we have a choice whether to join ourselves to Adam or Christ, Eve or the Mother of God.

In Genesis 1:26, God says, 'Let us make'. To St Basil the Great, among others, this mysterious plural speaks of the Trinity deliberating over the creation of the human person. The Father consults with the Son and the Holy Spirit.[1] The image of the Trinity is thus imprinted upon humans in their creation itself. This connection provides a patristic foundation for twentieth-century reflections about humankind as image of the Trinity.[2] Moreover, St Basil points to the contrast between the language of Genesis 1:26 and the 'Let there be' that echoes throughout the earlier parts of Genesis 1. The Trinity pauses to deliberate about the creative masterpiece.[3] Then, instead of simply calling the human person into being, like the sun and the stars, 'God fashioned the human being with his own hands and breathed in something of his own breath' (Gen 2:7), as Clement of Alexandria says. He adds that God loves the human being as his own image, and that, because God is good, his image is good. Indeed, he says, 'the love-charm is within the human being – that which indeed is called a breath of God'.[4] That is, God has shared his own breath with us, which forms a concrete connection between the divine and the human. This shared breath then attracts his love to us as well. Basil, Clement and the other Fathers find an affirmation of immense human dignity in Genesis.

The New Testament includes Christ in the theology of the divine image and likeness, thus encouraging reflection on relationships among God, Christ and humankind. In 2 Corinthians 4:4, St Paul speaks of 'Christ, who is the likeness of God'. Colossians 1:15 says of Christ, 'He is the image of the invisible God', and Hebrews 1:5 adds, 'He reflects the glory of God, and bears the very stamp of his hypostasis.'[5] It follows that the Son's person is the image of the Father's person. Indeed, this is a perfect image, since Father and Son are consubstantial, equal and thus alike, except in the distinctive features each bears such as begetting and being begotten. So Christ is the image of God *par excellence*. Other human beings, by contrast, are obviously less than the Father and unlike him in various ways, so the image of God in humanity must be imperfect. The Fathers coined the term *to kat'eikona* ('that which is according to the image'), to name those aspects of humanity that manifest the divine image and are thus the core and definition of what it is to be human. Here we will follow the modern shorthand and speak of 'the image of God' in the human person, but would ask the reader to bear in mind the differences between Christ and all other humans. Christ *is* the image, while we are made *according to* the image; the difference between Christ and all other humans is thus qualitative, not merely quantitative.

When Colossians and Hebrews speak of Christ as the divine image, they also speak of him as Creator. Thus, from the beginning he is the link between the Father and humankind and the source from whom the image of God in humans is derived. St Irenaeus speaks of God the Father, who is above time, looking to Christ incarnate as the model when first creating humankind.[6] St Athanasius says that Christ is like an artist painting God's image in the human person, yet is also the model sitting for the portrait.[7] For humans, the divine image is first of all a direct link at the very core of their being with Christ, and through him with God the Father. So, through prayer we can find Christ in our own hearts. So also we can receive from him, whom we can reach from within our own selves, moral excellence and eternal life, and thus come to bear the divine likeness.

Genesis 1:27 adds, 'So God created man in his own image, in the image of God he created him; male and female he created them.' Despite the androcentrism of the late antique Mediterranean world in which they lived, nearly all the Fathers conclude that men and women alike bear the divine image.[8] They add that Eve's creation from Adam's side (Gen 2:21–2)[9] shows her to be *consubstantial* with him. John Chrysostom quotes Genesis 2:18, 'Let us make him [i.e. Adam] a helper like himself', and comments that this means 'like him, of the same essence (*ousia*) as he, worthy of him, lacking nothing that is his'.[10] Thus, the unity of humankind and the likeness between human persons are affirmed with the same strong word used to affirm that in the Trinity the Son is fully God and is one in essence with the Father. St John Chrysostom draws the conclusion that in paradise Eve shares in all of Adam's cosmic kingship.[11] Thus human unity and diversity both have their origins in our creation. However, today Orthodox theologians debate each other about the status of gender in humankind, as we shall see below.

Orthodox theologians speak of nature, persons and energies in God.[12] It is useful also to think of *human* nature, persons and energies. Our *nature* is the foundation of what we are and is what everybody shares, what makes all people alike. Being according to the divine image is intrinsic to our nature. It gives us the capacity to become like God or not, to choose between good and evil, to live a life of virtue, to love God and neighbours, to be rewarded by God in the age to come or not, and to enjoy communion with God in heaven. Their nature thus makes people capable of likeness to God, communion with him, and eternal life in the age to come – that is, salvation. Yet as human beings we are also *persons*. Our personhood makes each of us unique and invites us into loving relationship with God and with each other. As persons we are free and unique, we each become different, we have distinctive characteristics we can share with each other. As persons we can choose to receive the grace God constantly offers us and thereby acquire more and more of God's likeness. As persons we can be saved and enter into eternal life. Yet as human we also have *energies* or activities. We are called increasingly to acquire and exercise the virtues as energies, to share them with God, thus to share in God's energies and collaborate in his activities. These shared energies are thus the very content of the divine likeness and the very life of those who are saved.

The Fathers identify a variety of human characteristics as the divine image and likeness. We can conclude that the divine image is multidimensional; it has many aspects. These include freedom and responsibility; spiritual perception and relationship with God and neighbour; excellence of character and holiness; royal dignity; priesthood of the created world; and creativity, rationality, the arts and sciences, and culture.

FREEDOM AND RESPONSIBILITY

Gregory of Nyssa emphasises the centrality of *freedom*. He notes that humans are free because they are images of God, who is free.[13] They are able to choose between good and evil. This is why they were able to misuse their freedom and to fall. The divine image is like a mirror at the core of our being that we can choose to turn in different directions. When we turn it towards God, we too are filled with light, but when we turned away from God we became filled with darkness.[14] To put it another way, we are like actors in ancient plays who wore masks that showed what characters they played. When we fall, we take off the mask that depicts God's image and instead put on a mask bearing the image of a savage beast, or even a demon.

Thus, we can misuse the powers given us in the divine image with devastating results. Adam and Eve were tempted to make themselves gods apart from God (Gen 3:5), and so they used their Godlike freedom for unwise purposes. As a result, all human beings, like their first parents, live in a fallen condition. Having turned away from God, the source of life, we are subject to moral and physical disintegration and to death.[15] Yet we still remain free, though it is more difficult to choose good. In Paradise God's collaboration was readily available to Adam and Eve. Now our task is to turn back towards God. With God's help, we must pray and struggle as we seek to find the way back to what we were originally created to be.

Moral and physical disintegration was never God's original purpose in giving us freedom. God loves us and would like us to love him in return, so he would not have been satisfied in creating puppets or robots. Our freedom is what enables us to love authentically, to enter into genuine relationships with God and our neighbours. Freedom also makes our virtues real and worthy of reward and our crimes worthy of accountability. It enables us to collaborate with God in his own creative activities. Indeed, as Basil says, 'In giving us the power to become like God, [the Creator] let us be artisans of the likeness of God.'[16]

For Orthodox Christians, divine freedom supports human freedom, and human freedom is called to cooperate with divine freedom. The divine will and the human will are not incompatible; we were created to unite our wills with God's will, so that together with God we can do good and creative things. So we do not have to choose either divine freedom or human freedom, either divine sovereignty or human independence; Orthodox Christians affirm both. Human freedom need not be compromised in order to confess the glory of God; rather, it is an expression of God's glory. Yet this does not mean that an abundance of choices is good per se, or that all choices are equally valid. For example, a choice among cocaine, heroin and God is not better than a choice between heroin and God because it offers more options. Human freedom is a good gift because it makes it possible for us to love God in return, to assist in God's work, to grow into the divine likeness.

SPIRITUAL PSYCHOLOGY AND THE DIVINE IMAGE[17]

In the ancient world, the soul was understood as engaging in a broader range of activities than are sometimes ascribed to it today. It gives life to the body, so that without a soul a body becomes a cadaver. It also is the locus of human mental and emotional faculties including reason, free choice and conscience, fear and desire, sorrow and joy. Plato formulated a tripartite model of the soul that became standard in popular philosophy during Late Antiquity. The Cappadocians and many of the other Fathers use it, modifying Plato's model to say that the soul and all its faculties are in harmony when a person obeys God, rather than simply one's own reason. This model remains the basis of the Eastern Christian tradition of spiritual psychology.[18]

What follows is a simplified overview of this psychology. It is important to note that it names distinct activities of the human person that interact in various ways, not separate, self-enclosed, static entities that form components of the self. The first or highest of the three parts is *nous*, which means reason, mind or intellect, though this is understood as something greater, deeper and broader than the 'reasoning brain' emphasised today. Its activities include cognition and reasoning but also moral insight and deliberation, and freedom of choice. The intellect perceives the material world through the senses and organises and evaluates these perceptions. Yet its highest and most important function is to perceive spiritual realities, including other people in their spiritual aspect, angels and ultimately God.[19] St Basil explains succinctly how the mind can be used for good, evil or morally neutral purposes, depending where it focuses its attention.[20] According to the Fathers, the *nous* is the focal point of the divine image in the human person. Gregory of Nyssa says that we were created able to see and give thanks for all the beauties of the earth around us; and by the majesty of what we see, to sense 'the power of the Maker which is beyond speech and language'.[21] In our fallen condition, we have lost awareness of these powers of spiritual perception. The Orthodox spiritual traditions gathered in the *Philokalia* guide people in the lifelong process of cleansing their faculties of spiritual perception so they can know and love God and neighbour.

Those who receive the divine light in the mirror at the core of their being can shine, for they pass along the same light to others around them. The saints can see God manifest in their own pure hearts, though for most of us the inner mirror is covered with the mud of our sins.[22] It can be cleansed over time through a life of ongoing transformation for the better. We can come to see the divine light in the faces of the saints, and even of people around us who manifest Christ's character in diverse ways. Besides seeing icons of angels and saints on the walls of the church, we come to see fellow members of the congregation, or strangers we encounter on the street, as living icons.

In a mature, well-balanced human life, our *nous* is supposed to discern, receive and obey the will of God, and to guide and bring order to the other two faculties of the soul, which are understood as including the instinctive and emotional impulses and drives. Like the mind, both of these non-rational faculties can be used for good or evil purposes, depending in which directions they turn and move. One of these is desire, which seeks to move a person towards various things or persons, or draw them towards the self. Desire is easily misdirected when obsessively focused on the flesh or material possessions, but it also serves as the necessary driving force in love for God and love for neighbour.

The other non-rational faculty is called *thumos* in Greek, a word that is difficult to translate. This faculty complements desire in that it pushes things away from the self and sets limits on other impulses, one's own or those of other people. Plato and Christian Fathers influenced by Platonism see well-ordered *thumos* as a useful ally to reason in curbing one's inordinate desires. Basil compares it to a loyal soldier who has left his weapons with his wise general – that is, reason – and is ready to serve at his commander's bidding.[23] *Thumos* is also the necessary driving force in virtues such as perseverance, courage, self-restraint, rejection of evil, and struggling for justice. Yet *thumos* is most closely associated with anger, and in some contexts this is what it means, though clearly it has a broader range of meanings.

When a person's life is rightly ordered, all these impulses and drives work together harmoniously in serving excellence of character, guided by reason and obedient to God's will. However, this harmony, which existed in the original human state in Paradise, has become disrupted in human-kind's fallen condition. Our soul's faculties pull us in different directions and are often in conflict with each other. It is the whole person, body and soul, who either turns towards God, turns away from him in sin, or turns back towards him in repentance. The centre of the human being, body and soul, in which all the mature person's faculties and drives become con-centrated, is called 'the heart'. When the heart and all the human faculties are again directed towards God, their original harmony is restored.

When the non-rational faculties of the soul, desire and *thumos*, are allowed to run away with a human person, they become passions. 'Passion' is a slippery word in patristic writings. Sometimes it simply means instincts and emotions; sometimes it is intrinsically sinful, which is how I mean it here. As we have seen, instincts and emotions are not necessarily sinful at all. When allied with God and human reason, they become virtues – love for God and neighbour, perseverance, courage and self-restraint. 'Virtues' are excellence of character, as found in Jesus Christ and the saints. When we imitate Christ and the saints and are united with them, we acquire God's likeness, since virtues are originally divine attributes such as wisdom, justice, humility, forbearance, com-passion and love; by grace God shares them with us. The divine likeness is the aim of human existence. So virtues have a central place in Orthodox anthropology. Throughout history, countless sermons and spiritual writ-ings have been devoted to teaching people how to overcome passions and grow in virtues, and the lives of the saints have provided many diverse examples. Monks and nuns love to reflect on this subject as they strive to put the teachings into practice.

ROYAL DIGNITY

As bearers of God's image, all men and women are endowed with royal dignity. To be sure, St Basil is careful to keep a balance. He warns the proud to reflect on the earth from which they were made and the poor to reflect that dignitaries who intimidate them are also made from the earth. Yet he also encourages the poor not to envy the rich, since they too are endowed with all the gifts of the divine image.[24] Early Christians such as St Gregory of Nazianzus and St John Chrysostom challenged Roman ideas of social hierarchy by stressing the royal dignity of the poor, slaves, the homeless, the ill, the disabled and all people.[25] Yet Gregory of Nyssa argues from the divine image to social justice most clearly. He asks slave owners how they can enslave others who are like themselves:

> You condemn to slavery the human being, whose nature is free and self-ruling, and you legislate in opposition to God, overturning what is according to the law of nature. For upon the one who was created to be lord of the earth and appointed to rule the creation, upon this one you impose the yoke of slavery, as if he were resisting and fighting the divine precept. You have forgotten the limits of your authority, a rule limited to dominion over the non-rational animals. For scripture says, 'Let them rule birds and fish and quadrupeds and reptiles' [Gen 1:26]. How can you bypass the slavery within your power and rise up against the one who is free by nature, numbering one of the same nature as yourself among the four-legged and legless beasts?[26]

Similarly, he argues for the dignity of one who is homeless, disabled and disfigured by disease:

> He is a human being, created according to the image of God, appointed to rule the earth, having within his power the service of the non-rational animals. In this misfortune he has indeed been changed to such an extent that from his appearance it is doubtful whether his visible form with the identifying marks it bears is clearly that of a human being or of some other animal.[27]

Of course, the most authentic dignity resides in virtues and the divine likeness. Those who have become like God will be manifest in the age to come, when the social hierarchies that preoccupy us in this life will have melted away.

In order to affirm the dignity of slaves and the homeless disabled, Gregory of Nyssa contrasts the human person who is made in God's image with other animals who are not. The concept of animals as slaves is shocking today, but slavery was taken for granted in the ancient world, and Gregory was writing in a rural economy. Farmers work with animals every day, respect them, and have to take care of them to maintain their livelihood. Gregory's point is like that made by my uncle, a dairy farmer, who visited farms in South Africa during the Apartheid era. He told me afterward that he was shocked at the contrast between the sleek, healthy cows and the black farm hands in ragged clothes.

The authority given to humans in Genesis 1:26 means a responsibility to care for animals and for the natural world. In order to understand how this responsibility manifests the image of God, we must consider the role of the human body, which links human beings with the natural world. The Fathers affirm the body's great dignity. It is, after all, designed to house the mind made in the divine image, and equips the soul with tools that it needs to perform acts of virtue. Gregory of Nyssa says that, just as the soul is the image of God, the body is the image of the soul, that is, an image of the image of God.[28] Gregory of Nazianzus says the soul is called to educate the body, so that instead of remaining a slave it comes to labour alongside the soul in serving God, and then God will unite both with himself in the age to come.[29] Thus, provided we use our bodies to work with God, they too come to share in his likeness. All the Fathers affirm that God will raise the body from the dead to enjoy eternal life. There can be no greater affirmation of its eternal value.

The human body in fact has an important function in uniting the created world within itself, and joining it to God. The human person is a *microcosm*, a small world: that is, one who shares in every level of reality in the cosmos. Our bodies are composed of the same elements as earth and sky, while our souls share in the spiritual world with the angels. Gregory of Nazianzus says that God created the heavens and the earth, then created the human being as a participant in both who can unite them together.[30] St Maximus the Confessor says that humans had the task of uniting Paradise and the inhabited earth, heaven and earth, the material and immaterial worlds, and finally the created and the uncreated. When we fell we failed in this task, but Christ has accomplished it and invites us to join again in his work.[31]

Being a microcosm also enables the human person to become a *mediator*, which is an essential function of the image of God. As human beings we are called with Christ to a cosmic priesthood[32] whose task is to offer the world to God and bestow God's blessing on the world. Metropolitans John Zizioulas and Kallistos Ware, mindful of the ecological crisis, have said that the 'dominion' God gave humankind over the earth (Gen 1:28) is best understood as a priesthood.[33] Yet it is also a royal task. Just as Adam's work was to care for the garden of Paradise, our work is to care for the earth and all its creatures, on behalf of God.

THE DIVINE IMAGE AND HUMAN CULTURE

The divine image also includes the practical reason that has enabled humankind to develop creativity, the arts and sciences, economics and politics, and cultures. Because we are endowed with inventiveness, humans have created prodigious variety. Here, perhaps above all, it is clear that human free will governs the powers given with the divine image, so they can be used for good or evil. Human culture can glorify God and assist in his work, or it can threaten to undo God's handiwork by destroying humankind and with it the earth on which we live.

In icons, the Church has made ordinary matter into images that shine forth with divine beauty.[34] Icons are a unique expression of Christian life, and they are not to be equated with art in general. Yet they do point to the true purpose of all the arts: to disclose beauty that is ultimately from God, not to hide or distort that beauty, producing idols or serving secular ideologies. Practical creativity has also invented skills that enable the world's economy, such as the crafts, agriculture, manufacturing and technology. Economic exchange enables humans to share with one another, yet it also produces many material things that can draw our attention away from God. Why do many find it easier to perceive God in the beauty of the natural world, which he has made, than in cities, which we humans have made?

Scientific reason is also a facet of the divine image. People can use the methods of science to discern the patterns of the natural world, thus to 'think God's thoughts after him', to discover with awe the vast inventiveness of the Creator. Yet, as Evagrius Ponticus[35] and his successors in monastic life have understood, there is a way of contemplating nature that goes beyond scientific method. It is possible through prayer to perceive God within everything he has made, and at the same time to see God's ultimate purposes and plans at the heart of each created thing. Science can measure the outward surfaces of objects, but prayer can plumb their depths. In the end, we can come to see the whole creation as a vast burning bush, alight with God's glory.

Humans are also called to use reason to organise and govern society by implementing wise and loving plans. Political, economic and organisational leaders can thus share in the work of divine providence. Yet such power is often misused in ways that frustrate God's purposes. More generally, we must guard against the danger of becoming self-enclosed in our own imagination, of creating a 'virtual reality' that becomes an alternative to God's reality. We have been given creativity so we can share directly in God's creative activity, not so as to invent our own reality in a way that excludes God and tries to put humans in his place. That, after all, was the sin in the garden.

THE HUMAN BEING IN MODERN ORTHODOX THOUGHT[36]

Panayiotis Nellas, one of the principal twentieth-century writers on Orthodox anthropology, expresses the point made above in terms of the 'garments of skin' of Genesis 3:21.[37] According to St Gregory of Nyssa's interpretation, these 'garments' stand for mortality and all that goes with it; and that includes law, family life, political and economic life. All these things belong to the world of the Fall; but they are given within that world as blessings and means of salvation, provided that God is the ultimate goal of our endeavours within these areas. If, however, these 'garments' are treated as autonomous, they work to our harm. This provides Nellas with a clear framework for both affirming human engagement in 'the world' and keeping such activity in perspective.

Growing into the divine likeness through use and understanding of the world, through science and economic activity, is a theme very prominent in the thought of Dumitru Stăniloae. Whereas Nellas uses the image of 'garments of skin', Stăniloae starts from the cosmology of St Maximus. For him, using the world is a matter of developing our reason (*logos*) by perceiving God's Word and rationality (*logos*) in all creation. That Word calls for response and responsibility towards both God and the human community.[38]

Modern Orthodox anthropology is extensively concerned with interpreting the Church Fathers, but this should not obscure the fact that much of it is responding directly to the challenges of modern humanisms. 'False, atheistic humanism is a question put to the Church', writes Sergius Bulgakov, 'and Christian humanism would be an answer'.[39] A part of that answer is the notion of personhood,[40] seen as a corrective to both the impersonal collective of Communism and the individualism of capitalism. In addition to the well-known 'personalist' theologians discussed later in this volume, we should note the significance of Archimandrite Sophrony (Sakharov). In this Russian Athonite, the personalist emphasis of Russian religious philosophy meets the ascetic tradition with its profound experiential knowledge of human nature, and of the potentials of that nature revealed in the saint. Fr Sophrony shows how Christian asceticism and obedience open the person up to his or her full personal potential; their goal is prayer for the whole Adam-humanity, in which the oneness of human nature is realised.[41]

A similarly bold vision of human potential is expressed by Nellas, who advances what he calls a 'theocentric humanism'. Drawing on Maximus, Cabasilas and Nikodimos of the Holy Mountain, he sees humanity as created for the sake of the Incarnation. In the Virgin Mary, human nature itself is revealed as 'Theotokos' ('Mother of God') – the creature through whom the Word of God comes into the world so that the human being can be deified.[42]

An aspect of this 'high' anthropology is the value it ascribes to the human body. Much more emphatically than most of the early Fathers, modern writers underline that the totality of the human being is created in the divine image. Important here is the influence of St Gregory Palamas; his emphasis on the Transfiguration and the actual vision of divine light inspires continuing exploration of the heights to which our bodily nature is called.

Honesty requires that an exalted view of the nature of the human creature must go hand in hand with a profound sense that our world is touched by a Fall: most of what we regard as 'natural' does not correspond to the Creator's original intent. This applies even to the apparently basic division of humanity into male and female. Certainly, men and women are both created according to the divine image; but does this mean that sexual differentiation is a necessary consequence of being in the divine image? Theologians influenced by Russian religious philosophy are more inclined to see masculinity and femininity as ontological components of the human being; Paul Evdokimov is one such who has explored anthropology in some detail, for instance in his *Woman and the Salvation of the World: Christian Anthropology on the Charisms of Woman*.[43] But other Orthodox theologians, particularly patristic scholars, are sceptical of the claim that sexual differentiation in humans is part of God's original intention and will persist in the resurrection. As Valerie Karras points out, this raises some perhaps unexpected points of contact between Orthodox and feminist anthropology. Within Orthodoxy, this aspect of theological anthropology and its implications are still a subject of lively debate.[44]

CONCLUSION

In the Orthodox understanding, the mystery of human identity is an image of divine mystery. Gregory of Nyssa observes that the incomprehensibility of the human mind is an image of God's incomprehensibility.[45] So although we have identified many features of the divine image in humankind in this chapter, this can only be a starting point. The image of God is multi-faceted and open-ended. There is always more to God, and thus more to God's self-manifestation within the human being, to be discovered; more than words can describe. This means that, as humans, we are invited to share increasingly in God for eternity, as our capacity stretches towards the infinite. The gifts God gives us at once fill us and increase our capacity so we can hope to receive more of his life.[46] This eternal growth includes an ever closer sharing in the divine likeness.

Further reading

Harrison, V. E. F., 'Gregory of Nyssa on human unity and diversity', *Studia Patristica* 41 (2006), 333–44.

'Male and female in Cappadocian theology', *JTS*, n.s., 41 (1990), 441–71.

'Women, human identity and the image of God: Antiochene interpretations', *Journal of Early Christian Studies* 9 (2001), 205–49.

*Nellas, P., *Deification in Christ: Orthodox Perspectives on the Nature of the Human Person*, Crestwood, NY: SVS Press, 1987.

*Sakharov, N. V., *I Love Therefore I Am: The Theological Legacy of Archimandrite Sophrony*, Crestwood, NY: SVS Press, 2002.

Ware, K. T. (Bishop of Diokleia), *Through the Creation to the Creator*, London: Friends of the Centre, 1997.

*'The unity of the human person according to the Greek Fathers' in A. Peacocke and G. Gillett (eds.), *Persons and Personality: A Contemporary Enquiry* (Oxford: Basil Blackwell, 1987), pp. 197–206.

Zizioulas, J. D., Metropolitan of Pergamon, 'Preserving God's creation: three lectures on theology and ecology', *King's Theological Review* 12 (1989), 1–5, 41–5; 13 (1990), 1–5.

Notes

1. Basil of Caesarea, *On the Origin of Humanity, Discourse* 1, 4.
2. See B. Bobrinskoy, 'God in Trinity', above, and A. Papanikolaou, 'Personhood and its exponents in twentieth-century Orthodox theology', below.
3. Basil of Caesarea, *On the Origin of Humanity, Discourse* 1, 3.
4. Clement of Alexandria, *The Instructor* I. 3.7.1–3.
5. Here I have modified the RSV according to the Greek text.
6. Irenaeus of Lyons, *Against Heresies* III.22.3.
7. Athanasius of Alexandria, *On the Incarnation* 14.1–2.
8. See V. E. F. Harrison, 'Male and female in Cappadocian theology', *JTS*, n.s., 41 (1990), 441–71; and 'Women, human identity and the image of God: Antiochene interpretations', *Journal of Early Christian Studies* 9 (2001), 205–49.
9. In Hebrew and Greek, the word customarily translated 'rib' can as easily be translated 'side', which shows that when Eve was made from Adam, they emerged as two 'sides' of the same human being.
10. John Chrysostom, *Homily 15 on Genesis* 1.

11. John Chrysostom, *Homily 10 on Genesis* 4–5.
12. See B. Bobrinskoy, *The Mystery of the Trinity. Trinitarian Experience and Vision in the Biblical and Patristic Tradition*, trans. A. P. Gythiel (Crestwood, NY: SVS Press, 1999), esp. pp. 55–63.
13. Gregory of Nyssa, *On the Creation of Humanity* 16.11–12.
14. Gregory of Nyssa, *On the Creation of Humanity* 12.9–11.
15. Athanasius, *On the Incarnation* 3.11–13.
16. Basil of Caesarea, *On the Origin of Humanity, Discourse* 1, 16.
17. Much of this section is taken, with modifications, from the Introduction to V. E. F. Harrison, *St Basil the Great: On the Human Condition* (Crestwood, NY: SVS Press, 2005), pp. 22–4.
18. One of the best brief descriptions of these psychological terms can be found in the glossary at the end of each volume of the English translation of the *Philokalia*. The spiritual psychology described here is presupposed throughout this treasury of Orthodox monastic spirituality. See A. Louth, 'The theology of the Philokalia' in J. Behr, A. Louth and D. Conomos (eds.), *Abba. The Tradition of Orthodoxy in the West. Festschrift for Bishop Kallistos (Ware) of Diokleia* (Crestwood, NY: SVS Press, 2003), pp. 351–61.
19. Basil of Caesarea, *On the Holy Spirit* 9.
20. Basil of Caesarea, *Letter* 233.
21. Gregory of Nyssa, *On the Creation of Humanity* 2.
22. Gregory of Nyssa, *Homily on the Beatitudes* 6.4.
23. Basil of Caesarea, *Homily Against Anger* 5.
24. Basil of Caesarea, *On the Words, 'Be Attentive to Yourself'* 5–6, and *On the Origin of Humanity, Discourse* 2, 13.
25. See Gregory of Nazianzus, *Oration* 14, *On the Love of the Poor*, which aimed to raise funds for the hostel that St Basil had founded. John Chrysostom advocated for the poor throughout his life. See, for example, his *Homilies on Wealth and Poverty* (Crestwood, NY: SVS Press, 1984).
26. Gregory of Nyssa, *Homilies on Ecclesiastes* 4.
27. Gregory of Nyssa, *On the Love of the Poor* 2.
28. Gregory of Nyssa, *On the Creation of Humanity* 12.9–11.
29. Gregory of Nazianzus, *Oration* 2, *In Defence of this Flight to Pontus* 17.
30. Gregory of Nazianzus, *Oration* 38, *On Theophany* 11.
31. Maximus the Confessor, *Ambigua*, trans. Louth, p. 41.
32. This refers to the 'royal priesthood' of all believers (1 Pet 2:9).
33. Kallistos of Diokleia, *Through the Creation to the Creator* (London: Friends of the Centre, 1997); J. Zizioulas, 'Preserving God's creation: three lectures on theology and ecology', *King's Theological Review* 12 (1989), 1–5; 41–5; 13 (1990), 1–5.
34. John of Damascus, *On the Divine Images* 1.16; cf. M. Fortounatto and M. B. Cunningham, 'Theology of the icon', below.
35. Evagrius Ponticus, *The Praktikos* 1–3.
36. This section, along with texts marked with an asterisk in 'Further reading', are contributed by Elizabeth Theokritoff.
37. P. Nellas, *Deification in Christ: Orthodox Perspectives on the Nature of the Human Person* (Crestwood, NY: SVS Press, 1987), pp. 93–104.

38. D. Stăniloae, *The Experience of God. Orthodox Dogmatic Theology*, vol. II, trans. I. Ionita and R. Barringer (Brookline, MA: Holy Cross Orthodox Press, 2000), pp. 21–63.
39. S. Bulgakov, *Social Teaching in Modern Russian Orthodox Theology*, included with *The Orthodox Church* (Maitland, FL: Three Hierarchs Seminary Press, 1935), p. 16.
40. See A. Papanikolaou, 'Personhood and its exponents in twentieth-century Orthodox theology', below.
41. N. V. Sakharov, *I Love Therefore I Am: The Theological Legacy of Archimandrite Sophrony* (Crestwood, NY: SVS Press, 2002) pp. 137, 204–21.
42. P. Nellas, 'The Mother of God and theocentric humanism' in *Synaxis*, vol. I (Montreal: Alexander Press, 2006), pp. 129–40.
43. P. Evdokimov, *Woman and the Salvation of the World: A Christian Anthropology on the Charisms of Woman*, trans. A. P. Gythiel (Crestwood, NY: SVS Press, 1994).
44. See further V. A. Karras, 'Eschatology' in S. F. Parsons (ed.), *The Cambridge Companion to Feminist Theology* (Cambridge: Cambridge University Press, 2002), pp. 243–60; Karras, 'Orthodox theologies of women and ordained ministry' in A. Papanikolaou and E. Prodromou (eds.), *Thinking Through Faith* (Crestwood, NY: SVS Press, 2008).
45. Gregory of Nyssa, *On the Creation of Humanity* 11.3.
46. Gregory of Nyssa, *On the Soul and Resurrection*.

6 Christ and salvation

PETER BOUTENEFF

Christian Orthodoxy has never restricted its doctrine of salvation to a single plane. Rather, the answers to the questions of how we are saved, and even what it means to be saved, rest simultaneously in multiple dimensions or paradigms. Salvation is understood as *theosis* ('deification'), as communion, as illumination of understanding, as freedom from captivity; it is achieved through Christ's Incarnation, his divine-humanity, his teaching, his sacrifice on the Cross, the Church. Yet the registers within which we consider salvation are distinct only in human logic, where each must be discussed within its own boundaries: in truth they are thoroughly interdependent and distil to one reality.

What unites all Orthodox thinking about salvation is the total focus on Jesus Christ. Christ is 'the way, the truth, and the life' (Jn 14:6); we know no other name by which we may be saved (cf. Acts 4:12). He *is* our salvation. But it goes the other way as well: our thinking about Christ centres on salvation. All of the patristic, conciliar and liturgical formulations about the person of Christ – some of which are abstruse and technical, some of which were arrived at through martyrdom – are ultimately concerned with our salvation. The pursuit of an understanding of the person of Christ utterly consumes Christian thinking precisely because *everything* is at stake. It is a matter of eternal life and death.

This chapter will therefore maintain a double focus: on soteriology – reckoning on salvation – and on Christology – reckoning on Christ: two sides of the same coin.

THE NEED FOR SALVATION

The first point to establish about salvation is that we need it. To many, whether believers or not, this is already obvious. We need not look far into the world or into our own selves to know that the world, and we human beings first and foremost, are not well. To a Christian, the idea that this earthly life is the best of all possible worlds is a case of having, to say the least, no imagination, no insight into eternity. Furthermore, we cannot lay the blame for the world's ills entirely elsewhere. To the extent to which we perceive the world, as well as our own sinful selves, our misguided choices, our skewed priorities, we will see the relationship between the two: there is evil in the world, and we human beings are systemically complicit in it.

The opening chapters of Genesis reveal an ordered process of creation culminating in the creation of the human person in the image of God. Orthodoxy does not focus in any way on a purported ideal or immortal state of humanity 'before' the Fall. In fact, St Maximus the Confessor implies that there is no such state at all, that the first-created humans 'fell together with their coming into being'.[1] Others, such as Irenaeus, Gregory of Nazianzus and Ephrem, say that we were a work in progress, like children who acted too early on something that was meant for us at a later stage. When the Fathers describe salvation as 'restoration' they do not mean a return to some historic, perfect and deified original state but the restoration of the essential will of God for a humanity united to him in perfect freedom and love. Moreover, the transgression and the expulsion from Paradise narrated in Genesis 3 never engendered in the Christian East a doctrine of 'original guilt' or 'guilt in Adam'.[2] Orthodoxy's strong emphasis on human freedom entails that people are personally guilty only for their own sins. Likewise the early Genesis narratives did not produce in the Orthodox East a doctrine of total depravity, which would run counter to the conviction that human nature is at root good, even though distorted. The Paradise account, together with the other 'decline narratives' of Genesis 1–11, testify to the state of exile in which we currently find ourselves: at odds with God, with each other and with the created environment, and therefore in need of saving.

The patristic heritage is consistent about the role of the human person both in the Fall and in the salvation of the world. Elaborating on ideas found in Classical philosophy, the Fathers teach that the human person is a microcosm, a summation of the composition of the created world. The human being is unique among all of creation in being both spiritual and physical, thus partaking of the nature of the angelic, bodiless powers as well as of the material creation. If a microcosm, then the human person is also a mediator between the material and the spiritual, between earth and heaven. The 'priestly' vocation that is common to all humanity is to offer up all of creation to God. Inasmuch as we sin in any way, we fail in this vocation, and the whole of creation suffers as a result (cf. Hos 4:1–3). Insofar as we fulfil our vocation (by the Spirit of God, in the crucified Christ), we fulfil our calling to 'till and keep the earth' (Gen 2:15), to make the 'chaos' of the disordered world into a God-ordered 'cosmos'. The whole of creation groans in travail (Rom 8:22) awaiting the fully realised salvation wrought by God, in Christ, and through us. Being microcosm and mediator of the created universe is no small calling.

THE DESIRE AND WORK OF GOD FOR SALVATION

God desires salvation for all (cf. 1 Tim 2:4; 1 Thess 5:9). It is impossible to isolate 'God's acts of salvation', as they are contiguous with the act of creation itself (e.g., Ps 73 [74]:13–18). The Fathers saw salvation embedded in the creation narratives, especially in their heavy use of typology: seeing in Paradise a type for the Church, in Eve a type for Mary, and especially seeing in Adam a type for Christ (Rom 5:14). But some of them take the concept of 'type' or 'prefiguration' still further. Leaving behind chronological time, they say, we may conceive of the first Adam as being created *because of*, and *according to* the model of, and in the image of Christ, the New Adam. 'It was not the old Adam who was the model for the new, but the new Adam for the old', wrote St Nicolas Cabasilas; 'The first Adam is the imitation of the second.'[3]

All that God does, he does for our salvation. The Nicene Creed speaks of Jesus Christ, who 'for us and for our salvation' became incarnate and was made human. In the festal life of the Church we close each service by asking Christ's mercy and salvation, and speak of him – depending on which feast we are celebrating – as 'He who was born in a cavern and lay in a manger for our salvation', 'He who deigned to be baptized by John in the Jordan for our salvation', and so on through all the works and events of Christ's life: 'who endured fearful sufferings, the life-creating cross, and voluntary burial in the flesh' *for our salvation*. There is no other reason God creates us, and there is no other reason that God creates or acts in the world. 'For', as the dismissal texts all continue, 'He alone is good, and *he loves humankind*'.

SALVATION IN CHRIST

In some scholarship of the nineteenth and twentieth centuries, especially that which built on medieval Western writing, it became common to reckon 'salvation history' in terms of a strictly linear chronological progression. There, one might trace a single line from the creation of perfect, immortal Adam and Eve to their surprising Fall, which in turn necessitated God's sending of his pre-existing Son into the world around the year AD 1 to restore us to the perfect immortality of the pre-fallen

Adam and Eve. In such thinking, 'Jesus Christ' comes to be identified with a 33-year-long episode in the eternal lifespan of the Logos. This is not how the Fathers and the liturgy exegete either Jesus Christ or the economy of salvation. True, they sometimes present a narrative beginning with creation, outlining the Fall, and culminating in Christ – as beautifully exemplified in the anaphora prayers in the Liturgy of St Basil the Great. But this is not a history in the 'forensic' sense of that word: it is better understood as a faith confession.[4] Read with an eye to their theological sense, the Fathers and the liturgy present history as 'beginning' with the apostolic understanding of Christ's Passion, from which point all scripture, all narrative and all history could be understood in terms of Jesus Christ.

Rather than seeing Jesus Christ as a trinitarian person who irrupted into linear history 2,000 years ago, the patristic and apostolic perspective is that of Jesus Christ as the foundation of all history ('by whom all things were made'),[5] the centre of creation, and the image of God (Heb 1:3; Col 1:15), according to whose image we are made – and not just as a 'pre-existent Logos', but eternally as the crucified one, the 'Lamb slain from the foundation of the world' (cf. Rev 13:8), 'destined before the foundation of the world but made manifest at the end of the times for your sake' (1 Peter 18:20): 'For in [Christ] all things were created, in heaven and on earth, visible and invisible, ... all things were created through him and for him. He is before all things, and in him all things hold together. He is the head of the body, the Church; he is the beginning, the first-born from the dead' (Col. 1:16–18). Jesus saves, indeed, in and through his life-giving Passion, as the foundation of creation, as the one in whose image humanity is made. He saves both in history – 'crucified under Pontius Pilate' – and also as the foundation of history.

HOW DOES JESUS SAVE?

To reiterate the opening statement of this chapter, an Orthodox doctrine of Christ and salvation will always be multidimensional in character. It will describe several strands, each of which can be followed on its own while also thoroughly intertwined with the others, all leading together to the same goal. An ancient and enduring codification of the dimensions of salvation – dating back to at least the early fourth-century Eusebius of Caesarea and drawing on earlier Jewish sources – describes Christ as fulfilling the three vocations at which human beings failed: *prophecy* (the understanding and proclamation of truth), *priesthood* (the offering of the world to God) and *kingship* (stewardship and humble dominion over the world).

This rubric can be helpful in exploring the various dimensions of salvation in Christ, both revelatory and constitutive.

Christ as prophet

The verse Deuteronomy 18:15, 'The Lord your God will raise up for you a prophet like me from among you, from your brethren – him you shall heed', testifies to a Hebrew expectation that the apostles saw as fulfilled in Christ (cf. Acts 3:22–3). The 'Christ as prophet' paradigm shows how salvation is linked with knowledge and understanding about God and about created reality. Jesus Christ, anointed by the Holy Spirit, the Spirit of Truth (Jn 15:26), shows us who God is and how God acts. He shows this, to be sure, in his acts of power. The gospels bear witness to Christ's divinity by describing his messianic works: he subdues the chaotic waters (as God does throughout the Bible), he heals the sick, he raises the dead, he forgives sins, he is called 'The Lord' (*kyrios*), which the Greek-speaking readers of the Old Testament recognised as the divine name, a translation of the Hebrew *adonai*. These are signs that first-century hearers would recognise as heralding the divine messiah himself. But nowhere does Jesus better reveal the love and the almightiness of God than when he is at his most vulnerable: voluntarily hanging on the Cross, abandoned by all, the icon of God's saving love for the world. Christ's outstretched hands are the open book revealing nothing less than the living God. When 'he who hung the earth upon the waters is hung upon the tree', as we sing on Holy Thursday, all of creation is amazed. Our liturgical formulations are full of the imagery of Christ dispelling ignorance, showing genuine human life as well as genuine divine life. At the Liturgy of the Presanctified Gifts celebrated during Great Lent, the Old Testament reading is followed by the celebrant's placing a candle over the gospel, exclaiming to the prostrated congregation: 'The light of Christ illumines all!' Even the rite of our entry into the Church, baptism, is called 'holy illumination'. These are expressions of the scriptural testimony that Christ, *being* the Truth, is the supreme revelation of truth to the world.[6]

Christ as priest

As an ancient liturgical formulation has it, Jesus Christ is both the offerer and the one who is offered. He is the sacrifice that he himself offers voluntarily. It was natural who Christians should adapt the *topos* of high-priestly sacrifice, so potent in Hebrew law and liturgy, as the Epistle to the Hebrews does throughout. However, when later thinkers would pose the question, 'To whom was the sacrifice offered?', their answers were varied, and rarely helpful. The idea that God sacrificed his Son to the Devil was soundly defeated. In reaction, eleventh-century Anselm of Canterbury said that the sacrifice was to God the Father – more on this below. But the answer from the Greek East was clear from long before: *there is no identifiable party that demanded the sacrifice or ransom of Christ.*[7] Yet it is a sacrifice nonetheless, which cleanses humanity with God's own humanity.

It is sometimes erroneously said that Orthodoxy does not teach 'the atonement', that it shuns transactional imagery in its understanding of salvation. If that were so, then Orthodoxy would be ignoring scripture itself, which is rife with the concept of human bondage and debt, and divine ransom, atonement and redemption.[8] Yet it is true that Orthodox theology differs from some of the teachings embedded in later Western theology. Anselm's teaching, that the sacrifice of Christ was offered to the Father, seemed to presuppose a God whose honour, justice and majesty were defiled and who demanded satisfaction or repayment. Not only is this an uncharacteristic portraiture of God, but the resulting 'substitutionary' theories of atonement so stressed the sacrificial death on the Cross that they undermined the comprehensive work of God in Christ and the Spirit for the salvation of the world. While substitutionary atonement models are these days frequently formulated in such a way as to sound close to Orthodox understanding (which agrees that Christ makes a sacrifice that mere humans are unable to), Orthodox theology renounces not only their distortions but their foundational principle that the sacrifice of the Son is in any way demanded by the Father.

The nature of Christ's sacrifice overcomes a condition best described as captivity to death or to sin. So when the Fathers did speak of a 'recipient' of the sacrifice, they spoke metaphorically: the debt was paid *to our condition* (in the words of Leo of Rome), or, as St Basil the Great has it in his liturgical anaphora, 'He gave himself as a ransom *to death*', so that Christ's death makes 'a path to the resurrection of the dead'. Human beings still die biologically, but death no longer has the final word: it is a death *in Christ*, filled with the hope of a resurrection in Christ (Rom 6:1–11).

Christ as King

The idea of Christ as King, in victorious authority over evil powers, in some senses stands on its own, particularly where scriptural, patristic and hagiographic literature engages the imagery of the 'unseen warfare' between forces of light and darkness. Viewing Christ as King also refers directly to the scriptural understanding of the Kingdom (or 'rule') of God,[9] the eschatological reign of Christ. But it also stems from both his role as prophet (for he defeats darkness – as ignorance – with the light of knowledge) and his priestly sacrifice, which defeats or 'tramples' death.

Indeed, all the models are naturally held together: the King is the one who offers himself up for his people in priestly, sacrificial death, which not only transfigures death itself but reveals and teaches to humanity the true nature of both God and humanity. In his treatise *On the Incarnation*, St Athanasius speaks of salvation as the entrance of a king into a city – almost as if the entrance (Incarnation) alone is what saves the city. But he immediately goes on to say that the King offers himself for the city and its inhabitants, and corrects their neglect by his teaching.[10]

Many of the Fathers also taught that Christ saves in such a way that 'like heals like': Christ has a human body because the body needed healing, and he has a human soul because the soul needed healing. As Gregory of Nazianzus famously wrote, 'That which is unassumed [by Christ] is unhealed.'[11] But we would be wrong to think that the Fathers' teaching was crudely physical, for they specify that it is not simply by technically possessing a soul that Christ heals human souls, but by suffering, by experiencing temptation and natural passions,[12] as only an ensouled being can. Christ passes through all ages of human life – again not magically to 'sanctify' every age, but to become an example for all ages, and in order truly to have led a human life unto death.[13]

THE LANGUAGE OF CHRISTOLOGY

Many, if not most, of the dimensions of salvation in Christ enumerated above are believed by Christians across confessional lines. But Orthodoxy's insistence on adherence to the precise and often technical definitions of the person of Christ is perhaps unique in its strength and persistence through the ages to the present. There are important reasons for that insistence, some of which follow from how Orthodox Christians understand the nature of theology and Church tradition. The chief reason that they care rightly to define the person of Christ is that every single dimension of salvation outlined above depends on a right understanding of Christ. They rely on the identity of this one person Jesus Christ, who is at the same time fully divine and fully human. A mere human being can die voluntarily for others to great effect, but he or she is not the saviour of the world. And the 'voluntary' suffering and death of Jesus, if he had no human life, soul, passions or vulnerability, would be mere play-acting.

In every age from the dawn of Christianity, people have been faced with the genuinely dazzling mystery of Christ, one which poses the question of how one person could in himself hold together two incommensurate modes of being: created and uncreated, beyond time and yet time-bound, beyond space and yet circumscribed, almighty and yet vulnerable. The answers, which often were responses to the periodic challenges to a saving doctrine of Christ, strove to evince Jesus Christ in a way that was genuinely faithful to the scriptural testimony about him. Christological formulations were drawn from the apostolic witness in scripture and from the Fathers and the ecumenical councils. But these in turn drew from the language and philosophical culture of the age, which, during the most formative period of doctrine, was the language of Classical Greek philosophy. For us today to arrive at a genuine and saving doctrine of Christ (which ought to be our goal), it is essential to familiarise ourselves with these seminal formulations and explore what they actually mean to say. Before saying more about the significance and necessity of this language, here is an attempt to elucidate one of the key terms employed in the teaching about Jesus Christ: nature.

When Christology uses the language of nature (*physis*), whereby people speak of Christ's 'two natures' or his 'one nature', there is a great deal at stake, and much tragic misunderstanding. Churches that split from each other over the council of Chalcedon in AD 451 remain out of communion with each other to this day. While many of the factors that divided and continue to divide them from one another can be attributed also to historical and political realities, it would not be an exaggeration to say that the chief theological issue concerns how the different parties use the word 'nature' in their descriptions of Jesus Christ.

The (Chalcedonian) Orthodox Church insists on being able to speak of Christ as being known in two natures, divine and human. The (non-Chalcedonian) Oriental Orthodox Churches see that language as leading too easily to a concept of Christ as two separate *persons* – one Son of God and one Son of Mary. As the modern dialogue between these Churches has shown, the matter comes down largely to how the word 'nature' is actually understood and used. The following paragraphs are an attempt to set out the issues.

Nature may be understood *generically*. Here, nature is a set of defining characteristics or qualities, specifically *the sum total of characteristics that make something what it is*. It is not always possible to agree on a definitive list of these qualities – it is not a simple matter to define the characteristics which constitute 'human nature', for example – but at least we know that a finite list hypothetically exists, and that such a list defines X as a human person, in contrast to Y as, say, a chimpanzee.

However, nature may also be understood *concretely*, in at least two ways. Nature may be concrete by definition, as in the enduring Platonic concept of concretely existing forms. Here nature is not merely abstract, nor only descriptive, for natures exist in actuality in the realm of ideals. But even if one rejects the Platonic ontology, nature may be reckoned concretely in another way: by association or by consequence. If one asserts that natures do not exist in and of themselves, but only as realised in concretely existing things (*hypostases*), then there is no abstract 'apple nature', there are only apples, which can be seen to share certain characteristics. On this basis it could follow that referring to a nature necessarily means referring to a specific hypostasis (a concrete thing or person). This logic, when applied to the person of Christ, can become thorny. For if asserting two natures in Christ indeed leads inexorably to positing two hypostases – two concretely existing beings or 'two sons' – we are on untenable ground.

The point is that the language of 'two natures', as well as the language of 'one nature', can be used about Christ only where it is properly defined. When terminology is used with care and precision, the divisions between the formulations dissipate. And the fact is that several Church Fathers, notably including St Cyril of Alexandria and St Maximus the Confessor (both of whom had a great deal at stake in this language), found it possible to use both 'two-nature' and 'one-nature' formulations about Christ.

Here is how they did, and how we may: speaking of Christ as known in 'two natures' means simply that this one person, Jesus Christ, is both fully divine and fully human. Nature is here understood *generically.* Jesus is properly described both by human nature (the characteristics that make someone 'human') and by divine nature (the characteristics that make someone 'divine'). This is effectively no different from the language of 'double consubstantiality', namely that Jesus is consubstantial (of the same essence or substance) with us humans, and also consubstantial with God the Father ('light from light').[14] He is truly divine as derived from God the Father and truly human as derived from Mary.

Speaking of Christ as known in 'one nature', or, to use Cyril's catchphrase, 'one incarnate nature of the divine Logos', is to speak of this single person, Jesus Christ, whose unique nature it is to be both divine and human. It is 'his nature' – i.e., it is characteristic of him – to be defined by, and observed to manifest, divine and human characteristics.

The word 'nature' thus does double duty. We are saying, in effect, that *it belongs to Christ's single incarnate nature to be a two-natured person.*

The language of 'composite nature' has in this sense been helpful in the dialogue process.

CHRISTOLOGY, FAITH AND WORSHIP

A few more words are in order about the language of Christology, for many people feel that it is needlessly complex, arcane or even impious in the face of the holy mystery of Christ. Why do we need to be versed in it? We no longer reckon along the lines of Greek ontological categories. Is this merely the language of theological hobbyists with nothing better to do? And is it not attempting to describe things that cannot be fully described?

While not every member of the Church needs to be immersed in the details of nature, essence and hypostasis, we ought to consider at least two points. Firstly, this language is neither random nor happenstance, nor does it represent just an idiosyncratic and antiquated phase in the history of the Church. It is the language of the ecumenical councils, and thus constitutes an enduring and definitive reference point. Furthermore, it is constantly sung in our liturgy, which gives it an ongoing currency in the life of the Church. When we sing or recite the Nicene Creed, we sing of the Son who is *homoousios* ('consubstantial') with the Father. The Vespers service includes a variable 'Dogmatic Hymn' to the Mother of God in which we often use explicit theological terminology:

> The Only-Begotten Son shone timelessly from the Father,
> But from you [O Virgin] he was ineffably incarnate:
> God by nature, yet human for our sake,
> Not two persons, but one, known in two natures![15]

This is the language of the Church – not just when it is in a technical mode, but when it is joyfully singing its doxology to God. It is not coincidental that such language takes place in hymnography dedicated to Mary, for the Church's dogmas about her, including her main title of '*Theotokos*' ('Mother of God'), point finally to Christ. As the human mother of the One who is divine, she is the link between Christ's human and divine natures, between the old and the new dispensations. Even as our praise and veneration of Mary stem very much from the heart, they also emerge out of the necessity to follow through with precision on the Church's teachings concerning the One to whom she gave birth.

Secondly, this language was the vehicle by which a process took place, one which we consider to be of life-and-death importance. It is language adapted and developed in the service of a clear teaching, articulated with all the precision that can be mustered, one that concerns nothing less than our eternal life in and with God. It may be, too, that this degree of precision and specificity would not have been necessary were it not for the fact that, in every generation, in every time and in every place, to this day, there are people who arise either from within the Church or from outside it who reason and teach *wrong* things about Christ. In every age someone teaches about Christ as if he were 'an exceptionally good human being with an extraordinary connection to the divine' or as 'God who took on the appearance of a human body and pretended to be hungry and tempted'. There must be language, backed by conciliar authority, that can show clearly and precisely why such opinions are outside the teaching of the Orthodox Christian Church.[16]

Finally, we ought to recall that, in contemplating the person of Christ, neither the apostles, nor the Fathers, nor the liturgy begin with the technical language; instead they begin with the vision of Christ, the King of Glory, crucified for our sake, and risen from the dead. The technical language of Christology exists in the service of that confession.

The world could be healed by none other than this God-man. But God saves the world not only by the fact of Jesus's divine-humanity, but through his voluntary death on the Cross, and through what the Passion reveals to the world. Put differently, Jesus's dying on the Cross is the *culmination* of his divine humanity (cf. Phil 2:8–11). The icon of Christ on the Cross is the icon of perfect divinity as well as of perfect humanity. In the apostolic preaching, the Cross reveals to us the God who creates the world and who is at the same time so involved with it in all its violent fallenness that he makes himself its victim, in complete solidarity with all suffering. It reveals to us the person who unwaveringly harmonises his human will to the divine, unto a bitter end. Here again though, if this were the mortal suffering of a mere human being, it would be meaningful, but it would not be the cosmos-shaking event of *the death of the divine Son*. If this were the pretended or merely apparent suffering of a divine phantom, it would be a mockery. The 'life-giving Cross' both relies on and reveals the full divinity and the full humanity of the one Jesus Christ.

WHAT IS SALVATION?

Salvation, as seen above, has to do with the reconciliation between God and creation, through the mediation of the central creature: the human being. It is a restoration of relationships that are marred, distorted from their true character. It has to do therefore with the forgiveness of sins, the loosening of the bonds of memory. It also entails illumination: in order to heal relationships, people had to be taught, shown how truly to live, how to relate to each other, to themselves, their created environment and their God. It also has a great deal to do with union: so many scriptural and liturgical exclamations about salvation are about integration, integrity and coherence in the face of division and brokenness – the work of the Devil (*ho diabolos*, literally 'the Divider'). Aside from all the texts that speak of reconciliation in Christ, Ephesians 1:9–10 sees the culmination of everything in terms of the union of all things, and Colossians 1:17–22 expresses Christ as the principle of unity and coherence of all things, in and through the Church. Maximus the Confessor understood salvation as the realisation in Christ of the human vocation, which he spelled out in terms of a five-fold scheme of the union and integration of divisions within the earthly plane, as well as between the earthly and the heavenly.[17]

The Church and its sacramental life are more than instrumental in the way of salvation. The word 'sacrament' or 'mystery' is understood in the Church as referring to the union of the uncreated and the created – thus Christ himself is the supreme sacrament, as is the divine-human Church.[18] And so are the sacraments which, by the Holy Spirit, unite the things of earth – bread, water, oil – to the things of heaven. The Church in its sacramental character is the space within which Christians – by the grace of God, in Jesus Christ, by the Holy Spirit – work out, elaborate and even experience the foretaste of salvation.

The idea of salvation as union is nowhere more thoroughly or more dazzlingly fulfilled than in the doctrine of the *theosis* ('deification') of the human person. The Fathers taught that the divine likeness is something towards which we strive; it is the realisation of the gift and vocation implanted in us with the divine image. St Athanasius's oft-repeated dictum, 'He [the Word of God] became human so that we could become divine', is but one iteration of a teaching that resonates throughout the Fathers. Although neither deification, nor life itself, is ours by right – it is a gift of God's grace – the Fathers saw it as the natural fulfillment of the human being: 'The life that bears a likeness to the divine is completely in accord with human nature.'[19] But however stunning and unimaginably mysterious this doctrine may (and should) sound, it also has a concrete moral dimension. St Gregory Palamas equated the divine energies with the divine will: participating in the energies is participating in God's will, doing his commandments. We naturally become more and more 'God-like' the more we harmonise our own will with his. As with everything else holy, good and saving, our supreme example for deification is Christ himself, who unites the human and the divine in his person, on every level, including that of the will. Deification can be understood therefore as 'Christification', or becoming ever-more Christ-like.[20] This is what is implied by the injunction to imitate Christ, especially in the taking up of his Cross, to become co-crucified with him – renouncing our will, living for and ministering to others, especially to the poor and outcast. In this way the scripture that says 'When he appears we shall be like him' (1 Jn 3:2) may be fulfilled.

Our vocation is to become by grace everything that Christ is by nature. In other words, our work is to participate in God's work and in his will, and in his light and his glory, to the point where, while remaining created human persons, we become also partakers of the characteristics of divinity itself. In that ascent – and through all the 'crosses' that it entails – we join the One who descended for our sake, who, while remaining uncreated and divine, became also a partaker of the characteristics of humanity.

Further reading[21]

Behr, J., *The Mystery of Christ: Life in Death*, Crestwood, NY: SVS Press, 2006.

Meyendorff, J., *Christ in Eastern Christian Thought*, Crestwood, NY: SVS Press, 1975.
'New life in Christ: salvation in Orthodox theology' in Meyendorff, *Rome, Constantinople, Moscow: Historical and Theological Studies*, Crestwood, NY: SVS Press, 1996.

Romanides, J. S., *The Ancestral Sin*, Ridgewood, NJ: Zephyr, 2002.

Russell, N., *The Doctrine of Deification in the Greek Patristic Tradition*, Oxford: Oxford University Press, 2004.

Ware, K. (Bishop of Diokleia), *How Are We Saved? The Understanding of Salvation in the Orthodox Tradition*, Minneapolis, MN: Light and Life, 1996.

Notes

1. Maximus the Confessor, *Questions to Thalassius*, 61.
2. Orthodox patristic, conciliar and liturgical formulations do not speak of the transmission of guilt from Adam. They emphasise rather that, although the figure of Adam represents the beginning of human sin, anyone who sins does so of his or her own free choice, and assign no culpability for Adam's sin. Cf. John Chrysostom, *Homilies on Romans* 10.
3. Nicolas Cabasilas, *The Life in Christ* 6.91–4. Cited in J. Behr, *The Mystery of Christ: Life in Death* (Crestwood, NY: SVS Press, 2006), p. 110.
4. See 'A premodern faith for a postmodern era' in Behr, *Mystery*, pp. 173–81.
5. Nicene Creed – see also Jn 1:3; Rom 11:36; 1 Cor 8:6; Heb 1:2.
6. Jn 8:31–2, 14:6, 17:3; Eph 4:21; 1 Tim 2:4; 1 Jn 5:20.
7. See especially Gregory of Nazianzus, *Oration 45, The Second Oration on Easter* 22.
8. Hos 13:14; Mt 20:28; Mk 10:45; Lk 1:68; 1 Tim 2:5–6; 1 Pet 18–20. The word 'atonement' simply means 'reconciliation', as its basic etymology (at-one-ment) confirms.
9. *Basileia* can denote 'Kingdom' as a place as well as 'kingship', 'rule' or 'reign'.

10. Athanasius of Alexandria, *On the Incarnation* 9–10.
11. Gregory of Nazianzus, *Epistle* 101.5.
12. The natural passions of zeal and desire are not sinful in themselves.
13. St Irenaeus feels so strongly about this that he extends Christ's lifespan into old age – see *Against Heresies* II.22.4.
14. The modern dialogues, begun in the 1960s, indicate that Chalcedonian and non-Chalcedonian Churches agree on the language of double consubstantiality.
15. Tone 6 Dogmatikon.
16. See P. Bouteneff, *Sweeter than Honey: Orthodox Thinking on Dogma and Truth* (Crestwood, NY: SVS Press, 2006), pp. 99–115.
17. This teaching is helpfully elucidated in A. Louth, *Maximus the Confessor* (London and New York: Routledge, 1996), pp. 72–4.
18. See P. Bouteneff, 'The mystery of union: elements in an Orthodox sacramental theology' in G. Rowell and Christine Hall (eds.), *Gestures of God: Explorations in Sacramental Theology* (London and New York: Continuum, 2004), pp. 91–107.
19. Gregory of Nyssa, *Homily 1 on Ecclesiastes*.
20. See P. Nellas, *Deification in Christ: Orthodox Perspectives on the Nature of the Human Person* (Crestwood, NY: SVS Press, 1987), esp. pp. 115–59.
21. These suggested readings vary in character, and to a degree in content as well. But they collectively provide a sense of the main lines along which Orthodox theologians today conceive Christ and salvation.

7 Eschatology

BISHOP HILARION ALFEYEV

All religions contain an eschatological dimension since they are directed not only towards the reality of the material world, but also to the spiritual world; not only to the present age, but also towards the future. In Christianity, however, eschatology plays such an essential role that, without the eschatological dimension, Christianity loses its meaning. Eschatology permeates the entire life of the Church: its services, sacraments and rites, its theological and moral doctrine, its asceticism and mysticism. The entire history of the Church is filled with eschatological expectations, beginning with the Resurrection and Ascension of Christ and continuing until the present day. Indeed, it is because the resurrection has taken place – because we live in the time of the resurrection – that eschatology is so fundamental to the Church.

As Fr Georges Florovsky notes, the Western liberal theological tradition beginning with the Age of Enlightenment ignored eschatology; to many, it seemed to be a remnant of the long-forgotten past. But modern theological thought – both Catholic and Protestant – has once again discovered eschatology, returning to the realisation that all dogmas of faith are directly related to it.[1]

As for Orthodox theology, it never lost its eschatological dimension. Yet the 'pseudomorphosis' of Orthodox theology in the eighteenth and nineteenth centuries could not but leave its mark on eschatology. The expositions of eschatology in Greek and Russian textbooks on dogmatic theology from this period mostly follow Catholic schemes. In this sense the twentieth century became also for the Orthodox Church a time for re-thinking eschatology, for returning to its patristic foundations.

According to Fr Alexander Schmemann, eschatology is a distinguishing characteristic of the Christian faith inasmuch as it is 'belief in God, belief in the saving power of certain historical events, and finally belief in the final victory of God in Christ and of the Kingdom of God'.

Picture
Kingdom

Eschatology looks to the future, to the mystical *eschaton* of the coming Kingdom. At the same time,

> as Christians we already possess that in which we believe. The Kingdom is still to come, and yet the Kingdom that is to come is already in the midst of us. The Kingdom is not only something promised, it is something of which we can taste here and now. And so in all our preaching we are bearing witness – *martyria* – not simply to our faith but to our possession of that in which we believe.

Schmemann writes that the true essence of the Christian faith lies in the fact that we 'live in time by that which is beyond time; living by that which is not yet come, but which we already know and possess'.[2]

These two aspects of Christian eschatology are developed in the New Testament teaching on the Kingdom of God. The expression 'to enter into the Kingdom of Heaven' (Mt 5:20; 7:21; 19:23–4), repeatedly used by the Saviour, points to the prospect for salvation after death. Christ gives his disciples the Kingdom which will come to fulfilment in the *eschaton*, at his second coming (cf. Lk 22:29–30).

On the other hand, Christ's preaching, like that of John the Baptist, began with the message that the Kingdom of Heaven was 'at hand' (Mt 4:17; 3:2), i.e. had truly approached the people. The news of the nearness of the Kingdom becomes a leitmotif of Christ's preaching: the Kingdom of God is not a reality of 'life beyond the grave', but rather an experience which is accessible to man already in his earthly life. The eschatological 'last times' begin with the first coming of Christ and his preaching on earth.

An event from Christ's life that had a special eschatological significance was his Transfiguration. The gospel account of this event begins with Christ's words that 'there are some standing here who will not taste death before they see that the Kingdom of God has come with power' (Mk 9:1), and these words are understood in the Orthodox tradition as referring to the Transfiguration. The vision of Christ in his glory and the experience of the divine light are at the very heart of both Orthodox mysticism and Orthodox eschatology. According to St Gregory Palamas, the light of the Transfiguration 'is not something that comes to be and then vanishes'. Rather, Christ's disciples experienced a transformation of their senses so that 'they beheld the Ineffable Light where and to the extent that the Spirit granted it to them'.[3] This was, therefore, not only a prefiguration of the eternal blessedness to which all Christians look forward, but also the Kingdom of God already revealed, realised and come.

The Kingdom is already present in the Church invisibly, being the foundation of its life. This experience is manifested in the Orthodox services, especially in the Divine Liturgy, which is not only an *anamnesis*, a remembrance of past events (the last supper, the suffering, death and resurrection of the Saviour), but also a participation in the future reality. During the Liturgy the Saviour's promise is realised: 'That you may eat and drink at my table in my Kingdom'. The words of the eucharistic prayer place events of the past, present and future into one continuous series: 'You brought us into being out of nothing, and when we fell, you raised us up again. You did not cease doing everything until you had led us to heaven and granted us your kingdom to come'. The Kingdom of God is 'the future', but at the same time it has *already* been given. The Liturgy *already* raises people into the heavens; it is *already* 'heaven on earth'.

Before discussing the most important aspects of Orthodox eschatological expectation, it is necessary to explain two things. First, we must note that eschatology is an area of questions, and not answers; of mysteries, and not of the obvious; of hopes, not of definite, final affirmations. Much of what concerns the future fate of the world and humankind has been revealed to us in holy scripture and the tradition of the Church, but much still remains in the hidden depths of God's mysteries.

The second explanation concerns the co-existence of two eschatologies in the Christian theological tradition – the 'personal' and the 'universal–historical'.[4] Personal eschatology deals with questions concerning death and the fate of the person after death. Universal eschatology, which will be the focus of this chapter, is concerned with future events relevant to the history of all humankind – the second coming of Christ, the general resurrection, the Last Judgement, the ultimate fate of the righteous and of sinners.

THE SECOND COMING OF CHRIST

The main focus of Christian eschatology is the second coming of Christ. The entire history of Christianity unfolds in the period of time between the first and second comings of the Saviour. The fate of all people – both the living and the dead – is woven into this history. Those who lived before Christ, including the righteous of the Old Testament, also remain in expectation of the second coming. In Eastern Christian patristic literature, the theme of the second coming of the Saviour was generally developed from two different perspectives. On the one hand, the spirit of the joyful anticipation of Christ's coming was never completely lost: this is the spirit expressed in the words of the apostle Peter about Christians 'looking for and hastening the coming of the day of God' (2 Pet 3:12), and in the exclamations 'Maranatha' (1 Cor 16:22) and 'Even so, come, Lord Jesus' (Rev 22:20), which reflect early Christian liturgical practice.

On the other hand, Church writers paid close attention to the fearsome and alarming events which, according to the New Testament, will precede Christ's second coming. The theme of the Antichrist (cf. 2 Thess 2:8, 1 Jn 2:18, etc.) was particularly developed in Eastern patristics. In the patristic tradition, the term 'Antichrist' points to the main enemy of Christ and the Church, 'who shall come at the end of the world'[5] in order to deceive the entire world and turn people away from the true faith. The main characteristics of the Antichrist will be apostasy, resistance to God and the desire to pass himself off as God.[6] St Paul writes that 'the mystery of iniquity doth already work' (2 Thess 2:7). The war of the Antichrist against Christ began at the moment of Christ's first coming but the final battle, vividly described in the Apocalypse, will take place at his second coming.

In the perception of modern human beings, the word 'apocalypse' (literally, 'revelation') is usually associated with the horrors and catastrophes that will precede the end of world history; and such a view can be found also among some Orthodox Christians. It would be an error, however, to lose sight of the fact that the main character of the second coming will be Christ, and not the Antichrist; and that the second coming itself will not be a moment of defeat, but a great moment of the glory of God, the victory of good over evil, life over death, and Christ over the Antichrist. It is not by chance that the theme of victory is one of the leitmotifs of the Apocalypse. All who have taken the side of good in the cosmic battle between good and evil will participate in this victory; their names will be written into the Book of Life (Rev 2, 3, 21).

The second coming of Christ will mark the completion of world history; yet this completion is not a tragic and painful breaking point in the fate of mankind, but the glorious goal to which history, through God's providence, is moving unswervingly. The Christian philosophy of history takes a view of the 'end of the world' with which 'apocalyptic' fears are incompatible, a view permeated by joyful expectation and hope.

THE GENERAL RESURRECTION

The doctrine of the general resurrection is one of the most difficult Christian beliefs for the rational mind-set. The power of death over everything and everyone, its inexorable and irreparable character, seems such an obvious fact that the doctrine of the resurrection can seem to contradict reality itself. The decay and disappearance of the body after physical death seems to leave no hope for its subsequent restoration. Moreover, the doctrine of the resurrection of the body contradicts the majority of philosophical theories that existed in the pre-Christian era, including Greek philosophy, which viewed liberation from the body as the highest good, a passage into a purely spiritual, noumenal state.

The apostolic *kerygma* ('proclamation') revealed the radical difference between ancient philosophy and the recently born Christianity, especially on this point. The book of Acts contains an account of St Paul's preaching on the Areopagus, which began very successfully and could have been quite convincing for the Athenian senators if only Paul had not begun to speak of the resurrection. For his preaching of 'Jesus and the resurrection' the Athenians called Paul a 'babbler' (Acts 17:32–3; 18). Yet the doctrine of the general resurrection is the heart of Christian eschatology. Without this teaching, Christianity loses its meaning, just as the Christian *kerygma*, according to St Paul, is in vain without faith in Christ's resurrection (1 Cor 15:12–13). St Paul was the first Christian theologian to systematise the doctrine of the resurrection of the dead: all subsequent development of this doctrine was based on the foundations laid by him. The apostle enlarges on this teaching most fully in the First Epistle to the Corinthians. Here he links the resurrection of the dead to Christ's resurrection, placing one event in direct dependence on the other (1 Cor 15:12–19). The resurrection of the entire human race follows from the resurrection of Christ with the same obvious logic as the death of all people following from the death of Adam (1 Cor 15:17–23, 47–9).

St Paul examines in detail the question of the nature of the bodies in which the dead will rise (1 Cor 15:35–53). Christ will 'change our vile body, that it may be fashioned like unto his glorious body' (Phil 3:20–1). In other words, the bodies of the resurrected will be similar to Christ's glorified body, i.e. his body after his resurrection.

In the third century, Origen and St Methodius of Olympus disagreed sharply over the nature of resurrected bodies. Origen's writings reflected the opinion that the bodies of the resurrected will be spiritual and ethereal. But Methodius rejected the view that human bodies will be destroyed, even if Christ had said that the saints will be 'as angels in heaven' (Mk 12:25; Mt 22:30) in the resurrection. According to Methodius, Christ's words should be understood not in the sense that the saints will lose their bodies after the resurrection, but in the sense that their state of blessedness will be like that of the angels.[7]

In the fourth century, St Gregory of Nyssa devoted much attention to the subject of the resurrection of the dead. In answering the question of what the 'mechanism' of re-uniting the soul with the body will be like at the general resurrection, and how the souls will recognise their own bodies, Gregory advances his opinion that there is a natural mutual attraction between the soul and body, an attraction which does not cease even after death.[8] Each body has its own *eidos*, its own appearance, which remains in the soul like the imprint of a seal even after its separation from the body. At the general resurrection, the soul will recognise this *eidos* and will re-unite with its body. In doing so, the scattered particles that once comprised the material substance of the body will re-unite, just as drops of spilled quicksilver gather together. The Bishop of Nyssa writes: 'If it is God's command that corresponding parts unite by themselves with that which is their own, this will present no difficulty for him who renewed nature'[9].

THE LAST JUDGEMENT

The notion that man will be judged for his actions can already be found in the Old Testament (e.g. Eccl 11:9); it is in the New Testament, however, that this teaching is developed in its fullness. Speaking with the disciples on the Mount of Olives not long before his death on the Cross, Christ draws a picture of the Last Judgement, when he will 'separate them one from another, as a shepherd divides his sheep from the goats'. The only criterion according to which the righteous will be separated from the sinners is works of mercy towards one's neighbour (Mt 25:31–46).

God's judgement will not be something forced upon humankind from the outside, and will not simply be a result of a 'just requital' by God. The necessity of judgement follows from the principle of man's moral responsibility before God and other people. The Last Judgement begins in the earthly life of the person and takes place every moment when one chooses or neglects to feed the hungry, give drink to the thirsty, visit those in prison, or share with those in need. Christ's words about the Last Judgement are not a threat of retribution, but a call to do good. This is how the Orthodox Church understands this parable, addressing the following words to its members on the Sunday of the Last Judgement:

> Having understood the Lord's commandments, let us live in
> accordance with them: let us feed the hungry, give drink to
> the thirsty, clothe the naked, give rest to strangers, visit the sick
> and those in prisons, so that he who will come to judge the entire
> world will say to us: come, blessed ones of my Father, inherit the
> Kingdom prepared for you.[10]

The Orthodox Church teaches that all people without exception will stand before the Last Judgement – Christians and pagans, believers and non-believers. However, the thought that Christians will be judged with special strictness is present already in the Epistles: 'Judgement must begin at the house of God' (1 Pet 4:17), i.e. beginning with the Christian Church. Regarding those who are outside the Church, St Paul writes that they will be judged in accordance with the law of conscience written in their hearts (Rom 2:14–15). Virtuous pagans, says Chrysostom, are astonishing because 'they had no need of the law but fulfilled everything contained in it, having inscribed in their minds not the letter, but deeds'.[11] And he draws a radical conclusion: 'If a pagan fulfils the law, nothing else will be necessary for his salvation.'[12] When acts committed during one's life are evaluated, moral criteria will be applied to all people without exception, the only difference being that Jews will be judged according to the Law of Moses, Christians by the gospel, and pagans according to the law of conscience written in their hearts. According to Basil the Great, the Last Judgement will be not so much an external as an internal event: it will take place primarily in the conscience of each person, in his mind and memory. Moreover, the Last Judgement will occur with lightning speed: 'It is probable that by some ineffable power, in an instant, all actions committed during our lifetime will be imprinted in the memory of our soul, as in a picture.'[13]

These explanations introduce an important corrective into the understanding of the Last Judgement that is reflected, for example, in Michelangelo's renowned frescoes in the Sistine Chapel. In these frescoes, the main idea is that justice is administered: each person receives according to his merits, and God's sentence is irreversible. But in the Orthodox understanding, the Last Judgement is not so much the moment of requital as the victory of truth. It is the revelation of God's mercy and love that is underscored. God will never cease to be love and light; but, subjectively, divine love and the divine light will be perceived differently by the righteous and by sinners.

'THE POWER OF LOVE WORKS IN TWO WAYS'

For most Christians in the West today, the very idea of 'torments of hell' will seem primitive, totally off-putting, and impossible to reconcile with the idea of a loving God. From the Orthodox point of view, hell is also irreconcilable with divine love. This is why Eastern Fathers stressed that God did not create hell: it was created by humans for themselves. The source of eschatological torment is the will of those humans who are unable to partake in God's love, to feel God's love as a source of joy and blessedness. Isaac the Syrian writes that:

> those who are punished in Gehenna are scourged by the scourge of love. Nay, what is so bitter and vehement as the torment of love? I mean that those who have become conscious that they have sinned against love suffer greater torment from this than from any fear of punishment. For the sorrow caused in the heart by sin against love is more poignant than any torment. It would be improper for a man to think that sinners in Gehenna are deprived of the love of God. Love … is given to all. But the power of love works in two ways: it torments sinners, even as happens here when a friend suffers from a friend; but it becomes a source of joy for those who have observed its duties.[14]

Fr Georges Florovsky writes that the possibility of hell is contained in the primordial paradox of creation: 'in the act of creation God posits something totally other than himself, "over against" himself. Accordingly, the world of creatures has its own mode of existence.' God gave the created world freedom, and thus autonomy. In this is revealed the 'kenotic self-limitation' of God, who 'as it were spares room for the existence of something different'. Yet 'the sting of the paradox, of the *kenosis*, is not in the existence of the world, but in the possibility of hell'. The world may be obedient to God, in which case 'it is not a "limitation", but an expansion of God's majesty. On the contrary, hell means resistance and estrangement, pure and simple.'[15]

According to many theological and liturgical texts of the Eastern Church, Christ in his descent into hell liberated all people from hell – without exception. Truly, hell has been 'abolished' by the resurrection of Christ: it is no longer unavoidable for people and no longer holds them under its power. But people re-create it for themselves each time sin is consciously committed and not followed by repentance.

This follows from one's understanding that hell consists in being tormented by sorrow for the sin against love. This 'sorrow' is a fruitless and belated remorse, to be distinguished from the repentance that one can bring forth during one's life. Repentance is remorse for sins accompanied by a *change of mind* (this is the literal meaning of the Greek *metanoia*), a change in one's whole way of living. Remorse, on the contrary, is sorrow over evil committed without the possibility of doing anything for its correction. One has the possibility of correcting mistakes only in earthly life. As Symeon the New Theologian writes, after death there begins a state of inaction, when nobody can do anything, good or evil. Thus, one will remain as one was at the end of one's earthly life.[16]

For many centuries, the doctrine of hell was a subject of theological discussion in the Christian East and West. During these debates, questions were asked such as: is liberation from hell possible? Are the torments of sinners eternal or temporary? How can one reconcile eternal torment with the notion of God's boundless and ineffable love towards man?

The Western and Eastern theological traditions did not always answer these questions in the same way. For example, in the West, under the influence of St Augustine and a number of other Latin Fathers, the doctrine of purgatory was conceived as an interim place between heaven and hell, or rather a special section of hell where sinners are exposed to the fires of purification.

The Eastern Christian tradition never recognised the doctrine of purgatory and never made a distinction between eternal torments from which liberation is impossible, and a fire of purgatory from which one can be saved. According to the Orthodox teaching, it is possible to be freed from the torments of hell: the practice of praying for the departed and even for 'those in hell' at Pentecost vespers is based on this. However, this liberation occurs not because of some automatic necessity and not because the sinner serves a kind of 'prison term' established for those who commit certain sins, but through the prayers of the Church and God's ineffable love for man.

The juridical nature of the doctrine of purgatory met with rejection in the Christian East, where it was always thought that God's mercy cannot be limited to just a certain category of the deceased. The Orthodox belief is based on the idea that, until the Last Judgement, changes for the better are possible in the fate of any sinner. In this sense one can say that Orthodoxy views the fate of the person after death with greater optimism than Catholicism, and never closes the door of the saving Kingdom of God to anyone. Until the final verdict of the Judge is pronounced, there is hope for all the departed to enter the Kingdom of heaven.

'THAT GOD MAY BE ALL IN ALL'

Does this mean that God's mercy will cover all human unrighteousness in the end? The Orthodox Church is far from the excessive optimism of those who maintain that all people will *necessarily* be saved. Origen took that stance in the third century, writing that all living creatures are arranged into a common hierarchy in which each is placed on a level corresponding to their spiritual perfection. In the end all of them will be brought into unity with God, with the difference between them only in the time it takes them to rise from one step to the next and, so to speak, in the degree of pain in this process. The supposition of the final salvation of the Devil and demons is made repeatedly by Origen,[17] although in other places he speaks directly of the impossibility of salvation for the Devil and demons:[18] obviously, this question remained unanswered for him.

Origen's teaching on the *apokatastasis* – the universal restoration – was already a subject of debate during his lifetime. He borrowed the term *apokatastasis* from the Acts of the Apostles (Acts 3:21), which speaks of the promised times of the 'restoration of everything' (*apokatastasis tôn pantôn*). Origen interpreted this term in the sense of a restoration to the primordial state,[19] according to the principle that 'the end is similar to the beginning'.[20] Following ancient philosophers, Origen viewed the universe as a cyclic process, as a succession of 'aeons', in each of which events that took place in previous aeons can be repeated. In this peculiar system, the *apokatastasis* is thought of as the completion of a full historical circle and return to the original state – to the state before the fall.[21]

This theory conflicts with traditional Christian teaching on several counts. It contradicts the vision of the historical process as a path to the final transfiguration and change into a better state, not as a return to the starting point. Secondly, it practically excludes the notion that one can follow Christ into eternal life only of one's free choice. As one modern theologian writes, 'to admit with Origen that evil will come to an end by exhaustion, whereas God alone is … able to satisfy the inexhaustible desires of human nature, is to forget the absolute character that belongs to personal freedom precisely because it is in the image of God'.[22] Thirdly, in Origen's system the *apokatastasis* is closely linked with the theory of the pre-existence of souls: the life of the soul in the body is viewed as a kind of punishment or trial, necessary for restoration to its primordial dignity. This theory has always been firmly rejected by the Church. Fourthly, Origen's version of the *apokatastasis* raises the question: what is the moral sense of the entire drama of human history, if good and evil are ultimately irrelevant before divine mercy and justice?

The council of Constantinople in 543 and the fifth ecumenical council in 553 condemned the teaching of Origen and his followers on the doctrine of *apokatastasis*. But having condemned Origen, the fifth ecumenical council said not a word about the teaching of Gregory of Nyssa, who also wrote of the total extermination of vice and the final salvation of all people.[23]

In the seventh century the teaching on universal salvation was developed in detail and decisively asserted by Isaac the Syrian. According to Isaac, all who have fallen away from God will eventually return to him: by undergoing purification in the fire of suffering and repentance, they will attain to the angelic state.[24] Isaac was strongly averse to the opinion that only a few chosen will enjoy the Kingdom of heaven. On the contrary, he was convinced that the majority will end up in the Kingdom of God, and that only a few evil-doers and sinners will end up in Gehenna, and this only temporarily, for the duration necessary for their sins to be forgiven.[25]

It can be argued that Isaac's view of Gehenna is in some way similar to the Western understanding of purgatory. The difference is that for Isaac, as it seems, there is no eternal hell at all: he only admits Gehenna as a place of temporary punishment. He warns, however, that Gehenna's torment is terrible and unbearable, even though it is limited in time. Gehenna is a reality that is in no way denied by him. Yet he understands it in the context of the gospel's message about God's unspeakable love and boundless mercy. For Isaac, God is primarily a householder making those who worked only one hour equal to those who have borne the burden of the whole day (cf. Mt 20:1–15). A place in the Kingdom of heaven is given to a person not on the basis of his worthiness or unworthiness, but rather on the basis of God's mercy and love towards humankind. The Kingdom of heaven is not a reward, and Gehenna is not a punishment: both are gifts of the merciful God 'who desires all men to be saved and to come to the knowledge of the truth' (1 Tim 2:4).

The teaching of Gregory of Nyssa and Isaac the Syrian on the final salvation of all people is not identical with the Origenism condemned in the sixth century: neither Gregory nor Isaac believed in the pre-existence of souls, nor did they teach that the *apokatastasis* will be a return to the primordial state. Nevertheless, even the teaching on universal salvation found in the writings of these authors can be viewed only as a hypothesis: as a Christian hope, not as a dogma. The key to understanding the idea of the possibility – in the final eschatological perspective – of the salvation of all people can perhaps be found in the words of John Climacus: 'although not all people can be completely free of passions, it is not impossible that all be saved and reconciled with God'.[26] People may be at different levels of spiritual perfection, but this does not mean that they cannot *all* attain salvation. The Lord said, 'In my Father's house are many mansions' (Jn 14:2), and these words have traditionally been understood as indicating various levels of closeness to God in the eschatological Kingdom of God.

St Paul writes that 'God will have all men to be saved' (1 Tim 2:4). God will always, *eternally*, wish for the salvation of all people; but God will always, *eternally*, respect the free will of the person, and cannot save people against their will. This is the great paradox of the mystery of salvation. If salvation depended only and exclusively on God, all people would be saved. But since salvation is a fruit of common labours, of the synergy (collaboration, cooperation) between God and man, man's participation in his own salvation is necessary.

In the twentieth century, the teaching on universal salvation acquired a number of authoritative exponents among the theologians and philosophers of the Russian diaspora. Archpriest Sergius Bulgakov and Nicolas Berdyaev consistently defended this theological opinion. Vladimir Lossky spoke more cautiously but nevertheless unequivocally in favour of this teaching. It was also repeatedly defended by Metropolitan Antony of Sourozh, who wrote that 'the certainty of the salvation of all people cannot be a certainty of the faith, since there are no clear assertions of it in holy scripture that might serve as proof; but it can be a certainty of hope since, knowing God as we know him, we have the right to hope for all things'. The gospel uses the expression 'eternal torments', but there is a difference between divine eternity and the eternity of the created world: the latter 'can be fitted into the confines of time'. If the Devil succeeded in 'creating an eternal kingdom independent of God', that would signify his victory over God.[27]

The Church's condemnation of Origen's teaching on *apokatastasis* in no way disaffirms the belief that in the end God will be 'all in all', that death will be vanquished and abolished for good, and that a 'new earth' and 'new heaven' will appear (cf. 1 Cor 15:22–8; 51–57; and the Book of Revelation). Thus scripture teaches that a certain 'restoration of all things' (Acts. 3:21) will occur, when God will be 'all in all' (1 Cor 15:28).

In this connection, St Silouan of Mount Athos could be remembered, who asserted that an Orthodox Christian must pray for the whole world and for every living creature: 'We ... must have but this one thought – that all should be saved'.[28] The merciful God, he says, 'makes the heart ache for the whole universe, that all men might repent and enter Paradise'.[29]

Once a certain hermit said to him: 'God will punish all atheists. They will burn in everlasting fire.' But St Silouan answered with sorrow: 'Love could not bear this. We must pray for all.' 'And he did, indeed, pray for all', writes Fr Sophrony, St Silouan's biographer: 'His soul was stricken by the realisation that people lived in ignorance of God and His love, and with all his strength he prayed ... for the living and the dead, for friend and foe, for all mankind'.[30]

In the Orthodox understanding, then, the question of the salvation of all humanity cannot be addressed theoretically: it invites not speculation, but prayer. As long as the Church lives – and it will live forever – the prayer of Christians for those outside the Kingdom of heaven will not cease. Every day the Church offers the Eucharist for all living and departed. And even when time is transformed into eternity and 'we shall all be changed', the Church will pray to the Lord for the salvation of all people who were created by him.

Further reading

Alfeyev, Bishop H., 'The life of the age to come', in Alfeyev, *The Mystery of Faith. An Introduction to the Teaching and Spirituality of the Orthodox Church*, ed. J. Rose, London: Darton, Longman & Todd, 2002, pp. 199–230.

'The life of the age to come', in Alfeyev, *The Spiritual World of St Isaac the Syrian*, Kalamazoo, MI: Cistercian Publications, 2000, pp. 269–97.

Daley, B., '*Apokatastasis* and "honorable silence" in the eschatology of St Maximus the Confessor', in F. Heinzer and C. Schönborn (eds.), *Maximus Confessor; Actes du Symposium sur Maxime le Confesseur*, Freiburg, 2–5 September, Freiburg: Éditions Universitaires, 1982, pp. 309–39.

Florovsky, G., 'The patristic age and eschatology', in Florovsky, *Collected Works of Church History*, Vol. IV: *Creation and Redemption*, Belmont, MA: Nordland Publishing Co., 1976, pp. 63–78.

Jevtić, A., Bishop of Herzegovina, 'The eschatological dimension of the Church', *GOTR* 38.1–4 (1993).

Lossky, V., *The Vision of God*, trans. A. Morehouse, London: Faith Press, 1963.

Ware, K. (Bishop of Diokleia), 'Dare we hope for the salvation of all?', in Ware, *The Inner Kingdom, Collected Works*, vol. I, Crestwood, NY: SVS Press, 2000, pp. 193–215.

Zizioulas, J. D., Metropolitan of Pergamon, 'The Eucharist and the Kingdom', *Sourozh* 58 (November 1994), 1–12; 59 (January 1995), 22–38; 60 (May 1995), 32–46.

Notes

1. Fr. G. Florovsky, 'The last things and the last events' in Florovsky, *Collected Works of Church History*, vol. III: *Creation and Redemption* (Belmont, MA: Nordland Publishing Co., 1976), pp. 243–5.
2. A. Schmemann, 'Liturgy and eschatology', *Sobornost* 7.1 (1985), 9–10.
3. Gregory Palamas, *Homily I on the Transfiguration* 4.
4. See N. A. Berdyaev, 'Eschatological metaphysics' in Berdyaev, *The Kingdom of the Spirit and the Kingdom of Caesar* (in Russian) (Moscow: Respublika, 1995), p. 277.
5. John of Damascus, *Exposition of the Orthodox Faith* 4.26.
6. Cf. Irenaeus of Lyons, *Against Heresies* v.25.1.
7. Methodius of Olympus, *On the Resurrection* 31.
8. Gregory of Nyssa, *On the Creation of Humanity* 27.
9. Gregory of Nyssa, *On the Creation of Humanity* 27.6.
10. *The Lenten Triodion*. Meat-fare Sunday, Great Vespers.
11. John Chrysostom, *Homily on Romans* 5.5.
12. John Chrysostom, *Homily on Romans* 6.1.
13. Basil of Caesarea, *Commentary on the Prophet Isaiah* 1.18.
14. Isaac the Syrian, *Homily* 28 (English numbering).

15. Florovsky, 'The last things and the last events', in Florovsky, *Collected Works*, I, pp. 245–6.
16. Symeon the New Theologian, *Hymn 1*.
17. Cf., *inter alia*, Origen, *Commentary on the Epistle to the Romans* 5.10; 9.41; *Commentary on the Gospel according to John*; *Commentary on the Gospel according to Matthew* 13.17.
18. Cf. Origen, *Homily on Joshua* 8.5.
19. Cf. Origen, *Homily on Jeremiah* 14.18.
20. Origen, *On First Principles* I.6.2.
21. Origen, *On First Principles* II.9.2–3.
22. O. Clément, *The Roots of Christian Mysticism* (London: New City, 1993), p. 301.
23. Gregory of Nyssa, *On the Soul and Resurrection* 7–10.
24. Isaac of Nineveh, 'The Second Part', II.40.5.
25. Isaac of Nineveh, 'The Second Part' II.40.12.
26. John Climacus, *Ladder of Divine Ascent* 26.
27. Metropolitan Antony of Sourozh, *Man before God* (in Russian) (Moscow, 1993), pp. 59–65.
28. Archimandrite Sophrony, *St Silouan the Athonite*, trans. R. Edmonds (Tolleshunt Knights: Stavropegic Monastery of St John the Baptist, 1991), p. 226.
29. Archimandrite Sophrony, *St Silouan*, p. 426.
30. Archimandrite Sophrony, *St Silouan*, pp. 48–9.

8 The Church

MATTHEW STEENBERG

Much as Orthodox theology is understood as the mystical encounter with the incarnate Christ, Son of the eternal Father, through the Spirit of Truth, so Orthodox ecclesiology is understood in incarnational and trinitarian terms. The Church is the body of Christ, offered 'for the life of the world',[1] in which the world finds life through communion with its incarnate Lord. It is first and foremost in the meeting of divine and human, of uncreated and created, in the Incarnation of the Son that the Church finds its own reality. It is in and as the living body of the 'one person in two natures' (to employ the language of the Chalcedonian definition) that it brings to fruition, through the Spirit, the saving will of the Father: that his Son become man, so that man might be united to him as God.[2]

The Church is seen primarily as a place of encounter, where God is not so much learned about as met, and where human lives are brought into an *ecclesia*, a community, of relation to this encountered God. At the beginning of its main service, the Divine Liturgy, the deacon proclaims to the celebrant bishop the intention of the Church's work: 'Master, it is time for the Lord to act' (cf. Ps 118 [119]:126) – announcing an act that culminates in the eucharistic encounter of the communicant faithful with the body and blood of Christ.

This focus on encounter establishes the nature of the Church as intrinsically sacramental. The sacraments stand at the centre of the Church's life and mission, not because of a symbolic significance or merit of ritual, but because in each sacrament the person is drawn farther into the encounter with God which transforms and transfigures.[3] These sacraments are more traditionally known as the 'mysteries', *mysterion* and *sacramentum* being two terms not quite identical in meaning, but both conveying the concept of the sacred and the depth of God's transcendence.

For all this, 'definitions' of Church in Orthodoxy are hard to come by. Whether this is because a tendency against dogmatic definitions is part of the Orthodox heritage is debatable; but a more significant reason is the perception of the Church as, above all, a living organism, Christ's very body, into which his creation is drawn through encounter and relation, rather than an institution or complex that can be neatly defined. The nearest thing to a 'dogmatic' claim concerning the nature of the Church comes in the phrase of the Creed of Nicaea–Constantinople through which the faithful confess belief in 'one holy, catholic and apostolic Church'. In its usual exegesis, this phrase is taken to indicate the cardinal principles of Orthodox ecclesiology: that it is unitive and singular; that it is holy, inasmuch as it is the Church founded and governed by Christ; that it is *katholike*, or 'universal'; and that it is apostolic, inasmuch as it preserves and provides the encounter with Christ first experienced by his apostles and handed down (literally, 'traditioned', from the Latin *traditio*, 'to hand over') to future generations. It would be incorrect to assume, however, that this phrase alone stands as the Church's definition of its structure and mission. Too often overlooked is the place this confession holds in the Church's functional life: the Creed is, in Orthodox *praxis*, not so much a dogmatic statement as an ascetical tool of liturgical preparation for the Eucharist. It is recited in the Liturgy after the gifts are brought into the altar, immediately before the prayers of the anaphora. So the statements of the Creed, including its confession of 'one holy, catholic and apostolic Church', are above all confessions of relational orientation, drawing the faithful into the encounter of the chalice. The Church is 'one' precisely here: in the chalice over which the *aër* (the large veil that usually covers the holy gifts on the altar) is waved while the Creed is recited, since the Church is the living body of the one there to be met. The Church is 'holy' in exactly this act of sacramental communion, the sanctification of the Spirit (often taken by commentators as signified in the waving of the same *aër* above the gifts). And the Church is both 'catholic' and 'apostolic' inasmuch as the eucharistic communion is understood as the singular encounter with the one Christ met and known by the apostles, brought to 'the whole inhabited earth' through the mystery of the Spirit at Pentecost.

It is thus in the Eucharist, the sacrament of sacraments, that the Church finds its fullest definition, and not chiefly in any creedal statement. This location of the Church at the chalice provides, in turn, the means to examine its structure; for as much as the Church is the living body of mystical encounter, it is also a community in creation, with its own structure, form and manner of operation.

TWO PERCEPTIONS OF ECCLESIAL STRUCTURE: HIERARCHY IN POWER AND HIERARCHY IN COMMUNION

It is characteristic of the Church that it is a structured entity, taking as its model the concept of a body made up of many parts in ordered relationship (cf. St Paul's analogy in Romans 12:3–18). The specific organisation of this body is modelled on the relationship of Christ to his apostles: namely, that there is but a single head (Christ), yet a conciliar community of leadership and evangelical work. The usual term for the organisational structures of the Church is 'hierarchy', a term that stresses order and ranks, but which the Church's theologians have always been wont to stress does not equate to a gradation of worth.[4] Hierarchies in the Church exist to ensure the right order and operation of the body as a whole, following Paul's reminder that in a body one organ is not of more worth than another by virtue of a seemingly more glorious function; and modern hierarchs (a title normally given to those in the episcopal ranks) such as Metropolitan Anthony of Sourozh have laid stress upon the fact that those of 'highest' authority are ultimately chief servants to the body of the Church. One is reminded of one of the titles customary to the pope of Rome since the time of Gregory the Great (sixth/seventh century): *servus servorum Dei* ('the servant of the servants of God').

Generally speaking, two models or perceptions of church hierarchy and organisation predominate in Orthodox discussion. The first, perhaps the most common, is of a linearity of power and authority, taken in the positive sense of the power given to the apostles by Christ (cf. Mt 9:8; 10:1; Mk 6:7; Lk 24:29) and authoritatively preserved through the generations. This pattern traces the episcopal lineage of the churches from the twelve apostles, through the ecclesiastical centres they founded, locating their authoritative structure in the unbroken connection to these first descendants. In each location a bishop, in direct succession to his predecessors, is surrounded by his priests and deacons, whose authority as ministers of the sacraments and teachers of the gospel encounter comes through the charismatic preservation of apostolic heritage and mission. From at least the second century the priests have been taken to symbolise the 'council of elders' – i.e. the apostles – and the deacons, the angelic ministers of the Word, or at times Christ himself. The local churches maintain communion with one another after the manner of the apostles' own interrelationships: equal heirs of the encounter with the living God, accountable to one another in terms of maintaining the universality of the one faith (i.e. that 'the truth and the contemplation of the apostolic tradition is manifested throughout the whole world'[5]). The common conviction of the early Church was that the apostles were organised in rank: Peter was first among the apostles, while James held a special place as overseer (*episkopos*) of Jerusalem. After the same pattern, the successors to these apostles are ranked in relation to each other: so within territories there are patriarchs, metropolitans, archbishops and bishops; and between territories there are rankings of honour and eminence. Yet such ranks are 'of equals', even as the apostles were as one before Christ, who reminded them that 'he who seeks to be first shall be last, and last first' (cf. Mk 9:35).

This perception of the Church's structure, and the means through which it is preserved as 'one, holy, catholic and apostolic', has been the explanation favoured over the past several centuries. Yet in recent decades, and in the past few years in particular, Orthodox theologians have come to question whether it is an adequate portrayal of the ecclesiology actually encountered in the Church's history and the writings of the Fathers. The questioning began with the works of the Russian theologian N. Afanasiev,[6] with his emphasis on the eucharistic celebration as the defining mark of the local Church, and has been most influentially furthered by Metropolitan John Zizioulas with the publication of his *Being as Communion* in 1985, which emphasised the communion of God the Father with the Son and Spirit, in trinitarian relation, as the foundation of Christian ecclesiology. As a result, the tide has been turning towards explanations of the Church that see the apostolic heritage more squarely in terms of communion.[7] It is in the apostles *as ministers of the living God* and of the encounter with him (i.e. in the sacramental work of the Spirit) that their 'authority' is grounded. And the Church is defined as 'apostolic' inasmuch as it carries forward that singular work of the apostles: to bring human creation into this same incarnational, eucharistic encounter. The unity of the Church is understood as residing not in the monadic structure of its organisational apparatus and history, but in the one encounter with the one God, into whose life the faithful are brought through a communion (or relation) of being, that images the eternal communion of the Father, Son and Spirit as Trinity.

More recent reflections on ecclesiological structure have taken pains to stress, too, that the Church is the communion of the faithful with the *crucified and risen* Christ, and that the eucharistic life of relation to God is enabled only through the sacramental connection to his death and resurrection.[8] So 'Church' is articulated more carefully as that reality in which the faithful are joined in the Eucharist to the crucified and risen Lord, united through the working of the Spirit to the sacrifice of Christ, which brings them into the authentic *ecclesia* of the apostles: the community of resurrected sons and daughters of the Father.

COMMUNITY AND CONCILIARITY – THE CHURCH
AS *SOBORNOST*

Both models of ecclesiology stress the conciliar nature of the Church, meaning that it is hierarchical but not monadic. There is not a single 'head' amongst the successors to the apostles (the bishops), even as there was no chief of that original apostolic communion, set up over the others. The inter-communion of catholicity (known in Slavonic as *sobornost*) involves an order of honour and ranks of organisation, but these exist precisely to facilitate conciliar leadership within the Church. The ultimate administrative authority in the Church is not a single episcopal head, but the communion of apostolic successors – the council or *sobor*.

If the Orthodox Church is sometimes known as 'the Church of the ecumenical councils', it is because this emphasis on conciliar oversight has been a characteristic of its organisation from its earliest days. The supreme dogmatic authorities of the Church are those councils deemed ecumenical, or universal, in scope (from the Greek *oikoumene*, 'world' or 'inhabited earth'), of which it recognises seven, dating from the fourth century to the eighth. These gatherings of bishops, whilst varied in focus, and at times of questionable political and social orientation,[9] nonetheless are considered by the Church to have been guided by the Holy Spirit into the 'right division of the Word of God's truth' (to paraphrase roughly 2 Tim 2:15 and the prayer for hierarchs said at the Divine Liturgy). As the Church proclaims when it commemorates them on the Sunday of the Fathers of the first six ecumenical councils (16 July):

> The apostles' preaching and the Fathers' doctrines
> have established one faith for the Church.
> Adorned with the robe of truth, woven from heavenly theology,
> it defines and glorifies the great mystery of Orthodoxy.[10]

As the council is a fraternal body in fellowship (*koinonia*, 'communion'), so it follows that the articulation of dogma in the Church is conciliar in nature. The ecumenical councils, like the local councils of which there are a great (and continually expanding) number, are forums of discussion and discernment amongst hierarchs; while presided over by the highest-ranking bishop of the assembly, they are nonetheless meeting places of canonical equals, determining in *sobornost* the articulations and practices of the Church. At the level of the ecumenical councils, these have included dogmatic statements (e.g. the Creed of Nicaea–Constantinople (325–81); the definition of Chalcedon (451)),

heresiological definitions (e.g. the anathemas of the second council of Constantinople (553)) and confessional documents (e.g. conciliar recognition of
the letters of St Cyril of Alexandria, St Leo of Rome, and others at the
council of Chalcedon). They have also determined affairs of ecclesiastical
order through laying down, modifying, rescinding and issuing canons
(from the Greek *kanon*, 'measuring stick' or 'rule, guideline') based on
situational and historical needs. Many of these delineate and refine precisely the conciliar structure of the Church: determining how bishops
are to meet in councils, that they are not to attempt to rule in other
bishops' territories, and so forth.

The same emphasis on conciliarity is found in the functional structure
of the Church's ministry. Bishops, as ministers of the apostolic encounter
with Christ in the Eucharist and other mysteries of the Church, are surrounded by their priests (also known as 'presbyters', from the Greek for
'elder') who serve as their councillors and ministers in a local territory.
Amongst the priests there is a similar hierarchy of equality to that found
in the episcopacy, with different ranks and orders in a common office of
ministry and service. Together with the priests are the deacons, serving
a distinct liturgical and pastoral function in the threefold ministerial structure of the Church. Deacons are primarily the ministers of the prayers
of the people in the Divine Liturgy, standing in their midst and lifting
up their petitions before the altar at which the bishop or priest stands
as celebrant.

If the ministerial structure of clerical leadership can be said to be threefold,[11] the full worshipping structure of the Church is fourfold, for ecclesiastical service is the work of the bishop, priest, deacon and the *laos*,
the 'people' of God. The term 'clergy' itself derives from *kleros*, meaning
'lot': those from the people to whom it is allotted to serve for and with
the people in the temple. This understanding of the clerical offices does
not allow the clergy to be separated from the body of the faithful of
which they are members and for which they are called to service – a call
taken up by the people in their proclamation of 'axios!' ('he is worthy!')
at ordinations to all levels of the clergy. In the services of the Church,
the clergy and the people pray and serve together: the people in affirmation
of the deacons' petitions in prayer, the priest in offering and blessing. That
in modern practice the people's role has become, in some places, markedly
passive in an external sense, with their 'office' of service being relegated
wholly to a choir who sings on their behalf, is a regrettable, if subtle,
form of clericalising ecclesiology. It should, however, be pointed out that
not all silence is passive. There are contexts in which silence is part of
an intentional practice of interior prayer and participation in the divine

services; and this must not be downplayed in favour of an emphasis on a 'lay participation', which is sometimes seen as authentic only if it is externalised.

COMMUNION, FELLOWSHIP AND LITURGICAL MEMORY

The conciliar nature of the Church, expressed in its councils, its clerical structure and its participatory understanding of worshipping life, grounds too the substance of its existence as sacramental and rooted in the common experience of prayer. As Metropolitan John Zizioulas has recently written:

> It is not by accident that the Church has given to the Eucharist the name of 'communion'. For in the Eucharist we can find all the dimensions of communion: God communicates himself to us, we enter into communion with him, the participants of the sacrament enter into communion with one another, and creation as a whole enters through man into communion with God. All this takes place in Christ and the Spirit, who brings the last days into history and offers to the world a foretaste of the Kingdom.[12]

The grounding of the Church in the experience of Christ, through the Spirit, which brings the faithful into conformity to the Father's will, establishes its identity in this communion with God. And as God is the Lord 'of ages past' (cf. Ps 89 [90]:1) as well as of the 'last days', the communion of the person, and of the Church, in this God is the communion too with the whole *pleroma* ('fullness') of humanity, beyond the confines of the time and space of human history. The Church exists as 'the communion of the saints', not merely by admiring the saints, but in living relation to the whole body of Christ, in the dimension of Christ's own eternity. The living and the dead are not merely common recipients of the Church's prayer, but common participants in it. Prayers are offered 'on behalf of all and for all', since it is for these that Christ died; and in him believers 'do not perish, but have eternal life'.[13] If in Christ 'those who have gone to their rest' are not dead but alive in him, then communion in Christ is communion, also, in the fellowship of this body. This is symbolised in Orthodox churches first of all by the iconography of the temple: one is surrounded, on entry into the church, by the images of those persons transfigured in Christ, understood as mystically present in the communion of his body. The continual commemoration of the saints throughout the services (nearly every litany ends with a commemoration of the Mother of God, together 'with all the saints') unites in liturgical memory the whole human race, brought to the sacrifice of Christ, who offered himself 'for the life of the world'.

This practice of *memory*, of drawing into the heart the redemptive work of God and making it alive and real to the present moment, is at the very centre of the human *synergeia*, or co-working, with God in the Church's liturgical life. It is 'in remembrance' of Christ, as he commanded, that the gifts of bread and wine become the very body and true blood of which the faithful partake;[14] it is in 'eternal memory' that the saints are ever alive and present to the faithful;[15] it is in 'remembering, therefore, this saving commandment and all that has come to pass for us – the cross, the tomb, the resurrection on the third day', that the faithful enter into the reality of these very things.[16] This is memory in the sense not only of recollection, but of calling into the present experience of the human mind and heart – or *nous* – the reality of God's redeeming work. Through the communion with this God who is beyond time, the Church *engages in the reality* of the thing remembered. So the Eucharist is not just a re-enactment of Christ's offering, but the real communication of his body and blood. The communion of the saints is not merely the recollection of past lives of holiness, but a genuine presence, the inter-communion of the living with the departed. The events of salvation are not simply called to mind, but in that remembrance they are *authentically experienced in the present*.

This perception lies behind the commemorative focus of the Church's worshipping cycle, and particularly its festal commemorations. When the Church celebrates Christ's resurrection, the hymns sung by the people 'in remembrance' of that unique and unrepeatable event are not hymns of the past, but of the present: '*Today* is the day of resurrection … A sacred Passover has been shown forth to us *today*.'[17] The same reality that grounds the communion of the saints beyond time and beyond death grounds the continual making-present of transformative moments of the divine economy in the Christian life. The Church is understood as the living body of Christ the eternal Son of the Father, which, through the Spirit, is united to the timelessness of this God's eternity.

So the Church has not only a historical dimension; it has also a dimension of the eternity of beginnings and ends that meet in Christ, who is understood as the one who declares 'I am the *alpha* and the *omega*, the beginning and the end' (cf. Rev 1:8, 11; 21:26; 22:13). We have already seen this in terms of the Church's eschatological dimension, its 'bringing the last days into history'; but this is equally true of its engagement with protology, with the 'first things'. The pinnacle of the Divine Liturgy is the participation in the Eucharist, accompanied by hymnography drawn primarily from the Book of Revelation (or 'the Apocalypse'); and similarly the liturgical day begins at Vespers with the hymn of creation, Psalm 103 [104], proclaimed with the priest standing outside the closed Holy Doors of the iconostasis, symbolising Adam outside the closed gates of Eden. In order to make real *in time*, i.e. at the present moment of worship, the full scope of human existence in God, the sacramental remembrance of the Church extends *beyond time*, into God's eternity, to draw together the full story of human creation, sin, redemption and perfection in the living Christ of the Church's sacraments.

THE CHURCH AS THE ARENA OF TRANSFIGURATION

In all of the above, it is clear that the *work* of the Church is the work of God in Christ: the transfiguration and deification of the human person and the whole of creation. The understanding of *theosis*, or deification, as the adoption into God of his own human handiwork, links it inextricably in Orthodox thought to the life and mission of the Church as the arena of human transfiguration. It is in sacramental communion with God that this conversion of life is wrought, and so the intensely *personal* reality of a deified life is – since personal being, like divine being, is relational – united to the work of the communion of the Church. The Church is thus understood as the place of light, in which creation is 'illumined' (a term traditionally applied to baptism), and the 'spiritual hospital' in which the disease of broken communion with God is healed.

The principal sacraments of the Church are characterised by their transformative character. The Eucharist is *par excellence* the mystery of restored communion; and with it, in practice as much as in theory, the sacrament of confession, which is the avenue for repentance and conversion leading to that communion. Confession is the liturgical 'removal of the log from one's own eye' before gazing upon the reality of another, even if (especially if) this 'other' is God himself. Baptism is the sacrament of a life received into the sanctification of the Spirit which unites one to the body of Christ; and similarly chrismation, the anointing with the 'seal of the Holy Spirit'. The sacrament of unction, or anointing of the sick, is an extension of the transformative mission of the Spirit in baptism and chrismation, united to confession of sins and communion in Christ's body and blood. The final two most common sacraments, marriage and ordination, may less obviously be transformative in orientation, but these too are understood in an ascetical context by the Church: marriage as the sacrament of *communal and relational* growth in Christ and struggle against sin; and ordination as the setting aside of a life for participation in a particular way in Christ's work in the world – the very conversion of the world in Christ.

A hesitancy to number the above as 'the seven sacraments', or to give a definitive catalogue of the Church's mysteries, may have something to do with the late arrival of such a classification (which seems to have entered into Orthodox liturgical handbooks around the time of the scholastic influence on traditional Orthodox lands, *circa* the seventeenth century). More significantly, it reflects a perception of sacraments as those means of transformative encounter in Christ, through the Spirit, that deify creation in the ministry of Christ's body. In this light, these seven sacraments may hold a certain pride of place, but they cannot be seen as categorically distinct from the extension of that encounter that fills many other dimensions of ecclesial existence. Hence a sermon, properly prepared, is sacramental inasmuch as it gives the hearer a deeper receptivity to Christ's presence in the Eucharist (and so its place, according to Russian practice, immediately before the entry of the holy gifts into the altar). So too the sacramental character of the veneration of icons, of prostrations and the sign of the Cross, of receiving the *antidoron* (blessed bread) at the end of the Liturgy. In the sense of transformative encounter, the Church sees the whole of its work, and not only certain acts, as deifying and transfiguring. This is a theme particularly developed in modern Russian thought, where it may be expressed in terms of the Church as the soul of the world, progressively transforming the world and the whole of life so that it 'becomes Church'.

THE CHURCH AND HUMAN SINFULNESS

In every dimension of its self-understanding, the Church is an organism of divine–human interrelation. Because this interrelation does not involve either an a-historical humanity or a generic deity, but the one human race begun in Adam and the God revealed fully in Christ crucified and risen, so the *redemptive* character of the Church correlates to the *sinful* reality of human experience borne up in it. The Church exists in a broken and fractured world, comprised of similarly broken and fractured people who constitute its life – for Christ has come to save not the healthy, but the sick (cf. Mt 9:13; Mk 2:17; Lk 5:32). As such, the Church may be holy with God's own holiness, but it also remains the hospital of the broken; it deals with the reality of sin as much as with its transformation and redemption.

In practical terms, the conciliar nature of the Church attempts to provide a structure capable of combating the inevitable encroachments of such sin into the life of the Church itself. The fact that there is no loca-lised dogmatic authority in the singular, but rather a connected family of episcopal communities, provides – at least in principle – a robust means for dealing with local and more widespread challenges to the belief and practices of the Church. In some sense the anti-heretical focus of most of the councils emphasises this para-local structure of conciliarity. So Arius, who preached in Africa, would be condemned by bishops gathered in Nicaea, and Nestorius, who ministered in Constantinople, would be condemned in Ephesus – signs of the Church's catholic response to local issues. In a similar manner, clerics and even bishops might fall into error, without necessarily carrying their whole community, or a whole *magisterium*, with them. Individual error is met by conciliar repair.

In practice, the strengths of this paradigm have been accompanied by weaknesses. Mention of Nestorius, who was condemned at the ecumeni-cal council of Ephesus in AD 431, raises both the issue of geographical de-localisation and the problem of universal conciliar agreement. Geogra-phy, as much as political agendas, might influence the practical consti-tution of councils (an issue of utmost relevance at Ephesus, and also at Chalcedon); and agreement secured at a council does not per se equate to acceptance at the level of the whole *oikoumene*. Ephesus initially engendered a division between the Eastern and Western portions of the Christian empire in the years immediately following 431, healed (in part) only thanks to careful negotiations between St Cyril of Alexandria and John, Bishop of Antioch. More tragically, the council of Chalcedon in AD 451 engendered a division in the Christian realm that has never fully healed, and remains to this day. That differing ecclesial traditions today regard different councils as ecumenical – Eastern Orthodox recognising seven and Oriental Orthodox three – bears witness to the lifespan of some of these issues. The resiliency of the conciliar model has to be coun-tered by this complexity of localisation and the problems it engenders. Many of the disputes of the early period, between AD 300 and 600, have at least partial grounding in different general approaches to exegesis and dogma between the geographic centres of Alexandria on the one hand and Antioch on the other; just as modern-day difficulties in canonical jur-isdiction and territory have substantial grounding in different understand-ings of canonical frameworks between the Church of Constantinople on the one hand and that of Russia on the other.

This has, in part, led to the present-day phenomenon of 'jurisdictional-ism' in the Orthodox Church. The ancient pattern of geographic evangeli-sation was (in simplified terms) for a new territory to be evangelised by a mission from one of the ancient patriarchates and to grow under that 'mother patriarchate's' guidance until such time as it be granted independence (autonomy) and self-governance (autocephaly); but the reality of Orthodox presence in much of the New World is quite different. Multiple mother churches have established ecclesiastical presences in single territories, at least in part through the desire of immigrants in such areas to have a Church 'from the homeland' in their new environments. But the situation of a single territory – Great Britain and North America are chief examples – having overlapping dioceses, multiple bishops in a single city, and a variety of churches in a single city divided wholly along jurisdictionally ethnic lines, is one for which the canons of the Church make absolutely no provision. Use of the canons in an attempt to redress such jurisdictional considerations, even if the motivation is divorced from the question of ethnic background and shifted to that of mission, is fraught with problems for precisely this reason, and local churches have often found themselves at loggerheads over the interpretation of specific canons that might be used to determine jurisdictional legitimacy in one way or another. Orthodox theologians over the past century have lamented this question of jurisdictionalism as chief among the challenges facing the Church in the twentieth and now twenty-first centuries; but it is unclear, at present, how the matter may eventually find resolution.

Damaging though jurisdictional divisions may be to the Church's witness, they only rarely and briefly impair the Church's unity in communion. To some, therefore, a still more fundamental question is that of ecclesiastical identity in a world of multiple Christian traditions and churches. If the Orthodox Church is understood as '*the one* holy, catholic and apostolic Church', what of those outside it? Suffice it to say that few voices in the Church would suggest anything apart from this foundational claim of ecclesial unity, yet nonetheless there is little by way of common agreement on how precisely to speak of boundaries, limits and relations. Georges Florovsky's article 'The limits of the Church', written in 1933, is considered by many to be a classic exploration of the tension between the canonical and the charismatic boundaries of the Church.[18] Orthodox Christians would generally accept the dictum of Cyprian of Carthage that 'outside the Church there is no salvation'; but this can be understood either in an exclusive sense, or as a tautological statement that all who are saved are *in some sense* within the Church. Orthodoxy understands the Church to be intrinsically one, and salvation to be united to the life and mission of this Church; yet it maintains with equal fervency the confession that Christ's sacrifice was for the life of all the world – a mystery easier to confess than to articulate in precise ecclesiological terms. As

Metropolitan Kallistos Ware puts it, 'There is only one Church, but there are many different ways of being related to this one Church, and many different ways of being separated from it.'[19] The divisions of Christendom, which the Orthodox Church understands as the fruits of human sinfulness, remain one of the most challenging aspects of its relationship to the modern world.[20]

CONCLUSION

On the human level, as Metropolitan Kallistos again points out, the Church's life is indeed 'grievously impoverished as a result of schisms, yet such schisms cannot affect the essential nature of the Church'.[21] Orthodox Christians firmly believe that the Church remains 'one, holy, catholic and apostolic', inasmuch as it is not the fracture of the sinful world that defines it in this way, but the reality of its headship in Christ, who is 'in our midst, now and always' – a proclamation shared between the clergy at the altar during the Liturgy. When the Church comes together at the defining moment of its self-identity, the reception of the body and blood of Christ, it hears the priest proclaim 'The holy things are for those who are holy', to which the people reply, 'There is but one who is holy, one who is Lord: Jesus Christ, to the glory of God the Father.' The Church is holy *in Christ*, in the very midst of its need for the redemption he brings. Because the Church is sanctified through the living encounter of a broken creation with Christ, an encounter that heals and transforms it, the Church is thus at its core both missionary and evangelical. Though the deacon proclaims at the Liturgy's beginning, 'It is time for the Lord to act', there follows no proclamation of its end – no *ite, missa est* ('the mass is finished'). The work of the Church is fundamentally a work for the world, and the people are summoned to 'go forth in peace, in the name of the Lord'. If the Church is truly one in the redemptive power of God's holiness, it is charged with the missionary task of making all the world one, joining itself to the intention of Christ before his Father: 'that they may be one, even as thou and I are one' (Jn 17:11). Its charge is nothing less than to bring the whole of creation into itself. The scriptural book of Revelation, so much the sourcebook of the Church's services, concludes with an eschatological vision of the 'new heaven and new earth' of Christ's redemption, in which a new and heavenly Jerusalem descends from heaven to be the abode of man; and it is fitting that in the vision of this perfected city, there is no temple, no Church. It is the Church's mission to take the whole of creation into itself, to bring all of God's handiwork into the life-giving encounter with the incarnate Son, so that the world itself becomes the Church of God, 'who will be all in all' (1 Cor 15:28).

Further reading

Florovsky, G., 'The limits of the Church' in Florovsky, *Bible, Church, Tradition: An Eastern Orthodox View*, Belmont, MA: Notable and Academic Books, 1987.

Hopko, T., 'On ecclesial conciliarity' in J. Breck, J. Meyendorff and E. Silk (eds.), *The Legacy of St Vladimir. Byzantium, Russia, America*, Crestwood, NY: SVS Press, 1990, pp. 209–25.

Meyendorff, J. (ed.), *The Primacy of Peter: Essays in Ecclesiology and the Early Church*, Crestwood, NY: SVS Press, 1992.

Schmemann, A., *Church, World, Mission*, Crestwood, NY: SVS Press, 1966.

Ware, T., *The Orthodox Church, New Edition*, London: Penguin Books, 1993.

Zizioulas, J. D., Metropolitan of Pergamon, *Being as Communion: Studies in Personhood and the Church*, Crestwood, NY: SVS Press, 1997.

  Communion and Otherness: Further Studies in Personhood and the Church, ed. P. McPartlan, London and New York: T. & T. Clark, 2006.

  Eucharist, Bishop, Church: The Unity of the Church in the Divine Eucharist and the Bishop During the First Three Centuries, trans. E. Theokritoff, Brookline, MA: Holy Cross Orthodox Press, 2001.

Notes

1. St John Chrysostom, *The Divine Liturgy*, Anaphora; cf. 1 Jn 2:2.
2. See Athanasius of Alexandria, *On the Incarnation* 54.
3. See V. Lossky, *The Mystical Theology of the Eastern Church* (London: James Clarke & Co., 1957; repr. Crestwood, NY: SVS Press, 1998), p. 181.
4. So the extensive hierarchical theology of, for example, (Ps-)Dionysius the Areopagite; cf. A. Louth, *Denys the Areopagite* (London and New York: Continuum International, 1989).
5. See Irenaeus of Lyons, *Against Heresies* III.3.1; cf. I.10.1, 2.
6. See his important 'The Church which presides in love' in J. Meyendorff (ed.), *The Primacy of Peter: Essays in Ecclesiology and the Early Church* (Crestwood, NY: SVS Press, 1992).
7. J. Zizioulas, *Being as Communion. Studies in Personhood and the Church* (Crestwood, NY: SVS Press, 1985).
8. So J. Behr, *The Mystery of Christ: Life in Death* (Crestwood, NY: SVS Press, 2006); and J. Zizioulas, *Communion and Otherness. Further Studies in Personhood and the Church*, ed. P. McPartlan (London and New York: T. & T. Clark, 2006).
9. In particular, the third (Ephesus, AD 431) and fourth (Chalcedon, AD 451) councils were fraught with political rivalry and motivations; see J. A. McGuckin, *St. Cyril of Alexandria and the Christological Controversy* (Crestwood, NY: SVS Press, 2004).
10. Kontakion for the Sunday of the Holy Fathers.

11. Which it has been since at least the middle of the third century, though other models, particularly a two-fold model of presbyter (equivalent to bishop) and deacon, are strongly evidenced in the early patristic corpus; cf. the *Didache* and Clement of Rome, *First Epistle to the Corinthians*.
12. Zizioulas, *Communion and Otherness*, p. 7.
13. Jn 3:15; St John Chrysostom, *The Divine Liturgy*, Anaphora prayers.
14. So his commandment to 'do this in remembrance of me' (cf. Lk 22:14–19; 1 Cor 14:24, 25), repeated during the Anaphora of the Divine Liturgy.
15. Cf. the prayer at the end of the funeral and memorial services of the Church: 'May his/her memory be eternal!'
16. St John Chrysostom, *The Divine Liturgy*, Anaphora.
17. From the *stikhera* of Paschal Matins.
18. In Florovsky, *Bible, Church, Tradition: An Eastern Orthodox View* (Belmont, MA: Notable and Academic Books, 1987).
19. T. Ware, *The Orthodox Church, New Edition* (London: Penguin Books, 1993), p. 308.
20. See further J. Jillions, 'Orthodox Christianity in the West: the ecumenical challenge', below.
21. Ware, *The Orthodox Church*, p. 245.

9 Theology of the icon

MARIAMNA FORTOUNATTO
and MARY B. CUNNINGHAM

WHAT IS AN ICON?

The Greek word *eikon* simply means 'image', but the word has come in Orthodox tradition to mean much more than simply a pictorial representation of a religious subject. Every icon, whether it depicts Christ, the Word and Son of God, Mary the Mother of God, a saint, or a biblical scene or feast, represents a confession of faith and a witness to the Incarnation. This is because the icon is a symbol, which manifests something greater than its physical limits allow. Like the written word, an icon expresses divine truth in a manner that humans can perceive and understand. As St John of Damascus asserted in the eighth century, when Orthodox Christians 'venerate images, it is not veneration offered to matter, but to those who are portrayed through matter in the images'.[1]

An 'icon' usually means a portable wooden panel, painted either with encaustic wax (especially before about the seventh century) or with egg tempera. However, the term refers in its widest sense also to the images portrayed in frescoes or mosaics on church walls, on sacerdotal vestments, altar vessels, Gospel and liturgical book covers, crosses and other media. Panel icons may be made not only on wood, but also on ivory, metal, textile and many other materials. Icons may serve decorative or pedagogic purposes, in addition to acting as liturgical or devotional objects. All of these forms of icons, however, share one important characteristic: they offer a window into eternal meaning and are thus worthy of honour and devotion. Such honour is not offered to the icon itself, but to what it represents.

The icon is also a microcosm, which links together the divine and created worlds. The world of matter is represented in various forms, including animal, plant, mineral and water, in the composition of the image. Frescoes are made of stone, lime and earthy pigments, for example, while panel icons may combine wood, mineral pigments, the egg that is used to bind these, and water. Thus the icon painter 'frees' matter as he offers it back to God in his reverent creation of an image. The subject, or prototype, that is depicted, however, provides the icon with its sacred meaning and presence. Because it represents an image of the transfigured, or divinised, world, the icon acts as a window, or passageway, between human beings and God.

As mediators of divine reality, icons represent focal points of prayer in the Orthodox Church. They are not intended to leave us passive and, indeed, they are not themselves passive. 'We do not watch like passive spectators', writes Metropolitan Philaret of Moscow, 'but we present our soul to the luminous face of Jesus Christ, like a mirror to receive his light' (cf. 2 Cor 3:18).[2] It is for this reason that the figures depicted in icons always face the beholder, making spiritual communion possible. Even narrative, or festal, icons have this quality: the figures turn outwards towards the world and nothing is hidden from the sight of the beholder. The icon does not merely depict unseen holy things; it invites us to enter among them.

THE DEVELOPMENT OF CHRISTIAN ART AND ICONOGRAPHY

Although Orthodox tradition maintains that icons were present in the Church from the very beginning, with the earliest one, according to legend, being an icon of the Virgin Mary and Christ child painted by the evangelist Luke, no examples survive from the first two centuries of the Christian era. Scholars still debate whether this reflects Christian adherence to an Old Testament understanding of the second commandment (Ex 20:4) or whether the lack of artefacts is due to historical accident.[3] Early Christian texts that seem to question the role of images should not be read out of context; these are in any case qualified by evidence that Christians accepted representational art, especially in funerary contexts, from a very early date.[4]

The pictorial language of the Church was established in its essential traits between the fourth and sixth centuries. This language of images, called iconography, was unified not only across national boundaries, but also throughout subsequent centuries, thus revealing artists' respect for a consecrated tradition. For all icons, the prototype, which is the transfigured world, remains unchanging; whether expressed in a scene or individual portrait, the deeper truth that it reveals is timeless.

Both symbolic and figurative depictions of Christ were employed in early Christian art. They could be based on Old Testament prophetic types, pagan figures such as Orpheus, or, more literally, on the historical Jesus who performed miracles such as the raising of Lazarus. The catacomb of Commodilla, dated to approximately the fourth century, contains a bust of Christ, flanked by the Greek letters alpha and omega (cf. Rev 1:8), which portrays him according to an iconographic type that would later become familiar as the *Pantokrator* ('All-Ruler').[5] This represents a theological statement, marking the victory over the Arian heresy; it was intended to leave the faithful in no doubt that Jesus is both the Son of God and the Son of Man. The use of more symbolic images for Christ was finally forbidden at the council 'in Trullo', sometimes called the 'Quinisext' council, in Constantinople (AD 692). This council decreed that symbols such as the lamb, along with Old Testament types for Christ, had been superseded by the Incarnation. Christ was incarnate and prophecy had been fulfilled; thus:

> the figure in human form of the Lamb who takes away the sin of the world, Christ our God, [should] henceforth be exhibited in images, instead of the ancient lamb, so that all may understand by means of it the depths of the humiliation of the Word of God, and that we may recall to our memory his conversation in the flesh, his passion and salutary death, and his redemption which was brought about for the whole world.[6]

ICONOCLASM AND THE THEOLOGY OF IMAGES

In the early eighth century, a reaction against the growing importance of holy icons in religious worship developed in the Byzantine Church. Scholars have suggested many reasons for the introduction of Iconoclasm (literally, 'the smashing of images') by a series of emperors beginning with Leo III in AD 730, including fear of God's wrath in the face of 'idolatry', Muslim or Jewish influence, or increased political and military disruption in the empire owing to the rise of the Islamic state. It is also possible, however, that the iconoclasts saw themselves as reformers from within, aiming to return Christianity to the pure, aniconic state which they believed had existed in the earliest Church.

Persecution in the first phase of Iconoclasm (AD 730–87) was severe, especially under Leo III's son Constantine V. After the death of Constantine's son, Leo IV, in 780, his widow Eirene called the seventh ecumenical council of Nicaea in 787 and, on the basis of its decisions, re-introduced icons in the Church. Adherence to the decrees of this council lasted only a generation, however: in 815, probably in response to a period of military setbacks and the memory of victories under iconoclast emperors of the eighth century, Leo V re-introduced iconoclastic policies. This second phase, which lasted until the 'triumph of Orthodoxy' in 843, was less severe than the first. Nevertheless, many defenders of holy images, including, above all, monks, were imprisoned or even tortured in the attempt to eradicate their belief in the importance of icons in religious worship. Although many early icons, wall paintings and mosaics were lost in this period, it did cause religious thinkers to work out a consistent and logical defence of icons and their veneration in the Church. Much of this debate centred on the depiction of Christ in holy icons, but the portrayal of the Mother of God, saints and feasts was also discussed. We know much less about iconoclast teachings than we do about the Orthodox position; nevertheless, it is possible to piece together some of their charges against icons from the writings of their opponents and from fragments of their writings that survive in the Acts of the seventh council of Nicaea.

It appears that the most basic, and probably earliest, charge levelled by the iconoclasts was that of idolatry. This reflects a literal interpretation of the second commandment, and iconophiles, beginning with St John of Damascus, answered it in two ways. First, argues John, an icon is not an idol. This argument stems from the nature of the object that is depicted and it is quite simple: an image of Apollo is an idol because this is an illegitimate – even nonexistent – pagan god; an image of Christ or the Mother of God, on the other hand, is holy because these subjects, or prototypes, are themselves holy.[7] Secondly, John uses the biblical argument that God overturned his own commandment when he ordered Moses to construct the tabernacle with all its decorations, including the cherubim that sit above the mercy seat or place of propitiation (Ex 25:18–20).[8] God delivered his commandment against idolatry in response to a particular situation, when the sinful Israelites were worshipping idols instead of the one, true God. This commandment is no longer applicable in any case since the old covenant has been replaced by a new order. As John puts it, quoting St Paul, 'We are not under the law but under grace (Rom 6:14), having been justified by faith (Rom 5:1), and having seen the one true God.'[9]

Christological arguments also featured in eighth-century debate, although they were developed more fully in iconophile writings of the second phase of Iconoclasm. Here it is worth noting that the debate focuses primarily on images of Christ. To begin with the iconoclast charge, this appears to have been as follows: if we depict Christ, the Son and Word of God, in an icon, then we are deviating from the doctrine that was defined at the council of Chalcedon (AD 451). Christ is in two natures; if we depict him in an icon as a human being, then we are either ignoring his divine nature or attempting to depict that which is invisible and uncircumscribable. If, on the other hand, we simply say that we are portraying his human nature, then we are guilty of Nestorianism, in that we are dividing the human and divine natures of Christ.

The iconophiles had several answers to this charge, including those that focused on the meaning of the Incarnation, which allowed human beings to see and depict Christ in his human body, and those that dealt with the nature of an image. To begin with the first category, John of Damascus stressed repeatedly in his three treatises the importance of the Incarnation in the history of God's saving dispensation. Accusing the iconoclasts of dualism, he perceived that their distrust of painted icons represented a denial of the goodness of creation and God's continuing presence in it (what might today be called 'panentheism'). Further, he argued, they denied the reality of Christ's human Incarnation, which allowed humans to see God here on earth for the first time.

John of Damascus also perceived that iconoclasts and iconophiles have a different understanding of what an image actually is. It is clear, on the basis of Constantine V's writings as well as the Acts of the council of Hiereia, that the iconoclasts confused images with their prototypes; in other words, like most other late antique people, they probably believed that the subject of an icon was in some way present in that image or that they shared the same essence or being. John points out that, after all, an image *is only an image*. In his third treatise in defence of icons, John lists six different types of images, ranging from the 'natural' image, which may be seen in Christ's relationship to the Father, to the painted icons that differ in substance from their prototypes. John is not denying the relationship of the latter form of image to its model, but rather pointing to the different manner in which images are connected with their prototypes. The Damascene also argues that a hierarchy of images in the divine and created worlds assists the faithful towards a greater apprehension of God. Many such images, including not only icons but also relics and signs, have been held as holy in the living tradition of the Church; they may not have been endorsed in scripture or in written documents, but they are authenticated by the living memory, the 'seasoned discipline' of the Church and, as such, act as potent reminders of divine power.[10] Theodore of Stoudios and the patriarch Nicephorus developed these as well as more philosophical arguments in defence of icons further, after Leo V re-introduced iconoclastic policies in 815. When this party triumphed in 843, with the help of the recently crowned Emperor Michael III and his regent mother, Theodora, the 'theology of images' had reached full maturity. Both ecclesiastical hierarchs and Christian rulers thereafter accepted that not only does the correct interpretation of the Chalcedonian definition allow the depiction of Christ and other holy figures in icons, but it positively requires this practice in Orthodox tradition.

ICONS OF CHRIST AND THE VISION OF GOD

In fact the problem of how to depict Christ, the Son of God, in an image had caused controversy well before the period of Iconoclasm. As we have seen, early Christians solved this by using symbolic imagery or types. After the end of the iconoclast period, icon painters took care to follow the directive of the council 'in Trullo', that is, to portray only the incarnate Christ. It is likely that the iconography that they followed was based firstly, in its physical attributes, on an existing image, which was believed to be authentic and which is attested first in the sixth century. This is the *mandylion*, a cloth on which Christ had miraculously imprinted his features before sending it to Abgar, a contemporary king of Edessa, who had sent for his healing presence. The *mandylion* image was subsequently treasured in Edessa as an icon 'made without hands'.[11] John of Damascus alludes to the story in his first treatise in defence of icons, as evidence that Christ himself authorised the existence of holy images.[12]

Although an icon of Christ depicts his human nature and not that which is unseen, according to John of Damascus, these two natures are 'acknowledged … without confusion, change, division or separation', as the Council of Chalcedon affirms.[13] This mystery is revealed throughout the Gospels, but perhaps most vividly in the story of Christ's Transfiguration. It is elaborated in the hymnography and icons for the feast of the Transfiguration, which emphasise the transfigured, or deified, state of Christ's humanity. St Gregory of Nazianzus believes that the light that shines in Christ's face, body and garments represents nothing less than his divinity,[14] while St John of Damascus refers to the 'splendour of the divine nature' and to the 'timeless glory of God the Son' in his homily on the Transfiguration. Icons of the Transfiguration depict the transfigured Christ standing on Mt Tabor in a shining garment. The *mandorla*, which may be inscribed with a geometrical figure representing the 'bright cloud' (Mt 17:5), is interpreted in Orthodox theology as the divine energies that suffuse Christ and, through him, the whole of creation.[15]

The idea that the faithful may be given the grace to see God in fact has biblical authority. 'He that has seen me has seen the Father', says Christ to Philip in John 14:9, and again, in the Beatitudes, he says, 'Blessed are the pure in heart, for they shall see God' (Mt 5:8). This awe-inspiring promise contradicts God's refusal in the old covenant to grant human beings any vision of himself, as we see in Exodus 33:20: 'you cannot see my face; for no one shall see me and live'. On the other hand, even in the Old Testament, there is a tradition that the 'light of God's countenance' (Ps 88 [89]:15) is accessible to humanity. In Numbers 6:25, God tells Moses to instruct Aaron and his sons to pray that 'the Lord make his face to shine upon you.'

The theme of the vision of God resurfaces in Hesychasm: that is, contemplative prayer in stillness and silence of soul. This ancient method of prayer came to prominence in the fourteenth century, when Gregory Palamas defended the claim of the Hesychast Athonite monks to see God as light, and his teaching was upheld by the council of 1347. This has momentous implications for how we see – and therefore depict – the human body and the world to which it belongs. As L. Ouspensky sums it up, 'the Church recognised that the divine action transfiguring man originates in the uncreated, imperishable light, the energy of the Divinity felt and contemplated in the body'.[16]

This theological reality is translated into icons, influencing their form as well as their content. The challenge for the iconographer is to paint human beings who already in their earthly lives have passed beyond the threshold of the Kingdom. The saints' experience of the divine must be translated so that the beholder may contemplate the Kingdom through the icon and acquire sanctification through the grace of the Holy Spirit, fulfilling what all God's creation is called to become. Thus, gold is used in haloes but also in backgrounds as a sign of deification. Under Hesychast influence, iconography acquired a new quality of light and transparency set against contrasting colours. As a contemporary Athonite expresses it, 'Light in an icon is not of the present age. It does not come from outside to give light in passing. An uncreated light that knows no evening is shed from within the icon itself, from the faces of the saints and transfigured creation'.[17] The saint is depicted 'in another form' (cf. Mk 16:12), in accordance with the transformation of human nature prefigured in Christ's Transfiguration or even after his resurrection. This 'other' physical aspect spilling over from the faces and bodies of the saints to their garments,[18] to everything they touched, and to the nature surrounding them, represents one of the most important characteristics of Byzantine and Slavic iconography.

It was during the discussions about the light of the Transfiguration and the deification of man that the boundaries of Church art were established.[19] There is asceticism and sobriety in the use of colours and the composition of the narrative icon. The purpose of this art is not to sweeten life with naturalistic depictions that would still leave the beholder in the world of decay: it is to represent the beauty of the world transfigured, to reveal the human as inseparable from the divine.

SOME ICONOGRAPHIC THEMES

Following the restoration of icons in the Church after 843, the iconography of Orthodox churches became increasingly formalised. The iconic decoration of a church reflects the symbolic meaning of this holy space, telling the story of the salvation of humankind. In other words, the church building itself is an icon, or an image of God's dispensation. Whereas individual icons put us in the presence of just one event, architectural painting provides the whole story.[20]

As St Maximus the Confessor argued in the seventh century, the church is an image of the cosmos, symbolising both the heavenly and earthly kingdoms: 'God's holy church in itself is a symbol of the sensible world as such, since it possesses the divine sanctuary as heaven and the beauty of the nave as earth'.[21] Thus, Christ, the Pantokrator or All-Ruler, occupies the dome at the top of the church, which represents the heaven that is brought down to earth in his Incarnation. The emphasis is placed here on Christ's majesty in his heavenly abode above the cherubim. The Divine Liturgy celebrates his exalted position, especially in the Cherubic Hymn, which evokes the hymn of the heavenly host (Is 6:3). The events of Christ's life, celebrated in the main feasts of the liturgical year, are placed in the highest vaults of the church, symbolising their place in both eternal and historical time. In the sanctuary of the church, the conch of the apse often contains an image of the Mother of God. This testifies to the christological doctrine expressed at the council of Ephesus (431), which affirmed Christ's divinity and humanity, and proclaimed Mary, his mother, as the 'one who bore God' (Theotokos). Portrayed in her motherly role with the Christ child in her arms, the Mother of God symbolises the mystery of the Incarnation itself. The register below the Mother of God in the apse may in classical sanctuary iconography depict Christ administering communion to the apostles. This represents a liturgical image since it emphasises Christ's priestly function, as the celebrant of the Eucharist, rather than the scriptural scene of the Last Supper. In Orthodox usage, the latter is usually described as 'the mystical supper', which in fact emphasises the identity between the two. Christ's supper with his disciples has its place among the dominical feasts and in the Passion cycle.

The screen between the nave and the sanctuary is called the iconostasis. This manifests symbolically the uniting of the eternal and temporal spheres, or heaven and earth, through the Incarnation. The boundary between these spheres is represented by the 'Royal' or Holy Doors, through which the clergy proceed in the course of the liturgy and from which they read the gospel and administer communion. The Doors in many Russian churches show the Annunciation and the four evangelists, which together symbolise the inauguration of the Kingdom. Taken together, the icons on the screen tell the story of salvation from the creation of Adam to the Last Judgement.

In its fullest form, found in some Russian churches, there are five tiers of icons, which are arranged as follows: (1) the forefathers from Adam to Moses, with the icon of the Holy Trinity (represented by an image of the three heavenly messengers at Abraham's table (Gen 18:1–15)) at its centre; (2) the prophets, from Moses to Christ, holding scrolls which prophesy the coming of the Messiah; an icon representing the Mother of God 'of the Sign' (Is 7:14) occupies the centre of this group; (3) the festival row, which depicts the lives of the Mother of God and Christ, as celebrated in the great feasts of the liturgical year; (4) the 'Deesis' (prayer), in which angels and saints are placed in relation to a central triptych which depicts Christ in glory flanked by the Mother of God and St John the Baptist in attitudes of intercession (this section of the iconostasis in fact represents the most ancient core of the sanctuary screen); (5) at the bottom, icons of locally venerated saints or the patron saint of the church, along with two large icons of Christ and the Mother of God on either side of the Holy Doors.

Turning to a more detailed analysis of individual icons, we may begin once again with that of Christ. As we saw earlier, the icon of Christ sums up the Church's teaching on the person of Christ, depicting his transfigured human nature. Iconographic and stylistic details in icons of Christ make this teaching clear. For example, the purple of Christ's tunic, which was reserved in Byzantium for the emperor alone, expresses Christ's kingship; later this purple, which had evolved into a purplish-brown, was considered symbolic of the earth, thus indicating Christ's human nature. His *himation*, or robe, on the other hand, is blue, symbolising (but not depicting) his heavenly, or divine, nature. Christ's halo is inscribed with a cross; often the arms of this cross bear an inscription in Greek which refers to the answer that Moses received when he asked God for his name. The Greek text here is translated variously as 'He who is', 'I who am', or even 'the Being' (Ex 3:14). Used in the icon of Christ, the phrase indicates his divine nature, as well as his manifestations as God in the Old Testament (cf. Jn 8:58).

The Mother of God, or Virgin Mary, also reveals her connection with Old Testament prophecy in some icons. As mentioned earlier in connection with the iconostasis, the iconographic type known as the Mother of God 'of the Sign' refers to Isaiah 7:14: 'Therefore the Lord himself will give you a sign. Look, the virgin is with child and shall bear a son, and shall name him Emmanuel.' The early Christian female figure of the 'orant' type forms the basis for this iconography. In the icon the Virgin faces the beholder, arms raised in an attitude of prayer. The child, who is contained in her womb wearing robes of light, is Christ the All-Ruler, blessing with his right hand and holding in his left the scroll containing his Word. St John of Damascus's hymn to the Virgin expresses this in words, celebrating Mary's womb as the temple of God and paradise: from you 'God was made flesh'.[22] The womb, as a form of *mandorla*, is symbolically depicted as three concentric circles of graded sapphire blue, which relate it to the throne and glory of God, or heaven itself (cf. Ezek 1:26, 10:1). In icons depicting his role as Messiah, known as 'Emmanuel' icons, Christ is shown wearing the garments of glory, covered with gold assist, indicating his divinity. He is the pre-eternal Son of God, who has become Son of the Virgin, while remaining the Logos who spoke to Moses from the cloud (Ex 19–32). In some 'sign' icons, cherubim rest below the mandorla or hover on either side of the Child in an attitude of adoration, referring us to Ezekiel's vision of the glory of God perpetually attended by the cherubim (Ezek 1–2). Signifying adoration of God, the Virgin's outstretched arms also invite the beholder to share the mystery of her love and experience of the divine.

The same openness is found in other iconographic types of the Mother of God, such as those of the *Hodigitria* and *Eleeousa*. *Hodigitria* signifies 'the one who points the way' to Christ; theologically, it reminds us of the role of the holy Virgin at Cana (cf. Jn 2:5), as she points away from herself to the Child on her arm as if to say, 'Look at him. He is your God and Saviour as he is my God and Saviour.'[23] The *Eleeousa* iconographic type is sometimes translated as 'loving kindness' (Russian *Umileniye*).[24] In this icon the heads of the Mother and Child touch: he looks at his Mother, but she looks at us. Never do they exchange intimate regards that would exclude the beholder. The tender embrace of the Virgin Mother and Christ makes real the physicality of her motherhood, but does not glorify 'sweet' maternity. As in the case of all other Virgin and Child icons, the *Eleeousa* image glorifies the Incarnation.

Festal iconography depicts events, but the icons, like the festal hymnography that celebrates these events, represent far more than simple illustrations of scripture. The iconography of an event may depart significantly from the scriptural account in order to emphasise particular aspects of a feast. A good example of this exists in the two different icons used for Pentecost. One of these depicts the three angels who visited Abraham (Gen 18:19), who symbolically represent the Trinity. In the hands of Andrei Rublov, who leaves out Abraham and Sarah and other narrative details, the 'Hospitality of Abraham' becomes the hospital-ity of God at his holy altar, whereby all the faithful are invited to enter with fear and love into the intimacy of God.[25] The chalice has become the symbol of the Eternal Banquet.

The icon of the Descent of the Holy Spirit is venerated on Monday, the day of the Holy Spirit. The iconography is dominated by a solemn calm, contrasting with the general turbulence described in Acts 2:1–13. Instead of the multitudes, only twelve persons are seated in a semicircle: the space at the centre belongs to Christ, the head of the Church, who is invis-ibly present. The figures always include St Paul and the evangelists, St Mark and St Luke, who are not numbered with the twelve apostles and who had not yet written the scripture rolls that they hold in their hands in the icon.[26] This festal icon, like all others, does not merely depict a historical event; it is an icon of the Church itself.

THEOLOGY OF THE ICON REDISCOVERED

From the sixteenth century onwards, the Orthodox icon witnessed a gradual decline, in content as well as in spiritual awareness. Traditional iconography was dismissed as old-fashioned and fit only for the unedu-cated, while more 'artistic' icons began to be painted by professionals who were often detached from the teachings of the Church. When scholars later began to study icons, they judged them from an art historical and qualitative point of view, rather than on the basis of their theological and liturgical content. For some Christians, icons represented mere decora-tion, while, for others, they were used habitually, but without proper understanding, during prayer. The understanding of the true meaning and place of icons in the Church had been to a large extent forgotten.

The nineteenth and twentieth centuries have, however, witnessed a renewal of interest in holy icons, which began in conjunction with revived interest in the medieval past, but which soon included a new appreciation of their theological importance in Orthodox tradition. Two figures especially stand out in this process of re-evaluation and both were icon painters as well as scholars: the Greek Fotis Kontoglou, and the Russian Leonid Ouspensky. Kontoglou was born in 1895. During a stay on Mt Athos in the 1920s, he discovered for himself the ancient tech-nique of Byzantine icon painting. From that time onward, he worked to revive traditional icon and fresco painting throughout Greece and pro-duced many books and articles on icons and sacred art.[27] Ouspensky was born in Russia in 1902 but came to Paris in 1926 where he formed a lasting friendship with another Russian painter, George Krug, the future monk Gregory. Both became interested in icon painting and proceeded to abandon secular art in order to dedicate themselves to religious art. In addition to painting icons, Ouspensky began in the 1940s to study their inherent meaning; eventually, towards the end of his life, he published his magisterial *Theology of the Icon*. The book is the first of its kind since it places the icon firmly within its originally intended place in the Church, expounding its doctrinal and liturgical content. Ouspensky taught the theology of images and trained icon painters in Paris and else-where, including Finland. Some of his students continue his work, striving to be true to the tradition and teaching of the Church.

Recent decades have seen the publication of a great number of illus-trated books on icons; unfortunately, in many of these the icon is simply evaluated along with other objects of art historical and cultural signi-ficance. Yet people who are starved of truth and spiritual values are begin-ning to look at icons and to find that they are not silent, but that they help to satisfy this yearning. Thus, these seekers wish to learn more about icons, their theological meaning and their origins. They discover that they are in fact meeting *someone*, not just seeing *something* in the icon. The icon has ceased being viewed merely as a beautiful curiosity from the past, but is recognised as a living presence before which one may pray.

Since the fall of Communism, a lively interest in icon painting has sprung up in Eastern Europe as well as in the West, among both Orthodox and non-Orthodox Christians. However, it is not always understood that icon painters require a continuous apprenticeship in churchmanship: this is a question not merely of attending services, but of being integrated into the whole, active life of the Church. A gifted, self-appointed painter of icons from a secular background misses something essential without this integration. Icon painters do not paint in their own names, but in the name of, and on behalf of, the Church. They must be aware that their work is holy, that it is solely for a sanctifying purpose, and that only the action of the Holy Spirit can give light to their inner sight to enable them to do their work. It is in this way that the icon comes to be in practice an expression of the theology of the Church.

Further reading

Baggley, J., *Doors of Perception. Icons and Their Spiritual Significance*, Crestwood, NY: SVS Press, 1988.

Doolan, S., *La redécouverte de l'icône: la vie et l'oeuvre de Léonide Ouspensky*, Paris: Editions du Cerf, 2001.

Evdokimov, P., *The Art of the Icon: A Theology of Beauty*, trans. Fr Steven Bigham, Redondo Beach, CA: Oakwood Publications, 1990.

Limouris, G., *Icons. Windows on Eternity. Theology and Spirituality in Colour*, Geneva: WCC Publications, 1990.

Ouspensky, L., *Theology of the Icon*, 2 vols., trans. A. Gythiel with E. Meyendorff, Crestwood, NY: SVS Press, 1978; repr. 1992.

Ouspensky, L. and Lossky, V., *The Meaning of Icons*, Crestwood, NY: SVS Press, 1983.

Parry, K., *Depicting the Word. Byzantine Iconophile Thought of the Eighth and Ninth Centuries*, Leiden, New York and Cologne: Brill, 1996.

Pelikan, J., *Imago Dei. The Byzantine Apologia for Icons*, New Haven and London: Yale University Press, 1990.

Notes

1. John of Damascus, *On the Divine Images* III.41.
2. Metropolitan Philaret of Moscow, *Sermons*, vol. II (Paris, 1866); L. Ouspensky, *Theology of the Icon*, trans. A. Gythiel with E. Meyendorff, vol. II (Crestwood, NY: SVS Press, 1978: repr. 1992), p. 214.
3. S. Bigham, *Early Christian Attitudes Towards Images* (Rollinsford, NH: Orthodox Research Institute, 2004); E. Kitzinger, 'The cult of images before the age of Iconoclasm', *Dumbarton Oaks Papers* 8 (1954), 83–150.
4. Sr M. C. Murray, 'Art and the early Church', *JTS* 28 (1977), 303–44.
5. For an illustration, see J. Elsner, *Imperial Rome and Christian Triumph* (Oxford: Oxford University Press, 1998), p. 157, pl. 104.
6. *Acts of the Quinisext Council 'In Trullo'*, Canon 82.
7. John of Damascus, *On the Divine Images* I.24.
8. John of Damascus, *On the Divine Images* I.15, II.9.
9. John of Damascus, *On the Divine Images* I.21.
10. John of Damascus, *On the Divine Images* I.23.
11. Evagrius Scholasticus, *Ecclesiastical History* IV.27.
12. John of Damascus, *On the Divine Images* I. For an illustration of this iconographic type, see L. Ouspensky and V. Lossky, *The Meaning of Icons* (Crestwood, NY: SVS Press, 1983), p. 70.
13. *Acts of the Council of Chalcedon* II.
14. Gregory of Nazianzus, *Oration 40, On Holy Baptism* 6.
15. Ouspensky and Lossky, *The Meaning of Icons*, pp. 209–12; illustration, p. 210.
16. Ouspensky, *Theology of the Icon*, II, p. 250.
17. Archimandrite Vasileos of Stavronikita, *Hymn of Entry. Liturgy and Life in the Orthodox Church* (Crestwood, NY: St Vladimir's Seminary Press, 1984), p. 85.
18. Cf. Lk 9:29.
19. Ouspensky, *Theology of the Icon*, II, p. 250.
20. A classic account of the iconographical scheme of 'cross-in-square' Byzantine churches may be found in O. Demus, *Byzantine Mosaic Decoration. Aspects of Monumental Art in Byzantium* (London and Henley: Routledge & Kegan Paul, 1948; repr. 1976), pp. 3–39.
21. Maximus the Confessor, *The Church's Mystagogy* 2–3.
22. Basil of Caesarea, *Divine Liturgy*.

23. M. Fortounatto, 'The veneration of the Mother of God and her icon,' *Priests and People* 2.4 (May 1988), 142. For an illustration of this iconographic type, see Ouspensky and Lossky, *The Meaning of Icons*, pp. 82–3.
24. Ouspensky and Lossky, *The Meaning of Icons*, pp. 92–3; illustration, p. 91.
25. For an illustration of this famous icon, see Ouspensky and Lossky, *The Meaning of Icons*, p. 198.
26. Ouspensky and Lossky, *The Meaning of Icons*, pp. 207–8.
27. See, e.g., F. Kontoglou, *Byzantine Sacred Art: Selected Writings* (Belmont, MA: Institute for Byzantine and Modern Greek Studies, 1985).

10 The spiritual way

JOHN CHRYSSAVGIS

INTRODUCTION: FROM *THEOSIS* TO *ASCESIS*

It has become fashionable, for Orthodox and non-Orthodox alike, to be infatuated with characteristic, even exotic, technical terms that define essential dimensions of Orthodox theology and spirituality. Scholars and students alike are generally enchanted, even distracted by the mystical or mysterious implications of such concepts as the way to *theosis* (namely, deification or divinisation), prayer of the heart (or the Jesus Prayer) and the vision of divine light. It may, therefore, be helpful to offer from the outset certain terminological clarifications of key theological concepts, mystical principles and spiritual practices as these translate into Orthodox life. Indeed, the term 'spirituality' itself assumes numerous meanings, being either loosely adopted sometimes or else completely dismissed at others. Some Orthodox theologians are quick to claim that there is no reference in the classical tradition to 'spirituality' as such and rightly emphasise the connection between the Spirit of God and the spiritual life. There is no doubt that the word 'spirituality' itself is vulnerable to misunderstanding and misuse unless carefully 'unpacked' and nuanced. Nevertheless, words communicate the pregnancy of divine life when we approach them in a spirit of humility and with a sense of awe. It is not surprising, then, to find that the literary classics of the early Church, and particularly of the early Egyptian and Palestinian desert, underline the rigorous discipline involved in personally appropriating, rather than merely arbitrarily describing, the spiritual way. In this regard, they prefer to speak more about *ascesis*, rather than about *theosis*.

Theological language is shaped very early in each person's life; in the Orthodox way, it is especially shaped by the lives of the saints, who have experienced the life of the Spirit. Therefore, in reclaiming our spiritual vocabulary, it is the saints of the Church who teach us the process of learning or re-learning what it is consciously to know and to reflect God's love in the world. In exploring, then, the writings of the 'Church Fathers', or in living with the tradition of the saints, we find that vocabulary comes to life and ultimately challenges the ways we perceive God and understand the world in our struggle towards personal holiness and social justice, namely in the journey towards personal salvation and cosmic transformation.

This chapter concentrates on some of the fundamental terms and concepts that are central to any understanding of Orthodox spirituality and endeavours to unveil their intrinsic value today. It constitutes a humble effort to translate an ancient faith into a modern language.

ESCHATOLOGY AND SPIRITUALITY: 'DYING, YET BEHOLD WE LIVE'

'I await ... the life of the age to come', proclaims the Orthodox 'symbol of faith', otherwise known as the Nicene–Constantinopolitan Creed, formulated in the fourth century and recited at each celebration of the Divine Liturgy. The technical term for talk regarding 'the age to come' is 'eschatology': it is the study of the 'last events' (*eschata*). Most of us assume that the 'last times' and the 'last things' imply an apocalyptic or even escapist attitude towards the world. Modern theologians had to disabuse themselves of the medieval legacy that eschatology is the last, perhaps unnecessary chapter in every manual or course of dogmatics. We appreciate more readily today that eschatology is not primarily the teaching about what *follows* everything else in this world. Rather, it is the teaching about *our relationship* to those last things and last times. In this way, eschatology is what properly defines and directs our spiritual ways and ascetic practices.[1]

In the formative years of Christian monasticism in the desert of Egypt and Palestine, the inhabitants of the desert there and in Sinai learned some of the fundamental insights about eschatology. The practice of asceticism is closely connected to the phenomenon of monasticism. In fact, the roots of Christian asceticism are, much like the origins of Christian monasticism, veiled in a cloud of mystery. Nonetheless, they are profoundly related to the effort of the early Christian Church to respond to Christ's call, recorded in the gospels, for his disciples to be 'perfect' and 'merciful', 'just as your heavenly Father is' (Mt 5:48; Lk 6:36). The entire concept of discipline was regarded not so much in terms of rigour as in terms of discerning ways to become disciples. Thus, asceticism looks to the transformation, and not the mortification, of the body and the world. Indeed, from the middle of the third to the late seventh centuries, the desert of Egypt, Palestine and Sinai became a laboratory for studying hidden truths about heaven and earth, as well as a place for drawing connections between the two. The hermits who inhabited those deserts experimented in and explored what it means to be human and how to reach the depths of the divine. To them, the word 'eschatology' was no longer otherworldly; the struggle to embrace their brokenness and vulnerability dispelled any division between heaven and earth, or between time and eternity. They recognised that what is far more difficult and far more important than learning to live is learning to die. They realised how dying and loss are the best lessons in how to live 'in abundance' (Jn 10:10) and how to love to the fullest.

Metaphysical and mystical reflections are fatally flawed if they do not begin with the reality of eschatology; it is eschatology which shapes the ascetic way and gives meaning to life in this world and to all of creation, including our tiny part in it. Living life to the full comes only when the ultimate concerns – namely, meaninglessness and death – have been honestly confronted and openly embraced. How we face or avoid these concerns has a profound consequence for our understanding of *ascesis* and *theosis*, as well as for our experience of solitude and community. For remembrance of death is a crucial virtue in the spiritual life, a daily and tangible reminder of human weakness and imperfection. If we want to come out of life nice and polished, we need simply to think of death. There is hardly an outward sense of perfection in nursing homes and hospices. Remembrance of death allows the reality of brokenness to be revealed truthfully, so that the lie that heaven is elsewhere may split wide open and genuine healing may begin. In the spiritual way, awaiting this fullness of the kingdom-to-come assumes the form of prayer, especially expressed through the silence of tears.

SILENCE AND TEARS: LEARNING TO LISTEN

In the same desert of Egypt, Palestine and Sinai, silence was described as the daughter of patience and the mother of watchfulness. For when all words are abandoned, a new awareness arrives. Silence awakens us from numbness to the world around us, from our dullness of vision.

Abba Poemen said: 'Be watchful inwardly; but be watchful also outwardly.'[2]

The early desert dwellers taught us that silence is a requirement of life; it is the first duty of love. Silence is a way of waiting, a way of watching, a way of noticing – instead of ignoring – what is going on in our heart and in our world. It is the glue that binds our attitudes and our actions, our belief and our behaviour. Silence reflects our ultimate surrender to God as well as our gradual awakening to new patterns of learning and living. When we are silent, we learn by suffering and undergoing, not just by speculating and understanding. Silence confirms our readiness to lead a counter-cultural way of life, to choose rather than to be led, to admit our limited perspective as possessors and consumers in society, and to appreciate another, unlimited perspective of the spiritual way.

What we learn in silence is that we are all mutually interdependent, that the entire world is intimately interconnected.

> Take a compass [says Dorotheus of Gaza in the sixth century] and insert the point and draw the outline of a circle. The centre point is the same distance from any point on the circumference … This circle is the world and God is the centre; the straight lines drawn from the circumference to the centre are the lives of human beings … The closer these are to God, the closer they come to each other; and the closer they come to each other and to the world, the closer they are to God.[3]

The truth is that all things are inseparably interrelated and closely inhering in each other – beyond our imagination. Nothing living is self-contained; the brokenness of one person or element reflects the fragility of the whole world: 'If one member suffers, all suffer together with it' (1 Cor 12:26). There is no autonomy – only a distinction between a sense of responsibility and a lack thereof. The result of any bifurcation between spirituality and reality is inevitably catastrophic.

One of the more tangible ways of expressing our vulnerability, at least according to the classical texts of Orthodox spirituality, is weeping or the shedding of tears. The gift of tears is 'native' to Christianity and may be traced from the New Testament through the early desert tradition; it has played a dominant role in various ascetical and mystical expressions throughout the centuries. The Eastern Church has in fact served as a cradle for this treasure given to Christianity by Jesus, who 'blessed those who mourn' (Mt 5:4).[4] Tears were accorded a particular priority in the East, perhaps on account of the emphasis on the heart as a vessel of the Holy Spirit. The gift of tears may not easily be understood in our world; then again, it may readily be misunderstood as an emotional outburst or confused with various kinds of tears, not all of which are the fruit of the Spirit and some of which are in fact the product of passions. For there are passionate tears of envy, just as there are natural tears of grief. Still, this spiritual teaching is in fact one of the more consistent doctrines practised and taught by the early Eastern Fathers.

Tears are another means of surrendering – of dying, although always in the context and in the hope of new life and resurrection. They are a way of embracing darkness in order to receive light. No wonder, then, that the wisdom of the early desert emphasised remembrance of death as an essential virtue in the spiritual way; it was another dimension to remembrance of God. The pioneer Fathers and Mothers of the desert embraced their mortality; they were comfortable with the concept and the experience of death. They recognised death as an important way of connecting to themselves, to their neighbours and to God. Unfortunately, so often, we endeavour to cheat death; we instinctively try to avoid or escape death: 'Abba Poemen said: "Weeping is the way that the scriptures and the Fathers give us: 'Weep!' Truly, there is no other way than this".'[5] The desert elders learned to embrace human shortcoming and welcomed human failure as the ultimate opportunity for receiving divine grace and strength, which can only be 'perfected in weakness' (2 Cor 12:9). Somewhere on that long trail between childhood and adulthood, many of us lose touch with the vital skills that permit us to know ourselves. Part of the problem is that we set impossible goals, which can be met only by angels. The spirituality of the desert taught its inhabitants that perfection is for God alone; we are called neither to forgo nor to forget our imperfection. Strangely, the fragility and vulnerability of life itself reveals the priority of confronting and embracing our innermost weaknesses. Life has a way of finally catching up with us – so that we can look it in the face! The truth is that God may be discerned in the very midst of every tension and trial. This understanding was part and parcel of desert wisdom. In the desert, the Gospel injunction to 'be perfect, even as your heavenly Father is perfect' (Mt 5:48) becomes a vision of realism precisely through the realisation and acceptance of human imperfection. The way of the ascetics is indeed the way of *theosis*; but it is understood only as the way of imperfection. *Theosis* is no less, and no more, than falling down and getting back up, starting anew. If our eyes enjoy the vision of God (the mystery of becoming God), it is because our tears can express the beauty and the mystery of being all too human. Tears are the closest companion of deification, our sure escape-route from death to life.

In light of this, therefore, the spirituality of tears becomes an overture of joy. In the seventh century, St John Climacus speaks of 'joyful sorrow'. Tears are at once the foretaste of death and of resurrection. They are not, as unfortunately they are often perceived, a negative aspect of the spiritual life, a way of merely regretting past sins or ongoing weaknesses. As symbols of imperfection, tears are in fact the *sole* way of spiritual progress. While it may be true that *theosis* is the culmination of Orthodox theology and spirituality, so eloquently articulated in the writings of such mystics as Symeon the New Theologian and Gregory Palamas, the great majority of classical patristic literature focuses not so much on deification as on the long journey of the spiritual way – namely, on the gradual stages, the painful steps towards this sublime goal. The saints know that this alone is what – realistically and uniquely – lies within our grasp. They are convinced that one silent tear will advance us further in the spiritual way than any number of louder ascetic feats or more visible virtuous achievements. In this way, tears signify fragility and woundedness, the broken window through which God enters the heart, bringing healing and wholeness to both soul and body.

Thus, the silence of tears prepares the heart for self-knowledge and compassion. It allows us the time and space to become alert to ourselves and to others. Unfortunately, however, we tend to confuse self-knowledge with self-absorption, whereas, in reality, self-knowledge leads away from self-absorption towards a sense of what, in the sixth century, Barsanuphius and John would call 'forgetting oneself'.[6] Curiously, while – in the church life generally and the spiritual way especially – we encourage the need for knowing and loving others through compassion, we less frequently reward the virtue of knowing ourselves through silence. Yet knowing why we do what we do facilitates the awareness also of why other people do what they do, and in the end leads to the acceptance of other people as they are. Narcissism is not too much self, but rather insufficient knowledge of our true self. People who are self-absorbed or self-centred normally suffer from too little rather than too much self. Moreover, we often seek intimacy by facing in the wrong direction: instead of looking inward, we turn outward towards others. Nevertheless, the isolation of solitude serves as the first step towards any intimacy or communion with other people.

Silence, then, is the great stabiliser; it resembles a secret compass in our relationships with God, with others and with ourselves. Silence is about being, and not simply doing; it renders the heart acutely attentive and uniquely receptive. Through silence, the heart is gradually refined and increasingly educated in the art of attentiveness. Silence provides the space and the capacity to listen to and soak up what another person is conveying. In brief, it is the skill as well as the tool whereby we acknowledge that what is going on in someone else's world matters.

Utter silence can almost feel like death; yet, in its essence, it too is associated with the desire for 'life in abundance' (Jn 10:10), beyond 'mere survival'. Most of us deny the relation between silence and death by entering a whirl of individual achievement and social activity that renders death improbable or impossible, at least in our own minds. By contrast, silence is like 'marking' – and not merely 'killing' – time! It is like standing respectfully and reverently before even the most frightening experience of failure and isolation. It is a renewed sense of anticipation and expectation of the last times and the age to come. In silence, we become aware of being alive, and not dead – of having needs and temptations, and of being able to face and embrace these without turning elsewhere, without turning away. In silence, we are not empty; we are not alone; we are not afraid. We simply 'know that God is' (Ps 45 [46]:10–11) – an experience that may occur in a split instant or take shape over an entire lifetime.

Finally, silence introduces an apophatic element to the way of intimacy and love. For through stillness comes the refreshing suggestion of approaching and acknowledging others by 'not knowing' them. If we are fixed to our preconceptions or fears of people, then we may never enjoy perfect silence. When we 'know' someone, we have already shut our eyes to that person's constant process of change and growth. We limit ourselves by rooting others in the past and not rejoicing in their potential. Therefore, through the power of silence, we can risk embracing the other person in his or her entirety, in his or her eternal dimension – beyond what we could ever comprehend or tolerate.

THE PASSIONS OF THE SOUL: GROWING THROUGH SUFFERING

Silence is the way we begin to notice what is happening inside and around us. However, progress in the movements of the heart takes toil and time. We do not change suddenly, magically becoming new people, our old faults forgotten. We can never run away from who we are; we shall never escape temptations and passions: our temper, vanity, ambition, fear, envy, delusion, resentment or arrogance.

In the spiritual classics of the early desert, knowing oneself means knowing one's passions; and knowing – at least, in the biblical sense – means loving. It implies being aware of one's behaviour, and particularly one's weaknesses. Indeed, in the ascetic tradition, there are two ways of understanding and responding to the passions. Sometimes, passions are perceived as negative; this derives from the Stoic concept of sins and vices, whereby these are regarded as a disorder or disease. Alternatively, passions may be perceived as positive; this conveys the Aristotelian understanding of sins or vices, whereby passions are considered neutral forces or natural impulses. According to the former view, passions are intrinsically evil; they are a pathological condition. The source of passions is the Devil; passions must, therefore, be eradicated or eliminated. According to the latter view, passions are intrinsically objective; they are neither good nor evil, neither right nor wrong. The source of passions is God; passions, then, must be redirected or transfigured. Indeed, in the second of his

Ascetic Discourses, in the fifth century, Abba Isaiah of Scetis claims that all passions – including anger, jealousy and even lust – are granted by God with a sacred purpose: namely, to reflect and reveal our 'passion-ate' love for God and 'com-passion' for God's creatures.[7]

Our passions and problems cannot be denied or concealed; for, potentially, they are the very resources for spiritual renewal and revitalisation. When our passions are misdirected or distorted, the soul is divided; we are no longer whole or integrated. So passions are never either quashed or quenched; they are fulfilled and transformed by God's loving grace. In the solitude of the heart, through common temptations and all-too-human tensions, we become painfully aware of what is lacking. There, we are haunted by the absence of love and begin to yearn for the depth of communion. The cell of the ascetic symbolises the safe haven of the heart, where one can always willingly return to discover more and more of the authentic self, irrespective of how painful an ordeal or how agonising a struggle this may be. Such a discovery through solitude eventually becomes a fountain of healing. Embracing solitude in the loneliness of the cell (or the soul) means knowing what you think, understanding how you behave, and finally accepting others without the need to defend yourself. It is assuming responsibility without the least sense of self-justification or self-righteousness. Ultimately, the measure to which we are able to acknowledge and accept others will depend on the degree to which we can understand and tolerate ourselves. This is because we are more united to each other through our weaknesses than through our strengths; we are more like one another through our shortcomings than through our successes. Passions are what connects us with one another; this is exactly why passions can be fully understood only through others.

SPIRITUAL DIRECTION: LEARNING WITH OTHERS

One way of recognising the spiritual unity that binds all human beings is silently embracing the reality of our passions and weaknesses. Yet in the early desert of Egypt and Palestine, both lay Christians and ordained clergy, novices and monastics alike, would travel long distances in order to visit renowned elders for a word of advice or, as they would call it, 'a word of salvation'. Inasmuch as they recognised how they were filled and formed by human passions, these same charismatic elders had become Spirit-filled and ultimately transformed. Thus, they were able to convey the lessons of their journey and communicate a word of healing to those who approached them. This self-knowledge – perhaps above all other qualifications, spiritual (such as great feats of fasting[8] and prayer[9]) or secular (such as education[10] or even age[11]) – was what rendered the *abba* ('spiritual father') or *amma* ('spiritual mother') uniquely skilled and prepared to guide the souls of others.

If there is one lesson learned in the early desert, then, it is the conviction that, in order to achieve self-knowledge, we also need to trust at least one other person. The desert elders spoke of obedience and spiritual direction. Obedience is essentially an act of listening; it is the art of listening attentively or closely, which is precisely the implication of the Greek word *hyp-akoe* ('obedience'). However, the goal of obedience is not to repress the will; it is in fact to stabilise the will. This is why obedience is the measure and criterion of authentic solitude and silence: Barsanuphius claims that 'when you hasten to do something on your own, then the resulting silence is from the devil'.[12]

While the fine balance between isolation and intimacy is actually impossible to attain without divine grace, it is extremely difficult to sustain without sharing with, or baring all before, a spiritual director. Through someone else's belief in our self, we begin confidently – i.e., by the act of confiding and confessing – to rediscover the solid ground within. Sharing our thoughts and temptations openly with at least one other person enables us to become familiar with the desires and conflicts that drive our behaviour. Furthermore, listening to and accepting the reality of our self renders us more aware of and more caring towards others, which is precisely the way of *theosis* or being 'like God'.

One reason for sharing with others is quite simply that most of us are harsher critics of ourselves, striking the most painful blows against ourselves at just the time when we most require tolerance and compassion – virtues that undoubtedly characterise the early desert elders, such as Arsenius and Macarius in Egypt, as well as Barsanuphius and John in Gaza.[13] Obedience clearly goes against the grain of so much in our contemporary society, which espouses such notions as individuality and independence. Nonetheless, when someone is unable to build up from even the smallest patch of solid ground, then terms like 'freedom' and 'will' have little resonance.

In addition to – or rather, as a consequence of – obedience, the desert elders (especially Barsanuphius and John) frequently cite Galatians 6:2 and emphasise that assuming responsibility for 'the burdens of others' is critical to growing spiritually. Acknowledging responsibility for the consequences of one's thoughts and actions implies not blaming others: 'To come to perfect silence, one must first endure insults from other people, as well as contempt, dishonour and hurt … in order that the labour may not be in vain (cf. 1 Thess 3:5)'.[14] The point is that we can be authentically attached only when we have become completely detached. This is essentially the experience of letting go and of trusting. It is the ability to forget oneself in an effort to reach out to another person.

In the spiritual way, one is called to liberation by way of the margins of self-renunciation, in the paradox of self-subjection to a spiritual elder. 'Those who seek to save their life will lose it, and those who lose their life will preserve it' (Lk 17:33); Christ speaks these words in light of the day of his glorious Second Coming. The Christian lives in the shadow of this day, in the light of the age that is both already at hand and yet to come.

This surrender of one's self is no easy task. The ascetic chooses to go to extremes because of the extremity of the fallen, self-enclosed condition. It is a limiting situation that requires equally unlimited measures. However, obedience to one's spiritual elder does not resemble the submission that one experiences in the world; for it subsists – or, at least, it ought to exist – in the context of love. Without this kind of personal relationship, one gains nothing but a feeling of guilt from obedience. And such guilt defeats the purpose of obedience, which is spiritual liberation.

The spiritual elder, then, does not aim at imposing rules and punishments. The elder never prescribes rules but rather becomes a personal rule or living model, not so much through his or her words as through example. 'Be their model, not their legislator' is the advice of Abba Poemen.[15]

In a unique and refreshing passage from the seventh-century *Ladder of Divine Ascent*, John Climacus describes the spiritual guide as a 'sponsor' (*anadochos*), the term used for a god-parent at the sacrament of baptism. The concept signifies someone who assumes responsibility for another.[16] The source of this doctrine is Pauline: 'We who are strong ought to bear the failings of the weak' (Rom 15:1). The spiritual elder does more than direct responsibly; he assumes direct responsibility for the disciple. Barsanuphius of Gaza writes to one of his disciples: 'I assume and bear you, but only on this condition: that you bear the keeping of my words and commandments.'[17] The process of spiritual direction clearly implies a profound sense of love for and solidarity with another human being, for the elder assumes the suffering of others and, therefore, 'bears the cross' (Lk 14:24) of Christ himself. This reveals the art of spiritual direction as a way of love.

Therefore, in opening up to a spiritual elder, one allows the divine other into the whole of one's life. In order to achieve this, it is necessary to allow at least one other into the deepest recesses of the heart and mind, sharing every thought, emotion, insight, wound and joy with another person whom we trust completely. For most people, however, this is a difficult venture. It is not easy to open up to another person, revealing the vulnerable and darker aspects of our life. Our culture encourages us from an early age to be strong and assertive, to handle matters alone. Yet, for the spiritual wisdom of the early desert, such a way is false; it is, in fact, the way of the Devil. For 'we are members one of another' (Rom 12:5), not islands unto ourselves. And the Orthodox spiritual way proposes a variety of contexts within which we may begin to open our hearts and affirm the communion that exists among us: these include the sacramental way of confessing to a parish priest and the spiritual way of sharing with an experienced elder, whether male or female.

People need others because often the wounds that they feel are too deep to admit to themselves; sometimes, the evil is too painful to confront alone. The sign, then, according to the Orthodox spiritual way, that one is on the right track is the ability to share with someone else. This is, of course, precisely the essence of the sacrament of confession or reconciliation. Yet repentance (or *metanoia*) should not be seen in terms of remorse, but rather in terms of reconciliation, restoration and reintegration. Confession is not some kind of transaction or deal; it defies mechanical definition and can never be reduced in a juridical manner merely to the – albeit significant – act of absolution. Confession is not some narcissistic self-reflection. Sin is always understood in Orthodox spirituality as a rupture in the 'I–Thou' relationship of the world; otherwise *metanoia* could easily lead to paranoia. Instead, genuine confession always issues in communion; it is ultimately the ability to utter, together with at least one person, 'Our Father'. It is the sacrament of the Eucharist, the mystery of communion, lived out day by day.

THEOSIS THROUGH *ASCESIS*: THE WAY OF AUTHENTICITY

The ascetic way, then, is a way of authentic liberation and communion. For the ascetic is the person who is free, uncontrolled by attitudes that abuse the world; uncompelled by ways that use the world; characterised by self-control, by self-restraint, and by the ability to say 'no' or 'enough'. Indeed, asceticism aims at refinement, not detachment or destruction. Its goal is moderation, not repression. Its content is positive, not negative: it looks to service, not selfishness; to reconciliation, not renunciation or escape: 'Without asceticism, none of us is authentically human.'[18]

Unfortunately, however, centuries of misunderstanding and abuse have tainted the concept of asceticism, identifying it either with individualism and escapism or else with idealism and angelism. Both tendencies verge on the point of dis-incarnation, promulgating enmity towards the world. Yet, at least in its more authentic expression, asceticism is a way of intimacy and tenderness, a way of integrating body, soul and society. In this respect, asceticism is essentially a social discipline. Moreover, it is never practised in a way that would insult the Creator. It is no wonder, therefore, that even after years of harsh and frugal living, the early desert Fathers and Mothers would emerge in their relationships as charming and compassionate, accessible and tranquil.

In the Orthodox spiritual way, one example of this may be seen in the discipline of fasting. Orthodox Christians fast from all dairy and meat products for half of the entire year, almost as if in an effort to reconcile one half of the year with the other, secular time with the time of the Kingdom. To fast is not to deny the world, but in fact to affirm the world, together with the body, as well as all of the material creation. It is to recall that humanity is not called to 'live by bread alone' (Mt 4:4) but rather to acknowledge that all of this world, 'the earth, and all the fullness thereof, is the Lord's' (Ps. 23 [24]:1).

Therefore, like every ascetic discipline, to fast is ultimately to learn to give, and not simply to give up. As another act of 'letting go', it is not an expression of denial, but in fact an offering of thanks. It is a way of breaking down barriers, established by selfishness, between myself and my neighbour, as well as between myself and the world around me. In a word, to fast is to love. It is to move away from what I want to what the world needs. It is to be liberated from greed, control and compulsion. Fasting is to value everything for itself, and not simply for ourselves.

In the final analysis, the aim of asceticism is to regain a sense of wonder, to be filled with a sense of goodness and of God-liness. It is to see all things in God and God in all things. And it is precisely here that *ascesis* encounters *theosis*. For the most divine experience is to discover the wonder of God in the beauty of the world and to discern the limitless nature of grace in the limitations of the human body and the natural creation. There are those among us who may well be converted 'suddenly with a light flashing from heaven' (Acts 9:3) or be 'caught up to the third heaven' (2 Cor 12:2). Yet such ecstasy is experienced by very few – 'scarcely one among ten thousand . . . indeed, scarcely one in every generation', according to Abba Isaac the Syrian.[19] It is no wonder, then, that the desert Fathers encourage their disciples to restrain someone rising to spiritual heights: 'The old men used to say: "If you see someone climbing toward heaven by his own will, grab his foot and pull him down; for this will be for his own good".'[20] The ascetic literature clearly demonstrates a preference for the more lowly experience of those who have known their passions and recognised their failures. John Climacus refers to them as 'blessed': 'I saw ... and was amazed; and I consider those fallen mourners more blessed than those who have not fallen and are not mourning'.[21] While the end of *ascesis* may be the vision of God or *theosis*, the way of *ascesis* is none other than the daily life of self-knowledge or integrity, carved out of the ordinary experience of everyday life perceived in the extraordinary light of the eternal kingdom. It is the gradual – and, as a result of our resistance, painful – process of learning to be who you are and do what you do with all the intensity of life and love. 'An old man was asked: "What is it necessary to do to be saved?" He was making rope; and, without looking up from the work, he replied: "You are looking at it".'[22] In this way, the ascetic way defines in a uniquely tangible and concrete manner the theological doctrines concerning the original creation of the world, the divine Incarnation of the Word, and the age to come that we expect.

Further reading

Behr-Sigel, E., *The Place of the Heart: An Introduction to Orthodox Spirituality*, trans. S. Bigham, Torrance, CA: Oakwood Publications, 1992.

Chryssavgis, J., *Light through Darkness: The Orthodox Tradition*, London: Darton Longman and Todd, 2004.

Evdokimov, P., *Ages of the Spiritual Life*, Crestwood, NY: SVS Press, 1998.

Gillet, L. (Archimandrite), *Orthodox Spirituality: An Outline of the Orthodox Ascetical and Mystical Tradition*, Crestwood, NY: SVS Press, 1996.

Krivochéine, B. (Archbishop), *In the Light of Christ: Saint Symeon the New Theologian. Life, Spirituality, Doctrine*, Crestwood, NY: SVS Press, 1986.

Meyendorff, J., *St Gregory Palamas and Orthodox Spirituality*, Crestwood, NY: SVS Press, 1974.

Sophrony, Archimandrite, *His Life is Mine*, London: Mowbrays, 1977.

Walker, A., and C. Carras (eds.), *Living Orthodoxy in the Modern World: Orthodox Christianity and Society*, London: SPCK, 1996.

Notes

1. See Bishop H. Alfeyev, 'Eschatology', above, for further discussion.
2. *Sayings*, p. 186: Poemen 137.
3. Dorotheus of Gaza, *Discourses and Sayings*, pp. 138–9.
4. See I. Hausherr, *Penthos: The Doctrine of Compunction in the Christian East* (Kalamazoo, MI: Cistercian Publications, 1982); K. C. Patton and J. S. Hawley (eds.), *Holy Tears: Weeping in the Religious Imagination* (Princeton and Oxford: Princeton University Press, 2005).
5. *Sayings*, p. 184: Poemen 119.
6. See J. Chryssavgis (ed.), *Barsanuphius and John: Letters*, vols. I–II (Washington, DC: CUA Press, 2006–7).

7. See J. Chryssavgis and P. R. Penkett (eds.), *Abba Isaiah of Scetis: Ascetic Discourses* (Kalamazoo, MI: Cistercian Publications, 2002). For more on passions and healing, see J. Larchet, *The Theology of Illness* (Crestwood, NY: SVS Press, 2002).

8. Cf. *Sayings*, p. 84: Theodora 6.

9. Cf. *Sayings*, p. 131: Macarius the Great 19.

10. Cf. *Sayings*, p. 10: Arsenius 6.

11. Cf. *Sayings*, p. 175: Poemen 61.

12. Barsanuphius, *Letter* 93.

13. On spiritual direction in the early church, see G. Demacopoulos, *Five Models of Spiritual Direction in the Early Church* (Notre Dame, IN: Notre Dame University Press, 2007); J. Chryssavgis, *Soul Mending: The Art of Spiritual Direction* (Brookline MA: Holy Cross Press, 2000).

14. Barsanuphius, *Letter* 185.

15. *Sayings*, p. 191: Poemen 174.

16. John Climacus, *Ladder of Divine Ascent* 4.104.

17. Barsanuphius, *Letter* 270.

18. Cf. K. Ware, 'The way of the ascetics: negative or affirmative?' in V. Wimbush and R. Valantasis (eds.), *Asceticism* (Oxford and New York: Oxford University Press, 1995), p. 13. See also P. Nellas, *Deification in Christ: Orthodox Perspectives on the Nature of the Human Person* (Crestwood, NY: SVS Press, 1987).

19. Isaac of Nineveh, *Mystic Treatise* 22.

20. Cf. C. Stewart (trans.), *The World of the Desert Fathers: Stories and Sayings* (Oxford: SLG Press, 1986), p. 37.

21. See John Climacus, *Ladder of Divine Ascent* 5.

22. Cf. Stewart, *The World of the Desert Fathers*, p. 35.

Part II

Contemporary Orthodox Theology: its Formation and Character

11 Church Fathers and the shaping of Orthodox theology

AUGUSTINE CASIDAY

It is a characteristic of Orthodox Christianity that its theological history is conceived of very broadly and valued very highly; in the eyes of many commentators, Orthodoxy quite simply *is* patristic Christianity. According to one anecdote, a recent visitor to Mt Athos was told by one of the monks there, 'Here it is still the fourth century.'[1] That claim is, of course, in many ways quite fatuous – but even so it reveals something very important about Orthodoxy. For to make such a claim is at once to present an important fact about how Orthodox Christians tend to think about the past: the past constantly flows towards the future and, in so doing, lives in the present. The past is not tidily compartmentalised and detached, as an object for disinterested study. This is not to deny the possibility of Orthodox Christians engaging professionally and seriously in historical study, even in the historical study of Orthodoxy. Rather, it is to make a claim about the process of continuously appropriating the past that animates Orthodox theology (and, perhaps, to shed light on why Fr Georges Florovsky regarded historical theology as having a special claim on the Orthodox).

This chapter will not attempt a history of Orthodox Christian doctrine; still less will it attempt a patrology. Both such projects are important and have their place, but what concerns us here is the exposition of patristic doctrine and that task is necessarily theological. Although it is important to be historically scrupulous in expositing that topic, our attention will be devoted less to historical detail and more to theological currents. For purposes of convenience, we will consider these currents as they were exemplified in the lives and writings of particular historical figures. The coverage will necessarily be selective, but it will register important developments in areas of doctrine such as Christology, trinitarian theology and iconography. In the following pages, key themes from the doctrinal heritage of Orthodox Christianity will be presented in a series of vignettes. The vignettes will be arranged in chronological order and, in most cases, the presentations will be anchored by brief biographical notes on particular people whose names have become closely associated with the doctrines in question.

ATHANASIUS THE GREAT (C. 296–373): ON THE DYNAMICS OF CHRISTIAN LIFE

Athanasius the Great, sometime Archbishop of Alexandria and formidable controversialist, gave us one of the truly great lapidary phrases from the Greek patristic tradition when he wrote of God the Word that 'he became human that we might be made divine'.[2] This pithy statement – which elegantly describes the dynamic underlying most Orthodox reflection on the doctrine of deification, or *theosis* – was penned probably before Athanasius was fully overwhelmed by the lengthy struggles he faced against the teachings about Christ advanced by the Alexandrian priest Arius.[3] It expresses in a positive way Athanasius's persistent claim (so important during the Arian controversy) that, to act as Saviour, Christ must be fully divine and fully human. Only thus could Christ bridge the absolute difference in essence that separates the divine from the created. For 'other things, according to the nature of things originate, are without likeness in essence with the Maker'.[4] Athanasius was similarly outspoken in insisting on the full divinity of the Holy Spirit, who is likewise deeply involved in the work of salvation. Indeed, the Spirit, no less than the Son, is implicated in deifying God's creation.[5] The actions of the Son and the Spirit are co-ordinated and consistent; it is through the Spirit that the Son's activity is accomplished: 'As then the Father is light and the Son is his radiance – we must not shrink from saying the same things about them many times – we may see in the Son the Spirit also by whom we are enlightened . . . But when we are enlightened by the Spirit, it is Christ who in him enlightens us.'[6]

Athanasius tirelessly asserted the full and equal divinity of the Father, the Son and the Holy Spirit against a range of other theological views. Athanasius's theological style was deeply philosophical. In furtherance of this cause, Athanasius employed the categories of middle Platonism and, through the 'interlocking' of history and salvation with ontology, he was able to present a coherent account of the Christian life.[7] Yet Athanasius had a critical attitude towards philosophy, which he subordinated to his theology. To paraphrase Gregory of Nazianzus's ringing praise for Athanasius, he was preoccupied with the 'true philosophy' that confers deification.[8] By contrast, Athanasius found pagan philosophy shamefully implicated in the problem of idolatry – a serious theological problem insofar as the making of gods amounts to a turning from God to self.[9] But the coming of Christ, and most especially the Cross of Christ, provokes a re-orientation towards God such that humans are made to participate in God's attributes, i.e. they are made gods.

The most fundamental divine attribute in which humans participate is also the most basic: reality itself. As Athanasius states, 'Now reality is the good, unreality what is evil. I call reality the good because it has its exemplar in God who is real; and I call unreality what is evil because what has no real existence has been invented by the conceits of men.'[10] The evils invented by human conceits are chiefly the false gods who litter the false cosmology developed by perverse imaginations – as Athanasius makes clear with a lengthy quotation from Wisdom 14:12–21.[11] In quoting that passage, Athanasius demonstrates a practice that he warmly advocates in his famous *Letter to Marcellinus* by entering into scripture and making its worldview his own. This is possible, Athanasius contends, precisely because the words of scripture were inspired by the Holy Spirit who animates the Christian spiritual life.

THE CAPPADOCIAN FATHERS: ON THEOLOGICAL FORMULAE

Athanasius is chiefly remembered for his contributions to Christology. Although, as we have seen, he contributed to several other key areas as well, he dedicated most of his considerable talent to defending the divinity of Christ. It was left to three of Athanasius's younger contemporaries – Basil the Great (*c.* 330 – 1 Jan. 379), his brother Gregory of Nyssa (uncertain: *c.* 330 – *c.* 395) and their friend Gregory of Nazianzus (329/30–389/90) – to apply the same care and diligence to defending the Holy Spirit. The three hailed from Cappadocia in Asia Minor and, as Gregory of Nazianzus proudly claimed, 'of all men in the world, [Cappadocians'] special qualities are firmness in the faith, and loyal devotion to the Trinity'.[12] Motivated by this loyal devotion, these three Cappadocian Fathers contributed to the development of patristic theology 'a full-scale doctrine of the Trinity, in which both the unity and the diversity could be precisely formulated within a systematic theory and with a technical terminology adequate to obviate misunderstanding or equivocation'.[13] To appreciate this accomplishment, we need to consider the terminological problems that they faced.

The divinity of the Father was axiomatic and, in AD 325, the council of Nicaea asserted the divinity of the Son. But the place of the Spirit was still obscure. Theologians such as Athanasius were happy to appeal to the Holy

Spirit in their writings and even to offer analogies in support of the divinity of the Holy Spirit. He had also claimed that the Spirit must be God because the Spirit does what only God can do (namely, save humans).[14] But several basic questions about the Holy Spirit still awaited a satisfactory answer. In one of his orations, Gregory of Nazianzus runs through a long list of competing claims that could be made about the Spirit, even by Christians who were prepared to acknowledge the Spirit as God:

> these agree with us that there are Three Conceptions [*tria ... nooumena*]; but they have separated these from one another so completely as to make one of them [the Father] infinite both in essence and power, and the second [the Son] in power but not in essence, and the third [the Spirit] circumscribed in both; thus imitating in another way those who call them the Creator, the Co-operator, and the Minister, and consider that the same order and dignity which belongs to these names is also a sequence in the facts.[15]

The problem could not be resolved by appeal to scriptures; to turn again to an observation from Gregory of Nazianzus: 'The Old Testament proclaimed the Father openly, and the Son more obscurely; the New manifested the Son, and suggested the deity of the Spirit.' The Bible does not spell out the truth about the Spirit; instead, as Gregory continues, 'Now the Spirit himself dwells among us, and supplies us with a clearer demonstration of himself.'[16]

Gregory thus explains the progressive disclosure of the Trinity as the revelation of the Holy Spirit dwelling in the midst of Christians. Basil offers this significant description of what happens as a result of the indwelling of the Holy Spirit:

> Just as when a sunbeam falls on bright and transparent bodies, they themselves become brilliant too, and shed forth a fresh brightness from themselves, so souls wherein the Spirit dwells, illuminated by the Spirit, themselves become spiritual, and send forth their grace to others. Hence comes foreknowledge of the future, understanding of mysteries, apprehension of what is hidden, distribution of good gifts, the heavenly citizenship, a place in the chorus of angels, joy without end, abiding in God, the being made like to God, and, highest of all, the being made God.[17]

Here, Basil links deification ('being made God') to the economic activity of the Holy Spirit, which can be contrasted to Athanasius's connection of deification to the Incarnation. But the contrast is superficial, since Basil's claim is in line with Athanasius's teaching (e.g., in his letters to Serapion) that the transforming effects of the Holy Spirit are evidence that the Spirit is fully divine.[18] These effects are demonstrated in greater understanding of God, to be sure, but it is precisely the same activity of the Holy Spirit that is manifest in care for the poor, service within the Christian community and other forms of pastoral involvement – and in all of these areas, Basil's contributions were renowned.[19]

But offering a systematic account of the divinity of the Spirit was difficult, because of the lack of conventional theological language. In surveying historical documents, we tend to expect key terms to be univocal and often supply such precision in instances where it is not warranted. Actually, Athanasius had treated essence (*ousia*) and subsistence (*hypostasis*) as synonyms,[20] and others carried forward this usage in a way that made it difficult to talk about the essential oneness of God.[21] So the Cappadocians roughed out terminological distinctions, which when subsequently refined would become landmarks of patristic doctrine. For instance, the hypostasis is that which is peculiar, rather than 'the indefinite conception of *ousia*'.[22] The distinctiveness of the Son and the Holy Spirit is further described using another technical expression – *tropos tês hyparxeôs* ('mode of existence') – that points to the different way in which each originates from the Father. The expression is found occasionally in Basil the Great's writings (e.g. *On the Holy Spirit* 18.46), but its refinement is to be credited to Gregory of Nyssa's *Against Eunomius*.[23] Gregory further contributed to the discussion by offering illustrations of their relation-in-distinctiveness in his letter to Ablabius entitled 'That there are not three gods'. There, he advances what is sometimes called, unsatisfactorily, the 'social model' of the Trinity by explaining how a single nature can be manifest in three (or, in the case of humans, a plurality of) persons. His main point is less social than grammatical: Gregory is delineating a proper grammar for theology. Hence, he concludes the letter by writing that, since 'the divine nature is apprehended by every conception as unchangeable and undivided, ... we properly declare the Godhead to be one, and God to be one, and employ in the singular all other names which express divine attributes'.

Perhaps the most famous theological formula associated with the Cappadocian Fathers is 'one nature, three *hypostases*' (or 'persons'): that is, the three divine persons are one in nature. That catch-phrase is exceedingly rare in their writings,[24] but it neatly expresses the direction of their combined influence on the development of trinitarian theology. And yet the Cappadocians had no fetishistic preoccupation with a form of words, however nice. Gregory of Nazianzus makes this clear in his somewhat embarrassed account of why Basil's *On the Holy Spirit* does not use the word *homoousios*: he writes, 'For our salvation is not so much a matter of words as of actions.'[25] Elsewhere, a similar note of reservation is sounded: 'Yet receive what I say as at best a token and reflection of the truth; not as the actual truth itself. For it is not possible that there should be complete correspondence between what is seen in the tokens and the objects in reference to which the use of tokens is adopted.'[26] The 'tokens' of theology refer us to God and are not to be mistaken for 'the actual truth itself'; and yet they are not for that reason useless or inaccurate, because they are inspired by the abiding presence of God.

EVAGRIUS PONTICUS (*c.* 346–399): ON THEOLOGY AS PRAYER

As we have seen, theology was for Gregory of Nazianzus more than a mere form of words, regardless of how important the right words are. Theology is actually an integral part of living a Christian life. How this is so can be seen clearly from the special case of living a Christian *monastic* life. The intimate connection between living and thinking is seen with exceptional clarity in the writings of a disciple of both Basil and Gregory: Evagrius Ponticus. Subsequent monastic theologians have taken up and developed this insight, and we shall consider some of them, too, in the next section.

Evagrius had known Basil and Gregory as a young man and, when Gregory became Archbishop of Constantinople, he travelled to the capital to aid his erstwhile teacher in promoting the Nicene cause. Shortly after Gregory left, Evagrius too departed – but Evagrius's journey took him ultimately to Egypt, where he was trained in ascetic practices that perfected the training that he had received in Cappadocia.[27] Evagrius was one of the many who came to Egypt to learn from the desert Fathers. We have writings from the same period that record travels in Egypt, sometimes lasting for several years, by John Cassian, Palladius of Hellenopolis, Rufinus of Aquileia and an anonymous group whose journey is related in the *History of the Monks of Egypt*. Evagrius stands apart from this group precisely because he came to stay. Although records suggest that he travelled from the desert to Alexandria upon occasion, and once (while fleeing the ordaining hands of a bishop) even left Egypt altogether, he embraced the life of Egyptian monasticism to such an extent that he did not so much as acknowledge the death of his father when it was reported to him.

It has been argued that Evagrius's theological writings, nearly all of which date from his time in Egypt, demonstrate a profound influence from the elder desert Fathers – men such as Pambo, Macarius the Egyptian and Macarius the Alexandrian. The extent to which Evagrius conforms to the conventional teaching of the desert Fathers is admittedly a difficult question to judge. This is in part because we have so little independent evidence of what they taught (they did not leave writings, for example) that we cannot be too confident that there even was a 'conventional teaching'. However, as Jeremy Driscoll has persuasively argued, Evagrius's writings resonate with themes that can be otherwise identified in accounts of the teachings of Pambo and others.[28] But even without attempting to generalise from Evagrius's works to a general theology of the desert, it is possible to acknowledge that those writings are a precious testimony to the experience of the desert Fathers as understood theologically by one of them.

At the risk of overstatement, we might identify Evagrius's lasting contribution to Orthodox theology in two clarion statements of his. The first is a pithy definition: 'Christianity is the teaching of our Saviour Jesus Christ, which consists of ascetic practice, natural contemplation and theology.'[29] Those words open the first book in a trilogy of his that was well known in the ancient world. The structure of the trilogy itself echoes that tripartite definition of Christianity: the first book is called *The Ascetic, or The Monk;* the second is *The Gnostic, or The One Who is Worthy of Knowledge;* the third is *Gnostic Chapters* (or *Gnostic Problems*). Form reinforces content.

In the first book, there is a marked emphasis on the foundational principles of ethical behaviour. In the second, more advanced themes such as the interpretation of scripture and advising other monks – both of which require profound understanding – come to the fore, though the importance of ethical practice is by no means ignored. In the third book, there is another shift in content so that the reader is presented with chapters about God, about the nature of creation and about the dynamics of salvation, all of which are put in a deliberately elliptical way. Quite apart from the positive content of these three works, Evagrius has in them identified three major modes of activity within Christianity – ascetical and ethical living; understanding of God's creation; converse with God – that are progressive, mutually reinforcing and illuminating. This identification of the interrelated areas of activity, culminating in theology proper, has been vastly influential in the Orthodox tradition.

The second statement from Evagrius that has been enduringly fruitful is this: 'If you are a theologian, you will pray truly, and if you pray truly, you will be a theologian.'[30] The first statement makes a proposition about how theology relates to life; this second statement makes a proposition about the character of theology. It is *prayerful*. As Evagrius puts it elsewhere, prayer is 'the mind's conversation with God'[31] – and so, by implication, true converse with God is theology. Furthermore, undistracted prayer is the mind's highest function when it functions naturally[32] – and so, again, the implication is that theology is the highest function of the mind doing what it does naturally.

THE MONASTIC CONTRIBUTION: ON LIVING THEOLOGICALLY

Students of early Christianity increasingly recognise Evagrius for the importance of his writings because they reveal a major, early synthesis of monastic practice and theology. He is, however, a divisive figure, and in the subsequent literature he is frequently castigated for succumbing to a problematic infatuation with philosophy that is associated with the name of Origen of Alexandria. In the Greek tradition, Evagrius's name is most closely associated with a network of abstract and speculative theological claims about creation and salvation that has been repeatedly condemned. But his practical teachings (and even some of his quite advanced writings, such as *Chapters on Prayer*) have been very influential, as has his integration of prayer and theology. It is particularly through the monastic tradition that this heritage has been preserved and disseminated. But a word of warning is needed: though it is clear that the traditional understanding of monastic theology in the Orthodox world is profoundly indebted to Evagrian categories of thought, it is definitely *not* the case that every later monastic theologian has been indebted to Evagrius.

One great monastic teacher who is certainly not assimilated to Evagrius but whose writings reveal a similar integration of practice and theology is known to us as Macarius, sometimes called 'pseudo-Macarius' or 'Macarius-Symeon', author of *Fifty Spiritual Homilies* and the *Great Letter*. For several decades, it has been a commonplace to contrast the 'intellectualism' of Evagrius with the 'materialism' of Macarius, though this contrast is overdrawn.[33] It is perhaps too easy to think of Evagrius as an intellectual monk, precisely because within Orthodox tradition he is sometimes condemned for speculation, and also too easy to think of Macarius as a pious but crude monk, because his *Homilies* have a complicated relationship with the Messalian movement (an ascetic movement of the late fourth century, known to us chiefly through the writings of its opponents).[34] But in both cases the easy generalities are unsatisfactory. The major problem with that attitude towards Macarius is that people are not accustomed to reading the works of such a 'spiritual' author for their theological content, but the effort to do so is (as Marcus Plested has recently shown) amply repaid by the results. The account of Christian life in Macarius's writings is both animated by a vivid awareness of the experiences of salvation and informed by a coherent theology in which teachings about the Trinity, the Incarnation, the gifts of the Spirit and other topics are integrated.[35] The homiletic structure of his writings may make the underlying theology less obvious to a casual glance, but it is no less real for that.

If Evagrius has a reputation for being too intellectual and Macarius for being too emotive, the monastic author who is usually credited with striking the right balance between those extremes is Diadochus, Bishop of Photike in New Epirus. His debt to the Evagrian tradition is clear in both the terms and the format that he uses (the genre is the 'century' of 'chapters', or group of 100 interconnected but discrete units); his affinity to Macarius is identifiable in the warmth and intensity that we find in his descriptions of the Christian life. His *One Hundred Practical Texts of Perception and Spiritual Discernment* analyses the experience of prayer as the major form of contact between God and humans, and its consequent effects for the one who prays.[36] The influence of Diadochus's theology has been perceived in Maximus the Confessor,[37] another monastic theologian about whom we will have more to say in due course. For now, what we need to notice is that Diadochus's century of chapters made available to monastic readers key insights into life precisely by applying theological teachings in order to understand the experiences of (for instance) temptation and isolation from God. In this respect, Diadochus stands in a distinguished line of monastic authors whose writings made the relevance of theology quite clear by bringing it to bear on the events of daily life. Even though Diadochus (like Evagrius, and indeed like John Climacus) was adept at using the 'chapters' genre to convey his teachings, monastic literature is not limited to any particular form. We have pastoral letters (e.g. from Barsanuphius and John of Gaza), anecdotes about the lives and deeds of great monks that are sometimes intense and sometimes amusing (e.g. from Cyril of Scythopolis and from Dorotheus of Gaza, respectively) and even a travelogue (e.g. from John Moschus). What all of this literature has in common is that it is *practical*, not in the quotidian sense that it explains how to make household repairs or the like, but in the etymological sense that it concerns the *practice of asceticism*, which is nothing other than the daily application of the theological doctrines of the Church.

THE AGE OF THE COUNCILS (325–842): ON DEFENDING THE FAITH

To return now to those doctrines, mention has already been made of decisions against Arius promulgated by the council of Nicaea (AD 325) – a council that within a generation was already being recognised as 'ecumenical' in scope and authority.[38] But the decisions at Nicaea did not calm the controversies, and for decades thereafter Christology was a contested and divisive issue in many ways;[39] even so, it was Nicene doctrine that the council of Constantinople (381) reaffirmed. That council itself was within seventy years being recognised as the second ecumenical council.[40] The 150 bishops at Constantinople revised the earlier Creed formulated at Nicaea, and it is this Creed that is popularly (if inaccurately) known as the 'Nicene Creed' – shortly thereafter to be described as a 'wise and saving symbol of divine grace' which 'sufficed for the perfect knowledge and confirmation of piety, for on the Father and the Son and the Holy Spirit its teaching is complete [or perfect: *teleion*]'.[41]

In debates during this epoch, there was a perceptible increase in the sense of deference to earlier figures, traditions and authorities.[42] Recourse to these sources was prominent in the debates between Cyril of Alexandria and Nestorius of Constantinople, concerning Christology and the veneration appropriate to the blessed Virgin. For example, in the course of these debates, on 22 July 341, the bishops effectively made the Nicene Creed the touchstone of orthodoxy. Under Cyril's direction, the council of Ephesus (431; third ecumenical) robustly asserted that Christ cannot be divided into two separate persons (i.e., a divine person filiated by the Father and a human person born of Mary), that Mary is thus the 'Birth-giver of God' (*Theotokos*) and therefore that to deny her the honour of that title is to blaspheme against Christ God. Cyril's success resonated and, in subsequent controversies about Christ, all sides would attempt to claim fidelity to Cyril's position. A strong consensus was forming.

But the stronger the consensus, the larger the rifts that followed. This generalisation is well illustrated in the events subsequent to the council of Chalcedon (AD 451; fourth ecumenical), which resulted in the estrangement of two large confederations of bishops that, for purposes of convenience, may be described as those in communion with the emperor and those who were not. (Because conforming and nonconforming bishops sometimes nominally held the same sees, communion is a better indicator than geography – although geographic patterns do emerge subsequently and survive to this day.) All of this is to say nothing of the survival of the Apostolic Church of the East, whose members do not attribute authority to the decisions of the council of Ephesus.[43]

Following Chalcedon, there were several turbulent decades of mutual recrimination during which, broadly speaking, Alexandrian theologians accused Antiochene theologians of heretically separating Christ into two persons ('Nestorianism') and Antiochenes retaliated by accusing Alexandrians of heretically collapsing Christ's two natures into a composite nature ('Monophysitism'). During the reign of Justinian I, a council convened in Constantinople (AD 553; fifth ecumenical) to re-assert the authority of Chalcedon, and also to condemn some writings by prominent Antiochene theologians. Around this time, perhaps in conjunction with the council itself, a system of beliefs inspired by the Alexandrian theologians Origen, Didymus the Blind and Evagrius Ponticus was condemned as 'Origenism'.

Still christological controversy continued, as indicated by unsuccessful attempts at constructing a mutually agreeable position; such were 'Monergism', which posited a single energy (or activity) in Christ, and 'Monothelitism', which asserted unity at the level of the will. Key figures who resisted these attempts were Emperor Constans II, Maximus the Confessor – whose cosmological vision of Christology has been enormously significant in Orthodox theology[44] – and Pope Martin of Rome. Imperial leadership favoured reconciliation, but some prominent churchmen resisted the implied compromise of Chalcedonian orthodoxy and held to that resistance to the point of death. For instance, during his trial Maximus explained that 'no being exists without natural activity. I mean that the holy Fathers say plainly that it is impossible for any nature at all to exist or to be recognised apart from its essential activity [*tês ousiôdôs . . . energeias*]'.[45] For Chalcedonian theology to be meaningful, the two natures of Christ must be expressed through their proper activities. This position was broadly endorsed by the council that assembled in 680–1 (Constantinople III; sixth ecumenical) and that condemned previous attempts at compromise, thus asserting that Christ's two natures implied Christ's two wills and two energies.

Though further debates emerged in which key issues already discussed were taken up again (as when, for example, essential energies figure prominently in the debates about Hesychasm), the next major crisis that required a theological solution provides a good example of how Orthodox theology proceeded through insightful and creative recourse to traditional themes that were deployed in response to new challenges. In this instance, the challenge came in the form of a principled rejection of religious imagery ('Iconoclasm') about a generation after the sixth ecumenical council and ran for over sixty years (AD 730–87). But in 787, Constantine VI and his mother Eirene convoked a council that established the theological basis for iconography (council of Nicaea II; seventh ecumenical). The major 'intellectual architect' of this theology was John of Damascus (approx. 650/5–750), whose *Three Treatises Against Those Who Attack the Icons* offer two collections of passages consolidated from earlier sources in support of Christian iconography, framed by a sustained theological analysis of imagery that is based on the Incarnation as an event that clarifies God's relationship to matter and so justifies Christian symbolism.[46]

Collectively the ecumenical councils produced a huge collection of canonical legislation, but they are particularly important for our purposes because of their doctrinal creeds and formulations. These doctrines centre on the mystery of Christ – but that mystery itself has cosmic ramifications and, of these, some are pursued in conciliar definitions and statements. Examples include the veneration appropriate to those creatures and things who are imbued with God's love – whether the 'Theotokos', the Gospel book, or graphic and plastic representations taken from salvation history; the divinity of the Son and the Spirit; good order within the communities that are being reconciled to God; the relationship between secular culture and sacred learning. Even during the centuries in which the great councils were occurring, the decisions of ecumenical councils were already becoming normative (if not sacrosanct) by long customary usage.

It is striking that all of these councils convened in the Christian East, though Western – or, more specifically, papal – involvement was always important; sometimes, it was decisive. (Maximus the Confessor's high regard for the Church of Rome was largely based on its exemplary record of supporting orthodoxy and challenging heresy: 'I love the Romans because we share the same faith, whereas I love the Greeks because we share the same language', as he said in his trial.)[47] But by the time of the iconoclast controversies, Rome and Constantinople were beginning to pull apart for cultural and political reasons, some of which can be traced to the Christianisation of non-Roman peoples.

To the north, Charlemagne asserted himself as a Christian leader with no less stature than the emperor in Constantinople. His theologians, though opposed to the destruction of religious imagery, attacked the theological case for iconography advanced by the Fathers of the council of 787 in four books (the *Libri carolini*) written c. 790–2. The books' aggressive tone is owed in part to faults in the Latin translation of the council to which they respond, but beyond that the Carolingians were overtly hostile towards icon-devotion, fearing that it admitted a return to pagan idolatry. Their strident and self-confident rejection of Greek theology should also be understood against the background of strained diplomatic relations between Charlemagne and the Byzantine empress, Eirene. Comparable political problems overflowing into theological controversies intensified in the following decades, so that relations between the East and West ebbed low during the patriarchate of Photius the Great (*sed.* 858–67, 878–86).

PHOTIUS THE GREAT (c. 820–893): ON PATRISTIC CONTROVERSY

Photius was an erudite man who was made patriarch in the midst of controversy. His domestic problems were compounded when he came into conflict with Pope Nicholas I (*sed.* 858–67), a stalwart advocate of papal primacy, since both Rome and Constantinople were laying claim to jurisdictional oversight of recently converted Bulgaria.[48] Open conflict was inevitable because Germans and Greeks brought different practices and observances to the Balkans. The most provocative divergence was the Carolingians' inclusion in the Nicene–Constantinopolitan Creed of the clause 'and the Son' (in Latin, *filioque*) to describe the procession of the Holy Spirit, or more precisely the Spirit's *dual* procession, from the Father *and the Son*. The clause had initially been introduced as an anti-Arian device in fifth-century Spain, where Catholic Christian bishops were confronted by conquering Germanic tribes whose faith fell short of Greek standards. By the time it came to be advocated by the Carolingians, the expanded Creed was widely accepted as a matter of tradition in the Latin Christian world. Even Western theologians who rejected the modification of the Creed, such as Pope Leo III, supported the theological claims implied by the *filioque*.

The Greeks objected categorically to the modification of a conciliar Creed, as part of their increasing conviction that their ecumenical councils (even councils that, when they convened, went largely unnoticed) were normative. Meanwhile, the Carolingians set about tracing their own genealogy of trinitarian theology and generated lists of earlier patristic sources to support the dual procession of the Holy Spirit. In his *Mystagogy of the Holy Spirit*, Photius challenged the Carolingians. According to Photius, his adversaries defended their position by invoking Ambrose, Augustine and Jerome, claiming, 'One ought not to charge the sacred Fathers with the crime of ungodliness [*dyssebeias*]. Either one agrees with their opinion because they taught piously and are acknowledged as Fathers, or they, together with their teaching, should be rejected as impious [*asebeis*] because they introduced godless doctrines [*dyssebôn*

... *dogmatôn*]'.[49] Photius's counter-argument exposes the crudity of their claim on two counts: first, it reduces teaching to a factor that is absolutely pure or impure and thus compels assent or rejection, respectively; and second, it asserts that those acknowledged as holy Fathers are therefore to be followed in every particular.

By contrast, Photius criticises the Carolingians for contentiously opposing patristic excerpts against 'the teaching of the Church'. Photius can accept that error (even 'godless error': *dyssebêma*) can be found from time to time in the teaching of those who 'were admirable by reason of many other qualities which manifest virtue and piety' and he is prepared to acknowledge that they are Fathers despite the error. This is a disarming claim, particularly since Photius was vehemently opposed to the *filioque*.[50] Photius believes that historical development gives us the benefit of hindsight, but also that we are obliged to be charitable.

Photius accepts that a venerable father is not *ipso facto* inerrant, that a saint can be in error and that holiness is distinguishable from accuracy even amongst the Greek Fathers (which nearly offsets his tendentious claims about the superiority of the Greek language).[51] He also accepts that, in matters of doctrine, standards of precision increase over time. So he can accept that, in the course of history, changing circumstances may invalidate earlier views, without therefore rejecting those who held to the invalidated views. In this way, Photius's polemic against the *filioque* outlines a critical approach to the reception of earlier theology that accepts the importance of historical development.

PETER OF DAMASCUS (*C.* 1027–1107): ON THE CONSOLIDATION OF TEACHINGS

As we have already seen through discussing some early monastic theologians, not all Orthodox teachings concern trinitarian or christological doctrines. Indeed, many theologians understand those doctrines as the summit of teaching that reaches down to practical and ethical instruction. An excellent example is preserved in Peter Damascene's *Treasury of Divine Knowledge*, a work infrequently studied but deeply important.[52] The *Treasury* reveals clearly that doctrine is not simply a set of interconnected propositions about God; it also includes practical guidance for daily life, so that one's entire life becomes a *theological* enterprise. Consider, for example, how Peter makes humility a principle of hermeneutics: he insists on recognising one's own limited understanding when reading the holy scriptures and on resisting the urge to conform the meaning of the Bible to our expectations.[53] To be able to learn, we have to accept that we are ignorant. Ethics and understanding are connected in that way. This basic insight is not limited to reading scriptures, however. Peter sees it at work in the Christian life as a whole. Initiation into understanding is a process that occurs when those who lack understanding put themselves in a position to learn from those who have more experience in theological living: 'It is on this account that with firm faith and by questioning those with experience we should accept the doctrines of the Church and the decisions of its teachers, both concerning the holy scriptures and concerning the sensible and spiritual worlds.'[54]

Peter's instructions outline the whole contents of theology – the 'doctrines of the Church and the decisions of its teachers' as they bear on the Bible and on creation. Even if it does not correspond to the standard divisions of modern academic theology, Peter's syllabus is basically familiar to students of Orthodox theology. What is interesting about it is that, in effect, it identifies his *Treasury* as an exemplary work of theology precisely because the *Treasury* is a compendium of those doctrines and decisions. Peter is of course not the first theologian to produce a massive collection of traditional theology. He has an eminent precursor in an earlier theologian from Damascus, St John Damascene, whose *Fountainhead of Knowledge* (or *Exposition of the Orthodox Faith*) is a famous, and rather more tidy but otherwise comparable, example.

In much the same way that the *Treasury* can be compared to John Damascene's *Fountainhead*, it can also be compared to earlier collections of monastic wisdom. Collected aphorisms from the desert Fathers were already circulating within a generation of their lives (as we know because Evagrius, who lived in their company, apparently cites such a collection) and their sayings would eventually become a major theological resource. But there is also evidence in old manuscripts that a larger canon of standard monastic literature had developed even before Peter Damascene's time.[55] The *Treasury* is an important milestone in the development of monastic theology that stands midway between the earliest records of that theology and the hugely significant modern collections like the *Philokalia* and the *Dobrotolyubie*; in fact, the *Treasury* has been rightly called 'a circle within a circle, a concentrated *Philokalia* within the more extended *Philokalia*'.[56] As such, it has an important place in the broad tradition of ascetic literature that has nurtured Orthodox theology for centuries, inspiring modern monastic fathers of the Church from St Nil Sorsky to Fr Cleopa of Sihăstria,[57] but also playing a key role in the modern re-vitalisation of Orthodox theology as a whole. So both directly, through the pastoral ministry of spiritual Fathers who are themselves steeped in the traditions recorded in ascetic literature, and indirectly, through the resurgence of a genuinely Orthodox theology that is inspired in large measure by the same literature, monastic theology has been felt even by secular Orthodox Christians.

Similarly, although Peter himself was a monk, he makes his teachings available to all Christians, as is clear from this remark in the preface to the *Treasury*:

> there is no object, no activity or place in the whole of creation that can prevent us from becoming what God from the beginning wished us to be: that is to say, according to his image and likeness, gods by adoption through grace, dispassionate, just, good and wise, *whether we are rich or poor, married or unmarried, in authority and free or under obedience and in bondage* – in short, whatever our time, place or activity.[58]

Peter's teaching aims to meet the contingencies of life. By grounding theology in spiritual practice, and theological insight into human life, Peter exemplifies the traditional mode of Orthodox theology. In his *Treasury*, earlier Orthodox doctrines are recapitulated in such a way as to make the riches of theory and discipline generally available.

GREGORY PALAMAS (c. 1296–1359): ON REDEFINING DOCTRINE

Like Peter, Gregory Palamas[59] was also the inheritor of a rich theological tradition – but the controversies in which he became embroiled demonstrate that, for all its broad-based stability, this tradition was neither mechanical nor hidebound. For instance, Palamas drew heavily from the Fathers to offer his theological account of and defence for the claims of certain Athonite monks about their life of prayer (known as hesychasm). These monks were accused of heresy by Barlaam the Calabrian for claiming that they physically experienced an encounter with God. Palamas insisted to the contrary that when humans experience the activities (or 'energies') of God, they thus come into direct contact with God; or, to put it negatively, God's energies are not created effects that mediate between God and creatures. Divine energy is itself 'ineffable, uncreated, eternal, timeless, unapproachable, boundless, infinite, uncircumscribable, invisible to angels and men; it is the archetypal and immutable beauty, the glory of God, the glory of Christ, the glory of the Spirit, a ray of divinity, and so forth'[60] – and as such, to contact it is to contact God. Consequently, the Hesychasts affirmed that our material bodies can directly experience contact with God.

Now divine energies were already a theme in Greek theology, but Palamas articulated a position that met the needs of contemporary debates in a way that developed on earlier writings. But Palamas's defence provoked further controversy, this time from Gregory Akindynos. Akindynos criticised Palamas sharply – not without some justification – for his interpretation of the Fathers.[61] The fact that a competent theologian, well versed in the Fathers, challenged Palamas's patristic argument indicates that Palamite theology is not a simple recapitulation of classical doctrine.[62] In his *Discourse before Patriarch John XIV*, Akindynos presents an alternative solution to the debates on Hesychasm that is sympathetic to Hesychastic practices and at the same time more doctrinally conservative with respect to the Fathers than Palamas's argument had been. In defending the Hesychasts as he did, Palamas was transforming – or, from Akindynos's point of view, deforming – the patristic doctrinal heritage, by refining and developing it through theological reflection on Hesychastic prayer and its meaning. He re-deploys patristic doctrine and his point of departure is a particular set of religious experiences. Although the resulting emphasis on divine energies is characteristic, the theological method that leads to this characteristic emphasis is well attested and virtually constant throughout Orthodox theology.

CONCLUSION

In surveying major developments in the history of Orthodox doctrine, we have noted several recurrent themes. We have seen that doctrine arises from, and remains in dialogue with, the experiences of the newness of life in Christ: theory guides practice, practice informs theory. The constant interaction of theory and practice in Peter Damascene's *Treasury* makes it possible for doctrine to be endlessly applicable by a general population. It also makes a central place in theology for ethics, since ethical living is basic for theological understanding. But ethics is not simply preliminary, something that is left behind after it has been put in order. As we learned from Photius, ethical considerations play an important part in articulating valid criticism within the tradition. Criticism fed by humility and charity enabled Photius to accept that mistakes are made, even by admirable and venerable teachers, and to avoid morbid preoccupation with a quest for abstract purity. His polemic against the Frankish theologians provides an example of how someone within the tradition can be constructively critical about the past, and thus of how the tradition itself can become self-critical.

This capacity for self-criticism (when it is exercised) has kept Orthodox doctrine from hardening into hidebound retrospection or atrophying into flaccid nostalgia. The accumulation of doctrinal insights is neither automatic, nor inevitable. Instead, it is deliberate and careful. Doctrine is validated by experience and corroborated by the witness of the saints. As circumstances change, it may become necessary to re-state the principles of Orthodox teaching. In proclaiming doctrine in a novel situation, or evaluating a proclamation that has arisen in that way, there is a criterion for criticism – and that criterion is Godliness. The goal of theology for the Orthodox is first and foremost communion with God. For this reason, life itself is a theological undertaking and doctrines are understood as expressions of the theological life. Even though it is possible (and in some cases necessary) to give a clear and precise statement of doctrine, Orthodox doctrine serves primarily to point the way towards God and so it takes on a distinctly experiential and practical flavour.

Further reading

Casiday, A. and Norris, F. (eds.), *The Cambridge History of Christianity*, vol. II: *From Constantine to c. 600*. Cambridge: Cambridge University Press, 2007.

Louth, A. and Casiday, A. (eds.), *Byzantine Orthodoxies*, Aldershot: Ashgate, 2006.

Meyendorff, J., *Byzantine Theology. Historical Trends and Doctrinal Themes*, London and Oxford: Mowbrays, 1974.

Pelikan, J., *The Christian Tradition*, vol. II: *The Spirit of Eastern Christendom (600–1700)*, Chicago: University of Chicago Press, 1974.

Ramsey, B., *Beginning to Read the Fathers*, New York: Paulist Press, 1985.

Runciman, Sir S., *The Great Church in Captivity*, Cambridge: Cambridge University Press, 1968, especially Pt I.

Notes

1. C. Stewart, '"We"? Reflections on affinity and dissonance in reading early monastic literature', *Spiritus* 1 (2001), 93–102, esp. 94.
2. Athanasius of Alexandria, *On the Incarnation* 54.
3. See K. Anatolios, *Athanasius. The Coherence of His Thought* (London: Routledge, 1998); on Arius, see R. Williams, *Arius: Heresy and Tradition* (London: SCM, rev. edn 2001).
4. Athanasius of Alexandria, *Against the Arians* 1.6.20.
5. E.g. Athanasius of Alexandria, *On the Decrees* 3.14.
6. Athanasius of Alexandria, *To Serapion* 1.19.
7. Anatolios, *Athanasius*, pp. 30–1.
8. Gregory of Nazianzus, *Oration* 21, *On the Great Athanasius* 2.
9. See Athanasius of Alexandria, *Against the Pagans* 19, and cf. *Against the Pagans* 10 (with reference to Plato); on his robust (and often

misunderstood) argument against idolatry at *Against the Pagans* 2–29, see Anatolios, *Athanasius*, pp. 26–84.

10. Athanasius, *Against the Pagans* 4.
11. Athanasius, *Against the Pagans* 11.
12. Gregory of Nazianzus, *Oration* 40, *On Holy Baptism* 33.
13. J. Pelikan, *The Christian Tradition*, vol. 1 (Chicago: University of Chicago Press, 1971), p. 218.
14. Athanasius, *To Serapion* 1.23.
15. Gregory of Nazianzus, *Oration* 31, *The Fifth Theological Oration on the Holy Spirit* 5.
16. Gregory of Nazianzus, *Oration* 31, 26.
17. Basil of Caesarea, *On the Holy Spirit* 9.23.
18. Athanasius, *To Serapion* 1.23.
19. See Gregory of Nazianzus, *Oration* 43, *Panegyric on St Basil* 34–5.
20. Athanasius of Alexandria, *Epistle to the Africans* 4; likewise, the Council of Sardica as well as Jerome and Epiphanius of Salamis: see J. T. Lienhard, '*Ousia* and *hypostasis*' in S. T. David, D. Kendall, SJ, and G. O'Collins, SJ (eds.), *The Trinity: An Interdisciplinary Symposium on the Trinity* (Oxford: Oxford University Press, 1999), pp. 99–121, esp. 103–4.
21. Thus (ps.-)Basil, *Letter* 38.1. Scholars now usually attribute this writing to Gregory of Nyssa; but since most Greek texts and English translations assign it to Basil, we follow that attribution, despite the possible inaccuracy.
22. (Ps.-)Basil, *Letter* 38.3.
23. Gregory of Nyssa, *Against Eunomius* 1.21; see further, B. Daley, 'Nature and the "mode of union"', in S. T. David, D. Kendall, SJ, and G. O'Collins, SJ (eds.), *The Incarnation: An Interdisciplinary Symposium on the Incarnation of the Son of God*, Oxford: Oxford University Press, 2002, pp. 164–96.
24. Thus Lienhard, '*Ousia* and *hypostasis*'.
25. Gregory of Nazianzus, *Oration* 40.68.
26. (Ps.-)Basil, *Letter* 38.5.
27. For details on Evagrius's life, see further A. Casiday, *Evagrius Ponticus* (London: Routledge, 2006), pp. 5–22.
28. J. Driscoll, *Steps to Spiritual Perfection: Studies on Spiritual Progress in Evagrius Ponticus* (Mahwah, NJ: Paulist Press, 2003).
29. Evagrius Ponticus, *The Praktikos* 1.
30. Evagrius Ponticus, *Chapters On Prayer* 62.
31. Evagrius Ponticus, *Chapters On Prayer* 3.
32. Evagrius Ponticus, *Chapters On Prayer* 35.
33. Thus, rightly, M. Plested, *The Macarian Legacy: The Place of Macarius-Symeon in the Eastern Christian Tradition* (Oxford: Oxford University Press, 2004), pp. 59–71.
34. A concise summary and evaluation of the evidence about the Messalians may be found in Plested, *The Macarian Legacy*, pp. 17–29.
35. Plested, *The Macarian Legacy*, pp. 30–45.
36. Diadochus of Photike, *One Hundred Practical Texts of Perception and Spiritual Discernment*.

37. Thus, e.g., A. Louth, *Maximus the Confessor* (London and New York: Routledge, 1996), pp. 25–6.
38. E.g., Athanasius of Alexandria, *Epistle to the Africans* 2.
39. See L. Ayres, *Nicaea and Its Legacy* (Oxford: Oxford University Press, 2004).
40. E.g. *Acts of the Council of Chalcedon*, Second Session § 2; Sixteenth Session § 18.
41. *Acts of the Council of Chalcedon*, Fifth Session § 34.
42. See P. T. R. Gray, '"The select Fathers"', *Studia Patristica* 23 (1989), 21–36; R. Lim, *Public Disputation, Power, and Social Order in Late Antiquity* (Berkeley: University of California Press, 1995), Ch. 5.
43. W. Baum and D. Winkler, *The Church of the East* (London: Routledge, 2003).
44. See E. Theokritoff, 'Creator and creation,' above.
45. Maximus the Confessor, *Record of the Trial* 7.
46. For further discussion, see M. Fortounatto and M. B. Cunningham, 'Theology of the icon', above.
47. Maximus the Confessor, *Record of the Trial* 11; see also Maximus's *Opusculum* 11.
48. See F. Dvornik, *The Photian Schism* (Cambridge: Cambridge University Press, 1948), pp. 91–131; R. Haugh, *Photius and the Carolingians* (Belmont, MA: Nordland Publishing Co., 1975); H. Chadwick, *East and West: The Making of a Rift in the Church* (Oxford: Oxford University Press, 2003), pp. 77–192.
49. Photius, *Mystagogy* 66. In fairness, it should be noted that the Carolingians also appealed to Athanasius, Didymus the Blind, Gregory of Nazianzus, Cyril of Alexandria and Hilary of Poitiers amongst others; see e.g. Theodulf of Orleans's *On the Holy Spirit.*
50. See, e.g., Photius, *Letter* 13.33: 'But also that blasphemy about the Spirit (or rather the Holy Trinity as a whole), which none surpasses, would suffice by itself – even if there were none of the aforementioned effronteries – to earn them a thousand anathemas.'
51. On Greek Fathers in error, see Photius, *Mystagogy* 75 and *Letter* 24.21; on the relative poverty of Latin, see *Mystagogy* 55 and *Letter* 24.5.
52. See G. Peters, 'Peter of Damascus and early Christian spiritual theology', *Patristica et medievalia* 26 (2005), 89–109; Peters, 'Recovering a lost spiritual theologian: Peter of Damascus and the Philokalia', *SVTQ* 49 (2005), 437–59.
53. Peter Damascene, *Treasury of Divine Knowledge* (*Philokalia*, III, p. 144).
54. Peter Damascene, *Treasury* (*Philokalia*, III, p. 138).
55. See further P. Géhin, 'Le Filocalie che hanno preceduto la "Filocalia"', in A. Rigo (ed.), *Nicodemo l'Aghiorita e la Filokalia* (Magnano: Qiqajon, 2001), pp. 83–102.
56. St Nikodimos the Hagiorite, as cited by Palmer, Sherrard and Ware (*Philokalia*, III, p. 72).
57. On Fr Cleopa, see N. Stebbing, *Bearers of the Spirit: Spiritual Fatherhood in Romanian Orthodoxy* (Kalamazoo, MI: Cistercian Publications, 2003), pp. 45–86.

58. Peter Damascene, *Treasury* (*Philokalia*, III, p. 76), emphasis added.
59. R. E. Sinkewicz, 'Gregory Palamas' in C. G. and V. Conticello (eds.), *La théologie byzantine et sa tradition*, vol. II (Turnhout: Brepols, 2002), pp. 131–88; J. Meyendorff, *A Study of Gregory Palamas* (Crestwood, NY: SVS Press, 1998).
60. Gregory Palamas, *Declaration of the Holy Mountain* 4.
61. See J. S. Nadal, 'La critique par Akindynos de l'herméneutique patristique de Palamas', *Istina* 19 (1974), 297–328.
62. N. Russell, 'Theosis and Gregory Palamas: continuity or doctrinal change?' *SVTQ* 50 (2006), 357–79.

12 The patristic revival and its protagonists

ANDREW LOUTH

THE 'NEO-PATRISTIC SYNTHESIS'

The history of Orthodox theology in the twentieth century is everywhere touched by the notion of a patristic revival. What this entails, however, is less than obvious. Predominantly it is bound up with the idea of a 'Neo-patristic synthesis' as characterising modern Orthodox theology, or more precisely the direction that modern Orthodox theology ought to be taking. The actual term seems to have been coined by analogy with 'Neo-Kantianism' (associated with such as Ernst Cassirer and influential on Husserl and Heidegger) or, more significantly perhaps, 'Neo-Thomism', associated with the promotion of Aquinas as a theologian by Pope Leo XIII and his advocacy by the French philosophers Étienne Gilson and Jacques Maritain. Like these two movements, the 'Neo-patristic synthesis' involved both *ressourcement* – a recovery of, in this case, the patristic witness – and an engagement with modern problems. It also had a particular polemical context in the reaction – associated especially with the names of two towering figures of twentieth-century Orthodox theology, Fr Georges Florovsky and Vladimir Lossky – against the general character of the 'Russian Religious Renaissance' that culminated in 'sophiology' and its condemnation in the 1930s. The decisive return to patristic sources that Florovsky and Lossky called for is certainly an important and influential aspect of twentieth-century Orthodox theology (which reverberated beyond the Russian émigré circles in which it originated), but is only part of a much more complex story, which this chapter will attempt to illuminate.

The programme of a 'Neo-patristic synthesis' was intended to recall Russian Orthodox theology from what Florovsky called the '"pseudomorphosis" of Russia's religious consciousness' or 'of Orthodox thought' – borrowing the geological term from Oswald Spengler's analysis of the 'decline of the West' – or more dramatically (echoing this time Martin Luther) 'the "Babylonian captivity" of the Russian Church', which was held to be evident by the eighteenth century, and led, via the Slavophiles and wayward genius of Vladimir Soloviev, to what Florovsky regarded as the near-paganism of sophiology. Florovsky's *Ways of Russian Theology* recounted the errant wanderings of Russian theology to the point where it needed to be recalled to the 'patristic style and method' which had been 'lost'. This 'patristic theology must be grasped from within', he declared.[1] Florovsky spoke of 'intuition' as well as 'erudition', and argued that, to regain this patristic way of thinking, or *phronema*, 'Russian theological thought must still pass through the strictest school of Christian Hellenism'.[2] The way forward he sketched on the last page of his book:

> A prayerful entry into the Church, a fidelity to Revelation, a return to the Fathers, a free encounter with the West, and other similar themes and elements make up the creative postulate of Russian theology in the contemporary circumstances ... The way of history has still not been fully travelled; the history of the Church is not yet finished; Russia's way has not yet been closed. The road is open, though difficult. A harsh historical verdict must be transformed into a creative call to complete what remains unfinished ... Russia's way has long been divided. It is a mysterious way of spiritual labour (*podvig*), a way of secret and silent labour in the acquisition of the Holy Spirit. There is also a separate way for those who have left this one.[3]

These 'two ways' refer back to Psalm 1:6 ('The Lord knows the way of the righteous, but the way of the ungodly shall perish'), quoted on the title page of the Russian original (but omitted in the English translation): Florovsky's *Ways of Russian Theology* is mostly about the way that will perish, and the final chapter recalls Russian theology to the 'way of the righteous', but at the same time, in the book, he tells a more complex story of the history of Russian theology, and this we need to understand, if we are not to confuse rhetoric with reality when thinking of the 'Neo-patristic synthesis'.

EARLIER PATRISTIC REVIVALS

For the 'patristic revival' of the twentieth century was not life from death; it built on a deep engagement with the Fathers, that Florovsky reveals in his book, even as he passes over it. Even if we cast a disapproving eye over the initial encounters between Orthodox theology and the West in the seventeenth century that issued in the so-called 'Symbolic Books' (semi-official confessions of faith, drawn up in the seventeenth century, and much influenced by Western theological categories) – and we may be wrong to do so – the eighteenth century certainly saw the beginnings

of a *ressourcement* associated with the traditionalist movement among
the Athonite monks, known as the 'kollyvades', and manifest in the
publication of the *Philokalia* in 1782 and other labours associated with
the names of its compilers, St Makarios of Corinth and St Nikodimos
of the Holy Mountain. Simply to summarize some of the achievements
of these monks gives an impression of the extent of this *ressourcement*.
The *Philokalia* itself is an anthology of mostly ascetic texts from the
fourth to the fourteenth centuries, with extensive selections from
St Maximus the Confessor and St Gregory Palamas – two of the theologians whose stars preside, as we shall see, over twentieth-century Orthodox theology. But Nikodimos also published an edition of the *Synagoge*
of Paul Evergetinos, a vast anthology of ascetic texts; (with St Makarios)
a work *Concerning Frequent Communion*; the *Heortodromion*, containing commentaries on the liturgical canons for the principal feasts; his
vast and influential collection of, and commentary on, the ecclesiastical
canons, the *Pedalion* or 'Rudder'; an edition of the works of St Symeon
the New Theologian; and he prepared an edition of St Gregory Palamas
(the publication of which was frustrated for political reasons by the
Viennese police). From these few highlights, we see that, for St Nikodimos,
renewal of the life of the Church involved all its aspects, and included a
careful understanding of the liturgical texts, a deepened spiritual life involving practice of the Jesus Prayer, the restoration of the role of the spiritual
father and the practice of confession, return to frequent communion in the
holy gifts, and the re-establishment of the life of the Church on the canons
of the Synods and the Fathers. Although firmly based on Orthodox,
Byzantine sources, Nikodimos's attention was not confined to them: he
translated works of Western, Counter-Reformation spirituality, notably
Lorenzo Scupola's *Unseen Warfare*, and was interested in the scientific
developments of his day (Harvey's discovery of the circulation of blood,
for instance). For Nikodimos, theological renewal was part of a renewal
of the whole life of the Church, which had implications for how he understood theology: it was no merely academic accumulation of philosophical
and historical learning, nor simply a moral enterprise, but an engagement
with God himself, who has communicated himself to humankind through
the Incarnation and in the sacraments, a participation in the life of the
Trinity through prayer and ascetic struggle, leading to *theosis* or deification, as the very title page of the *Philokalia* makes clear, when it speaks
of the ways 'by which the *nous* [or intellect] is purified, illuminated and
perfected'. Of Nikodimos's works, the *Philokalia* has perhaps been the
most influential (though the influence of the *Pedalion* can scarcely be
underestimated). Although its influence has not been uniform, indeed it
has been rather patchy and inconsistent, it could be claimed that it is

the vision of the *Philokalia* that has come to inform all that is best in twentieth-century Orthodox theology.

The influence of the *Philokalia* was not, at first, felt in Greece – in the nineteenth century the Greeks were perhaps too occupied with securing their freedom from the Ottoman yoke – it was rather in the Slav lands that the seed first germinated. In 1793, only eleven years after the publication of the original Greek, a Slavonic translation was published by St Païssy Velichkovsky of most of the texts (the texts of Maximus the Confessor and Palamas being the most notable omissions). Païssy himself had been a monk on Mount Athos since 1746, but by the time the *Dobrotolyubie* (as the Slavonic translation was called) was published he had left the Holy Mountain for Moldavia. For Païssy, too, the *Dobrotolyubie* was part of a movement of renewal in monasticism, characterised by an emphasis on prayer and asceticism (including the practice of the Jesus Prayer), the monastic office and the institution of spiritual fatherhood, *starchestvo*. Païssy's influence spread throughout the Slav lands, and in Russia the Monastery of Optino, re-founded in 1800, just over 100 miles south-west of Moscow, became a spiritual centre and a place of pilgrimage for Russian intellectuals from the Slavophiles to Dostoevsky and Tolstoy. Encouraged by the Slavophile Ivan Kireevsky, the Monastery of Optino published translations of the Fathers, mostly spiritual authors of the 'Philokalic' tradition. For Kireevsky himself, the Fathers had a kind of originary significance; as he put it, 'The holy Fathers speak of a country they have been to'; in their writings the Fathers bear 'testimony as eyewitnesses'.[4]

It was not, however, simply the labours of those connected with Optino that made the works of the Fathers readily available in nineteenth-century Russia. In the theological academies, too, the works of the Fathers of the Church were translated into Russian. These combined endeavours meant that, as Olivier Clément has put it, 'at the end of the nineteenth century, Russia had at its disposal, in its own language, the best patristic library in Europe'.[5] Russia had distinguished patristic scholars, too: the church historian, Vladimir Bolotov, for instance, and, on the very threshold of the revolution, scholars such as Epifanovich and Dobroklonsky, whose work on Maximus the Confessor and Theodore the Stoudite, respectively, has been assimilated by scholarship only in recent years.

THE PATRISTIC REVIVAL OF THE TWENTIETH CENTURY

The 'patristic revival' of the twentieth century, therefore, was far from being the rediscovery of something completely lost, and the realisation of this must qualify the severity of Florovsky's judgements of those 'religious philosophers' whose works he so deplored: Soloviev, Florensky and Bulgakov. They were by no means ignorant of the Fathers, and, in particular, Bulgakov's patristic learning was impressive. Nevertheless, there was a genuine patristic revival in the twentieth century, though it was not a purely, or even mainly, Orthodox phenomenon. The Roman Catholic contribution was striking, perhaps as a result of the limitations placed on biblical scholarship and dogmatic theology by the anti-Modernist oath. Issued in 1910 and required of all Roman Catholic theologians, this denied the validity of modern critical thought, especially in relation to scripture. 'Patristics' seemed safe (though after the Second World War, de Lubac's articulation of his patristic perspective on grace led to his censure). The principal fruit of this revival was not so much translations of the Fathers as critical editions of their texts, and the consequent discovery or rediscovery of Fathers of the Church who had hitherto been overlooked or forgotten. This included both those whose reputation had been dubious, e.g., Evagrius or the author of the homilies ascribed to Macarius – both of enormous importance for the Orthodox/Byzantine tradition – and Fathers whose works were scarcely known in reliable editions, e.g. Symeon the New Theologian, Gregory Palamas, and even Maximus the Confessor. The quest for the 'Neo-patristic synthesis' in the years after the Second World War was fuelled by this wider movement of patristic renewal, which lent it an aura of excitement. In the post-war years, a symbol of this revival of patristic scholarship was the series of International Patristic Conferences held in Oxford every four years from 1951. These conferences were from the beginning ecumenical in character, and attracted Orthodox scholars, both academics and monks.

ORTHODOX – ROMAN CATHOLIC ENGAGEMENT

The seeds of this revival were sown in the period *entre deux guerres*. In Paris there were contacts between Catholic thinkers and the Russian émigrés, particularly through the so-called 'colloquium', hosted by Nicolas Berdyaev. Daniélou has spoken warmly of the influence on him of, first, the articles, and then the person, of Myrrha Lot-Borodine, the Russian émigrée who married the famous French medieval historian, Ferdinand Lot:

> What made the work of Myrrha Lot-Borodine of exceptional value was not simply her dedication to learned research, but that she had rediscovered the living expression of Byzantine mysticism and she

knew how to make it felt. Her work was nourished by her reading of the great spiritual authors and theologians of the Greek and Byzantine world. One found there echoes of Gregory and Evagrius, of Maximus the Confessor and Pseudo-Dionysius, of Symeon the New Theologian and Nicolas Cabasilas. She mentioned these authors often, but not by citing them. Her articles had the minimum of scholarly apparatus. That made them difficult to use. The boundaries between the experience of the author and that of her sources were difficult to trace.[6]

Much that was important to the Orthodox in the twentieth-century patristic revival was the result of collaboration between Orthodox and, especially, Catholic scholars. Daniélou speaks of the sense of inwardness to the Fathers that he found in Lot-Borodine. The Catholic contribution included making available texts of the Fathers that enabled the attainment of that inwardness, but these Catholic scholars also possessed an inwardness to their own tradition.

The early representatives of this Orthodox patristic revival were the three figures already mentioned: Florovsky, Lossky and the somewhat older Myrrha Lot-Borodine, who had been in Paris since 1906. Lot-Borodine was, like her husband, a specialist in the Latin Middle Ages (as was, professionally, Vladimir Lossky), especially courtly love and the legend of the Holy Grail (on which her only book was published, posthumously).[7] Her patristic scholarship took the form of articles, especially collections on deification (mostly published 1932–3)[8] and on Nicolas Cabasilas (published 1936–7),[9] both published in book form after her death, and a translation (again as a series of articles) of Maximus the Confessor's *Mystagogia*. It was spirituality, both liturgical and ascetic, that was at the heart of her patristic scholarship. As such, she anticipates the central concerns of the patristic revival, which we might also call 'Philokalic'.

FLOROVSKY

The notion of a 'Neo-patristic synthesis' has been especially associated with the name of Fr Georges Florovsky; but rarely, if ever, did he address directly the question of what such a Neo-patristic synthesis would entail.[10] After the Second World War, he moved to the United States and taught there at a succession of academic institutes, but he also became increasingly caught up in the ecumenical movement, which doubtless absorbed energies that might otherwise have been spent on clarifying, and expounding, his understanding of this synthesis. The bulk of his patristic output is to be found in the lectures he gave in Russian at the St Sergius Institute of Orthodox Theology in Paris in the 1930s and published privately.[11] They present the teaching of the (Greek and Byzantine) Fathers of the Church from the fourth to the eighth centuries in the manner of a textbook intended for students (which they were), supplemented by a further volume on the ascetic and spiritual Fathers. More light is perhaps shed in the various lectures and articles given and published in the 1950s and 1960s and collected in the first four volumes of his *Collected Works*. There he discusses issues such as the place of the Bible and tradition in theology, the doctrine of creation and the nature of evil, the relation of Church and state, Christianity and culture, eschatology and a host of more specific topics. There is a repeated emphasis on the doctrine of creation out of nothing as determining the discourse of theology, which is a dialectic of the uncreated God and the creature called into being from nothing by God, rather than a dialectic of nature and grace. The same emphasis takes another form in his insistence on the personal nature of God and therefore theology. God is a person, not a principle, and theology springs from a personal encounter with God. Both these themes are from time to time expressed in terms of the Palamite distinction between God's essence and his energies, the unknowability of God's essence a consequence of the ontological gulf between God and creation which results from the doctrine of creation out of nothing, while it is through the energies, which are God himself, that God encounters his creatures personally.

LOSSKY

A sharper sense of what the 'Neo-patristic' synthesis might amount to emerges from the slender patristic *œuvre* of Vladimir Lossky. He died young, in his mid-fifties, his massive work on Meister Eckhart, which he would have submitted for his *doctorat ès lettres*, being published posthumously.[12] His *Mystical Theology of the Eastern Church*, published in 1944 (when Lossky was barely thirty years old), has become for many virtually a handbook of the Neo-patristic synthesis. Lossky begins by tackling what he means by 'mystical theology' (though Lossky's term, 'la mystique', here translated 'mysticism', is not perhaps quite the same thing):

> The eastern tradition has never made a sharp distinction between mysticism and theology; between personal experience of the divine mysteries and the dogma affirmed by the Church ... To put it another way, we must live the dogma expressing a revealed truth, which

appears to us as an unfathomable mystery, in such a fashion that instead of assimilating the mystery to our mode of understanding, we should, on the contrary, look for a profound change, an inner transformation of the spirit, enabling us to experience it mystically . . . There is, therefore, no Christian mysticism without theology; but, above all, there is no theology without mysticism . . . Mysticism is accordingly treated in the present work as the perfecting and crown of all theology: as theology *par excellence.*[13]

Mysticism and theology relate as experience and theory. But experience of what? Ultimately of God, but that is not where Lossky begins: he begins by speaking of 'personal experience of the divine mysteries', the term 'mysteries' being precisely ambiguous, designating both the sacraments of the Church and also mysterious – that is, unfathomable – truths about the Godhead. That double meaning is no chance homonymity; the two meanings are closely related for Lossky, because the mysterious truths about God – his existence as a Trinity of love, his creation of the world, his care for the world and his redemption of it, preeminently in the Incarnation – are truths that we experience and celebrate in the divine mysteries, or sacraments, of the Church. This is what gives Lossky's presentation such a different orientation from what is normally associated with mysticism in the West: it is not detached from dogma, but rooted in the dogmatic truths of the Christian tradition; it is not indifferent to church organization, hierarchy and sacraments, but rooted in the structured life of the Church; it is not individualistic, but rooted in the experience of the eucharistic community.

There is much overlap between the concerns of Lossky and of Florovsky: they share an insistence that theology springs from an encounter with God, manifest in the Incarnation, found in the Church; they have in common a personalist emphasis (which they may owe to the Russian roots they affected to despise). But there are some profound differences, notably in connection with the immense stress Lossky lays on the 'apophatic' character of Orthodox theology (an emphasis that has since become all but universal among Orthodox theologians). 'Apophatic' and 'kataphatic' theology were terms introduced into Christian usage (from Neoplatonism) by the mysterious figure who wrote under the name of Dionysius the Areopagite, to mean the use of affirmation ('kataphasis') and negation ('apophasis') in assertions about God. He had a profound effect on Byzantine theology, and especially on Maximus the Confessor and Gregory Palamas. The demonstration at the turn of the twentieth century of the pseudonymity of the works ascribed to the Areopagite cast a shadow over his reputation, and some notable twentieth-century Orthodox theologians (Meyendorff, Schmemann) have sought to distance themselves from him. Not Lossky, however: he delighted in Dionysius's thought, and especially his sense of the apophatic dimension of theology. Lossky accused the West of misunderstanding Dionysius's apophatic theology by treating it as a corrective to kataphatic theology, rather than a more fundamental dimension of theology that actually undergirded kataphatic theology. Furthermore, for Lossky apophatic theology was not in the least confined to a question of logic ('apophatic predication'). The use of negation disclosed the unfathomable nature of God, before which the human person stood in awe, and found his own self-understanding interrogated and called to repentance, *metanoia*. As Lossky put it in a famous passage:

> apophaticism, so far from being a limitation, enables us to transcend all concepts, every sphere of philosophical speculation. It is a tendency towards an ever-greater plenitude, in which knowledge is transformed into ignorance, the theology of concepts into contemplation, dogmas into experience of ineffable mysteries. It is, moreover, an existential theology involving man's entire being, which sets him upon the way of union, which obliges him to be changed, to transform his nature that he may attain to the true *gnosis* which is the contemplation of the Holy Trinity. Now, this 'change of heart', this *metanoia*, means repentance. The apophatic way of eastern theology is the repentance of the human person before the face of the living God.[14]

STĂNILOAE

Another major figure who must be mentioned in connection with the 'Neo-patristic synthesis' is the Romanian theologian Fr Dumitru Stăniloae. Born in 1903, he died in his ninetieth year in 1993. As a young man, he studied in Paris, working on the manuscripts of St Gregory Palamas, on whom he wrote a doctorate which was published in 1938. Stăniloae was, then, in the very vanguard of the twentieth-century discovery of Palamas. He spent the rest of his life in Romania, teaching first at Sibiu in Transylvania, and then at Bucharest from 1947 until his retirement, save for the years he spent in prison and concentration camp under the Communists. He was enormously prolific as a writer and translator. Perhaps the most important of his translations was his Romanian version of the *Philokalia*, which he expanded and complemented with commentaries. He thus made available in Romanian a vast library of the

'philokalic' Fathers, presented in such a way that the division between dogmatic theology and spirituality was transcended. His own writings were
voluminous, ranging from short popular articles to major theological
works. Amongst the latter, most important were his three-volume *Teologia dogmatică ortodoxă*[15] and his *Spiritualitatea ortodoxă ascetică şi
mistică.*[16] From these volumes one can discern the lineaments of a veritable 'Neo-patristic synthesis', developing over the whole canvas of dogmatic
and spiritual theology (never allowed to be divorced), a vision very much in
the line of Vladimir Lossky. Dionysius the Areopagite, Maximus the Confessor and Gregory Palamas are, as in the case of Lossky, the peaks of Stăniloae's patristic landscape – Maximus, perhaps, being the one closest to
his heart. His theology is personalist and apophatic, though he distinguishes his interpretation of the apophatic from Lossky's, seeing the
apophatic in the tacit dimension of experience, beyond expression
(which is perhaps not that far from Lossky's seeing the apophatic as fundamentally *metanoia*). What is particularly distinctive of Stăniloae's theology is its cosmic dimension, which he thinks through especially in
dialogue with Maximus. Taking the patristic notion of the human as
microcosm, Stăniloae turns it on its head and asserts that the cosmos is
a 'macranthropos' – the human writ large – for the cosmos is understood
from the perspective of the human and not vice versa. On this basis he
develops a far-reaching understanding of the human responsibility for
the cosmos. The Cross, too, is central to his vision: the created order is
God's gift, inscribed with his Cross, for it is through an asceticism of self-
denial that we can properly receive God's gift. He also develops Maximus's
notion of the *logoi* (principles, meanings) of creation, all united in the one
Logos of God, made known to us on the Cross as sacrificial love.

THE PLACE OF SCHOLARSHIP

There are other ways of perceiving the patristic revival in modern
Orthodox theology. The scholarly revival in patristics in the twentieth
century enabled Orthodox theologians to read Fathers whose works had
been hitherto either inaccessible, or accessible in unsatisfactory ways.
This is perhaps particularly true of ascetic theologians like Evagrius and
the author of the Macarian Homilies ('pseudo-Macarius' or, for a time,
'Symeon'), Barsanuphius and John of Gaza, Symeon the New Theologian
and even the Desert Fathers, but it is also true of 'dogmatic' theologians
such as Gregory of Nyssa, Maximus the Confessor, John of Damascus,
Gregory Palamas and, in rather a different way, Dionysius the Areopagite.
In all these cases there have been major editions of their works that either

have revealed texts hitherto unknown, or not associated with their real authors, or have presented a much more authentic text than had been known until then – a text that has often opened our eyes to a fresh under-standing of the authors, or completely revised our appreciation of them. Texts of Evagrius, for instance, hitherto preserved under a pseudonym or in translation (in this case into Syriac, mostly), have enabled us to grasp something of the real importance of this remarkable monk, disciple at once of the Cappadocians and of the great Macarius of Egypt. A similar revolution has occurred in our understanding of the author of the Macarian Homilies. Symeon the New Theologian, Maximus the Confessor, John of Damascus, Gregory Palamas: all these are now better and more accurately known than ever before. John Meyendorff opened up the study of St Gregory Palamas in his edition of the *Triads*[17] and in his monograph.[18] This has been followed on two fronts: on the one hand, further mono-graphs, mostly by Orthodox, deepening our understanding of Palamas, and, on the other, editions, largely by Western scholars, of other protago-nists in the hesychast debate, which reveal further perspectives on the con-troversy. The rediscovery of St Maximus the Confessor is a remarkable story of ecumenical collaboration, initiated by Catholic scholars like Hans Urs von Balthasar and Polycarp Sherwood, continued by the Lutheran scholar Lars Thunberg, and later the Orthodox scholar Jean-Claude Larchet – culminating in a critical edition of his works, edited entirely by Western scholars (though the first critical edition of the *Dialogue with Pyrrhos* is the work of Russian scholars).[19]

WIDER INFLUENCE OF THE PATRISTIC REVIVAL

There are other ways of seeing how Orthodox Christians have drawn on the Fathers as they have sought to articulate their vision in a rapidly changing world. One important area is that of spirituality: the vision of the Fathers, their quiet confidence in God's creation and providence, and their wholeness, inform attempts to develop a spirituality that would heal the anxieties and divisions of the modern secularist and consumerist West. Bishop (now Metropolitan) Kallistos has been especially associated with this dimension of the 'Neo-patristic synthesis'; he and others have pursued this in relation to modern ecological questions (e.g. the various initiatives of the current Ecumenical Patriarch, and the writings of Metropolitan John of Pergamon, John Chryssavgis, Elizabeth Theokritoff and others). In this connection, too, we find something deeper: no mere patristic revival or survival, but a veritable continuation of the patristic tradition, mediated largely through the monastic liturgical office, in the teaching of monastic spiritual Fathers, such as Elder Cleopa of Sihăstria (Romania) or St Silouan of Athos.

Other examples can be found in Orthodox reflection on ecclesiology in the twentieth century. In the diaspora, Orthodox theologians (Russians, especially, to begin with) found the question of ecclesiology particularly pressing. For centuries, Orthodox had lived with a Byzantine ('Justinianic') understanding of the relationship between Church and state as being characterised by *symphonia*. Even under the Ottomans, this understanding was only modified (though 'distorted' might be a better word). With the experience of diaspora, and also of atheist Communism, such an ecclesiology became untenable. Orthodox theologians looked back, behind the 'Constantinian revolution', and found in St Ignatius of Antioch, who died a martyr in the Flavian Amphitheatre under the Emperor Trajan, the outlines of a 'eucharistic ecclesiology', according to which the Church, gathered together under the presidency of the bishop, is constituted by the eucharistic celebration. 'The Eucharist makes the Church': this understanding of the Church made sense of church as it then (and now) existed – a gathered community, not the religious dimension of a political entity. The first to sketch out such a eucharistic ecclesiology was Fr Nicolas Afanasiev, one of the professors at the St Sergius Institute in Paris. His insights were developed in the fifties and sixties by the Greek theologians, Fr John Romanides and Metropolitan John Zizioulas. The idea of the Church as rooted in the Eucharist was developed in a different way, drawing its inspiration from the patristic understanding of the Divine Liturgy by Fr Alexander Schmemann, Dean of St Vladimir's Orthodox Seminary until his death in 1983.

THE PATRISTIC REVIVAL AND PHILOSOPHY

The patristic revival is also manifest in renewed philosophical reflection on human existence and the meaning of life. This is not at all restricted to the Orthodox world: a good example of a modern philosopher drawing inspiration from the Fathers may be found in the modern French philosopher, Jean-Luc Marion.[20] But Orthodox examples may be found in Greek philosophers such as Stelios Ramfos and Christos Yannaras, and in a rather different way in the Russian Sergei Averintsev (†2003).[21] Ramfos draws his inspiration for a series of reflections on the nature of human existence from the sayings of the Desert Fathers,[22] while Yannaras's philosophical pilgrimage has been deeply marked by his reading of the Fathers. In his early book, *Heidegger and the Areopagite: On the Absence and Unknowability of God*, Yannaras found in Dionysius the Areopagite's apophaticism a fundamental rejection of the 'ontotheology' that Heidegger had argued was central to the understanding of God in the Western metaphysical tradition – a tradition that had finally lost credibility, leading to Nietzsche's claim that 'God is dead' and the inexorable descent of the Western philosophical tradition into nihilism. In that book are found the beginnings of what Yannaras would later call (especially in his major work, *Person and Eros*) an 'apophaticism of the person', according to which knowledge of persons is inexhaustible, incapable of being captured in concepts and categories (and in that sense 'apophatic'), and only found in ecstatic encounter with another in the ecstasy of *eros*.[23] As Yannaras developed these ideas, he drew on the way Maximus articulated the distinction canonised at Chalcedon between person (or *hypostasis*) and nature in terms of the mode of existence (*tropos tēs hyparxeōs*) expressing the person and the essential definition (*logos tēs ousias*) of the nature. Furthermore, Yannaras correlates this distinction to the Palamite distinction between essence and energies: the essence corresponding to the essential definition and energies to the personal mode of existence. He thus draws a contrast between conceptual knowledge of natures and knowledge of persons by participation, which he illustrates from the experience of listening to music:

> Listening to a piece of music, for example, we come to know one of the creative – poetic – capacities or energies of human kind, of the human essence or nature. However, only by listening to music of Mozart (only by *participating* in his musical creation) can we distinguish his personal expression (his otherness in act) from the music of Bach or Beethoven.[24]

In his reading of the Fathers, Yannaras has been criticised for reading back into their writings ideas that developed much later, not least the modern notion of personhood. Nonetheless, in this creative use of the Fathers, Yannaras exemplifies the way in which the patristic revival may go beyond a merely academic *ressourcement* to a rediscovery of the patristic *phronema*, 'cast of mind', which draws on the richness of their wisdom and tackles the problems of existence that are pressing on us today. In seeking to realise this, the patristic revival becomes more than a fashion characterising a particular period of Orthodox history, and reveals itself as an enduring relevant principle of renewal.

Further reading

Blane, A. (ed.), *Georges Florovsky: Russian Intellectual, Orthodox Churchman*, Crestwood, NY: SVS Press, 1993.

Cavarnos, C., *St Nikodemos the Hagiorite* (Modern Orthodox Saints 5), Belmont, MA: Institute for Byzantine and Modern Greek Studies, 1974.

Clément, O., *The Roots of Christian Mysticism*, London: New City, 1993.

Felmy, K. C., *Orthodoxe Theologie: Eine Einführung*, Darmstadt: Wissenschaftliche Buchgesellschaft, 1990.

Jakim, B. and Bird, R. (trans. and eds.), *On Spiritual Unity. A Slavophile Reader*, Hudson, NY: Lindisfarne Books, 1998.

Lossky, V., *The Mystical Theology of the Eastern Church*, London: James Clarke & Co., 1957; repr. Crestwood, NY: SVS Press, 1998. (Trans. of *Essai sur la théologie mystique de l'Eglise d'Orient*, Aubier: Editions Montaigne, 1944.)

Turcescu, L. (ed.), *Dumitru Stăniloae. Tradition and Modernity in Theology*, Iasi: Center for Romanian Studies, 2002.

Notes

1. G. Florovsky, *Collected Works of Church History*, vol. VI: *Ways of Russian Theology*, vol. II (Vaduz: Büchervertriebsanstalt, 1987), p. 294.
2. Florovsky, *Collected Works*, II, p. 297.
3. Florovsky, *Collected Works*, II, p. 308 (the translation there is lacunose and otherwise faulty, so I have modified it by reference to the Russian text: G. Florovsky, *Puti Russkogo Bogosloviya* (Paris: YMCA Press, 1981; repr. of 1937), p. 520).
4. From Kireevsky's 'Fragments': translation in B. Jakim and R. Bird (trans. and eds.), *On Spiritual Unity. A Slavophile Reader* (Hudson, NY: Lindisfarne Books, 1998), pp. 248, 243.
5. O. Clément, 'Les Pères de l'Église dans l'Église orthodoxe', *Connaissance des Pères de l'Église* 52 (December 1993), 25–6, quoted by Boris Bobrinskoy in 'Le renouveau actuel de la patristique dans l'orthodoxie' in *Les Pères de l'Église au XXe siècle. Histoire – littérature – théologie* (Paris: Cerf, 1997), 437–44, here 440 (though England, as a result of the endeavours of the Fathers of the Oxford Movement, must have run Russia a close second).
6. Jean Daniélou in his introduction to M. Lot-Borodine, *La déification de l'homme selon la doctrine des Pères grecs* (Paris: Cerf, 1970), p. 11.
7. M. Lot-Borodine, *De l'amour profane à l'amour sacré. Études de psychologie sentimentale au Moyen Âge* (Paris: Librairie Nizet, 1961).
8. Lot-Borodine, *La déification de l'homme selon la doctrine des Pères grecs* (Paris: Cerf, 1970).
9. M. Lot-Borodine, *Un maître de la spiritualité byzantine au XIVe siècle: Nicolas Cabasilas* (Paris: Éditions de l'Orante, 1958).
10. For this question, see G. H. Williams, 'The Neo-patristic synthesis of Georges Florovsky' in A. Blane (ed.), *Georges Florovsky: Russian Intellectual, Orthodox Churchman* (Crestwood, NY: SVS Press, 1993), pp. 287–340.

11. They are published in English translation as vols. VII–X of Florovsky's *Collected Works*.

12. V. Lossky, *Théologie négative et connaissance de Dieu chez Maître Eckhart* (Paris: Vrin, 1960).

13. V. Lossky, *The Mystical Theology of the Eastern Church* (Cambridge and London: James Clarke, 1957), pp. 8–9.

14. Lossky, *Mystical Theology*, p. 238 (*Essai*, p. 237).

15. D. Stăniloae, *Teologia dogmatică ortodoxă*, 3 vols. (Bucharest: Editura Institutului Biblic şi Misiune al Bisericii Ortodoxe Române, 2nd edn, 1996–7; 1st edn, 1978); German translation (3 vols., Zurich: Benziger Verlag / Gütersloh: Gerd Mohn, 1985–95); English translation of vol. I, only: *The Experience of God. Orthodox Dogmatic Theology*, 2 vols., trans. I. Ionita and R. Barringer (Brookline, MA: Holy Cross Orthodox Press, 1994–2000).

16. D. Stăniloae, *Spiritualitatea ortodoxă ascetică şi mistică* (Bucharest: Editura Institutului Biblic şi Misiune al Bisericii Ortodoxe Române, 1992; originally published as *Teologia morală ortodoxă*, vol. III: *Spiritualitatea ortodoxă* in 1981); English translation, *Orthodox Spirituality. A Practical Guide for the Faithful and a Definitive Manual for the Scholar* (South Canaan, PA: St Tikhon's Seminary Press, 2002).

17. G. Palamas, *Défense des saints hésychastes*, 2 vols., trans. and ed. J. Meyendorff (Louvain: Spicilegium Sacrum Lovaniense, 2nd revised edn, 1973; originally published 1959).

18. Jean Meyendorff, *Introduction à l'étude de Grégoire Palamas* (Paris: Éditions du Seuil, 1959); abridged English translation (London: The Faith Press, 1964).

19. *Disput c Pirrom* (Moscow: Khram Sofii Premudrosti Bozhiei, 2004).

20. Perhaps most obviously in his *L'idole et la distance* (Paris: Grasset, 1977).

21. Little of the work of Averintsev – a polymath best known perhaps as a Byzantinist – is available in translation in any Western language. For an introduction, with a select bibliography, see Constantin Sigov, 'L'Esprit et le Verbe dans l'œuvre de Serge Averintsev', *Contacts* 57 (2005), 36–50.

22. Stelios Ramfos, *Like a Pelican in the Wilderness* (Brookline, MA: Holy Cross Orthodox Press, 2000), an abridged translation by Norman Russell of *Pelekanoi Eremikoi* (Athens: Ekdoseis Armos, 1994).

23. Christos Yannaras, *To Prosopo kai o eros* (Athens: Domos, repr. of 4th edn, 1992; first edn, 1970), esp. pp. 38–42.

24. Christos Yannaras, *On the Absence and Unknowability of God: Heidegger and the Areopagite* (London: T. & T. Clark, 2005), p. 84. Cf. Yannaras, *To Prosopo kai o eros*, pp. 88, 94, 158.

13 The Russian religious revival and its theological legacy

MICHAEL PLEKON

Over forty years ago Nicolas Zernov, himself a product of the religious revival of the Russian emigration, produced a still important overview of its personalities and accomplishments. He called it a 'renaissance', and this it truly was – a wave that rose and broke over several generations, bringing theological creativity of diverse kinds, liturgical renewal and a profound rediscovery of the Church and Christian life. Yet this renaissance was anything but a purely internal event, for it was expressed in the desire to be engaged with the culture and society of the time, and in the commitment to seek for unity in the Church. The Russians' discovery of so many other brothers and sisters in the Lord from the Western Churches was one of the main impulses for this ecumenical dimension.

It has been customary to connect the work of the thinkers of this renewal with their enforced flight from the Russian revolution and their subsequent encounter with the Catholic and Protestant clergy and laity who welcomed them. However, this overlooks the reality that many were already producing a renewal of religious thought and churchly practice before the revolution. In the nineteenth century, thinkers such as Khomiakov, Metropolitan St Filaret (Drozhdov) of Moscow, Soloviev and Bukharev had begun to write about the conciliar or 'sobornal' nature of the Church, to probe the meaning of God's presence in the world in the Incarnation – the 'humanity of God' (*Bogochelovechestvo*) and to argue for dialogue between the Church and modern culture. The ferment for renewal and reform in official church circles began in 1905 with the solicitation of the hierarchy's assessment of the state of the Church, and culminated in the Moscow council of 1917–18, a monumental attempt to renew the Church's life. Some of the council's reform proposals were implemented in other countries of the Russian emigration. However, due to the violence of the revolution and the destruction of so much of the Church, these initiatives were never put into practice in Russia itself.

With support from the American YMCA and the Church of England, the émigrés were able to establish the first Orthodox theological school in Western Europe, the St Sergius Institute of Orthodox Theology in Paris. There, they were also able to set up the YMCA Press, still in operation, for publication of the writings of the St Sergius faculty and other thinkers. The journal *Put'* ('The Way') was founded, under the editorship of Nicolas Berdiaev, for the exchange of ideas, along with several other periodicals such as *Novy Grad* ('The New City') and the *Vestnik* ('Messenger') of the Russian Student Christian Movement, also assisted by the YMCA. A ground-breaking ecumenical group was established in England, called the Fellowship of St Alban and St Sergius, and it became, along with its *Journal* (later renamed *Sobornost*), one of the most important forums for theological exchange.

Looked at historically, the meeting up of the émigrés with their Western confrères should be seen as part of the *ressourcement*, the 'return to the sources' of the scriptures, liturgy, and the writings of the Fathers that was developing in the years between the two world wars and which came to fruition in the 1950s and in the Second Vatican Council. 'Reassessment of tradition' is also an accurate description of the work of the theologians of the Russian renaissance and it underscores the ecumenical efforts in such areas as the rediscovery of the people of God and the priesthood of all the baptised, the rediscovery of the eucharistic ecclesiology of the early Church in the work of Nicolas Afanasiev, and the renewal of eucharistic liturgy and life by his protégé, Alexander Schmemann. Others who were close to Bulgakov, including Lev Gillet, Paul Evdokimov, Mother Maria Skobtsova and Elisabeth Behr-Sigel, also contributed. The most significant contributions can be gathered into several themes which in reality are seamless – interconnected in the intentions of the writers and overlapping in practice.

DIALOGUE AND ACTION IN THE MODERN WORLD

Without a doubt, the most creative and important of the theologians of the renewal is Fr Sergius Bulgakov (1871–1944). John Milbank calls him one of the twentieth century's most creative theologians.[1] Bulgakov's project, like those of Soloviev and Bukharev before him, was the encounter between the Church's tradition and the consciousness of modernity; and his training in the social sciences shaped his theological thinking for such dialogue. The central intention of his efforts was to probe the many consequences of the Incarnation, as expressed in the christological dogma of Chalcedon, both for humankind and for God himself. Since

Christ has entered time and space, we then experience in him the 'humanity of God' and nothing ever can be the same after this. Bulgakov felt that there was much to be said in positive terms about the consequences of the Incarnation beyond the Chalcedonian definition of Christ as God and human 'without confusion, without change, without division, without separation'.

Bulgakov's exploration of the 'humanity of God' thus took him in many directions. Throughout his writings, he tracked the presence of God in creation and in the Church, both of the Old and New Covenants. In his smaller trilogy he examined the significance of the angels, the Mother of God, and John the Baptist. For Bulgakov, it was the Church that opened the way for dialogue with the world, with politics, culture, philosophy, the arts and, in particular, with other Christians long divided. In his contemplation of the Church, in the liturgy and in history and beyond it in the heavenly Kingdom, the New Jerusalem, Bulgakov set the stage for his colleagues Afanasiev and Florovsky, and later Schmemann and Meyendorff, to extend and deepen this rediscovery of the Church. For Bulgakov, the Church began even before creation and extended into the eschatological realm which was the subject of his last writings, *The Bride of the Lamb* and *The Apocalypse*. Bulgakov saw salvation history in sum as the 'churching' (*votserkovlenlie*) of the cosmos, and in this he was in company with many others who passionately wanted to restore the Church to the centre of life, from the compartments such as the 'rites of passage' to which Russian custom and cultural rejection had exiled it. In thinking through the way the mysteries of death and resurrection had been ritualised as well as imprisoned in scholastic theology, Bulgakov revisited the thinking of Gregory of Nyssa, Origen and others in affirming the impossibility of anything but the total triumph of Christ, in his resurrection, over the Devil and the kingdom of death and hell. Hence his proposition, in hope and prayer, of the resurrection of all.[2] But here in this life, he celebrated the Eucharist as the continuing action of the Incarnation, with the Church as the 'perpetual Pentecost', the outpouring of the Spirit on all to bring all back into union with God. He raised the issue of the freedom of God reflected in human freedom and action, the relationship between Creator and creature being a consistent theme in his theological reflection.

What is striking, despite the density of Bulgakov's prose and conceptual inconsistencies from one book to the other, is how these themes are indeed connected: all are brought back to their root in the abyss of the Father's love, the sacrificial death of the Lamb of God from before the world's beginning and the continual descent of the Holy Spirit upon the Church, which is the Bride of the Lamb, and upon all of creation. The cosmic meaning and expanse of the Incarnation is a consistently recurring theme in Bulgakov's thinking. As in the anamnesis or 'commemoration' prayer in the Eastern liturgy, Bulgakov saw all the salvific actions: the Cross, the tomb, the resurrection, the second coming as well as Pentecost – not as events of the historical past, but real and efficacious in the present. Most controversial in his lifetime – in fact the object of accusations of heresy, and exoneration by a panel of his peers – was his constant appeal to the biblical figure of Wisdom/Sophia as the presence of God in the world in both created and uncreated forms.

Bulgakov's ecclesiological and eschatological vision led him to his contention that, despite all the centuries of division and the accompanying mistrust, God had been gracious enough to keep strong bonds of unity among Christians. He argued this in conversations and as part of ongoing study in the Fellowship of St Alban and St Sergius – which he had helped found – particularly in the essay, 'By Jacob's well'. His contribution to the important anthology *Zhivoe predanie* ('Living tradition') was his discerning claim that theological reflection and expression, to be faithful to the tradition and the Fathers, had to be as open and creative as they had been for the great teachers of earlier centuries. This was the challenge Bulgakov issued in 'Dogma and dogmatics', and like his challenge concerning the continuing unity in the Churches, it was largely ignored or rejected at that time by the Russian Church Abroad and the Roman Catholics, among others. He could see only sectarian ignorance in the condemnation of others who confess Christ as Lord. The saints, he believed, saw beyond the walls of division and dwelt in communion with each other in the Kingdom of heaven. The real presence of that Kingdom here and now was Fr. Sergius's great eschatological realisation and contribution, a vision that would transform Orthodox theology and churchly life.

REDISCOVERY OF THE CHURCH AND LITURGY AND THE 'CHURCHING' OF THE WORLD

In addition to Bulgakov, there were others concerned for ecclesiology, given the experience of ecumenical work and the jurisdictional divisions that emerged among the émigrés. Nicolas Afanasiev (1893–1966), according to Alexander Schmemann, was marked by a 'hidden fire, a consuming love for the Church'. In his work many of Bulgakov's themes are taken further, often into more specific and practical applications. Afanasiev was the only Orthodox theologian explicitly cited in the preconciliar *acta* of Vatican II, and though his name is not always remembered, his rediscovery has helped to reshape how many Christians think about the Church. His major work, *The Church of the Holy Spirit*,[3] paints in careful historical strokes the early Church's charismatic love from which later clericalism and legalism have distanced us. The early Church's community recognised the dignity of each Christian as a priest, prophet and king through baptism. The Church's very structure then was (and should be, Afanasiev argued) one of mutuality, of love incarnate in service, the rule of love not of law. At the same time, he also stressed the sociological and theological importance of every community as a 'local Church'. Contrary to charges of 'congregationalism', Afanasiev never pitted the local Church against the whole Church of God in Christ or the regional communions of Churches in a particular province or nation.[4] Every assembly that gathers around the Eucharist and lives that liturgy thereafter is the Church in all its fullness. The local Church, however, cannot authentically experience this unless in full communion with the rest of the Churches.

From just these ecclesiological realisations, Afanasiev achieved a radical sense of what it would take to heal the divisions of the Churches. Like Bulgakov and others in the Fellowship studies and debates of the 1930s, Afanasiev retrieved the Church's historical determination to be one again in the eucharistic bread and cup and in all the faith, prayer and work this presupposes, the pattern of healing used by Polycarp and Anicetus and others in ancient days. Afanasiev's studies of the councils and their canons confirmed his insistence that these canons can never be unchangeable. The Church is living, the bearer of a 'living tradition' of Christ and the gospel. Afanasiev also examined the ways in which the celebration of the liturgy drifted from the communal participation of the early centuries into individual piety, legalistic patterns and pious custom. Seen as a whole, his efforts affirmed the vision of Bulgakov, that of the Church transforming the world and making present the Kingdom; it set the direction for Schmemann's 'liturgical theology', as well as Meyendorff's approach to the Church in the world. What is more, the 'eucharistic ecclesiology' which Afanasiev excavated is a powerful indictment of the ecclesiological chaos into which international Orthodoxy has descended since the last years of the twentieth century.[5] The rise once more of Church–state alliances; of appeals to Churches of a particular national or ethnic tradition to unite solely on that basis; the resurgence of a clericalism, centred in the hierarchy, that threatens to obliterate all the concilar or sobornal aspects of church structure; the rejection of liturgical renewal; the abandonment of ecumenical dialogue and work as 'heretical', and the subsequent retreat into sectarian behaviour – these are but a few of the prevalent trends to which Afanasiev's vision (and that of the rest of the revival's thinkers) offer substantial theological challenges.

THE RECOVERY OF THE SOBORNAL/COMMUNAL AND EUCHARISTIC CHARACTER OF CHRISTIANITY: 'FOR THE LIFE OF THE WORLD'

For decades, Fr Alexander Schmemann (1921–83) was the face and voice of Orthodox Christianity in North America. A student of Bulgakov at the St Sergius Institute, a protégé of Afanasiev, he became in America a seminary dean, advisor to bishops, scholar, teacher and spokesman for the Orthodox Church. He single-handedly led an unparalleled liturgical and ecclesial renewal that reached far beyond Orthodox borders. Because of his work, today the prayers of the liturgy are read aloud and in the language of the people. The faithful can join in the liturgy and receive communion regularly as Christians had done centuries earlier. The services of Lent, Holy Week, Easter and the other great feasts have been revived, along with the communal celebration of baptism. Schmemann built on Afanasiev's teachings so as to help make clear the ecclesiological dimensions of liturgical celebration once again.

With Schmemann there was far more, though, than performative change; there was an entirely different approach to liturgy as the *theologia prima*. Worship is not just the locus of symbolism and rubrics but the very source of theology. And it is through this enactment in liturgy, in the 'corporate action' of the Church, that theology thereafter becomes mission in the lives of Christians. Schmemann stressed above all the eschatological sense of the Kingdom that is present in the living Church; this was a vision that he had inherited from Bulgakov. His sense of the Church's eucharistic and conciliar/sobornal character compelled him to pursue the question of the role of the Church in American life. His writing and lecturing bore fruit in the establishment of an autocephalous, truly 'local church' in America; not an ethnic club, or a poor imitation of Byzantium or 'holy Russia'. Schmemann's love for literature, his insistence that great writers expressed theology better than the academic texts, was manifest over and over again in his eloquent essays, books and talks. In the now classic *For the Life of the World*,[6] he drew readers away from liturgy as rule-dominated and obligatory, revealing the sacramental nature of all of Christian life and liturgy as a living relationship with God and his kingdom. In addition to his mentor Afanasiev's eucharistic ecclesiology, Schmemann emphasised the baptismal dimension of the church.

He stressed, as did Afanasiev, the priesthood of all the baptised and the vocation of all to mission in the world.

NEW COMMITMENT TO VARIETIES OF CHRISTIAN SERVICE AND WITNESS IN THE MODERN WORLD

For others too, the rediscovery of the Church and the renewal of the liturgy did not remain internal events but produced a new commitment to mission, that is, to Christian witness and service in society. Two other students of Bulgakov furthered his sense of the life of the Church as grounded in the Incarnation and the Spirit's continual Pentecost. Lay theologian Paul Evdokimov (1900–70) and the social activist nun Maria Skobtsova (1891–1945) both wrote about the relationship of the Church to the world and put into practice what they wrote. They showed how the 'liturgy outside the church' is celebrated, the 'sacrament of the brother/sister', that is, loving service of the neighbour. Their fidelity to church tradition and creative implementation of it show us much about how the gospel is to be lived out in the world of our time.

Evdokimov did not immediately enter academic life upon completing graduate study. After work with the Resistance during the Nazi occupation of France, for over two decades he directed hostels for the displaced, the homeless, and for third-world students. His theology was thus rooted both in the Church's tradition and in the everyday life of the modern world, and most particularly in the Church's outreach to those in desperate need. Evdokimov took his original interest in the theology of writers such as Dostoevsky and Gogol in a number of directions. His writing ranges over such areas as iconography, prayer, the spiritual life, liturgy, the place of the Mother of God and the Holy Spirit in the economy of salvation, and the Church's social programme. Yet central to it all is God's kenotic, even 'absurd love' for us (*l'amour fou / eros manikos*), as Cabasilas called it.[7] Like his contemporary, Maria Skobtsova, he did not just launch projects for social assistance but explored the basis for diaconal work from the early Church onward, in the examples of Fathers and monastic leaders such as Basil the Great, Benedict, Sergius of Radonezh, Joseph of Volokolamsk, and others such as Juliana Lazarevskaya the Merciful and the Grand Duchess Elizabeth Feodorovna.[8]

Because of his consistent, deliberate reliance on scripture in his theology, Evdokimov was called 'our Protestant Orthodox' by Vladimir Lossky. While the Orthodox tradition was dear to him, Evdokimov constantly led his readers back to the great tradition of the undivided Church in which it was rooted, a vision that he worked and prayed for – the healing of the divisions among the Churches. Evdokimov wrote what remains one of the best surveys of contemporary Russian theology. His historical analysis of the spiritual life is unmatched in its discernment of the patterns of holiness in the past and the more diverse, ordinary ones of the present. Taking a phrase from the spiritual writer of the nineteenth century, Tikhon of Zadonsk, he argued that every form of Christian life was a kind of 'interiorized monasticism'. Again, like Maria Skobtsova and Lev Gillet, he saw the diversity and development of spiritual practices in the past as the precedent for adaptation, for creativity in the present. Evdokimov suggested that Christians of the present era could fast from conspicuous and thoughtless consumption, as well as from addiction to work and entertainment. In his study of the social theology of the Church, he proposed redistribution of global income as a contemporary form of asceticism, in the spirit of the desert Fathers and Mothers, fully consonant with the radical political criticism of Fathers such as John Chrysostom.

Evdokimov's study of marriage shows that, in the view of the Eastern Church, there is no question of opposing a 'higher' vocation to a 'lower' one. Both monastic and married life are paths of living out the gospel. There is no end to the diversity of vocations, of forms that the Christian life might take in our time. As much as he spoke for the dynamic and open Christian life in the world, Evdokimov was also one of the finest interpreters of the riches of Christian tradition, the liturgy, iconography, spirituality and, above all, the word of God.

Evdokimov's colleague in Paris, similarly dedicated to *diakonia* ('service'), Mother Maria Skobtsova, was made a saint in May 2004 along with her son Yuri, the chaplain of her hostel, Fr Dimitri Klepinine, and their treasurer, Ilya Fundaminsky. A child prodigy, a gifted young poet, essayist and social activist, Mother Maria had a life that encompassed much of the tumult of the early twentieth century. Almost executed by both the Bolsheviks and the White Army, she was Russia's first woman mayor and was among the first women to attend lectures at the St Petersburg Theological Academy. Twice married and divorced, she was professed into monastic life by Metropolitan Evlogy, with the admonition that 'the whole world will be your monastery'. She established hostels in Paris for the homeless and sick, as well as a nursing home for the elderly in the suburbs. She took time from church services to rummage for food at the municipal market as well as to visit cafés in the evening, urging the homeless to come to the hostels. But whatever creativity she demonstrated in her monastic life, this paled in comparison with the rich, dynamic intellectual existence that she maintained in addition to administering the hostels.

Mother Maria's essays provide some of her most rigorous thinking about God's action for us and our response, avenues for exploration that she took from her teacher and spiritual father, Sergius Bulgakov. She explored the model of the Mother of God's discipleship and further probed the 'motherhood of God' (*Bogmaterintsvo*), God's radical self-giving and forgiving.[9] She challenged the traditionalism of Orthodox Christianity, especially with respect to monasticism and liturgical services, as well as the association of the Church with middle-class values and lifestyle. Her essay 'Types of religious lives' is still provocative after seventy years, with its discerning description and sharp criticism of what she viewed as the frequently empty piety of some contemporary Christians. In this same essay she also sketches out the radical discipleship she finds in the gospels and makes the strong connection, as did Evdokimov, between the liturgy and service of the neighbour.

An intellectual circle met each Sunday at Mother Maria's hostel, consisting of the board of her supporting agency: Berdiaev, Bulgakov, Mochulsky, Fedotov and Zenkovsky, among others. Mother Maria produced for their gatherings (as well as for the journal *Put'* and other publications) some very challenging ideas about how the 'liturgy outside the church' is a test of the authenticity of that celebrated within. What she wrote about was ultimately validated by the fate that she and her companions shared in the killing machine of the Third Reich.

A NEW VISION OF HOLINESS, OF CHRISTIAN LIFE IN THE MODERN WORLD

One of the last living links to the theological figures of the Russian religious renaissance described here was Elisabeth Behr-Sigel (1907–2005). Sergius Bulgakov was her first spiritual father, while Lev Gillet received her into the Orthodox Church and presided at her wedding. She was a life-long friend of both, as well as of Paul Evdokimov; as a young woman in Paris, she knew and assisted Maria Skobtsova. In the early 1950s, hers was the first effort by a Westerner to describe and assess the Russian Church's history of spirituality. She repeatedly stressed the linkage of prayer and liturgy to life, tracing this, much like Mother Maria Skobtsova and Paul Evdokimov, in the lives and examples of saints like Sergius of Radonezh and Seraphim of Sarov. She emphasised the use of the Jesus Prayer as a concrete example of this linkage, and further stressed the place of honour given to the scriptures and *lectio divina*, their prayerful reading. She lectured and wrote extensively on the place of women in the life and ministries of the Church. She called for the restoration of women deacons and further challenged the theological arguments for denying priestly ordination to women. In time Bishop Kallistos (Ware) came to agree with her that much of the contemporary Orthodox argument against the ordination of women is cultural rather than theological and, as she argued, even theological arguments such as female impurity or the physical male resemblance to Christ are not recognised by John Chrysostom or Gregory of Nazianzus, among others. If, as Chrysostom says, the priest supplies a voice and hands to Christ's words and actions, could not a woman do this?[10] Her work on women in the Church is without parallel in Orthodox theology and the source of inspiration for a generation of women theologians. Called the 'mother' or even 'grandmother' of the Orthodox Church in France, she centred all of her various concerns in the question she surely received from Bulgakov, Lev Gillet, Evdokimov, Maria Skobtsova and the rest – namely how to be open to the world as well as faithful to the Church, and, as she put it constantly, 'to become permeable to Christ'.

Known best as 'the Monk of the Eastern Church', his literary name, Lev Gillet was originally a Benedictine monk. He later joined Metropolitan Andrey Sheptytsky's Greek-Catholic monastic community near Lviv and was received into the Orthodox Church by Metropolitan Evlogy by concelebration of the liturgy. He was rector of the first francophone Orthodox parish in Paris, then served as chaplain in Maria Skobtsova's hostel at 77 rue de Lourmel and, after the Second World War, to the Fellowship of St Alban and St Sergius in London. Fr Lev was trained in psychology (he was the first French translator of Freud), and his great insight, apparent throughout his essays, retreat talks and preaching, is the recognition of God as 'Limitless Love', as he called him – his reaching out to human hearts. Always somewhat marginal to the institutional Church, Fr Lev spent his monastic life outside monastic communities, a kind of nomadic monk in the world, not unlike Maria Skobtsova, with Parisian cafés, London coffee-houses, and park benches serving as the locations of his immense pastoral ministry. His contact with so many people both inside and outside the Church enabled him to develop a language of talking about God that was accessible, free of religious jargon and pietisms. God as 'Limitless Love' was precisely the kenotic God which Bulgakov and Evdokimov recognised, the 'Lover of mankind' (*Philanthropos*) which the Eastern liturgy so often invokes; a God who seeks us out, to share our life and sufferings.

THE CONTINUING PRESENCE (AND PROBLEMS) OF THE CHURCH IN THE MODERN WORLD

The list of the remarkable figures of the Russian religious revival could go on, and it includes others whose thinking was rather different from that of those discussed hitherto. For some, it is either Vladimir Lossky or Fr Georges Florovsky who best represents contemporary Orthodox theology. Florovsky was in fact opposed to the theological perspectives of most of the people with whom he worked when he was at the St Sergius Institute in Paris. His *Ways of Russian Theology* makes clear his distance from their slavophile origins, their use of modern Western philisophical sources such as Schelling and Hegel, their theological creativity and their interest in dialogue with modern culture and society. For example, Florovsky opposed Bulgakov's use of the figure of Sophia, the Wisdom of God, to elucidate the relationship of God to the world, and his expansive understanding of dogma.[11] He did not follow up Soloviev's focus on the 'humanity of God', even though he appreciated the importance of ecclesiology and its christocentricity. Yet Florovsky himself, starting in the Fellowship of St Alban and St Sergius, remained an active participant in ecumenical work, particularly in that of the WCC from the 1950s till the end of his life. Like Lossky, Florovsky worked in the Greek patristic tradition, and in some extreme statements he virtually equated classical Christian theology with hellenism. Yet the breadth of his work extends far beyond such an assertion. Despite his differences, he nonetheless concurred with colleagues at the St Sergius Institute such as Bulgakov and Afanasiev in seeing the Church as eucharistic and sobornal, especially in his essay 'The Eucharist and Catholicity' (1929). He addressed the essential question of where the Church begins and ends in 'The limits of the Church', an essay which recent scholarship has identified as much influenced by Bulgakov.[12]

Vladimir Lossky sought to put the thinking of patristic authors into dialogue with the modern world. Thus, though disagreeing with some of those we have reviewed above, in theological method as well as substance – Bulgakov's use of Sophia and his creativity being notable examples – he nevertheless was one with them in the commitment to openness to the world and especially other Churches. The Church's distinguishing feature for him was 'catholicity', its fullness in truth but also extension or universality in the world. Towards the end of his life he recognised Bulgakov's efforts, which he had criticised and opposed years earlier, to track the cosmic presence and work of God. Lossky himself pursued this in his studies of the Holy Spirit in action and of the problem of the *filioque*. Fundamental to his approach was his concentration on the person.[13]

Another notable patristic scholar, who like Florovsky spent much of his life in America, was John Meyendorff. Internationally known as a Byzantinist and for his role in the 'rediscovery' of Palamas, he was also one of the most perceptive and critical commentators on religion in public life. He was not afraid, in any of the avenues of his scholarship, to offer sharp criticism, whether of the Soviet treatment of dissidents, of the Russian Church's reluctance to oppose such harassment during the Soviet era, or of the complacency and passivity of American Christians when faced with the witness of Dr Martin Luther King Jr. A resolute opponent of retreatism and fanaticism, he promoted a Christian faith that was engaged in the world. While he could critique some aspects of secularism in the American and international contexts, he cherished the freedom of religion from the state and the diversity of religious expression that this supports. He rejected the idea of Orthodoxy in America as merely a 'diaspora' phenomenon, cast into an alien environment and too spiritually immature to constitute an effective religious presence. The only 'diaspora' for him was that of Christians' distance from the Kingdom of God. While he respected the Russian Church and culture in which he was raised, he saw it as unnatural to yearn for a 'holy Russia' rather than seeking a Church planted in the social world of America, united in the faith and not divided or defined by ethnic particularities.

In recent years, the spirit of the Paris revival has begun to have an impact in Russia too. Fr Alexander Men spent virtually all of his life under the Soviet regime; yet when Gorbachev's reforms provided an opening for the Church, he became, even if only briefly until his murder in 1990, the principal face and voice of Orthodox Christianity in Russia, a frequent radio and TV guest and popular lecturer. Yet he had been writing, preaching and teaching for some time beforehand, just below the official Soviet radar. His grounding in tradition was combined with an ecumenical and eschatological openness. He claimed that 'Christianity was only in its beginning', a vision based not on the decades of Soviet repression but on a discernment of the cultural domesticity of the faith in many historical periods. Christ and his gospel cannot be captured and held prisoner by any community of faith or rite. Echoing the most popular of his books, *The Son of Man*, Men finds Christ as much a resident of the music and film, the politics and human service efforts of today as he was of the towns of Palestine through which he and his disciples walked. Recordings provide vivid witness of the spontaneity, clarity and power of his teaching. Like Bulgakov, Men promoted a generous ecumenism, looking for what still united Christians despite their divisions.[14] Likewise, he sought to stress the link between liturgy and life, a theme beloved of many figures discussed here.[15] Though Men was a student of Bulgakov, Afanasiev and the others of the revival only by reading smuggled copies of their writings, he himself became an important figure in the ongoing Russian religious revival and his legacy is continued by parishes, schools, conferences and the Hosanna community, which put his vision into practice.

This still does not exhaust the procession of figures who could be considered part of the revival of the twentieth and twenty-first centuries. We cannot but mention ecumenical leaders such as Lev Zander and Nicolas Zernov; church historians Anton Kartashev and Boris Sové; philosophers Symeon Frank and Nicholas Berdiaev; theologians such as Basil Krivosheine, Cassian Bezobrazov, Basil Zenkovsky and Alexis Kniazeff; and great renewers of iconography such as Sister Joanna Reitlinger, Fr Gregory Krug and Leonid Ouspensky.

Today, many of the thinkers named thus far occupy a puzzling position. 'Traditionalists' in the Orthodox Church either condemn them as 'modernists', 'ecumenists', 'innovators' or, worse, 'heretics', or else simply ignore them, as do even many 'mainstream' Orthodox Christians. Yet there remains a strong interest in their work, especially among Western Christians as well as many Orthodox. It would not be an exaggeration to say, with the recent work of Paul Vallière, Antoine Arjakovsky, John Milbank, Brandon Gallaher, Aidan Nichols and Paul Gavrilyuk, among others, that a movement of serious scholarly interest is taking place, a renewal of appreciation for a veritable treasure of theological contributions to the entire Church.

Further reading

Afanasiev, N., *The Church of the Holy Spirit*, trans. Vitaly Permiakov, ed. Michael Plekon, Notre Dame, IN: University of Notre Dame Press, 2007.

Arjakovsky, A., *La géneration des penseurs religieux de l'émigration russe*, Kiev and Paris: L'Esprit et la Lettre, 2002 (English translation forthcoming, University of Notre Dame Press).

Bulgakov, S., Society of Memphis, www.geocities.com/sbulgakovsociety/.

Gavrilyuk, P., 'The kenotic theology of Sergius Bulgakov', *Scottish Journal of Theology* 58 (2005), 251–69.

'Universal salvation in the eschatology of Sergius Bulgakov', *JTS*, n.s. 57.1 (2006), 110–32.

Hackel, S., *Pearl of Great Price: the Life of Mother Maria Skobtsova, 1891–1945*, Crestwood, NY: SVS Press, 1981.

Nichols, A., *Theology in the Russian Diaspora: Church, Fathers, Eucharist in Nikolai Afanas'ev 1893–1966*, Cambridge: Cambridge University Press, 1989.

Plekon, M., *Living Icons: Persons of Faith in the Eastern Church*, Notre Dame, IN: University of Notre Dame Press, 2002.

(ed.), *Tradition Alive: On the Church and the Christian Life in Our Time*, Lanham MD: Rowman and Littlefield / Sheed and Ward, 2003.

Sergius Bulgakov, SVTQ 49.1–2, (2005).

Vallière, P., *Modern Russian Theology: Bukharev, Soloviev, Bulgakov – Orthodox Theology in a New Key*, Grand Rapids, MI: Eerdmans, 2000.

Williams, R., *Sergii Bulgakov: Toward a Russian Political Theology*, Edinburgh: T. & T. Clark, 1999.

Zernov, N., *The Russian Religious Renaissance of the Twentieth Century*, New York: Harper & Row, 1963.

Notes

1. J. Milbank, 'Sophiology and theurgy' (paper presented at the conference 'Radical Orthodoxy and Eastern Orthodoxy', Institute of Orthodox Christian Studies, Cambridge University, 2005).
2. See B. Jakim, trans., *Sergius Bulgakov: Apocatastasis and Transfiguration* (New Haven, CT: The Variable Press, 1995), pp. 7–30.
3. N. Afanasiev, *The Church of the Holy Spirit*, trans. V. Permiakov, ed. M. Plekon (Notre Dame, IN: University of Notre Dame Press, 2007).
4. Critics of Afanasiev include J. D. Zizioulas, *Eucharist, Bishop, Church: The Unity of the Chruch in the Divine Eucharist and the Bishop During the First Three Centuries*, trans. E. Theokritoff (Brookline, MA: Holy Cross Orthodox Press, 2001).
5. For his sources, see Afanasiev, *The Church of the Holy Spirit.*
6. A. Schmemann, *For the Life of the World: Sacraments and Orthodoxy* (Crestwood, NY: SVS Press, 1973).
7. N. Cabasilas, *The Life in Christ* 6.3; M. Plekon and A. Vinogradov (eds. and trans.), *In the World, Of the Church: A Paul Evdokimov Reader* (Crestwood, NY: SVS Press, 2001), pp. 175–94.
8. After the assassination of her husband in 1905, Elizabeth founded a monastery of nuns dedicated to social service.
9. R. Pevear and L. Volokhonsky (trans.), *Mother Maria Skobtsova: Essential Writings* (Maryknoll, NY: Orbis, 2003), 'On the imitation of the Mother of God', pp. 61–74.
10. E. Behr-Sigel and K. Ware, *The Ordination of Women in the Orthodox Church* (Geneva: WCC, 2003), pp. 78–90.
11. See Bulgakov's essay from the 1937 *Living Tradition* anthology: 'Dogma and dogmatic theology' in M. Plekon (ed.), *Tradition Alive: On the Church and the Christian Life in Our Time* (Lanham, MD: Rowman and Littlefield / Sheed and Ward, 2003), pp. 67–80. Also see A. Klimoff, 'Georges Florovsky and the sophiological controversy', and S. V. Nikolaev, 'Spiritual unity: the role of religious authority in the disputes between Sergii Bulgakov and Georges Florovsky concerning intercommunion', in *Sergius Bulgakov, SVTQ* 49.1–2 (2005), 67–100, 101–24.

12. Brandon Gallaher, 'Catholic action: ecclesiology, the Eucharist and the question of intercommunion in the ecumenism of Sergii Bulgakov', (unpubl. M.Div. thesis, St Vladimir's Seminary, 2003). Also see Gallaher, 'Bulgakov's ecumenical thought' (Pt 1), *Sobornost* 24.1 (2002), 24–55, and 'Bulgakov and intercommunion', (Pt 2), *Sobornost* 24.2 (2002), 9–28.

13. For further discussion of this topic, see A. Papanikolaou, 'Personhood and its exponents in twentieth-century Orthodox theology', below.

14. See, e.g., *Christianity for the Twenty-first Century: The Prophetic Writings of Alexander Men*, ed. and trans. E. Roberts and A. Shukman (New York: Continuum, 1996), pp. 68–74, 151–63, 179–92.

15. A. Men, *Orthodox Worship: Sacrament, Word and Image*, trans. C. Masica (Crestwood, NY: SVS Press, 1999); Men, *Seven Talks on the Creed*, trans. C. Masica (Crestwood, NY: SVS/Oakwood, 1999); Men, *About Christ and the Church*, trans. A. Vinogradov (Crestwood, NY: SVS/Oakwood, 1996); Men, *Awake to Life! Sermons from the Paschal Cycle*, trans. M. Sapiets (Crestwood, NY: SVS Press / Oakwood, 1996).

14 Some key themes and figures in Greek theological thought

ATHANASIOS N. PAPATHANASIOU

A TURBULENT LEGACY

The Greek state was founded in 1830, after approximately 400 years during which the Greeks were subjugated to the Ottoman Turks. In modern times, therefore, theology in Greece had developed under political conditions of occupation and under the influence, broadly speaking, of two intellectual factors. On one hand it had inherited the multi-faceted and creative theology of the Greek Fathers which had dominated the Christian East for twelve centuries before the fall of the empire. On the other, there was what Fr Georges Florovsky called the 'pseudomorphosis' of Orthodox theology: the gradual obscuring of its own criteria, and the influence, as early as the fifteenth century, of characteristics of Western theology such as legalism and an institutional understanding of the Church. These characteristics overshadowed the more existential character of Eastern theology.

These two factors in the shaping of Greek theology operated in parallel: sometimes one was in the ascendant, sometimes the other. The circumstances of Ottoman domination and the antagonisms between Christian confessions often made Orthodox theology defensive; this hampered its creativity, whether in engaging with new ideas or in developing themes already present in Eastern thought (e.g. the tension between mysticism and history, or the relationship between the authority of scripture and that of the Church Fathers). In their response to changes in Europe such as the Reformation or the Enlightenment, clergy and lay scholars veered between dialogue and rejection. This can be seen in some of the initiatives intended to secure Orthodox identity, which, however, had the effect of establishing non-Orthodox influences. Thus we have Patriarch Cyril Loukaris (1572–1638), whose anti-Roman Catholic position was condemned as profoundly influenced by Calvinism; while the 'Confession' of Peter Mogila (1597–1646), approved by the four Eastern Patriarchs, reflected a manifestly Roman Catholic spirit.

218

Popular piety, on the other hand, retained valuable Orthodox sensibilities; but it often suffered from a lack of education and tended towards ritualism. Important church figures such as Makarios Notaras, Bishop of Corinth, and Nikodimos of the Holy Mountain (representatives of the monastic movement known as the 'Kollyvades' around the turn of the nineteenth century) tried to remedy the situation; their efforts were broadly welcomed within the church body, but encountered resistance from certain church circles. For instance, Nikodimos (a serious scholar who on some points was very conservative and on others exhibited a daring critical mind) worked on the canons of the Orthodox Church and made a diffident attempt to clean up the text in order to publish them as a corpus; he was criticised for this by churchmen who maintained that every text belonging to the tradition possessed divine authority and was beyond criticism.[1] He also encountered suspicion in his attempts, on the basis of Fathers such as Maximus the Confessor, to express a theology in which the culmination of the divine economy is the eschatological recapitulation of all things in Christ.

A few years after the formation of the Greek state, the University of Athens was established, with its theological faculty (founded 1837) organised on mainly Protestant German models. Dogmas were understood as ideological principles; as revealed truths, but with no organic connection to ethics, which was seen as an individual code of behaviour. Academic theology, pursued almost exclusively by lay professors, was thus often at odds with the sensibilities of traditional religious feeling with its emphasis on the worshipping community and experience of divine presence in the heart. But academic theology did represent an attempt to engage with the cutting edge of international education and research. On the other hand, the Greek state was set up in a way that echoed the prevalence of nationalism in Europe. In 1833 its Church broke with Constantinople and declared itself autocephalous; the result was a schism, until the Ecumenical Patriarchate canonically granted autocephaly in 1850. In the Church's consciousness, the tension between ecumenical identity and the sense of being a national Church continues under various guises.

In 1907, the Zoe ('Life') brotherhood of theologians was set up with the aim of reforming church life. It was not the first such attempt, but it was the most organised; and it raised the issue of religious organisations, which, through various phases, has been alive in Greece ever since. The religious organisations promoted a conscious religious life, freed from superstition; they put the Bible into the hands of ordinary laypeople and encouraged lay participation in church life, both sacramental and administrative, which in turn led to a flowering of liturgical, biblical and other studies (e.g. the scholarship of Panayiotis Trembelas, 1886–1977). The primary characteristics of the organisations' theology, however, were legalism and an emphasis on individual piety and moral purity. In combination with the very nature of the organisation (an association with its own legal basis, independent of the church structure of diocese and parish), these characteristics contributed to a sense among the members of belonging to a separate, elect and superior body.

The first half of the twentieth century in Greece saw a theology that was in many ways idealist in character, centred on an opposition between matter and spirit. Yet there were also important theological figures working in such fields as biblical and patristic studies, science of religion, canon law and dialogue with philosophy (Gregorios Papamichael, Nikolaos Louvaris, Hamilcar Alivizatos, Leonidas Philippides, Vasileios Vellas *et al.*). Side by side with the pietistic spirit and the confusion of national and religious identity, contacts were also being made with developments in the broader Orthodox and ecumenical worlds. But the spectacular nature of what followed, particularly in the 1960s, is one reason why the contribution of earlier theologians has not been adequately explored.

THE 1960S: AN EXPLOSION

The 1960s saw much of the world in ferment. The trend of returning to indigenous identities was gaining momentum, and there was a revival of interest in cultural particularities and indigenous religions. In various parts of the Greek theological world and particularly within the Zoe movement, there was a developing interest in discovering authentic Orthodox criteria, and struggling to articulate a theology that distanced itself from the prevailing individualism and legalism. Some members of Zoe came into contact with the theology of the Russian diaspora, but this movement was not able to produce radical reform in the organisation. For internal reasons, Zoe split up in 1960. Young members left in droves to serve theology and church life from different perspectives. Some took the lead in publishing a new journal, *Synoro* ('Boundary') (1964–7), which brought a new spirit to theology; notable among them was Christos Yannaras. Characteristics of this upheaval, which has come to be known as the 'theology of the '60s', include the understanding of the Church as a eucharistic community, interest in apophatic theology, focus on deification as the destiny of humans, attention to the cultural particularity of the Christian East, rediscovery of Byzantine iconography, interest in monasticism, and dialogue with contemporary thinking.

The fortunes of modern Greek theology do not coincide precisely with those of the religious organisations. Yet the dominance of the organisations, the attempts on the part of official church circles to respond to them and the 'explosion' of the 1960s largely defined the theological course that followed. In every case, what came out of the 'theology of the '60s' was not a uniform current but a ferment of at times conflicting trends and perspectives. We may now turn to some of the main theological themes discussed.

THE BATTLE OVER ETERNITY: THE WORLD, HISTORY AND ESCHATOLOGY

From the 1960s onwards, the centre of gravity seems to have shifted. Up to that time, the broadly prevailing idea was that life is simply tribulation, and that salvation – the reward for dealing with the trials of life – means the eternity of the soul, freed from the body after the death of the individual. The Kingdom of God was therefore envisaged as a disembodied life for the soul with God. Inevitably, almost nothing was said about the eschatological renewal of all creation. The doctrine of the Second Coming and the ultimate general resurrection was not, of course, abandoned (theology being constitutionally conservative); but it was unable to take a central place and give meaning to theological issues.

Since the '60s, various currents in Orthodox theology which had turned to study of the patristic tradition and also encountered contemporary European theology (e.g. Oscar Cullmann's *Christ and Time*, first published in German in 1946) contributed to a rediscovery of the fundamentally eschatological character of the Christian faith. A significant figure in the recovery of eschatological consciousness was the biblical theologian Savvas Agourides, whose studies on the subject were published in 1955–9.[2] Further light was shed on the eschatological nature of the Church by the development of liturgical theology and the study of Orthodox worship (especially the structure of the eucharistic liturgy); characteristic are the writings of Ioannis Foundoulis, as well as more recent liturgical scholars.[3] Despite the distortions that it has undergone over the years, worship has remained a witness to the eschatological consciousness of the Church.

Eschatology is closely connected with the dialectic of *created* and *uncreated*, which has become a central axis of contemporary theology. History is understood as an open and free progress on the part of creation towards the Kingdom, which is its future renewal, its liberation from corruption and death and its transition to a different mode of existence – its transformation into a communion of love. In this perspective, the Kingdom is not simply the final outcome of history, but the very *raison d'être* of the entire creation. The future is the cause of all that comes into being. This eschatological conclusion is the original will of God, and it is to this conclusion that God's work in history guides history and creation.

The 1957 doctoral thesis of future professor of dogmatics John Romanides (1927–2001), *The Ancestral Sin*, dealt a mortal blow to the idea of Christ's work as 'satisfaction' for an offence against divine justice (cf. Anselm of Canterbury *et al.*), and elaborated the patristic teaching on the renewal of human nature. There is now growing support for the doctrine of 'unconditioned' Incarnation, as it is called: the belief that the Incarnation did not take place simply on account of the sin of the first-created humans, but would have occurred even if the Fall had never happened. In other words, the Incarnation is regarded as the first-fruits of God's pre-eternal will that all creation should be in communion with him. Various theologians such as Andreas Theodorou (1922–2004) discussed this point[4] (responding to the challenge of Georges Florovsky's study 'Cur Deus Homo?'), but it was decisively brought to the fore by Panayiotis Nellas (1936–86),[5] who founded the theological journal *Synaxi* in 1982.[6] Nellas maintains that, according to the biblical and patristic tradition, man is created precisely as an image of the second Person of the Holy Trinity, and is thus a being created to be united with the Son. In consequence, man will be fully human when he is 'christified'. This eschatological perspective embraces the whole of creation, which is called to become the 'flesh' of the Son and, ultimately, a partaker in the Holy Trinity.

Increasingly prominent in recent years are the few theological voices that relativise the Fall still further, in the sense that they dispute its historicity and that of a pre-fallen state.[7] In this perspective, the imperfections associated with the world (corruption and mortality, resulting in the need for salvation) are not attributed to some ancient transgression, but to the very fact of createdness – a position that has been argued at length by Zizioulas.[8] The universe has been brought into existence not by some necessity, but by the free will of an Other; and in consequence, it does not possess of itself and by its own nature the power to exist, but tends towards disintegration. This inadequacy can be transcended, therefore, only if the created order comes to partake in God, so becoming a participant in a life that cannot arise out of that order's own self.

In these theological developments, the emphasis placed on the theology of St Maximus the Confessor, with his doctrine of the *logoi* or 'inner principles' of all that exists, has been of especial importance. Studies of Maximus have seen a remarkable increase, thanks in part to modern translations of his work with scholarly introductions by Fr Dumitru Stăniloae. Since, according to Maximus, things come into being through God's creative initiative, they are a materialisation of their 'ideas' which are held in the 'mind' of God. It is thus not only God's miraculous activity in the world that is a *theophany*, but the very existence of the world and history itself. 'Natural revelation', therefore, cannot be sharply distinguished from 'supernatural revelation', as in the medieval West. Maximus's doctrine has been connected with St Gregory Palamas's teaching that the energies of God are both uncreated and participable by creatures. When humans come into contact with these energies, therefore, they are united with God himself, despite the fact that they are not united with the divine essence. Modern writers[9] have explicated this theology in response to criticisms from non-Orthodox theologians who maintain that Palamite doctrine understands the uncreated energies as impersonal, so diminishing or obviating the distinctive role of the three Persons in salvation. The response is to clarify that the divine energies are 'enhypostatic': they are expressed and manifested through the three hypostases or Persons. In history, therefore, neither the incarnate dispensation of the Son nor the action of the Spirit can be replaced by a mystical pantheism.

Looking at the Greek theological spectrum, one finds that eschatology is indeed at the forefront: but it is not actually understood in a uniform way. Sometimes it is emphasised that the Kingdom belongs to the *future*, so that church life is seen as a foretaste of the Kingdom; in other cases, however, the Kingdom is understood as the experience of God here and now, for instance through the church community. In this case, the dimension of the future and its expectation as a basic element of Christian life is attenuated. The Kingdom tends to be identified with personal sanctity or purification from the passions, in such a way that the perspective of the promised future renewal of all creation is lost.[10] In other cases (perhaps under the influence of existentialism), history itself is understood as a fall and an impoverishment ('objectification') of existence; in consequence, the objective is not to take a positive approach to history and look for its transfiguration, but rather to escape from history. In many of these cases, we have a repetition of the clash between mysticism and history or, one might dare to say, Neoplatonism and biblical thinking. But 'transfiguration of history', too, is not always understood in the same way. Sometimes it is seen as a change to be brought about at some point in the future by God's almighty initiative; sometimes it is understood in connection with the synergy of God and man within history. In the first case there is a lurking danger of an eschatological excess which downplays history, often even to the point of overlooking man's responsibility within it; the same may sometimes apply even to the historical mission of the Church. In the second case, human praxis (solidarity, environmental commitment, etc.) is considered as a way of cooperating with God's initiative; it sees the world as the raw material of the Kingdom and brings into history the signs of the eschatological times.

Rediscovery of the connection between creation and eschatology is reflected also in the growing interest in dialogue with science, especially quantum mechanics, and in the ecological implications of theology. Contributors include Professor of Comparative Religion Marios Begzos,[11] Christos Yannaras[12] and other physicists and theologians.[13]

ECCLESIOLOGY: UNITY AND DIVERSITY

An understanding of the Church centred on the Eucharist has now generally replaced the idea that it is an institution which incidentally performs sacraments. Starting from Nicholas Cabasilas's saying that the Church is 'indicated' in the Eucharist, there is an emphasis on the Church becoming what it is when it celebrates the Eucharist. It is on the Eucharist that all the other parameters of the community – structure, administration, morality, sacraments – depend for their meaning and the form they take. In this perspective, the Eucharist is not simply a spiritual medicine to fortify believers in their spiritual struggle: it is the event from which every member of the Church draws his or her identity. It is a manifestation and foretaste of the Kingdom which will be fully realised in the future, in its cosmic dimensions.[14]

Church membership does not mean recruitment into an ideological faction, but above all a change in one's mode of being. The church event itself should form an icon, a manifestation and realisation of the trinitarian mode of being. This point, and particularly the use of the Trinity as a model for human life, has sparked debates about patristic thought and the possibilities for using contemporary personalistic categories in theology: the biblical theologians Ioannis Panagopoulos (1938–97) and Savvas Agourides have both expressed disagreements, from differing viewpoints, with the positions of Metropolitan John Zizioulas of Pergamon and Christos Yannaras.[15] Another issue is raised by the view (introduced principally by John Romanides[16]) that the Church is a 'hospital' where humans are healed of their passions, their existential sicknesses. The consequence of this view seems to be the belief that, in reality, to be a member of the Church is not simply to accept the faith or participate in the eucharistic community, but depends on one's degree of spiritual progress (through the stages of purification, illumination and deification).

In his 1965 doctoral thesis,[17] John Zizioulas maintains that the celebration of the Eucharist (and hence also the very constitution of the Church) are organically and indissolubly linked to the singularity of the president of the Eucharist, i.e. the bishop. Zizioulas disagrees with such theologians as Afanasiev and Meyendorff, whom he interprets as saying that the Church is actualised in its fullness wherever the Eucharist is celebrated, so that the parish, as eucharistic community, constitutes the catholic Church. In Zizioulas's view, the Church is actualised only in the eucharistic assembly under the bishop (and hence the existence of parishes is a concession to the presbyters on the part of the bishop). This eucharistic assembly around the bishop, however, has to be celebrated in canonical relationship with all other eucharistic assemblies. These issues continue to be the subject of lively debate and research. Professor Vlasios Pheidas has maintained[18] that the bishops' responsibility for ordaining the bishop of a neighbouring diocese was a catalyst for the formation of the system of the 'Pentarchy' in the fifth century. More recent theologians[19] show an interest in relativising the monarchical episcopate, looking to the ancient role of the college of presbyters which would promote a fellow-presbyter to be president of the Eucharist; this then developed into the position of bishop.

There is also discussion concerning charisms and ministries of service within the church body. Are charisms bestowed by the bishop (since no ecclesial ministry is legitimated independently of the Eucharist)? Or are they direct gifts of the Spirit and Christ to the members of his Body, in which case the bishop's job is to see that the gifts are not lost and the members do not atrophy? There is a similar tension in the debate over lay participation in church governance (election of pastors, participation in decision-making, etc.). According to some, such participation is not a basic right; where it appears, it is a temporary concession.[20] Others, however, maintain that the participation of all members of the Church (with differing positions and responsibilities) needs to be re-examined, since it is required by the very nature of the Church as a body. There is similar disagreement concerning the way councils operate. Some stress that councils express the experience and the faith of the ecclesial body as a whole;[21] others maintain that councils are true to the extent that they express the experience of those members of the Church who are at the stage of deification.[22]

'Patromonism' and particularly 'Christomonism' are terms coined in the early 1960s by Nikos Nissiotis (1924–86), who served for many years at the World Council of Churches, to describe the ecclesiologies prevailing in Western Christianity.[23] He sees some of these ecclesiologies as emphasising the role of God the Father at the expense of the other two Persons; while, according to others, Christ laid down the administrative succession on the basis of which the Church would continue to exist after Christ's departure from the earth. Thus the Roman Catholic tradition gives a central place to a 'vicar of Christ' who continues Christ's historical work, and this understanding leads inevitably to a centralised and autocratic church structure. In the Protestant world, on the other hand, emphasis on personal relationship with Christ has destroyed the cohesion of the body and led to the privatisation of charisms. These models neglect the activity of the Spirit, who makes present the eschatological Christ. The need for a fertile synthesis of christology and pneumatology has since been fulfilled especially by Zizioulas. In his thought, the 'economy of the Spirit' is not understood simply as the phase of history following the 'economy of the Son' (which is more or less how it is presented in Vladimir Lossky's *Mystical Theology of the Eastern Church*); it is the constant breath that makes whatever it touches into an event of communion. The very creation of the world took place 'in the Holy Spirit'; the Incarnation of the Son is Spirit-conditioned; and church life has a radically *epicletic*[24] character. This means that the church ceaselessly seeks the action of the Spirit, which is also what makes the body of believers into the Church. This is especially clear in the anaphora prayer at the liturgy, where the celebrant prays for the Spirit to be sent down not only upon the eucharistic gifts but upon the community as well. Furthermore, when the term 'spiritual' occurs in patristic writing it does not refer to 'spirit' in the sense of the human soul (i.e. as opposed to the body). 'Spiritual' relates to the Holy Spirit, and in consequence indicates the human being in its entirety when it becomes the dwelling place of the energies of the third Person of the Holy Trinity.

All of this has repercussions in actual church life. For example, some disregard asceticism (to the extent that God's eschatological initiative takes centre stage); others see asceticism as man's response to what God asks of him, an effort aimed not at acquiring individual virtue but at living in an ecclesial manner, being in communion. Furthermore, as interest in the Orthodox tradition has grown in Greece in recent decades and parish life has undergone a certain revival, significant ecclesiological problems have come to the fore. For example, the Christian's relationship with a spiritual father (a married or celibate priest) has sometimes been shaped by the transfer of monastic models to urban life, often with the result that the confessor is turned into a sort of guru. There is tension over who takes precedence, the spiritual father or the bishop: this is in reality a continuation of the long-running struggle between institution and charism in church life. There is also a heated theological debate over the relationship between spiritual fatherhood and psychoanalysis.[25]

CULTURE AND MISSION: A SENSITIVE LIAISON

As a continuing incarnation within history, the Church addresses itself to the whole human being. It judges cultures, it contributes to the creation of culture and it claims a presence in public life. John Zizioulas's study 'Hellenism and Christianity: the meeting of two worlds',[26] for example, has demonstrated the arduous but fruitful process whereby the Church adopted hellenic categories of thought, as well as the ruptures in the hellenic worldview resulting from this encounter.

Since the early 1980s, there has been a strong current of thought that gives especial emphasis to the cultural particularity of traditionally Orthodox peoples. For most of those involved, ecclesial and cultural identity are inseparable. Romanides constructed an interpretative framework according to which the Christianisation and cultural hellenisation of the Roman empire made all the peoples that it comprised into 'Romioi' (as distinct from non-Christian 'Romans'): they became participants in the culture of *Romiosyni* (the quality of being a *Romios*). For the Orthodox Eastern Roman empire, Constantinople was none other than the New Rome. According to this scheme, the West's deviation from right faith could be traced definitively to the fall of the Western empire in the fifth century, since when the barbarians developed a passionate rivalry with the Christian Roman empire and particularly the Orthodox East. This model has been adopted and developed to varying degrees and in different ways by Fr George Metallinos, Metropolitan Hierotheos Vlachos, Fr Theodore Zisis, Christos Yannaras and others.[27] Its specifications are anti-nationalist, and it disapproves of the nineteenth-century fragmentation of multi-ethnic *Romiosyni* into nation states with national Churches. On the other hand, it has difficulty accepting the possibility that an Orthodox Church can be constructed on the basis of a culture that is not Byzantine. It should also be noted that, while the *Romiosyni* model shifts the centre of gravity from race to culture, nationalism does not cease to be a perennial presence in church discourse. One sometimes hears voices identifying the Church's mission with the ideals not only of the nation, but also of the race.[28] Finally, the emphasis on seeking cultural particularity sometimes means giving absolute priority to cultural identity, to the detriment of the gospel priority of practical love and solidarity.

This whole discussion has brought to the fore the important truth that the Church does not exist in history in disincarnate form, as an ideological system unrelated to cultural realities; nor can its historical flesh, whether Hebraic-biblical or Hellenic, be discounted. In this discussion, however, it is often assumed that culture is a static quantity, as if it were a given and unchanging 'essence'; this makes it difficult to think seriously about the relationship of the gospel to cultures, and to the rapid changes taking place today. Thus conversion to Orthodoxy is often understood inevitably as a cultural conversion to *Romiosyni*.

Interest in foreign mission saw a revival in Greece in the early 1960s, when the Inter-Orthodox Mission Centre Porefthendes ('Go ye') was set up in Athens under the umbrella of Syndesmos (World Fellowship of Orthodox Youth). Protagonists of the missionary awakening included Anastasios Yannoulatos (later Professor of the History of Religions at Athens University and now Archbishop of Albania) and the first and only Professor of Missiology at Athens, Elias Voulgarakis (1927–99). For about a decade, Porefthendes cultivated a robust discussion of missiological issues, as well as following the changes taking place on the ecumenical front. Yannoulatos, whose doctoral studies were concerned with African indigenous religion, formulated a mission theology with eschatological backbone, and a readiness for fruitful encounter between gospel and cultures. He has also published important studies on Islam and interfaith dialogue.[29] Voulgarakis emphasised the universality of love, and the necessity of reformulating the Church's message in contemporary language.[30] Subsequent decades saw the rise of a folkloric and ethnocentric view, which put a brake on study of such burning issues as inculturation, restricting the discussion to triumphalistic evocations of the glories of Cyril and Methodius in the ninth century. Nevertheless, missiological thinking about vital issues continues. These include ecumenical missionary concerns and the relation between mission and liturgics;[31] the connection of mission to the nature of the Church (rather than simply to a secondary activism); issues raised by post-modernity and cultural anthropology, mission and solidarity; and the distinction between genuine conversion and proselytism.[32]

All this demonstrates that contemporary Orthodox theology in Greece is heir to a rich inheritance; and the differences and opposing tendencies within it have helped it develop considerable potentialities. The great challenge facing it is that of meaningful participation in discussion of the major themes that today preoccupy a globalised world.

Further reading

Hadjinicolaou, J. (ed.), *Synaxis: An Anthology of the Most Significant Orthodox Theology in Greece Appearing in the Journal Synaxi from 1982 to 2002*, 3 vols., Montreal: Alexander Press, 2006.

Nellas, P., *Deification in Christ: Orthodox Perspectives on the Nature of the Human Person*, Crestwood, NY: SVS Press, 1987.

Nichols, A., *Light from the East: Authors and Themes in Orthodox Theology*, London: Sheed and Ward, 1995.

Papathanasiou, A. N., 'Theological challenges facing the Church of Greece', *Koinonia, The Journal of the Anglican and Eastern Churches Association*, n.s., 49 (Summer 2004), 11–20.

Vassiliadis, P., 'Greek theology in the making. Trends and facts in the 80s – vision for the 90s', *SVTQ* 35.1 (1991), 33–52.

Yannaras, C., *The Freedom of Morality*, trans. E. Briere, Crestwood, NY: SVS Press, 1984.

'Theology in present-day Greece', *SVTQ* 16.4 (1972), 195–214.

Yannoulatos, Archbishop Anastasios, *Facing the World: Orthodox Christian Essays on Global Concerns*, Crestwood, NY: SVS Press, 2003.

Notes

Please note that all works cited in notes to this chapter are in Greek, unless otherwise indicated.

1. See further A. (T.) N. Papathanasiou, *Canons and Freedom: The Metamorphoses of the 108th Canon of the Local Council of Carthage (419) and the Fortunes of Free Acceptance of Christianity* (Katerini: Epektasis, 2005), esp. pp. 105–25.

2. For bibliography, see P. Vassiliadis (ed.), *Christ and History: A Symposium in Honour of Professor Savvas Agourides* (Thessaloniki: Paratiritis, 1993), pp. 267–70.

3. E.g. Georgios Filias, Panayiotis Skaltsis, Pavlos Koumarianos. Cf. also J. D. Zizioulas, Metropolitan of Pergamon 'The Eucharist and the Kingdom' (English), *Sourozh* 58 (November 1994), 1–12; 59 (January 1995), 22–38; 60 (May 1995), 32–46.

4. A. Theodorou, 'Cur Deus Homo? Unconditioned or Conditioned Incarnation of the Word of God', *Epistimoniki Epetiris tis Theologikis Scholis tou Panepistemiou Athinon* 19 (1972), 297–340 Theodorou has considerable reservations about an 'unconditioned' Incarnation.

5. P. Nellas, *Deification in Christ: Orthodox Perspectives on the Nature of the Human Person* (Crestwood, NY: SVS Press, 1987); Nellas, 'Redemption or deification? Nicholas Kavasilas and Anselm's question "Why did God become Man?"' in *Synaxis: An Anthology of the Most Significant Orthodox Theology in Greece Appearing in the Journal Synaxis from 1982 to 2002*, vol. 1: *Anthropology, Environment, Creation* (Montreal: Alexander Press, 2006), pp. 79–98 (both in English).

6. The name means 'assembly', especially that of the Church gathered for the Eucharist.

7. E.g. S. Agourides, *Myth, History and Theology* (Athens, 1988); J. D. Zizioulas, Metropolitan of Pergamon, 'Preserving God's creation: three lectures on theology and ecology' (English), *King's Theological Review* 12 (1989), 1–5, 41–5; 13 (1990), 1–5; C. Yannaras, *The Ontology of Relationship* (Athens: Ikaros, 2004); *Synaxis* 94 (2005), with articles by M. Konstantinou and A. Vletsis.

8. See discussion between John Zizioulas and Philip Sherrard, 'Christology and existence' (English) in *Synaxis*, I, pp. 23–61.

9. E.g. S. Yiangazoglou, *Communion in Deification: The Synthesis of Christology and Pneumatology in the Work of St Gregory Palamas* (Athens: Domos, 2001).

10. See the criticisms voiced by S. Papalexandropoulos, *Essays in the History of Religions* (Athens: Ellenika Grammata, 1994).

11. M. Begzos, *Dialectical Physics and Eschatological Theology: The Contemporary Philosophical Dialogue between Physics and Theology based on the Scientific Work of W. Heisenberg* (Athens, 1985).

12. C. Yannaras, *Post-modern Meta-physics* (Athens: Domos, 1993).

13. See, e.g., *Orthodoxy and the Natural Sciences* (Athens: Savvalas / Union of Greek Physicists, 1996), which includes contributions by Fr G. Metallinos, Fr A. Meskos and G. Pavlou; K. Zakhos, *Lost Familiarity: The Ecological Crisis in the Light of the Thought of St Maximus the Confessor* (Larisa: Ella, 1998).

14. Cf. P. Kalaitzidis (ed.), *Church and Eschatology* (Athens: Kastaniotis, 2003), a collection of essays by eighteen writers giving a broad overview of aspects of eschatology.

15. See Panagopoulos, 'Ontology or theology of the person?', *Synaxis* 13 (1985), 63–79; 14 (1985), 35–47; S. Agourides, 'Can the persons of the Trinity provide the basis for personalist views of man?' *Synaxis* 33 (1990), 67–78; J. Zizioulas, 'The being of God and the being of man' (English) in *Synaxis*, I, pp. 99–120; C. Yannaras, 'On a corpse sheltered from fire, or, existentialist and personalist aberrations', *Synaxis* 37 (1991), 37–45. See, further, A. Papanikolaou, 'Personhood and its exponents in twentieth-century Orthodox theology', below.

16. See J. Romanides, *An Outline of Orthodox Patristic Dogmatics* (English) (Rollinsford: Orthodox Research Institute, 2004).

17. J. D. Zizioulas, *Eucharist, Bishop, Church: The Unity of the Church in the Divine Eucharist and the Bishop During the First Three Centuries* (English), trans. E. Theokritoff (Brookline, MA: Holy Cross Orthodox Press, 2001).

18. V. Pheidas, *The Institution of the Pentarchy of Patriarchs* (Athens: Armos, 1977).

19. E.g. N. Loudovikos, *The Apophatic Ecclesiology of the Homoousion. The Primitive Church Today* (Athens: Armos, 2002); Dimitris Moschos, *From Osiris to the Son of David: The Origin and Primitive Constitution of Christianity in Egypt* (Athens: Parousia, 2002).

20. See T. Zisis, *The Laity in the Orthodox Church* (Thessaloniki: Vryennios, 1989).

21. N. Matsoukas, *Dogmatic and Symbolic Theology*, vol. ii (Thessaloniki: Pournaras, 1985), pp. 440–8.
22. J. Romanides, *Dogmatic and Symbolic Theology of the Orthodox Eastern Church*, vol. i (Thessaloniki, 1983), pp. 127, 222.
23. N. Nissiotis, *Die Theologie der Ostkirche im Oekumenischen Dialog* (Stuttgart: Evangelisches Verlagswerk, 1968), pp. 22–5, 64–85.
24. I.e. related to the *epiclesis*, the invocation of the Holy Spirit upon the eucharistic gifts.
25. See, for instance, A. Avgoustidis, V. Thermos and D. Kyriazis (eds.), *Theology and Psychiatry in Dialogue* (Athens: Apostoliki Diakonia, 1999); P. Faros, *The Myth of Mental Illness* (Athens: Armos, 2001).
26. In the contributory volume *History of the Greek Nation* (Athens: Ekdotiki Athinon, 1976), pp. 519–59.
27. See, for example, G. Metallinos, *Tradition and Alienation* (Athens: Domos, 1986); H. Vlakhos, *Romioi Born and Bred* (Livadeia: Nativity of the Theotokos Monastery, 1996); T. Zisis, *We have Become Franks: Our European Captivity* (Thessaloniki: Vryennias 1994); C. Yannaras, *Orthodoxy and the West* (English), trans. P. Chamberas and N. Russell (Brookline, MA: Holy Cross Orthodox Press, 2006).
28. See the critique in P. Kalaitzidis, 'The temptation of Judas: Church and national identities' (English), *GOTR* 47 (2002), 357–79.
29. E.g. A. Yannoulatos, 'The purpose and motive of mission from an Orthodox point of view', *International Review of Mission* 54 (1965), 298–307; *Various Christian Approaches to the Other Religions* (Athens: Porefthendes, 1971) (both in English).
30. See E. Voulgarakis, *Mission: Paths and Structures* (Athens: Armos, 1989); *Christianity and the World: In Search of a Contemporary Christian Discourse* (Athens: Armos, 1993).
31. E.g. P. Vassiliadis, *Eucharist and Witness: Orthodox Perspectives on the Unity and Mission of the Church* (English) (Brookline, MA: Holy Cross Orthodox Press, 1998).
32. See, further, Athanasios N. Papathanasiou, *Future, the Background of History: Essays on Church Mission in an Age of Globalization* (Montreal: Alexander Press, 2005); 'Reconciliation: the major conflict in post-modernity. An Orthodox contribution to a missiological dialogue', *Sobornost* 28.1 (2006), 8–20 (both in English).

15 Personhood and its exponents in twentieth-century Orthodox theology

ARISTOTLE PAPANIKOLAOU

After centuries of neglect, Christian theologians renewed their attention to the doctrine of the Trinity in the latter half of the twentieth century. This revival of interest in the Trinity was not restricted simply to an understanding of God; perhaps for the first time in the history of Christian thought, Christian theologians were claiming that the affirmation that God is Trinity has radical implications for theological anthropology, i.e., for thinking about what it means to be human. Christian thinkers, of course, had always linked the understanding of being human to the being of God, but only in the twentieth century was the more explicit claim made that, since God's being *is* persons in communion, then human 'personhood' must be defined in terms of relationality and communion. In other words, humans are truly persons when they image the loving, perichoretic communion of the persons of the Trinity.

Orthodox theology in the twentieth century was very much a part of this revival and its influence is noticeable both in the theologies of the Trinity and in the attempt to relate the doctrine of the Trinity to theological anthropology. The Russian Sophiologists of the late nineteenth and early twentieth centuries were the first to forge the link between Trinity and personhood. Beginning with Vladimir Soloviev, the father of Russian Sophiology, Russian sophiological understandings of person can be interpreted as applying a trinitarian corrective to the German idealist philosophy of the transcendental ego. The Russian Sophiologists, especially Pavel Florensky and Sergius Bulgakov, identified the 'person' with the absolute freedom and irreducibility of the transcendental ego that philosophy discovers through an analysis of self-consciousness. They argued, however, that such an understanding of 'person' is incomplete without the trinitarian notions of love and relationality. This theological understanding of person reaches its most developed form in the work of Bulgakov who, according to Michael Meerson, establishes 'the Trinitarian structure of both the created and the divine personality, by moving from

Fichte's *Ich*-philosophy through the Feuerbachian "I-Thou" thesis to the methodological "We" in the Russian notion of *sobornost'*.[1]

These themes of freedom, irreducibility, love and relationality and their identification with the concept of person, minus, however, the reliance on German idealist notions of the transcendental ego, are all evident in contemporary Orthodox theology. Such an affinity is especially evident in the theology of Vladimir Lossky, the Russian émigré theologian best known to both Eastern and Western Christians. Lossky, however, was largely unsympathetic to Russian Sophiology; it is, thus, likely that Lossky critically filtered Russian sophiological understandings of personhood into his own apophatic framework. It was Lossky's theology of personhood that influenced the Greek theologians Christos Yannaras and John Zizioulas, whose own writings evince no sign of Russian sophiological influence.

In the 1950s, theology in Greece is described as undergoing a liberation from captivity to the scholastic models inherited from German universities after Greek independence from the Ottomans in 1821.[2] Both Christos Yannaras and John Zizioulas situate themselves in this group of theologians who hoped to rescue Orthodox theology from its scholastic slumber by returning to the Church Fathers. Yannaras was also influenced by the Russian émigré theology, particularly that of Vladimir Lossky.[3] Their differences notwithstanding, I will show that these theologians share a consensus on two points: (1) the doctrine of the Trinity implies an understanding of human personhood in terms of *ecstasis* (freedom) and *hypostasis* (uniqueness) that is constituted in particular relations of loving communion; and (2) such an understanding of personhood emerges from what constitutes the core of the Orthodox tradition – the affirmation of divine–human communion.[4] Unlike in contemporary Protestant and Roman Catholic theologies, there is a remarkable consensus among Orthodox theologians that the very starting point of theology is the affirmation of divine–human communion. There is no disagreement on this point, but rather on the implications of this central axiom for thinking about God, Christ, theological anthropology, ecclesiology and epistemology. Lossky, Yannaras and Zizioulas share the consensus that divine–human communion could not be otherwise expressed than through the concept of personhood.

VLADIMIR LOSSKY

The beginning of theology, according to Vladimir Lossky, is the Incarnation understood as the event of the union of the divine and the human natures in the person of Christ.[5] It is this event which reveals the antinomic God, i.e., the God who is simultaneously transcendent to and immanent in creation. Given this revelation of God, theology must be apophatic. Lossky, however, means much more by apophatic than simply the assertion that one 'knows' God through the affirmations of what God is not. Apophaticism also does not mean that one can never make positive statements about God. Drawing primarily on Dionysius the Areopagite, Lossky explains that insofar as God reveals himself, kataphatic or positive names can be attributed to God, such as 'God is good.' God, however, is simultaneously the *transcendent* and immanent God; hence, language used to express what God is cannot be construed as literal. God's revelation is always excessive, which means that there is always a gap between our language about God and what God is. In an apophatic approach, theology attempts to stretch language in order to express the central antinomy revealed in the Incarnation – God's transcendence and immanence. As Lossky states:

> . . . [t]he existence of an apophatic attitude – of a going beyond everything that has a connection with created finitude – is implied in the paradox of the Christian revelation: the transcendent God becomes immanent in the world, but in the very immanence of His economy, which leads to the incarnation and to death on the cross, He reveals himself as transcendent, as ontologically independent of all created beings.[6]

The purpose of theology is not to resolve the antinomy, but to express it in order to lead one to union with the God who in his transcendence is radically immanent in Christ.[7] Dogmas are essentially, for Lossky, antinomic expressions of the mystery of the Incarnation whose purpose is to guide the believer towards an experience of divine–human communion. In the end, true knowledge of God is not propositional or conceptual; it is mystical knowledge that goes beyond reason without denying it, and is given in the experience of God – in *theosis*.[8]

The Incarnation reveals not only the antinomy of the transcendent and immanent God, but also the 'primordial fact' that God is Trinity.[9] Apophaticism is a necessary condition for expressing God as Trinity insofar as the Trinity is the antinomic affirmation that each of the three is simultaneously the same yet irreducible to the other.[10] The challenge to theology is to choose the proper language for expressing the Trinity. The distinction that is widely accepted in the Christian tradition is that between 'nature' and 'person'.[11] The language of the Trinity is the product of the Christian controversies over the person of Christ, often referred to as the 'trinitarian controversies'. On Lossky's reading, the nature/person distinction is the product of the genius of the Cappadocian Fathers. Nature (*ousia*) referred to what was the same among the Father, the Son and the Holy Spirit; person (*hypostasis*) referred to what is irreducible either to the nature or to the other persons. For Lossky, *hypostasis* was an especially suitable term since it was also used synonymously with *ousia*, and as such, when used for the Trinity, indicates that the three are the same *ousia*. The Cappadocians did, however, have to 'deconceptualise' *hypostasis* of its traditional philosophical content so that it can refer to the irreducibility of the three either to the *ousia* or to the other persons. In a deconceptualised form, *ousia* and *hypostasis* express the antinomy of God as Trinity, i.e. the simultaneity of sameness and irreducible particularity.[12] In characteristically apophatic fashion, Lossky asserts that this is all that the distinction is meant to convey – the antinomic truth of God's being as Trinity. Lossky, however, has difficulty remaining faithful to his own apophatic restrictions, and in his interpretation of the antinomic use of the person/nature distinction for expressing the doctrine of the Trinity, he gives one of the constitutive aspects of his theology of personhood – uniqueness as irreducibility to nature. To be a person is to be more than simply the nature common to persons.

To be irreducible to nature, however, also implies another constitutive feature of personhood – freedom from nature. This latter aspect of personhood is developed by Lossky in relation to his understanding of the *monarchia* of the Father. In, again, characteristically apophatic fashion, Lossky affirms the monarchy of the Father – the Father is the principle of unity in the Trinity. If either the nature of or the communion between the persons of the Trinity were the principle of unity, this would give priority either to what is the same or to what is particular in the Trinity. For Lossky, responding to Théodore de Régnon's axiom that theologies of the Trinity have started either with the one or with the three, it is necessary that both what is common and what is particular in the Trinity be thought simultaneously.[13] The monarchy of the Father accomplishes this antinomic condition of theology of the Trinity. He argues that '[t]hus the monarchy of the Father maintains the perfect equilibrium between the nature and the persons, without coming down too heavily on one side . . . The one nature and the three hypostases are presented simultaneously to our understanding, with neither prior to the other.'[14]

Although he affirms the monarchy of the Father on the basis of his apophatic understanding of theology as expressing an antinomy, Lossky cannot help but go beyond this apophatic restriction. It is clear, especially in Lossky's later writings, that the monarchy of the Father does more than simply serve an antinomic function; it implies something for the meaning of personhood. If the Father is the principle of unity of the Trinity, then, for Lossky, the 'cause' of the Son and Spirit is a personal principle. It is only, however, as a personal principle that the Father can be 'cause' of the other persons of the Trinity, since it is only as person that the Father is not reducible to the divine nature, and, thus, free from nature in such a way as to give the divine nature to the Son and the Spirit.[15] This free movement beyond nature in order to give it to the other persons of the Trinity Lossky cautiously identifies as *ecstasis*, while wary of 'introducing an expression too reminiscent of "the ecstatic character" of the *Dasein* of Heidegger'.[16] The Father as personal principle also implies that the movement towards the Son and Spirit is one of love.[17] To *be* a person of the Trinity is to be irreducible to nature, i.e. unique, in a movement of freedom from nature that is defined as love. Uniqueness is given when freedom exists as love.

Lossky's apophatic sensibilities are evident when he addresses the question of whether there can be an analogy between 'person' as understood in the Trinity and human personhood. It is clear, for Lossky, that there cannot be a direct analogy. What philosophical anthropology normally understands as 'person' really amounts to individualism. 'Person' is not so much what humans *are* as what they can become. There are two basic components to salvation for humans: the objective and the subjective.[18] The former is accomplished in the person of Christ who deifies human nature. This deified human nature is accessible in baptism. Unity with the deified nature of Christ is, however, only the precondition for the true goal of the human being, which is deification. Divine–human communion is effected by the work of the Spirit who communicates the divine energies; it is also, for Lossky, an event of personhood insofar as it is a movement of freedom beyond the limitations of human nature in communion with God, a movement which can only occur as love and which constitutes the person as uniquely irreducible to nature. Personhood, thus, is an event of human communion with God who, as Trinity, is the one who makes possible this communion as the transcendent and immanent God.

CHRISTOS YANNARAS

The general contours of Lossky's theology of personhood, together with his attack on Neo-scholasticism, are all prominent in the thought of Christos Yannaras. Yannaras affirms all that Lossky does about personhood in terms of irreducibility, freedom (*ecstasis*) and love. He adds, however, three distinctive elements: (1) an engagement with Heidegger who, he argues, provides the justification for a re-appropriation of Dionysian apophaticism; (2) an identification of *ecstasis* with *eros*; and (3) a much more explicit – rather than implicit, as it is in Lossky – identification of person as a relational reality.

Heidegger's singular contribution to the history of philosophy, according to Yannaras, was to discern how philosophical discourse on the question of God is essentially 'ontotheological'. God was reduced to the first cause of creation, but, as such, was reduced to the highest 'thing' within creation, thus leading to conceptual idolatry. Heidegger's critique, thus, opens the door for a revival of Dionysian apophaticism which emphasises knowledge of God as an experiential event. Apophaticism regarding the knowledge of God is really an apophaticism of the person insofar as the event of communion between God and humans is one between persons. In such an event humans are encountered as uniquely irreducible to nature, and, hence, to conceptual knowledge; they are constituted as unique and free beings in relations of freedom and love with the trinitarian persons who eternally exist as a communion of persons.[19] Yannaras much more explicitly crosses the apophatic boundary between human and divine personhood in drawing an analogy between the persons of the Trinity and human personhood. This allows him to emphasise the element of relationality in personhood: *imago dei* becomes *imago trinitatis* for Yannaras, which means that personhood is not a quality of human nature, but a relational event analogous to the communion which exists between the persons of the Trinity. Humans can image the life of the Trinity only in community: specifically, the ecclesial community, i.e. the Eucharist.

The knowledge in the experience of union with God is, according to Yannaras, an '*erotic* affair' and the 'gift of an erotic relationship'.[20] Person is an event of freedom, or *ecstasis*, from the limitations of nature in a movement of love which Yannaras identifies with *eros*. This movement is simultaneously a self-transcendence from the limitations of nature, a self-offering to the other, and a desire to be united with the other for the sake of the other.[21] *Eros* is a divisive and acquisitive force only in fallen humanity; when redeemed, it is a unifying force that does not annihilate but constitutes true otherness. Creation itself is a manifestation of God's *eros*, a desire for loving union with what is other than God and which inflames the human desire for return to God.

JOHN ZIZIOULAS

Zizioulas and Yannaras are contemporaries, but Yannaras was the first of the two theologians to form a developed theology of personhood in his small book *On the Absence and Unknowablility of God: Heidegger and the Areopagite* (1967 in Greek), and then more fully in his *Person and Eros* (1970 in Greek). Zizioulas's first attempt at a developed theological account of personhood appeared in 1975 in the article 'Human capacity and human incapacity', though one can detect traces of his theology of personhood in his dissertation, *Eucharist, Bishop, Church* (1965 in Greek). In his early writings, he continued to develop his theology of personhood primarily in relation to his ecclesiology. Zizioulas credits Yannaras and Martin Buber with influencing his own understanding of personhood.[22] There is thus a continuity of thought on personhood that can be traced from Lossky through Yannaras to Zizioulas. The early work on the Eucharist and ecclesiology is, however, key for understanding Zizioulas's own approach to personhood. The experience of God in the Eucharist is both the ground and the realisation of human personhood. Zizioulas here is linking personhood to the eucharistic ecclesiology of twentieth-century Orthodox theology most evident in the work of Nicolas Afanasiev and Zizioulas's own mentor, Georges Florovsky. Zizioulas also links his theology of personhood to a theology of the Trinity in a way that is more developed than in Yannaras and less apophatic than in Lossky.

For Zizioulas, theology begins with the experience of God in Christ, by the Holy Spirit, in the Eucharist. From the time of the early Christians, 'Church' was identified with the eucharistic assembly. If the Church is the Body of Christ, then the Church *is* the Eucharist since it is there that the community of the faithful is constituted as the Body of Christ. The Pauline expression, 'Body of Christ', is not metaphorical for Zizioulas: the Eucharist is quite literally the event of the resurrected Body of Christ.[23] It is such an event because of the presence of the Holy Spirit, who constitutes the faithful as the Body of Christ. The Holy Spirit does not simply inspire or empower individual Christians, but completes the work of Christ by making present the divine–human communion accomplished in the person of the resurrected Christ. The Holy Spirit's role is thus primarily communal and eschatological, in that it constitutes the Eucharist as the eschatological unity of all in Christ. This understanding of the interrelation of ecclesiology and Christology is what Zizioulas refers to as a 'pneumatologically conditioned Christology'.[24]

It is this experience of God in the Eucharist that forms the basis for the early Christian affirmation of the divinity of Christ and the Spirit. The challenge during the early Christian controversies was to find the proper language to express the eucharistic experience of God in Christ, and, hence, of the Trinity itself. Like Lossky and Yannaras, Zizioulas credits the Cappadocian Fathers with the *ousia*/*hypostasis* distinction which expresses what is the same and what is particular in the Trinity. For Zizioulas, however, the language of the Trinity must express more than what is the same and what is particular; it must signify the event of divine–human communion in Christ as experienced in the Eucharist, which is simultaneously an event of communion among the Father, Son and the Holy Spirit. This event of divine–human communion is inherently a relational event which occurs in the *hypostasis* of Christ. *Hypostasis* cannot simply mean, according to Zizioulas, that which signifies particularity; it is a relational category insofar as it is *in* the *hypostasis* of Christ that the eschatological unity of all creation occurs. This unity is not an absorption of human personhood in the person of Christ, but the constitution of human personhood in its eternal uniqueness by being brought into relation to the Father through the Son by the Holy Spirit. Christ is, by the Holy Spirit, the one and the many in whom the many are constituted as children of God, and, as such, eternally unique. It is only in Christ that humans are true persons, i.e. unique and irreducible beings.[25] This personhood, however, is also a relational and an *ecstatic* event in which the human person transcends the limitations of finite nature towards an eternal communion with the Father in Christ by the Holy Spirit.

According to Zizioulas, *hypostasis* by itself cannot convey all that is accomplished in Christ, and all that is revealed about God in Christ, primarily because *hypostasis* is not a relational category. *Prosopon* ('person'), however, is a relational category, but in both the ancient Greek and Roman contexts it lacked ontological content. The singular genius of the Cappadocian Fathers, according to Zizioulas, was to identify *hypostasis* and *prosopon* so that the relationality and freedom signified in *prosopon* was now given ontological content.[26] In doing this, the Cappadocians were not initiating an 'ontological revolution' so much as giving expression to the revolution in ontology implied by the divine–human communion in Christ. Such an ontology is mutually exclusive with the Greek philosophical ontology of substance in that the priority shifts to relationality, freedom, otherness and communion. The latter are no longer accidents, but what being *is*; human personhood *is* as a relational event in which the person is constituted as eternally unique, other and free. *Hypostasis*, thus, both human and divine, is not simply that which is 'particular', but a relational event of otherness and communion: 'The Person is otherness in communion and communion in otherness'.[27]

Identifying being with relationality, freedom, otherness and communion is not restricted to created being, but to divine being as well. For Zizioulas, this is the implication of the Cappadocian insistence on the monarchy of the Father, which itself logically follows, according to Zizioulas, the eucharistic experience of God in Christ. In what is probably his most controversial theological move, Zizioulas argues that the being of God as Trinity is 'caused' by the person of the Father. Being, thus, is the result of the freedom of the Person of the Father: 'God, as Father and not as substance, perpetually confirms through "being" His *free* will to exist. And it is precisely His trinitarian existence that constitutes this confirmation: the Father out of love – that is, freely – begets the Son and brings forth the Spirit.'[28] The Father as person, as a being who is *hypostatic*, i.e. unique and irreducible to nature, and *ecstatic*, free from the necessity of nature, is the *aitia*, the 'cause', of the persons of the Trinity who are themselves *hypostatic* and *ecstatic* beings in and through an eternal communion of each with the others. For Zizioulas, only by asserting the monarchy of the Father can one ground the possibility of freedom from necessity, which is itself the condition for the possibility for uniqueness and irreducibility. Thinking of God in terms of a primordial concept of an eternal communion would subject the being of God to a 'given' and, hence, to necessity. If God gives what God *is*, and if the experience of salvation in the eucharistic experience of God is a personal uniqueness constituted as freedom from the given, i.e. the necessity of finite humanity, then God's very being must *be* as freedom from necessity.[29]

It is in Zizioulas's reflections on the monarchy of the Father that one sees clearly how his relating a theology of the Trinity to a theology of personhood cannot be labelled as a simple social trinitarianism, nor as a top-down approach. The constitutive aspects of Zizioulas's theology of the Trinity are grounded in the eucharistic experience of God in Christ by the Holy Spirit. This bottom-up approach is even more evident in Zizioulas's discussion of the tragic state of created existence. There is a deep-seated longing, according to Zizioulas, in all of humanity for uniqueness and particularity. Such a longing is manifested in works of art,[30] in sexual desire[31] and in the analysis of the question 'who am I?'[32] In the end, such a longing is thwarted by death – the great leveller of uniqueness and otherness in rendering all the same. Salvation in Christ, experienced in the moment of the Eucharist, is the overcoming of this tragic longing insofar as it fulfils it. But the fulfilment of this longing, in the form of freedom from the necessity of finite nature, reveals that God's very being is freedom from necessity. It is not so much that, because of human salvation, God *must* be conceived as freedom from necessity; rather, for Zizioulas, the eucharistic communion reveals that God's being *is* this freedom insofar as it is this freedom as love that is given in Christ. Since the salvific experience is in Christ by the Holy Spirit, then the freedom of God is conceptualised in the form of the freedom of the Father to constitute the *way* or the *how* (*tropos hyparxeos*) of God's existence as Trinity.[33]

Personhood is the controlling category for Zizioulas's theology and he applies it consistently throughout to other aspects of theology. We have already seen how 'person' is the key to understanding his eucharistic ecclesiology which identifies the Church with the eucharistic assembly. Zizioulas synthesises the eucharistic theology of Nicolas Afanasiev, which one can also detect in Georges Florovsky, with the theology of personhood initiated in Lossky. The understanding of person as a *hypostatic* (unique) and *ecstatic* (free) being constituted in relations of loving communion informs Zizioulas's understanding of ministry. Ordination, as an example, is defined as 'assignment to a particular "ordo" in the community', and, as a result, personhood reveals 'the nature of baptism and confirmation as being essentially an ordination'.[34] This understanding also informs his reflection on the relation of the local to the universal Church, and on the understanding of the role of primacy in the Church. According to Zizioulas, since 'person' is understood in terms of the simultaneity of the one and the many, there is need to express this institutionally in the person of the primate of the universal Church; but the theology of person would preclude an understanding of this primacy in the form of universal jurisdiction.[35] Finally, the influence of his theology of personhood is evident in his writing on the environment. All humans, for Zizioulas, are 'priests of creation', called to personalise all of creation, i.e. to render it unique and free, by offering it eucharistically back to God.[36]

FUTURE ISSUES

The theology of personhood as developed from Lossky through Yannaras to Zizioulas has left at least two issues which future Orthodox theologians must confront. The first is a perennial question for Orthodox theologians and it deals with how one is to read the writings of the Church Fathers. Lossky's, Yannaras's and especially Zizioulas's attempt to root their theologies of personhood in the Fathers, particularly the Cappadocians, has recently been criticised.[37] The criticism keeps in the foreground the ongoing debate on how Orthodox Christians should 'theologise'.

The more substantial issue concerns the centrality of apophaticism and the essence/energies distinction within Orthodox theology in the twentieth century. Zizioulas's theology is a movement away from such a centrality and is, in the end, what separates his theology of personhood from that of Lossky and Yannaras. It is often unclear in Lossky how the understanding of salvation in terms of the essence/energies distinction (which is rooted in the antinomy of God's transcendence and immanence) and his theology of personhood (which is grounded in the antinomy of God as Trinity) relate to one another. This results in a tension in his thought. It is not as self-evident as Lossky and Yannaras assume that the logic of deification demands the essence/energies distinction or leads to the understanding of apophaticism given in their theologies. Regarding the latter, their theologies of personhood, insofar as they are grounded in God's being as Trinity, would appear to transgress their own apophatic sensibilities.[38]

These issues, however, will probably not threaten the consensus that Orthodox theologians share, which is the truth that humans were made to be in communion with God and that this communion has something to do with understanding the meaning of 'person', both divine and human. Orthodox theology, then, will continue as a history of debate not so much on the substance as on the details of conceptualising being as communion.

Further reading

Lossky, V., *In the Image and Likeness of God*, ed. J. H. Erickson and T. E. Bird, Crestwood, NY: SVS Press, 1974.

The Mystical Theology of the Eastern Church, Crestwood, NY: SVS Press, 1976.

Orthodox Theology: An Introduction, trans. Ian and Ihita Kesarcodi-Watson, Crestwood, NY: SVS Press, 1978.

Papanikolaou, A., *Being with God: Trinity, Apophaticism, and Divine–Human Communion*, Notre Dame, IN: University of Notre Dame Press, 2006.

Yannaras, C., *Elements of Faith: An Introduction to Orthodox Theology*, trans. Keith Schram, Edinburgh: T. & T. Clark, 1991.

On the Absence and Unknowability of God: Heidegger and the Areopagite, ed. A. Louth, trans. Haralambos Ventis, Edinburgh: T. & T. Clark, 2005.

Person and Eros, trans. Norman Russell, Brookline, MA: Holy Cross Orthodox Press, forthcoming.

Zizioulas, J. D., Metropolitan of Pergamon, *Being as Communion. Studies in Personhood and the Church*, Crestwood, NY: SVS Press, 1985.

Communion and Otherness, ed. P. McPartlan, London and New York: T. & T. Clark, 2007.

Notes

1. M. A. Meerson, *The Trinity of Love in Modern Russian Theology* (Quincy, IL: Franciscan Press, 1998), p. 174. In his *Modern Russian Theology: Bukharev, Soloviev, Bulgakov – Orthodox Theology in a New Key* (Grand Rapids, MI: Eerdmans, 2000), Paul Vallière cautions that

Bulgakov's personalism must be understood within the framework of his Sophiology.

2. C. Yannaras, 'Theology in present-day Greece', *SVTQ* 16.4 (1972), 195–214; *Orthodoxy and the West*, trans. Peter Chamberas and Norman Russell (Brookline, MA: Holy Cross Orthodox Press, 2006). Also, John Zizioulas, 'The ecumenical dimensions of Orthodox theological education' in *Orthodox Theological Education for the Life and Witness of the Church* (Geneva: WCC, 1978) pp. 33–40.

3. For Lossky's influence on Yannaras and on Greek theologians in general, see Basilio Petrà, 'Personalist thought in Greek in the twentieth century: a first tentative synthesis', *GOTR* 50 (2005), and Yannaras, *Orthodoxy and the West*. In spring 1996, Christos Yannaras explained to me in a private conversation that 'I [Yannaras] started with Lossky.'

4. Some challenge to the centrality of this axiom for theology, and not necessarily to its truth, is emerging in the Orthodox world, especially in the work of John Behr. See his *The Mystery of Christ: Life in Death* (Crestwood, NY: SVS Press, 2006).

5. V. Lossky, 'Apophasis and trinitarian theology' in V. Lossky, *In the Image and Likeness of God* (Crestwood, NY: SVS Press, 1974), p. 14.

6. Lossky, 'Apophasis and trinitarian theology' in *Image and Likeness*, p. 15.

7. For Lossky on antinomy, see 'Theology of Light in Gregory Palamas' in *Image and Likeness*, pp. 51–2, and 'Apophasis and trinitarian theology', p. 26.

8. 'Apophaticism is not necessarily a theology of ecstasy. It is, above all, an attitude of mind which refuses to form concepts about God: . . . The way of knowledge of God is necessarily the way of deification': Lossky, *The Mystical Theology of the Eastern Church* (Crestwood, NY: SVS Press, 1976), pp. 38–9.

9. Lossky, *Mystical Theology*, p. 64.

10. See Lossky's 'Apophasis and trinitarian theology' in *Image and Likeness* pp. 23–9.

11. On this distinction in Lossky, see his *Mystical Theology*, pp. 51–4; also, *Orthodox Theology: An Introduction* (Crestwood, NY: SVS Press, 1978), pp. 40–1.

12. 'It was a question of finding a distinction of terms which should express the unity of, and the differentiation within, the Godhead, without giving the pre-eminence either to the one or to the other' (Lossky, *Mystical Theology*, p. 50).

13. On Michel René Barnes's misreading of Lossky's use of de Régnon, see discussion in A. Papanikolaou, *Being with God: Trinity, Apophaticism, and Divine–Human Communion* (Notre Dame, IN: University of Notre Dame Press, 2006), p. 181, n. 101.

14. Lossky, 'The procession of the Holy Spirit in Orthodox trinitarian doctrine' in *Image and Likeness*, p. 81.

15. Lossky, 'The procession of the Holy Spirit in Orthodox trinitarian doctrine' in *Image and Likeness*, p. 83.

16. Lossky, 'The theological notion of person' in *Image and Likeness*, p. 120. See also Lossky, *Mystical Theology*, pp. 122–3.

17. See Lossky, *Orthodox Theology*, pp. 46–7.

18. Lossky, *Mystical Theology*, pp. 135–73.

19. 'The experience of personal relationship, the experience of *participation* in the *active* manifestation of the otherness of the other, *may be expressed*, but *is never exhausted* in verbal formulation': C. Yannaras, *On the Absence and Unknowability of God: Heidegger and the Areopagite*, ed. A. Louth (Edinburgh: T. & T. Clark, 2005), p. 86.

20. Yannaras, *On the Absence and Unknowability of God*, p. 99.

21. 'Eros is the dynamics of ecstasy, which finds its consummation as personal reference to supreme Otherness': C. Yannaras, *Person and Eros*, trans. N. Russell (Brookline, MA: Holy Cross Orthodox Press), forthcoming. See also his *Elements of Faith: An Introduction to Orthodox Theology*, trans. K. Schram (Edinburgh: T. & T. Clark, 1991), and *The Freedom of Morality* (Crestwood, NY: SVS Press, 1984).

22. In a private conversation in the summer of 1998 in London, Zizioulas was less receptive to my suggestion that, in light of the fact of Yannaras's own confession of 'beginning with Lossky', perhaps he was indirectly influenced by Lossky through Yannaras.

23. For a succinct summary of Zizioulas's understanding of the identification of the Church with the Eucharist, see his *Being as Communion. Studies in Personhood and the Church* (Crestwood, NY: SVS Press, 1985), esp. pp. 143–69.

24. For Zizioulas's pneumatology, see his 'Implications ecclésiologiques de deux types de pneumatologie' in *Communio Sanctorum: Mélanges offerts à Jean-Jacques von Allmen* (Geneva: Labor et Fides, 1981), pp. 141–54. Also see Zizioulas, *Being as Communion*, pp. 123–40.

25. On Zizioulas's understanding of salvation in the *hypostasis* of Christ, see his *Communion and Otherness*, ed. Paul McPartlan (London and New York: T. & T. Clark, 2007), pp. 13–112.

26. For Zizioulas's interpretation of the *hypostasis, prosopon* and *ousia* in the Cappadocian Fathers, see *Communion and Otherness* in its entirety, and *Being as Communion*, pp. 27–122.

27. Zizioulas, *Communion and Otherness*, p. 9.

28. Zizioulas, *Being as Communion*, p. 41.

29. Zizioulas, *Being as Communion*, p. 43. Also, Zizioulas, *Communion and Otherness*, pp. 113–54.

30. Zizioulas, *Communion and Otherness*, pp. 206–49.

31. Zizioulas, *Being as Communion*, pp. 49–65.

32. Zizioulas, *Communion and Otherness*, pp. 99–112.

33. The clearest expression of Zizioulas's understanding of the distinction between *what* God is and the *way* in which God exists appears in his 'The being of God and the being of man' in J. Hadjinicolaou (ed.), *Synaxis*, Vol. 1: *Anthropology, Environment, Creation* (Montreal: Alexander Press, 2006), pp. 99–120.

34. Zizoulas, *Being as Communion*, p. 216.

35. J. Zizioulas, 'Primacy in the Church: an Orthodox approach', *Eastern Churches Journal* 5.2 (1998), 7–28.

36. J. Zizioulas, 'Preserving God's creation: three lectures on theology and ecology', *King's Theological Review* 12 (1989), 1–5, 41–5; 13 (1990), 1–5.

37. A. de Halleux, '"Hypostase" et "personne" dans la formation du dogme trinitaire (ca. 375–81)', *Revue d'histoire eccléstiastique* 79 (1984), 313–69, 625–70. See also J. Behr, *The Nicene Faith* (Crestwood, NY: SVS Press, 2004); L. Ayres, *Nicaea and Its Legacy: An Approach to Fourth-Century Trinitarian Theology* (Oxford: Oxford University Press, 2004); and the recent criticism by L. Turcescu, '"Person" versus "individual", and other modern misreadings of Gregory of Nyssa', *Modern Theology* 18.4 (December 2002), 97–109, as well as the response by A. Papanikolaou, 'Is John Zizioulas an existentialist in disguise? Response to Lucian Turcescu', *Modern Theology* 19.3 (2004), 587–93.

38. For more on this tension between the essence/energies distinction and the doctrine of the Trinity, see Papanikolaou, *Being with God*, esp. pp. 106–27.

16 The witness of the Church in a pluralistic world: theological renaissance in the Church of Antioch

NICOLAS ABOU MRAD

It is not fortuitous that the followers of Jesus were first called 'Christians' in Antioch (Acts 11:19–26). It was only natural for a city that gathered believers from both Jewish and Gentile backgrounds in one eucharistic community to be linked to the very nature of Christianity. Referring to Antioch, the apostle Paul stresses in Galatians 2 the importance of the universality of the gospel of Christ, its ability to address Jews and Greeks alike, as a *sine qua non* for the veracity and credibility of his mission.

This 'pluralistic dimension' has always characterised the Orthodox Church of Antioch and shaped its theological discourse. From its first years, Antioch has had a unique experience of multiplicity and diversity; it has always represented a rich human and cultural tapestry, resulting from the encounter of the civilisations of the ancient Near East with Greek and Roman cultures. Later in its history Antioch co-existed with Islam, experiencing both the tolerant openness of the early Islamic rulers and the strict control of the Ottomans. Due to cultural and historical circumstances, the Christians of Antioch did not experience the triumphant dominance of an established Christianity such as we see in both the Byzantine world and medieval Western Europe.

ANTIOCH IN MODERN HISTORY: EMERGENCE FROM GREEK DOMINATION

The Antiochian schism in 1724, which resulted in the rise of the 'Greek Catholic' or 'Melkite' Church, led to intensive involvement by the Ecumenical Patriarch in the affairs of the Orthodox Antiochian Church. For well over a century, Orthodox patriarchs of Antioch and several other bishops were chosen from the ranks of Greek-speaking clergy from Constantinople, Jerusalem or Cyprus. In the second half of the nineteenth century, however, the Antiochian Church experienced an educational revival, thanks largely to Russian support. In 1848 the tsar dedicated a special budget to finance the education of the Antiochian clergy, and the Palestinian Imperial Russian Society (founded 1882) supported education in the Church of Antioch in addition to Russian pilgrimage to the Holy Land.

Crucial to the modern renaissance of the Church of Antioch was its emergence from Greek domination, when at the end of the nineteenth century Meletius Al-Doumani (*sed.* 1899–1906) was elected as the first Arab patriarch since 1724. This emergence coincided with the increasing weakness of the Ottoman state, and the rise, towards the end of the nineteenth century, of the Arab renaissance movement, within which Antiochian Christians played a leading role. Many of these Christians were prominent advocates of a secular state, secularists with important cultural ideas, who were active in the fields of literature, poetry and journalism, championed the Arab cause and resisted Western forms of colonisation.

Once Antioch was free to elect its own hierarchs, religious life witnessed a remarkable flowering. Church leaders saw the need for an educational movement to make believers more aware of their religious and cultural identity. Feeling the importance of having a theological educational institution like other Christian denominations in the region, in 1901 Patriarch Meletius founded the Balamand seminary, though it later had to close temporarily because of the First World War. Several other institutions for theological education were opened in monasteries such as St George's Monastery in Humeira (Syria) and the Monastery of Our Lady of Bkeftine (Lebanon). Publications have been issued in the form of magazines and newspapers, which were edited by some of the most prominent theologians of the Antiochian Church.

Meletius's successor Gregorius IV (*sed.* 1906–28) focused his activity on pastoral issues, including the establishment of 'denomination councils', consisting mainly of laypersons, to support the bishops in their work. These councils even had the right to participate in the election of the patriarch and the bishops.

The Church of Antioch suffered immensely during the Second World War and in its aftermath, as the re-drawing of national boundaries in the Middle Eastern region divided its flock between Syria, Lebanon and Turkey. However, the emergence of the Orthodox Youth Movement in 1942 breathed fresh life into the Church, bringing a serious commitment to ecclesial life and openness towards the challenges of the modern age.

THE ORTHODOX YOUTH MOVEMENT: A SPIRITUAL REVIVAL

The rise of the Orthodox Youth Movement or MJO (for 'Mouvement de la Jeunesse Orthodoxe') in 1942 was one of the most obvious signs of revival in Antioch's modern history. The founders of this movement, led by Georges Khodr (now Metropolitan of Byblos and Botris (Mt Lebanon)), were disturbed by the state of their Church, which was riven by inner tensions and dominated by confessional and sectarian ambitions fomented by Western powers. Inspired by religious zeal and the discovery of Orthodox spirituality, mainly through the writings of Russian émigrés, these young people called for a revival based on a 'rediscovery' of the richness of the Bible and the Orthodox tradition. They were convinced that a genuine Christian life is distinguished by a true commitment to prayer and a conscious participation in the sacraments, which went hand in hand with a deep desire to strengthen theological education, with the aim of crystallising a committed Orthodox awareness, caring for the poor and the needy, rejecting sectarianism and opening up to other Churches and to Islam.

After its recognition by the Antiochian Synod, the MJO spread rapidly. Youth groups were formed in the dioceses of Lebanon and Syria. Sunday Schools were established almost everywhere to teach children of all ages the basics of the Orthodox faith. The MJO has created an incomparable dynamic in Church involvement and ecclesial awareness that has touched almost every active member of the Antiochian Church. Under the influence of the MJO, and with a growing awareness of the importance of monasticism in the life of the Church, several monasteries were re-opened in Lebanon and Syria to welcome new brotherhoods of monks and nuns. These monasteries have since played a crucial role in counselling and spiritual guidance.

In a theological perspective, Georges Khodr considers the rise of the youth movement a response to the call of divine grace.[1] It is a prophetic movement whose main responsibility is the proclamation of the Word of God in word and deed, regardless of whether or not its members are ordained ministers. It is a spiritual movement complementing, not conflicting with, the activity of the clergy; for the Church cannot be but one Body, the members of which function in full harmony and cooperation. In an age of rigid clericalism, Khodr believes that spiritual matters are not the responsibility of the pastors alone; Christian witness 'in word and deed, in love and faith, and in purity' (1 Tim 4:12) is a responsibility which must be shared by all members of the Church.

As a fully Orthodox movement, the MJO invites individuals and communities to participate with full awareness in worship and sacramental life, to understand Christian doctrine and to live according to the gospel and the tradition. The Movement has no teaching of its own beyond that of the gospel, nor is it a separate body within the Church.

Revival, for Khodr, means appreciation of the Orthodox faith and the rediscovery of the rich heritage of the Church in the service of a more effective Christian mission and witness. The Church is understood as the heart of the world, fulfilling a prophetic function: it speaks for God. The community of believers living in history is stirred from within by the prophetic words of the New Testament, and its witness should therefore call the world to repentance. The main duty of Christians is, according to Khodr, to communicate this witness through charity and love for the poor, who are, in the words of St John Chrysostom, the 'altar' where believers can offer their sacrifices at all times.

In the same spirit Deacon Ignatius Hazim (now Patriarch Ignatius IV of Antioch), writing in 1946, urged Antiochian Christians to be aware of their responsibilities and commitments as members of the Church. He presented them with two choices: either to be indifferent to spiritual revival and to remain outside Orthodoxy, or to make every effort to revive the Antiochian Church and bring it out of the miserable state to which it was reduced after the Second World War. He made the striking affirmation that each committed Christian should care for others spiritually as if he were their pastor.[2]

Within the circles of committed and educated youth, the MJO has triggered a large scale re-thinking of the Church's witness and its role in society, and of the interaction between the Church and the challenges of modern trends and thoughts. The MJO has produced a number of authors who, in their turn, have enriched it with their insights.

Costi Bendali (born 1926) is probably the most prolific author whose name is closely associated with the MJO. Originally a specialist in applied psychology with a doctorate from the University of Lyon III (France), Bendali has dedicated his writing to reconsidering the relation of the latest approaches in psychology, philosophy and education to religious awareness and commitment. Bendali's fundamental premise is that faith constitutes a principal dimension in human existence. His *Fasting and Orality*,[3] for example, is a remarkable attempt to study Orthodox asceticism making critical use of the contribution of human sciences. In a clear allusion to Freud, he speaks of fasting as a means to liberate the 'desire' from the 'needs' within which the culture of 'consumption' wants to confine it. Desire would thus be freed to return to its origin, namely to become a desire of God, an aspiration to perfection. In this way, desire opens up to *agape* so as to become a loving attitude towards the beings and the things of the world.

In *Shadows and Splendours of the Spirit of Childhood*, Bendali embarks on a critical reading of a narrow and biased psychoanalysis, which claims that faith is a mere echoing of people's childhood need for authority.[4] Bendali distinguishes between childhood as understood in Jesus' saying that believers should be like children to inherit the Kingdom of God (cf. Mt 5:5), and childishness as a vague inclination towards a self-centred existence led by instincts. The spirit of childhood, according to Bendali, must accompany human beings throughout their lives, so that they may look at the divine mysteries with transparency and admiration. Genuine spiritual childhood enables humans to be aware and watchful, so that they may free themselves from childishness. Once the human being is liberated from childishness, he will be able to go beyond the self and await the perfection that comes from God.

In the field of education, Bendali believes that the ultimate goal is to lead human beings to the resurrected Christ. Whether it is religious, scientific, social, civic or sexual, education must respect the dignity of the human being and his vocation to be the image of God, regardless of religion and race. Costi Bendali has also written several remarkably accessible expositions of the Orthodox faith, which have made him one of the most popular authors within MJO circles.

Ecclesial concerns have also preoccupied other leading figures of the modern renaissance in Antioch, such as Georges Nahas (former MJO Secretary and now Vice President of the University of Balamand and Dean of the St John of Damascus Faculty of Theology). In his *Come and See*,[5] Nahas considers the active presence of the Church in the world and warns of the danger of falling into 'institutionalism' in the management of church affairs. 'Institutionalism', according to Nahas, arises from the influence of secular thought on the life of the Church. He reminds his readers that the Church's main role is the sanctification of human beings in their daily life, and this cannot be accomplished through mere forms. Neglecting the 'essence' in prayer, fasting, celebration of feasts or sacraments, or in financial matters, leads to a rigid 'formalism' which will eventually nullify the Church's witness to Christ. The Church in the world must be a milieu of revelation, through a life of humility and sacrifice in its service and obedience to its Lord.

With a prophetic spirit, Nahas invites the Orthodox Church in Antioch to be aware of the human, technical and intellectual changes that are taking place around it; to dispose of many residues from the past and find new ways of witnessing. The Church's vocation to witness requires it to reconsider its educational approaches, seeking less to inform the people than to strengthen them in Christ. All Christians are invited by God to a life of holiness: education must be practised in a way that respects this divine call.

The educationalist and former MJO General Secretary, Chafiq Haydar, also stresses the fact that Christian education presupposes the freedom of the person. Its goal is to help the person to discover him- or herself and his or her value as the image of God, and to learn to live out the freedom which this entails.[6] Church educational institutions should be built upon the basis of love and service so that they become places where human beings can meet God and know his holy face.

THE ST JOHN OF DAMASCUS INSTITUTE OF THEOLOGY

The most prominent landmark in the educational revival is the achievement of the Antiochian Holy Synod, which decided to turn the seminary of Balamand into an institution of higher theological education in the late 1960s. The Institute of Theology became one of the founding faculties of the Orthodox University of Balamand. Most of those who wish to work in the Church either in the ordained ministry or as lay-persons pursue their theological studies here.

Coupled with its role in preparing candidates for priesthood and service, the Institute aspires to be a place where the Orthodox heritage is re-discovered and fostered by further academic studies. In its relatively short history, the St John of Damascus Institute of Theology has made remarkable steps forward in theological education and research. In addition to Patriarch Ignatius IV and Metropolitan Georges Khodr, whose theological input is described elsewhere in this chapter, other professors at the Institute have made valuable contributions to their respective fields.

In the field of Biblical Studies, Paul Tarazi, who taught Old and New Testament from 1971 to 1996 (also Professor of Old Testament at St Vladimir's Seminary in New York since 1980), has contributed to the advancement of biblical research. In his three-volume introduction to the Old Testament,[7] he shows how the Old Testament authors use a variety of means and traditions to describe God's revelation, challenging the readers to accept God as Lord and Master of their lives. Interesting in Tarazi's approach is how he relates the historical traditions of the Pentateuch to the prophets, contesting the prevailing separation of these two parts of the Old Testament into two distinct theological dimensions, law and prophecy. For Tarazi, the 'historical language' used extensively in the Pentateuch and the historical books does not remotely reflect what would classically be considered a 'real perspective on history'. Actually, the so-called 'histories' of the kingdoms of Israel and Judah are concerned with the stories of interactions between the prophets and kings; this makes biblical history God's story of his kings rather than the kings' story of themselves. This 'anti-historical' approach to the Bible is important insofar as it reflects God's message to human beings. Hence the Old Testament is thoroughly prophetical, in the sense that it conveys the word of God in its full authority and power.

In his subsequent introduction to the New Testament,[8] Tarazi questions the prevailing idea that the New Testament contains different theological approaches (Pauline, Johannine, synoptic and so on). For Tarazi, the New Testament contains but one view, namely the true gospel which is based on the message of the Old Testament prophets. The organic relation between the Old and New Testaments is clear in the fact that the New Testament represents the only 'legitimate' interpretation of the Old Testament. For this reason, the texts of the New Testament have the same authority as those of the Old Testament, and from the moment they were written they were intended by their authors to be read as scripture, conveying to the believers the true message of the gospel of Jesus Christ. Following the tradition of the Church Fathers, Tarazi holds that Old and New Testament do not contain distinct 'theologies'; they represent together the one Bible, containing the saving word of God which was revealed through the prophets and which found its ultimate expression in the Incarnation.

Another biblical scholar, Daniel Ayuch, Professor of New Testament at the Institute, offers a modern reading of the narrative texts of the New Testament. He stresses the importance of reading the biblical texts in their final shape, and of analysing the level of the reader's response. In two studies, Ayuch offers a critical and analytical reading of biblical studies in the Orthodox Church and their crucial role in the shaping of the Eastern tradition.[9] Throughout his work, he combines exegetical methods with educative strategies in order to enhance communication between academic circles and parishes.

In the field of the Old Testament, Nicolas Abou Mrad, Professor of Old Testament and Biblical Languages at the Institute, has provided new insights on how to read the Bible, especially concerning the relationship between the narratives of the Old and the New Testaments. In 'Abraham: *typos* of the Christian believer',[10] Abou Mrad shows that the idea of the New Covenant, as it is described and presented in the New Testament, is rooted in the story of Abraham, which introduces the reader of the Old Testament to the newness of God's dealing with humankind, over against the 'oldness' of human attempts to imprison God within the framework of 'Ancient Near Eastern' religious categories.

In a study of the notion of 'Covenant' in the Old Testament,[11] Abou Mrad challenges the view of the Covenant as a relationship of obligations and rights between two partners, God and the people. For Abou Mrad, the images of marriage and sonship in Hosea 1–3 and 11 show that the relationship between God and the people is presented in such a way that the important point is God's position vis-à-vis his people. The ultimate meaning of the Covenant is to underline God's authority and lordship over his people.

Abou Mrad's approach to the Old Testament's books is based on his conviction that they present, in narrative form, the fundamental guidelines which will be used later by the New Testament authors to write their own narratives preaching Jesus Christ as the full revelation of the saving God.

In systematic theology, Georges Atiyeh, Professor of Dogmatics until 2006, has stressed the importance of Orthodox faith and practice as a necessity for salvation. On the question of the relation between faith and biblical interpretation, Atiyeh argues for the unity of the 'holy tradition' of the Church delivered by the apostles and disciples of the Lord in two ways, oral and written. The apostolic tradition was adopted by the Church and became the very mystery of its life and practice, through which the faithful are saved; and it is through this tradition that believers come to understand the scriptures. Atiyeh was also interested in showing the pastoral dimension of doctrine. On the basis of real debates with Jehovah's Witnesses and other sects, he published two books in which he refutes the arguments used by these sects to undermine the Orthodox faith.

On the question of women in the Church, Marlène Kanaan, Professor at the University of Balamand and Lecturer of Philosophy at the Institute, has a particular interest in the position of women in the writings of the Church Fathers. In a study of two patristic texts from the fourth century,[12] Kanaan discusses the significance of the expression 'woman', relating the anthropo-theological view of the Fathers on woman to their historical and social context. She deduces a universal anthropological vision of human beings which does not distinguish between male and female. Then she relates the notions of 'male' and 'female' to sexual particularities and organic differences which do not impose on 'males' and 'females' any special patterns of behaviour, but enable the person to go beyond his or her biological reality to achieve perfection through virtue.

In the field of philosophy, Adib Saab, Professor of General Philosophy and Philosophy of Religion from 1971 to 2000, published between 1983 and 2003 a tetralogy (in Arabic) in the field of Religious Studies. The third and main volume, entitled *Prolegomena to the Philosophy of Religion*, triggers a new field of study in modern Arab culture. It is noteworthy that Saab, in this tetralogy, writes as a philosopher, not as an apologist. He defends theism in general rather than his own faith and puts religions on an equal footing, adopting the socio-philosophical concept of 'mere difference'.

ANTIOCH AND ISLAM

The Church of Antioch encountered Islam just a few years after the appearance of that religion in the Arabian Peninsula. In the course of the Middle Ages, representatives of the two religions would confront one another, as Christian theologians attempted to defend the basic dogmas of the faith and to refute Islamic beliefs. However, many Christian apologists tried to expound their faith more positively, in order to assert themselves as monotheists.

In its modern theological discourse, the Church of Antioch has always insisted on the importance of both a dialogue of life and one of thought with the Muslims. This conviction is rooted in the experience of common history and in the necessity for understanding the other more deeply.

For this reason, the Orthodox University of Balamand founded in 1995 a Centre for Christian–Muslim Studies. Its initiatives included, among others, an annual Christian–Muslim summer school and a research project on the mutual images that Christianity and Islam have of each other today. The Centre has also convened an international Consultation on Christian–Muslim Studies. Georges Massouh, Director of the Centre and Lecturer in Islamology at the St John of Damascus Institute, emphasises faith in the same one God and also the common values and virtues shared by the two religions. In both, caring for the poor and for suffering persons and 'bearing one another's burdens' are the utmost expressions of religious piety. Moreover, in both Christianity and Islam the human being is the highest value; he is God's 'image and likeness' in Christianity, and God's 'representative on earth' in the Qur'an. Both religions call for an expectation of 'blessings to come' (Heb 9:11) and their realisation in the present world through genuine service.[13]

Patriarch Ignatius IV[14] has always insisted on the fact that Arab Christians belong to the Middle East: they are not guests. They have been living and witnessing in that region, proclaiming belief in the one God, since long before Islam conquered and established itself there. Patriarch Ignatius speaks in terms of Christians and Muslims believing in one God who embraces in his providence all peoples, regardless of their beliefs. Despite the historical difficulties that have led to mutual rejection, the Patriarch sees that life goes beyond mere controversies and disputes.

And Muslims and Christians in the Arab world have experienced a common life: they both trust in divine providence, and attach the same value to humility and the need to surrender oneself to God, which is what 'Islam' really means.

Ignatius IV speaks of plurality in the framework of love. For him, plurality is a form of obedience to the divine will. He invites Eastern Christians to share with Muslims the concerns of justice and peace and affirms that when one humbles oneself, one permits life to bear fruit despite the violence and disappointments of history. The Christians of the East have not shared the spirit of the Crusades, but that of the Cross. They did not make Christianity a closed, separate identity, but 'the humble and radiant presence of the life-giving Cross'. Hence they must always be in solidarity with those around them 'without naivety, yet without hate; without compromise, yet without fear'.[15]

This solidarity should be expressed in the attitude of Antiochian Christians towards the issues troubling the Arab East to which they belong, such as the question of Palestine. Patriarch Ignatius invites Eastern Christians to acknowledge Jerusalem as the heart of humanity, a crucible where many religions and religious values interact and co-exist; he describes racism and apartheid in Palestine as 'a stain on the brow of truth and justice'.[16] In the context of the troubles that shake the region, he speaks of the Church of Antioch standing in the midst of the 'bloodbath of the Middle East' as 'an unarmed, non-violent and confessing Church'.[17]

Like Patriarch Ignatius, Metropolitan Georges Khodr invites Eastern Christianity to express its faith and formulations in such a way as to become closer to Islamic thought and mentality, and to produce a living culture that would address the Muslims in their concerns and preoccupations, including Palestine, Iraq and the anti-Islamic trends in the West which characterise Islam as a terrorist religion. Crucial in his approach to such issues is the belief that the Old Testament is fully realised in Christ. In consequence, God's promise is no longer associated with the possession of territory, but with a Kingdom that will be inherited by the meek.[18]

Metropolitan Georges Khodr attempts a Christian theology of non-Christian religions.[19] He sees that the Church is not simply an institution in history but a charismatic place, the instrument of the mystery of the salvation of the nations. It is not in the world by accident. For this reason the Church is not a closed society, just as it is not a society whose progress can be measured in numbers. It does not constitute a 'Christian nation', a sociologically defined community. For Khodr, the same Christ who is present in the Church is also present outside its historical limits. Witness among non-Christians, therefore, is a matter of naming the Christ whom others have already recognised as the Beloved.

Following Vladimir Lossky, Khodr draws a clear distinction in this context between the economy of the Son and that of the Spirit. Pentecost signifies that creation has become capable of receiving the Holy Spirit.[20] It is the Spirit who makes Christ present within us; but the Spirit operates according to his own economy, and Khodr argues that we could see his inspiration at work outside the visible Church, in non-Christian religions. He also refers to the Christian values 'sown', like Justin's 'seminal word', in various places. In one of his best-known phrases, Christians should 'awaken the Christ who is sleeping in the night of religions'.

On this basis, Khodr affirms that the Logos is not confined to his Incarnation. Following St Maximus the Confessor, he points out that the Logos was incarnate in the biblical word before the coming of Jesus in the flesh. The Logos also became incarnate in the created world: the economy of Christ begins with creation as the manifestation of God's *kenosis*. The key to mission, therefore, is a 'kenotic' reading of scripture – one in accord with the voluntary self-emptying of Christ in which he does not cease to be God, but his divinity is not manifest. This means, conversely, that any reading of religions is a reading of Christ, since he is hidden everywhere in the mystery of his lowliness.

In addition to this theology aimed at understanding Islam from a Christian point of view, Khodr insists, like Patriarch Ignatius IV, on the co-existence of Christians and Muslims in a 'creative osmosis'. The main issue for the Christians remains how to live in the 'Land of Islam', even in countries where Islam is adopted as a state religion.

In this context mention should be made of Tarek Mitri, Professor at the Institute of Theology, former Coordinator of Inter-Religious Relations and Dialogue at the World Council of Churches and Programme Secretary for Christian–Muslim Dialogue. Mitri's principal area of interest is the history and sociology of Christian–Muslim relations and of Christianity in the Arab and Muslim world. For Mitri, the universal principles of co-citizenship, equality, the rule of law and human rights must be at the heart of the 'dialogue of life' between Christians and Muslims. Co-citizenship is the encounter of persons as equal actors in society and polity; while influenced by culture, religion and ethnicity, these persons cannot be reduced to the roles assigned to them in the name of communal identities, loyalties and perceived interests. Muslims and Christians need to learn that Christianity and Islam are not two monolithic blocks confronting each other. In dialogue with each other, they must understand justice to be a universal value grounded in their faith. They are called to take sides with the oppressed and marginalised, irrespective of their religious identity.[21]

ANTIOCH AND THE ECUMENICAL DIMENSION

The twentieth century has seen a process of mutual openness on the part of the Churches, and the ecumenical movement has emerged as one of the principal dimensions of the Christian presence in the world. Churches became aware that their encounter can make a great contribution to the realisation of world peace, as it increases the credibility of Christians' witness to their crucified and risen Lord in a rapidly changing and fluid world. At the beginning of the twentieth century, the Ecumenical Patriarchate played a crucial role in urging 'the Churches of Christ everywhere' to live out the 'fellowship' (*koinonia*) that exists between them.[22]

The Church of Antioch was one of the first Orthodox Churches to join the WCC. The present Patriarch Ignatius, then Metropolitan of Laodikia, gave the opening speech at the fourth general assembly held in Uppsala (1967), and later became one of the Council's presidents. Antioch has also participated in the official dialogue between the Catholic and Orthodox Churches since its foundation in the early 1980s. St John of Damascus Institute of Theology hosted the 1993 meeting of the dialogue, which issued the well-known Balamand document rejecting proselytism and calling for the abandonment of uniatism as a way of achieving unity between the Orthodox and Roman Catholic Churches.[23]

On the local and regional level, the Middle East Council of Churches (MECC) was founded in Nicosia (1974). The MECC is an independent regional structure which concentrates on facilitating unity and allowing the Churches to work together. The Church of Antioch has been a member of MECC since its foundation. Some of its members, particularly Patriarch Ignatius IV, played an important role in leading the MECC and orientating it. Achievements within the context of the MECC include work on common textbooks for religious education to be used in schools in Lebanon, agreements between Orthodox and local Catholic Churches on mixed marriages, religious education in schools and first communion, and the important agreements on pastoral matters between the Antiochian Orthodox Church and the Syriac (non-Chalcedonian) Orthodox Church in 1991.

Patriarch Ignatius IV sees Antioch as having a special role to play on the ecumenical level. Faithful to the spirit of its best-known bishop, St Ignatius, it always recalls that the genuine Christian is one who loves others and feels concerned with whatever befalls any other Christian, wherever he or she may be. It therefore has something to say regarding the ecumenical reconciliation of other Orthodox or non-Orthodox Churches, and on other live issues preoccupying the Church today, such as the challenges of modernity.

FINAL REMARKS: THE CHALLENGE OF MODERNITY

Many, including some Orthodox Christians, are troubled by modernity. They feel that it is tainted with nihilism, that it is an emptiness filled by the idolatries of image, market, eroticism or drugs. While unifying the planet materially, modernity seems to some to be incapable of sharing the world's resources justly or of embracing cultural diversity. It would sometimes appear to be imposing a spirit of globalism, rather than a globalisation that respects local cultures. Modernity is not strange to Christians, however. Antecedents of it are found in ancient Hellenism and in the biblical affirmation of a creaturely conscience penetrated by divine Wisdom, enabling humans to assume responsibility for themselves. It would therefore be false and dangerous to see only the negative aspects of modernity, for it is a strangely complex and heterogeneous phenomenon. Some of its positive insights are respect for others, freedom of spirit, democratic pluralism and openness. At their best, these are ultimately rooted in the evangelical revelation of the person and the liberating distinction made by Jesus between the Kingdom of God and that of Caesar.

Antioch, with its long experience of pluralism, has always expressed and lived the conviction that the Church is the conscience of the world, and that its role lies in proclaiming, prophetically, the will of God for human life and dignity. With loving openness, it has a word to say in today's rapidly changing world.

Further reading

Ignatius [IV], Patriarch of Antioch, 'The dichotomy between theological speculation and the reality of the Church', *Sourozh* 20 (1985), 10–16.
  Orthodoxy and Other Issues, Balamand, Lebanon: Balamand University Press, 2006.
  'Three sermons: a theology of creation; a spirituality of the creation; the responsibility of Christians', *Sourozh* 38 (1989), 1–14.
  'Uniting ourselves in the Truth: in someone, not in a theory or abstraction', *Sourozh* 33 (1988), 37–42.
Khodr, Metropolitan Georges, 'Christianity in a pluralistic world', *Ecumenical Review* 23 (1971), 118–28.
  'Exorcising war', *Sourozh* 49 (1992), 8–18.

'The Orthodox in the Lebanon: to be witnesses to the meekness of the Gospel', *Sourozh* 2 (1980), 42–9.

Rizk, Raymond, 'The role of the Orthodox in Lebanon', *Sourozh* 38 (1989), 15–30.

Notes

Historical sections of this chapter draw on Assaad Kattan, *Orthodox Antioch: Its thought and Life* (in Arabic) (Balamand: Balamand University Press, 2006).

1. G. Khodr, *The Orthodox Youth Movement: Light and Vocation* (in Arabic) (Beirut: Annour, 1992).
2. Deacon I. Hazim, 'The revival of the youth', in *Antioch in Revival* (Beirut: Annour, 1992), pp. 45–8.
3. C. Bendali, *Jeûne et oralité* (Beirut: Annour, 2007).
4. C. Bendali, *Ombres et splendeurs de l'esprit d'enfance* (Beirut: Annour, 2007).
5. G. Nahas, *Come and See* (in Arabic) (Beirut: Annour, 2001).
6. C. Haydar, *Thoughts on Orthodox Education* (Beirut: Annour, 2002).
7. P. Tarazi, *The Old Testament: Introduction*, vols. I–III (Crestwood, NY: SVS Press, 1991–6).
8. P. Tarazi, *The New Testament: Introduction*, vols. I–IV (Crestwood, NY: SVS Press, 1999–2004).
9. D. Ayuch, 'The Orthodox and the Protestant methods for biblical exegesis' (in Arabic) in *Orthodox and Evangelicals in the Arab East* (Balamand: University of Balamand and Near East School of Theology, 2006), pp. 265–85; 'Modern biblical criticism and the Orthodox Church' (in Arabic) in A. Chehwan (ed.), *The Dogmatic Constitution: Verbum Dei*, Biblical Studies 28 (Beirut: The Biblical Federation in the Middle East, 2004), pp. 203–15.
10. N. Abou Mrad, 'Abraham: *typos* of the Christian believer; the New Covenant in the Old Testament' in *Genesis and the History of Salvation* (in Arabic), Biblical Studies 26 (Beirut: The Biblical Foundation in the Middle East, 2002), pp. 271–82.
11. N. Abou Mrad, 'The notion of Covenant in the Old Testament. An exegetical study of the images of marriage and sonship in Hosea 1–3 and 11' (in Arabic) in A. Chetwan (ed.), *Studies in the Oriental World and the Lebanese History* (Beirut: The Biblical Federation in the Middle East, 2002), pp. 89–98.
12. M. Kanaan, 'Visages de femmes chez les pères cappadociens. D'après deux textes de Grégoire de Nysse et Grégoire de Nazianze: "La vie de Macrine" et "Gorgonie"', *Annals of the St. John of Damascus School of Theology* 4–5 (2003), 238–48.
13. G. Massouh, *The Coming Blessings* (in Arabic) (Beirut: Annour, 2003).
14. See his *Orthodoxy and Other Issues* (Balamand: Balamand University Press, 2006).
15. Ignatius IV, *Orthodoxy*, p. 21.
16. Ignatius IV, *Orthodoxy*, p. 108.
17. Patriarch Ignatius IV, 'Uniting ourselves in the Truth', *Sourozh* 33 (1988), 39.

18. Metropolitan Georges Khodr, 'The Orthodox in the Lebanon: to be witnesses to the meekness of the Gospel', *Sourozh* 2 (1980), 46.
19. See, for example, Metropolitan Georges Khodr, 'Christianity in a pluralistic world', *Ecumenical Review* 23 (1971), 118–28.
20. V. Lossky, *The Mystical Theology of the Eastern Church* (London: James Clarke & Co., 1957; repr. Crestwood, NY: SVS Press, 1998), p. 159. See further Khodr, 'Christianisme dans un monde pluraliste. L'économie du Saint-Esprit', *Irénikon* 44 (1971), 191–202.
21. T. Mitri, *Straight Lines in Curved Letters* (in Arabic) (Beirut: Balamand University Press and Annahar, 2007); see also T. Mitri (ed.), *Religion and Human Rights: A Christian–Muslim Discussion* (Geneva: WCC, 1996).
22. Constantin G. Patelos (ed.), *The Orthodox Church in the Ecumenical Movement: Documents and Statements 1902–1975* (Geneva: WCC, 1978), pp. 40–3.
23. 'Uniatism, method of union of the past and the present search for full communion', *Document of Joint International Commission for Theological Dialogue Between the Orthodox Church and the Roman Catholic Church*, 23 June 1993.

17 Russian theology after totalitarianism

LEONID KISHKOVSKY

No 'neutrality', no simple prosaic matters or questions any longer exist in the world. Everything has become disputed, ambiguous, and divided. Everything must be contested with the Antichrist, who lays claim to all things, hastening to fix his seal on them. All people stand before a choice – faith or unbelief – and the 'or' has become a burning issue. 'He who is not with me is against me, and he who does not gather scatters' (Mt 12:30). The revolution revealed a harsh and painful truth about the Russian soul, uncovering the utter abyss formed by faithlessness, apostasy, affliction, and depravity. The Russian soul was poisoned, disturbed, and lacerated. Only by the ultimate effort of open spiritual striving, by the light of Christ's reason, by the word of sincerity and truth, and by the word and power of the Spirit can a soul that is afflicted, bewitched, and disquieted by evil doubts and deceptions be healed and strengthened.[1]

In one of the final chords of his *Ways of Russian Theology*, Fr Georges Florovsky (1893–1979) passionately reflected on the meaning of events in Russia. His thoughts led him beyond the political, to the deeper level of spiritual and theological reflection. He wrote these words in the 1930s. In the Soviet Union the Russian Orthodox Church was suffering unprecedented persecution. The closing and destruction of churches and monasteries, the state atheism imposed on all aspects of life, the arrest, imprisonment, exile and execution of bishops, clergy, monastics, theologians and tens of thousands of active members had brought the Church to prostration. The voice of the Church in society was silenced, its teaching mocked, its extinction predicted.

The system of state atheism endured for some seventy years. The violent persecution came in waves and took varying forms. Yet the pressure was unrelenting. Millions of prisoners were released from the Gulag in the 1950s and 1960s, a welcome reversal of the mass terror of the Stalin era. Nevertheless, after a period of relative peace for the Church during the last decade of Stalin's rule, the persecution of religion was renewed, and the number of Orthodox churches was reduced from approximately 14,000 to some 7,000. This demonstrated the strength of the ideological commitment of the Communist party to the eradication of religion.

One of the consequences of state atheism and persecution of religion was the silencing of theology. There were many deficiencies and deformations in Russian society before the Communist period. There were also deficiencies and deformations in the life of the Church. Yet there was open discussion and lively debate about the role of the Church and the challenges faced by theological thought. Theologians, religious thinkers and philosophers reflected on mission and evangelism and on the place of the Church in state and society. These discussions and debates were not only occurring in Church circles, but had a resonance in the society at large, in newspapers and public debates and controversies.

QUESTIONS AT THE BEGINNING OF THE TWENTIETH CENTURY

Among the burning questions at the beginning of the twentieth century was the alienation of educated people from the Church. The Russian intelligentsia was characterised by a sense of social responsibility and social conscience. Their representative voices – writers and essayists, religious and philosophical thinkers – were as a rule both distant from the Church and critical of it. The alienation was mutual. The Church and its representative voices were as a rule hostile to and critical of the intelligentsia. The Church and 'society' as represented by the intelligentsia did not have a common language, and therefore did not speak to one another. At the beginning of the twentieth century, in St Petersburg, conversations between representatives of Church thought and representatives of the secular intelligentsia were organised in the form of 'religious-philosophical meetings'. These were promising, though difficult, efforts to overcome mutual alienation. During the years before the Communist revolution, a deep intellectual and spiritual quest continued to challenge the Russian intelligentsia, leading some towards religious faith. Sergius Bulgakov, a powerful thinker first as a political economist, then as a philosopher, and finally as a theologian, bore witness to the spiritual quest in his generation. He saw his intellectual and spiritual journey as the return of the prodigal son to the Father's house.

Another burning question in Russia in the early years of the twentieth century was that of church reform. In a questionnaire sent to all the diocesan bishops of the Russian Orthodox Church, all dimensions of ecclesial life were offered for discussion and review. In their responses, the bishops assessed the state of the Church, and were candid in their criticisms of the organisation and structures of the Church, diocesan administration, mission and theological education. The questionnaire was intended to be a stage on the way towards the convening of a council of the Russian Orthodox Church. It was hoped by many that the council itself would free the Church from its role as a state bureaucracy, liberating it for its appropriate ecclesial role.

Due to the reluctance of Emperor Nicholas II to allow a council which would lead to reforms in Church life, it was only after his abdication in 1917 that such a council was convened. At the council, the decision was taken to restore the patriarchal office which had been abolished by Peter the Great some 200 years earlier. Other reforms in church government and structure were instituted, and reforms in other spheres were discussed.

Due to the violence and chaos of the Communist coup and the civil war that followed it, the council was not able to complete its work. Communist repression and violence drove the Church out of the public arena, silencing its theologians. A radical reformist movement under the name 'Living Church' was used by the Communist regime and its secret police to disorientate and divide the Church. The legacy of the Living Church was to make all ideas of reform deeply suspect as potential manifestations of disregard for Church tradition and of faithlessness.

PERSECUTION AND MARTYRDOM

It should be noted that the system of repression in the Soviet Union was universal in scope. All classes and professions suffered – peasants and workers, educated and professional people, Communists and socialists, monarchists and liberals. It was the explicit intent of the Communist ideology to bring religion to extinction. Theologians, philosophers and religious thinkers either disappeared in the concentration camps, or went into forced exile.

A significant and symbolic personality was Fr Pavel Florensky, a scholar and thinker in many fields, from theology to art to the exact sciences, often called a 'renaissance man'. In his thought and person, as priest, religious philosopher, theologian and scientist, he held together these often separated worlds. And he held together also Church as liturgy and Church as theology, 'secular' thought and scholarship and 'religious' thought and scholarship. The style of his theological thinking and writing was personal and intimate (in the words of Fr Georges Florovsky), even idiosyncratic, yet he was a noted participant in the theological conversation and dialogue in Russian society and the Russian Orthodox Church. Imprisoned and sent to the concentration camp at the Solovetsky Monastery in the far north, he died in the Gulag in 1937.

Theological thought in Russia was effectively hidden for many decades. In the aftermath of the Second World War two theological academies (Moscow and Leningrad) were permitted, as well as several seminaries. During the persecutions of the Khrushchev period, seminaries were closed. Until the early 1990s there were five theological schools – the Moscow and Leningrad academies, the Moscow and Leningrad seminaries, and a seminary in Odessa. Theological books and studies were not easily available, even in the theological schools, and such books as could be found were old and outdated. In society at large, books of theology and religious philosophy were rarities, coming either from personal libraries or from sympathetic foreigners visiting the Soviet Union.

Two important but inadequate sources for theological works were the monthly *Journal of the Moscow Patriarchate* and the theological journal (*Bogoslovskye Trudy*) periodically issued by the Publications Department of the Moscow Patriarchate. In the prevailing conditions of censorship and self-censorship, the theological horizons of what could be published were extremely narrow. The number of copies printed was not enough to provide even one copy for each parish.

Out of sight of society and the authorities, individual believers and small groups of committed Orthodox Christians certainly did their best to keep alive both religious faith and religious thought. Yet the absence of open space for publication, discussion, debate and dialogue created conditions for many distortions and deformations. It was easy to fall into intellectualism or anti-intellectualism, aestheticism or pietism, belief in ritual or belief in imminent apocalypse. These deformations could often be intricately combined with one another.

Even in these circumstances of an imposed state atheism, the voice of lucid and public witness to God, the gospel of Christ, the image of God in man, and the presence of God in history and in civilisations could be found by those who had ears to hear. A vivid example of such a voice and personality was Sergei Averintsev (1937–2003). Averintsev was a philologist by education, a scholar by temperament, and an apologist by vocation. His writings and lectures were so grounded in scholarly integrity, historical truth and moral clarity that he became a witness to the Christian worldview prohibited in Soviet society. It was a unique achievement that Averintsev's writings – books and articles – were published despite the pervasive ideological control exercised by the Communist party and its Soviet state. His studies in Byzantine civilisation and in other cultures, as well as his entries in the *Philosophical Encyclopedia*, were uncompromising in their scholarly truthfulness, therefore bearing witness to God. Perhaps it was their scholarly truthfulness which allowed them to be perceived not as religious propaganda, but rather as a dispassionate and objective scholarly account.

The implosion of the Soviet Communist regime and the disintegration of the Soviet Union removed state atheism from the 'commanding heights' of Russian life. This dramatic change offered religious freedom in Russia for the first time in more than seventy years. The movement towards religious freedom began with the celebration of the Millennium of the Baptism of Rus' in 1988. While restrictions were still in operation at that time, little by little the public space opened for truth about religion and the violent persecution of religion in the Soviet period. One of the first signs of this change was a documentary film about the Solovetsky concentration camp and the imprisonment and executions there of Orthodox believers and many others.

THE RECOVERY OF MEMORY

The last decade of the twentieth century and the first decade of the twenty-first have become a time for gathering together again the lost, forgotten and dispersed Russian theological inheritance. This process has not been a co-ordinated one. Many new publication projects have emerged, involving existing publication houses as well as numerous new publishers. Some of these are directly or indirectly related to the Orthodox Church, others have no connection to the Church or to Church-related institutions. The incremental result has been the re-publication of many theological and philosophical works written and published before the Communist regime's total control was imposed. The reading public in Russia now has access to the theological and philosophical ideas of the nineteenth century and to the thinkers of the Russian religious renaissance of the early twentieth century. In addition, the books of the theologians of the emigration, especially the teachers at the St Sergius Institute of Orthodox Theology in Paris and St Vladimir's Seminary in New York, are now easily available.

Among the new publications in Russia are works written during the Soviet period and read by some clandestinely, but never before published. A good example of the emergence of this 'silent witness' under the Soviet regime is the recent publication of the collected works of Sergei I. Fudel. The three volumes (compiled by Fr Nicholas Balashov and Ludmila Saraskina, with notes and commentaries, and published by Russkiy Put' in 2001 and 2003) include memoirs, letters and essays on patristic, liturgical, literary and cultural themes. Sergei Fudel, the son of Fr Iosif Fudel, a well-known Moscow priest at the turn of the twentieth century, suffered imprisonment and exile, always remaining a faithful layman of the Russian Orthodox Church. The publication of his works brings to Russian readers a glimpse of the hidden spiritual and theological life under totalitarianism.

Yet another pastoral, spiritual and theological testimony in today's Russia was given by Metropolitan Anthony Bloom (1914–2003), Russian Orthodox priest and bishop in London from 1950 until his death. Metropolitan Anthony, a Russian émigré first in France and then in the United Kingdom, was a witness to Christ both in the West and in Russia. His visits to the Soviet Union as a bishop of the Moscow Patriarchate enabled many in Russia to hear his sermons and lectures and, through them, to appreciate the authenticity and depth of the Orthodox faith. During the years since the demise of Soviet totalitarianism, collections of Metropolitan Anthony's sermons and lectures have been constantly in print in Russia, and his voice continues to be heard as a living testimony.

The importance of the All Russian Church Council of 1917–18 is universally recognised in connection with the restoration of the office of patriarch and the election of Patriarch Tikhon (now canonised) as the first Patriarch in over 200 years. Most other aspects of this council are in dispute. Some see the council as the proper touchstone for the life and structure of the Russian Orthodox Church, affirming conciliarity, the convening of regular councils, the participation of priests and lay delegates as council members, and the creation of a mixed Supreme Church Council, composed of elected hierarchs, priests and lay members. Others denounce the council as a paradigm which led to the Living Church movement and proposed structures of church organisation poisoned by democratic ideas which are foreign to the Orthodox Church. In most cases, however, both the supporters and the critics of the council hold to their opinions on the basis of their ecclesial orientation, and not on the basis of deep and documented knowledge of the council's actual work.

Serious, detailed studies of the council's work are now being written and published. The authors do not limit their assessments to the plenary sessions, but take a close look at the work and minutes of the council's sections and subsections. In a recent book, Fr Nicholas Balashov offers a deep analysis of the liturgical problems and challenges in the Church of Russia, and of how the council of 1917–18 approached these challenges in honest and open discussion and debate, within the 'Section on divine services, preaching, and the church temple'.[2] It is clear that the question of reforms in the liturgical life of the Russian Orthodox Church was high on the priority list of challenges before Russian Orthodoxy, and that the word 'reform' was not at all taboo. An interesting and significant discovery in this study is that the supporters of liturgical reform were to be found in a very wide spectrum of opinion and orientation. We discover, for example, that future confessors and martyrs were among those who supported liturgical reforms. In another recent work, E. V. Beliakova gives us a vivid and descriptive assessment of the state of church life at the time of the council of 1917–18.[3] The problems of canon law and its application, marriage and divorce, mixed marriages, the second marriage of priests, celibacy, the monastic episcopate, women in the Church (including the question of deaconesses), the discipline of fasting, prayer for the heterodox and with the heterodox – all these were among the topics on the agenda of the council. Finally, a recent work by Sergei Firsov presents a history of the Russian Orthodox Church in connection with the growing demand for reform, the attitude of church leaders and the government towards reform, the plans and efforts to convene a council, the 'revolutionary destruction', and the council as a movement towards reform in a time of revolution.[4]

It is noteworthy that these three books are published as part of a series called 'Church Reforms', with the general title 'Discussions in the Orthodox Church in Russia at the beginning of the twentieth century'. The books in the series are genuine works of historical scholarship, and yet are written with sensitivity to the inner life of the Church.

The important work in progress is the recovery of memory. Recovered memory offers lessons both positive and negative. A truthful memory of Russian Orthodoxy before the Communist revolution shows that the seemingly well-established Church was not able to prevent the descent of Russian society into violence, totalitarianism and genocide. The pervasive presence of the Orthodox Church in the schools and in the military, its extended network of parishes, and its numerous monasteries and seminaries clearly did not have the spiritual strength to educate and enlighten Russians in the spirit of the gospel. Russian theology, with all of its scholarly resources and intellectual possibilities, was not able to influence the moral and social climate of Russian society. Instead, the illusions prevalent in Russian society affected many in the Church, to the extent that revolutionary slogans and ideology were pervasive in seminaries. The present challenge, therefore, is to recover truthful memory, without illusions and stereotypes.

THEOLOGICAL AND SPIRITUAL DISCERNMENT

This spiritual and intellectual effort will require an open space in the Church for discussion and disagreement, for collaboration and discernment, for careful and inspired theological scholarship as well as the creation of theological community. Since the demise of Communist totalitarianism there have been tendencies towards extremism in Russian society and polarisation in the Church. In the early and mid 1990s it seemed that the polarisation in the Church might well prevent open and honest conversation about the problems and challenges of Orthodox life and mission in Russia. At a 1994 conference in Moscow on the subject of 'church unity', the tone and style of the proceedings were reminiscent of political gatherings governed by ideology and not by theology and pastoral discernment. Another disturbing, even ominous, event was the burning in Ekaterinburg of theological books written by Frs Alexander Schmemann and John Meyendorff (prominent theologians of America and the Russian emigration whose theological writings are known and appreciated in Russia) and Fr Alexander Men (Russian Orthodox pastor, religious thinker and Christian apologist, murdered in 1990 near his home not far from Moscow by an unknown assailant).[5] If events such as these proved to be a general tendency, the witness of Russian Orthodoxy would be damaged in a fundamental way for a long time. That the tendency towards extremism has not become the governing reality of the Church of Russia is shown by the subsequent publication in Ekaterinburg of the same authors whose books had been consigned to flames in 1998.

A central role in providing an open space for genuine theological discussion and exploration has been assumed by the Synodal Theological Commission, guided and led by its chairman, Metropolitan Filaret of Minsk. The Commission has convened several conferences on theological themes such as 'Orthodox Theology on the Threshold of the Third Millennium' (2000); 'The Teaching of the Church about Man' (2001); 'Orthodox Teaching on the Church' (2003); 'The Eschatological Teaching of the Church' (2005); and 'Orthodox Teaching on the Sacraments of the Church' (2007). These conferences have become an open forum for the presentation of scholarly papers and ideas. At the conferences, there is no 'ideological spirit' present. There is no imposed or presupposed theological uniformity. Theologians and scholars of different orientations have the opportunity to prepare and present papers for discussion and debate. What is noteworthy is the spirit of openness in the discussions. When disagreements have been articulated, this has not been in the spirit of mutual exclusion or denigration. The conferences are slowly building a community of theological discourse in Russian Orthodoxy and beyond. It is not only Russian Orthodoxy which has suffered from the lack of open forums for competent and thoughtful discussion of crucial themes in theology and church life. Orthodoxy as a whole is suffering from the absence of regularly convened consultations and conferences at which ideas, views and convictions can be explored for mutual understanding and for the development of adequate and timely Orthodox responses to current questions, problems and challenges. The theological conferences held at the invitation of the Synodal Theological Commission of the Moscow Patriarchate are now also providing a service and ministry at the inter-Orthodox level.

In the post-atheist Russian situation there are specific challenges for Christian faith and Orthodox thought in response to the totalitarian experience. The most adequate response will require theological reflection, honesty and humility. It will also require scrupulous historical accuracy.

A major theme among Orthodox believers in Russia today is the witness of the martyrs and confessors. On the outskirts of Moscow is a place called Butovo. From the early 1930s to the early 1950s this place was a secret-police site, with executions occurring there throughout the period. Mass executions took place at Butovo in 1937–8, when more than 20,000 people were shot there. Approximately 1,000 of these were executed for their Orthodox faith, and more than 300 of these have been canonised as martyrs. Discovered as a killing field in the early 1990s, Butovo became a place of pilgrimage and a memorial site. A church has been built there, and was recently consecrated. The central altar is dedicated to the Resurrection of Christ, and the side altars are dedicated to St Tikhon, Patriarch and Confessor of Moscow, and the New Martyrs. In the lower church, the walls at the entrance display selected prison photographs, obtained in KGB files, showing the faces of men and women, old and young, religious and atheist, Russians and people of other nationalities – all victims of the totalitarian genocide. There are also selected personal items of those who died. Some of these victims had themselves been persecutors and killers – yet their own death was by no means intended as punishment for these crimes. Most of the victims were innocent of any wrongdoing. Some were genuinely faithful and steadfast as martyrs. Others were Christian believers who succumbed to torture and betrayed their fellow believers. The steadfast and faithful are now canonised saints, whose witness is held up as a model of Christian behaviour under persecution and whose memory is reverently honoured. Patriarch Alexy II of Moscow comes every year to the Butovo site on a

Saturday after the celebration of the Resurrection to preside at a Divine Liturgy. He has noted that Butovo is only one of the many Russian Golgothas. The priest of the Butovo church is the grandson of a priest martyred there seventy years ago.

The impulse and intuition to memorialise and honour the suffering of the martyrs is the first and proper Christian response. The labours dedicated to establishing the stories of killing fields are needed both by Orthodox faithful and by Russian society for moral accountability. These labours are also an important testimony offered to the whole Orthodox Church, and beyond that to people and societies everywhere. What will be needed for years to come is theological reflection on the meaning of martyrdom; on the responsibility of Christians to be witnesses *for* Christ and witnesses *against* ideological, political and national idolatries of any kind; and on the vocation of Christians to be articulate defenders and protectors of the human person as image and likeness of God.

In connection with the theological defence of the human person, there is an urgent need to defend human freedom. Freedom is today a concept easily abused and manipulated. Some of what Western culture today proposes as freedom is, in reality, an abuse of the person and an assault on the image and likeness of God. Sometimes, those who critique Western culture for its wrong understanding of freedom can become apologists for the denial of freedom. In cultures shaped by the Orthodox faith, freedom was often not understood as a religious and social value. And in the Orthodox Church itself, the understanding of freedom is too often superficial. Wherever the Orthodox Church abides today – in post-totalitarian societies such as Russia, in democratic states such as Greece, in Muslim societies such as Syria, or in Western democracies – a common reflection on the subject of freedom as a gift and as a task is of urgent importance.

We return to Sergei Averintsev, who continued to make his contribution as a Christian scholar and Orthodox thinker after the demise of the Soviet Union. Among his themes was the overcoming of the totalitarian past. His approach to this question was, as always, nuanced and subtly aware of irony. For example, he saw that there are forms of struggle against the totalitarian temptation which are themselves totalitarian:

> There is only one antidote for a new totalitarianism, and that is a sense of individual responsibility for every word and action, and consequently, distrust of inculcation, of mass suggestion, and of the spirit of abstraction . . . The only way to prevent totalitarianism

from coming back today is to be open to questions, to be completely honest and sober, as far as questions are concerned.[6]

Another characteristic concern was language, its corruption by the totalitarian mentality, and the need to use language with sobriety, honesty and lucidity. Sergei Averintsev saw that these concerns flow from the Christian worldview and are central to the Orthodox witness to the gospel of Christ.

As the system of state atheism withered, Russian society experienced a dramatic and enthusiastic renewal of interest in religion. The Orthodox Church, its traditions and rites, its feasts and fasts, became interesting to millions of people. During the early 1990s some Orthodox Christians wondered whether the Church would be able to respond convincingly and persuasively to the questions asked by millions of interested but profoundly ignorant people, people whose consciousness was formed by the pervasive materialistic ideology of Communism. Even when Soviet citizens found this ideology to be unpersuasive and senseless, they were still shaped by it. It is a fact that in due course the mass appeal of the Orthodox Church and of religion waned. The tasks of daily living and daily struggle took their toll. The Church was in many respects unprepared to persuade, to teach, to guide. Much of the popular reading material about the Orthodox faith was primitive, reducing the faith to ritual. While this style of reading material attracts some people, and is therefore indeed popular, in reality the burning questions of the meaning of human life and the meaning of Christian faith are left unaddressed and unanswered. The serious works of theology and spirituality are most often too scholarly and academic for 'ordinary people', or people whose normal interests and concerns are not in 'professional theology'.

Yet it is also true that a genuine human testimony to the spiritual effort and quest is capable of striking a resonant chord in today's Russia. One such testimony came in the form of Fr Alexander Schmemann's *Journals*, published in Moscow in 2006.[7] There have been round tables to discuss this book, conversations on television, book reviews. The interest has not been confined to 'church circles', but has reached the wider public. Fr Alexander's voice is heard in the Russian 'public arena' almost a quarter-century after his death.

An essay with the title 'What happiness it was!' discusses the *Journals*. The authors are Grigory Yavlinsky (Russian politician and economist, founder and leader of the liberal Yabloko party) and Tatiana Morozova (author of many articles about literature and film). What resonates with special force and clarity for the authors of the article is *honesty*. It is noted that Fr Alexander valued above all 'honesty with himself, with people, with life'. This honesty, the authors observe, was for Fr Alexander the criterion of a man's integrity, of the presence of God in him. And '. . . conversely, phony piety – the falsehood with which religions, Christianity and church life are permeated, repels me more and more. All this pseudo-depth, pseudo-problems, pseudo-spirituality; all these pretensions to loftier understanding! All these declamations! . . . can drive a man so far from Truth'. The authors speak of those for whom Orthodoxy is not so much a faith as an ideology, bringing them to a passage from the *Journals*:

> On my way home I was thinking, what primitive and unnecessary barriers our 'Orthodoxy' has placed before . . . people. This is the time it could be purified, renewed; it could shine! But that would require renouncing the idols, and especially the idol of the past, which is something Orthodoxy is least capable of doing since these idols are what they most cherish in Orthodoxy.

Yavlinsky and Morozova conclude: 'A religious renewal of Russia, like a political or socio-economic renewal, has yet to happen. For it to happen, we need to hear what Fr Alexander Schmemann has to say today on the pages of his journals.'[8]

It is obvious that the many in Russia who rejoice in the substance and tone of the *Journals* of Fr Alexander Schmemann are contradicted by others who reject the book. This disagreement is not destructive. The disagreement is creative. Both those who delight in the book and those who criticise it are engaged in a meaningful discussion about profoundly important and theological questions, what Russians (after Dostoevsky) call *damned* questions – the 'ultimate questions' of religious and philosophical dilemmas.

The state of Russian Orthodoxy today is complex and contradictory. The rebuilding of churches and monasteries, the creation of seminaries, the emergence of Christian education and publishing, the rediscovery of charity and social assistance to the poor – all this is evidence not only of the survival of the Church during some seventy years of oppression, but of the vitality of the Church. Yet this vitality is not without its dark side. There are temptations and trials to face which are painfully difficult to overcome. Not only is the 'old man' of the totalitarian Russian past very present in institutions both secular and ecclesial; the struggle and tension between the 'old man' put aside in baptism in order to put on the 'new man' is never far from our human and historical experience, our personal and collective realities.

In its encounter with contemporary challenges and problems the Russian Orthodox Church is compelled to pay attention to political and social issues. An effort to reflect on the intersection of Orthodox faith, conscience and worldview with today's moral, political and social questions is seen in the 'Basis of the social concept' document approved by the Bishops' Council of the year 2000.[9] It is to be noted that the document is not a 'social doctrine'. The choice of the title signifies the Church's desire to begin a conversation about articulating a social teaching on the basis of the Orthodox faith, tradition and worldview. Those who have interpreted the document on behalf of the Russian Orthodox Church have emphasised its role as a guideline and framework – as the beginning of a reflection rather than the final word.

The effort to address contemporary problems means that internal challenges in church life and practice must also be the subject of reflection. During the first years of the twenty-first century, questions of spiritual life and the role of elders and spiritual guides, the practice of the sacrament of confession, the practice and norms of the sacrament of marriage have all become themes for discussion at round tables and other forums. Questions which in the 1990s were regarded as closed questions, in the new millennium, are discussed as open questions requiring further discernment.

THE TASK OF THEOLOGY IN THE MISSION OF THE CHURCH

For the Church to be fully adequate in its inner life and in its public witness, theology is a necessity. This needs to be said today, since there are popular views suggesting that learning and the life of the intellect are actually unnecessary, and quite possibly harmful, for the Orthodox Christian. This was not the view of the Cappadocian Fathers and many other great teachers and saints. The characteristic affirmation was that all of human nature and experience – the whole human being and the whole human society – are to be dedicated to the service of God. Theology is necessary for the witness and mission of the Church so that the catholic, universal truth is the criterion of church life, and not habit or custom or provincialism of any kind.

After decades of state atheism and the oppression and suppression of religious faith, Russian theology has much work to do in order to strengthen its scholarly capacities, to reform its theological schools, to publish fundamental studies in patristics, dogmatics, liturgical theology, pastoral care and biblical studies. At the same time, the Russian Orthodox Church can regard its survival under Communist rule and its miraculous revival subsequently as a foundation on which to build. What is clear is that theology is a matter of life and death. If Russian theology develops its potential as a purely academic and scholarly vocation, it will fail to fulfil its task and calling. Russian theology, and all Orthodox theology, must strive to hold together all the dimensions of Christian faith and Orthodox life and witness, and must not allow the division of these dimensions into separate categories and compartments existing in isolation from one another.

This does not mean and cannot mean uniformity of thought or uniformity of theological teaching. It has been observed that the unity of the Church and the unity of the faith do not necessarily imply or demand uniformity of theology. Orthodox theology at its best times was able to accommodate different approaches to the same Truth, different theological paths to the same proclamation of the Faith, different voices bearing witness to the same Christ.

We will conclude as we began, with a passage from Fr Georges Florovsky's *Ways of Russian Theology:*

> Theology is ceasing to be a personal or 'private affair', in which each person is free to participate or not, depending on one's personal gifts, inclinations, and inspirations. In this present time of deceit and judgment, theology must once again become a 'public matter', a universal and catholic summons. Each person must be clad in complete spiritual armor. The time has come when theological silence, perplexity, inconsistency, or inarticulateness is tantamount to treason or flight before the enemy. Silence can be just as disastrous as a hasty or unintelligible answer; it can be even more thoroughly seductive and poisonous when one crawls into hiding, as if faith was a 'frail and not quite reliable thing' . . . Theology must resound with the Good News, the *kerygma*. The theologian must speak to living people, to the living heart.[10]

Further reading

Alfeyev, Bishop Hilarion, 'Orthodox theology on the threshold of the 21st century: will there be a renaissance of Russian theological scholarship?', *Ecumenical Review* 52.3 (July 2000), 309–25.

Bobrinskoy, B., "The Church and the Holy Spirit in twentieth-century Russia', *Ecumenical Review* 52.3 (July 2000), 326–42.

Clément, O., 'Martyrs and confessors', *Ecumenical Review* 52.3 (July 2000), 343–50.

Davis, N., *A Long Walk to Church: A Contemporary History of Russian Orthodoxy*, Boulder, CO: Westview Press, 2nd edn, 2003.

Ellis, J., *The Russian Orthodox Church: A Contemporary History*, Bloomington and Indianapolis, IN: Indiana University Press, 1986.

Hamant, Y., *Alexander Men: A Witness for Contemporary Russia (A Man for Our Times)*, Torrance, CA: Oakwood Publications, 1995.

Kirill of Smolensk and Kaliningrad, 'The Russian Orthodox Church and the third millennium', *Ecumenical Review* 52.3 (July 2000), 300–8.

Plekon, M., *Living Icons: Persons of Faith in the Eastern Church*, Notre Dame, IN: University of Notre Dame Press, 2002.

Pospielovsky, D. V., *A History of Soviet Atheism in Theory and Practice, and the Believer*, 3 vols., New York: St Martin's Press, 1987–8.

Vallière, P., *Modern Russian Theology: Bukharev, Soloviev, Bulgakov – Orthodox Theology in a New Key*, Grand Rapids, MI: Eerdmans, 2000.

Notes

1. G. Florovsky, *Collected Works of Church History*, vol. vi: *The Ways of Russian Theology* (Vaduz: Bucherrertrielasanstalt, 1987), pp. 304–5.
2. Archpriest N. Balashov, *On the Way to Liturgical Rebirth*, Round Table on Religious Education and Diakonia, *Church Reforms* (2001).
3. E. V. Beliakova, *The Church Court and Problems of Church Life*, Round Table on Religious Education and Diakonia, *Church Reforms* (2004).
4. S. Firsov, *The Russian Church on the Eve of Change (The End of the 1890s–1918)*, Round Table on Religious Education and Diakonia, *Church Reforms* (2002).
5. See M. Plekon, 'The Russian religious revival and its theological legacy', above.
6. S. Averintsev, 'Overcoming the totalitarian past', *Russian Magazine* (June 2001). The text is available on: http://english.russ.ru/politics/20010608.html.
7. The English version is available as *The Journals of Father Alexander Schmemann*, trans. J. Schmemann (Crestwood, NY: SVS Press, 2000).
8. G. Yavlinsky and T. Morozova, 'What happiness it was!' *Orthodox Church* 431/2 (January–February 2007); www.oca.org/PDF/DOC-PUB/TOC/2007/JAN-FEB.pdf.
9. See http://orthodoxeurope.org/page/3/14.aspx.
10. Florovsky, *Collected Works*, vi, pp. 305–6.

18 Orthodox Christianity in the West: the ecumenical challenge

JOHN A. JILLIONS

> Orthodoxy has the plenitude of life in Christ, but it does not have an exclusive monopoly on the truth.
>
> Metropolitan Kallistos Ware, *The Inner Kingdom*[1]

One of the striking features of Eastern Orthodox theology in the twentieth century was the role played by the West in the thinking of its most authoritative writers as theological context, as realm of fascination, and as focus of criticism. Georges Florovsky was a founder of the modern ecumenical movement and was at home in Western theological institutions and debates. But he also saw the West as the source of a troubling 'pseudomorphosis' or 'Babylonian captivity' of Orthodox theology. Vladimir Lossky learned much of his theology at the Sorbonne and had a lifelong interest in Meister Eckhart. But his *The Mystical Theology of the Eastern Church* (1944), the first systematic presentation of the Neo-patristic synthesis championed by Florovsky, underlined the deformations in Western theology that the *filioque* had introduced into Western Christian thought. Almost all the leading names of modern Orthodox theology studied in the West, engaged its ideas and became friends with the very theologians whose ideas they rejected. Indeed, at the opening of a centre for ecumenical studies in Cambridge, attended by many veteran ecumenists, Fr Ephrem Lash (one of the contributors to this volume) gave a talk entitled 'Now We Are Friends'. His point was that, after fifty years of the modern ecumenical movement, the Orthodox and their Western counterparts had become colleagues and friends to the extent that they could move beyond mere civilities and get to the heart of the very real theological issues that continue to divide us. So we may expect that the debates may become sharper. But such honesty can be fruitful only in an atmosphere of genuine friendship and respect.

Twentieth-century ecumenical contacts – particularly with Russian theologians – were in large part made possible by the dispersion caused by the terrible aftermath of the Bolshevik revolution and then the

276

Second World War. Various centres of Orthodox theology in the West have further contributed to this cross-pollination; but it remains true that most Western seminaries and university faculties of theology or religion offer no programmes and few (if any) courses in Eastern Christianity.

While the Orthodox theological mainstream is long accustomed to discussions with Western Churches and scholars, there is no doubt that large parts of the Orthodox world still have a hostile view of the West. This was a key observation made by Victoria Clark in *Why Angels Fall: A Journey Through Orthodox Europe from Byzantium to Kosovo*. But she also found much that was attractive among these Orthodox people – including remarkable hospitality shown to the very Westerners whose influence they were rejecting.[2] Like other Western observers, she is sometimes led astray by her own preconceptions, but outsiders like Clark are not the only ones to observe this anti-Western phenomenon. In reflecting on the start of the third millennium of Christianity, John Zizioulas (Metropolitan of Pergamon), a leading Orthodox bishop and theologian, hopes we can get beyond the past's polemics for which all Churches bear some responsibility:

> Today there is a tendency among the Orthodox to stress the responsibility of the Western Christians for the evil of division and for the wrongs done to the Orthodox Church by our Western brothers. History is, of course, clear in witnessing to the fact of a great deal of aggressiveness against the Orthodox on the part of the West. Deep however in the tragic reality of Christian division lies also an inability of the Orthodox to overcome and rise above the psychology of polemic in a true spirit of forgiveness and love. Confessional zeal has often proved stronger than forgiveness and love. The second millennium has been in this respect almost an unfortunate period of the Church's history.[3]

MUTUAL INFLUENCE, MUTUAL LEARNING

There is little doubt that Orthodox theologians have benefited from Western theological scholarship in numerous ways. Aside from their advanced training in Western universities, the very sources they use – biblical, patristic, canonical, conciliar and liturgical texts – come through editions and scholarly aids made possible by mainly Western scholars. And while it may have been true in the past that the Orthodox used this tradition with little attention to critical questions of historical context and interpretation, this is no longer true today. As Orthodox scholars and theologians participate in international academic forums, they have also come to appreciate the cross-confessional convergence that can occur in these areas of study.

The Western context in which many Orthodox theologians work is helping to shape their scholarship in various other ways as well. There is attentiveness to clear and rational argument and explanations, in contrast to mere assertion of Orthodox positions. There is an instinct for fairness, freedom of thought and expression, creative debate, due process, collaboration, discussion, civility and compromise. Western theologians are often the first to tackle issues that will sooner or later also affect Orthodox believers in 'traditional' societies. They can lead the way in reflecting theologically on how to live in secular, democratic and pluralistic societies and in wrestling seriously with the tensions between past tradition and the needs of the present. Most Orthodox countries are coming out of decades or centuries of political oppression (some are still living under those conditions) and can learn from the West something about living liturgy lived outside the walls of the Church, about social justice and social ethics and about creating mission, educational and social service institutions to serve society in the name of Christ and the Church. Even feminist theology, although it has not yet made substantial headway in the Orthodox world, has sensitised Orthodox Christians to the influences of 'patriarchy' and violence in the history of the Church and the development of doctrine. Orthodox theology is increasingly listening to unfamiliar points of view. At an international congress of Orthodox theological schools held in Sofia, Bulgaria, in 2004 it was reported that John Zizioulas

> aroused considerable interest and liveliness among Congress participants, stating that, 'If the Church wants to speak to the world, it also has to listen to it', adding that 'we cannot self-define ourselves by opposing others, but can only do so through establishing a connection with them. The new realities, especially in the context of the European Union, require active cooperation with the heterodox and the other religions.' The Metropolitan of Pergamon also stressed the need for revision in the theological educational itinerary regarding the insertion of modern problems such as bioethics and ecological ethics.[4]

But the learning is not all one way. The Orthodox are also contributing to reshaping the theological landscape today. In 2004, the *Christian Century* reported that 'It is difficult now to do serious theological work without extensive reference to ancient and modern Orthodox sources.'[5] It highlighted a number of Western theologians whose work has been deeply influenced in this way, including Geoffrey Wainwright, Sarah Coakley, Rowan Williams (who wrote the section on Eastern Orthodox theology for David Ford's influential *The Modern Theologians*), John Milbank (and also Catherine Pickstock, Graham Ward and other champions of 'Radical Orthodoxy'), Wolfhart Pannenberg, Jurgen Moltmann, Miroslav Volf, Robert Jenson, Eugene Rogers and Kathryn Tanner. One could also mention Thomas C. Oden, who gives a passionate account of the contemporary rediscovery of patristic faith across denominational lines.[6] Evangelical theology too is being marked by this phenomenon, as seen in a spate of books and articles in evangelical circles – including *Evangelicalism and the Orthodox Church*, edited by David Hilborn – and in the Emergent Church movement as exemplified by Brian McLaren's *A Generous Orthodoxy*.[7]

CHARACTERISTIC EMPHASES OF ORTHODOX THEOLOGY

Part of the attraction of Orthodox theology for Western Christians is that it takes shape outside historical Catholic and Protestant polemics, and can therefore often bring a new perspective to divisive issues. Some of the features that are repeatedly mentioned as characteristic Orthodox emphases include the following, most of which have already been encountered in this volume.

Theology, spirituality and liturgy are firmly bound together in Orthodox thought. Intellectual life cannot be understood apart from the Church's inheritance of worship and prayer. Indeed, where others speak of contextual theology in terms of geography, gender, ethnicity, sexual orientation, etc., the Orthodox think of the Church as the universal context that transcends these secondary milieux. We are first and foremost members of the Body of Christ. This deep sense of the Church gives theology a communal dimension that cuts across time and geography as a corrective to rampant individualism.

The worship experience of generations has shaped liturgy as the theological source par excellence, *theologia prima*. Ancient scripture and patristic writings are filtered through and stamped with the corporate life of prayer which remains in every age 'ever full of sap and green' (Ps 91 [92]:14). This accounts for the universal Orthodox experience of the liturgy as 'today' in spite of its ancient form. John Zizioulas has called this 'liturgical dogmatics' Orthodoxy's particular gift to the twenty-first century.[8] This point is an important counterbalance to the emphasis on theology as an intellectual discipline somewhat divorced from prayer and worship.

Closely connected to liturgy is the Orthodox sense of mystery, the priority given to apophatic theology and the reticence to over-dogmatise. This has been especially influential in Western circles ('Radical Orthodoxy' most specifically), for, as the *Christian Century* put it, 'after centuries of working in rationalistic categories, in the wake of the Enlightenment, Protestants [and we could add Catholics] have reason to welcome negative theology'.[9]

Orthodoxy has a vivid awareness that the Incarnation, the very fact of God's entry into the world, has changed everything: materiality is now infused with the divine. This is relevant not only to sacramental theology, but also, for instance, to the contemporary quest for spiritual underpinnings to environmental responsibility. A sacramental cosmology grounded in the Incarnation acts as a counterbalance to some of the more exotic 'green spiritualities', which lead many people of Christian background away from the Church. This is also bearing fruit in discussions between theology and science, as seen in recent discussions of 'panentheism'.[10] Closely related to this are the various environmental symposia, mainly under the Ecumenical Patriarch's auspices, in which Orthodox Christians are working with other Christians and other faiths to explore the spiritual dimensions of how humans live in the world. Yet another way in which Orthodox theology is helping Western Christians to overcome the split between matter and spirit can be seen in the explosion of interest in icons. Another aspect of reflection on the Incarnation is the divine *kenosis* ('Self-emptying'). This was perhaps the leading theme of twentieth-century émigré Russian theology, taken up by such diverse writers as Nicholas Berdyaev, Sergius Bulgakov, George Fedotov, Sophrony Sakharov (building on St Silouan) and Anthony Bloom. It was based on the self-emptying of Christ, who 'though he was in the form of God, did not count equality with God a thing to be grasped, but emptied himself (*eauton ekenosen*), taking the form of a servant' (Phil 2:6–7). But *kenosis* was also closely connected with the experience of the Russian émigrés who had lost everything, and as a result rediscovered what it means to have no abiding city. And hearing the beautifully haunting texts of Holy Week in the midst of suffering and exile would have reinforced this message. This would seem to be a precious lesson to be passed on both to Churches in Orthodox countries (whether or not they are listening), and to Christians in the West, who may think of themselves as 'post-Constantinian' but who are actually very keen to have influence in the public sphere, and are sometimes quite at home in the middle-class comfort of Western society.

Also connected with *kenosis* is the Orthodox focus on maximalism, living the Christian faith without compromises. This is linked with the consciousness of martyrdom: living, witnessing and, if necessary, suffering and dying faithfully for Christ under totalitarian regimes and oppression. Both of these are found in the Russian émigré experience of conscious (as opposed to social) Church membership, but also in the wider Orthodox experience of hostile non-Christian societies, as in the witness of Churches in the Arab world. And the 'post-Christian' West is now looking much more like the non-Christian societies in which most Orthodox Churches have lived for most of their existence.

Another characteristic emphasis of the Russian émigré theology of the Paris School was the notion of *sobornost*. This is variously translated as 'conciliarity', 'catholicity' or even 'togetherness', but it conveys the conviction that church life is a collaborative and yet hierarchal ordering of life in which the different gifts of laity and clergy are used for the building up of the Body of Christ without oppressing or impeding each other. The question of women priests throws into sharp relief the contrast between *sobornost* and an implicit clericalism in some Western thinking. As one woman theologian recently told me, 'I don't think I am the only Orthodox woman to feel rather affronted at the suggestion [from non-Orthodox] that because I cannot be ordained a priest, I am somehow less than a full member of the Church.'

Synergy is a characteristic word that helps define what is central in Orthodox theology: cooperating with God in an unending relationship that leads 'from glory to glory'. There is no authentic human life independent of this divine–human communion. Synergy thus seems to provide a vital missing element in much Western activism. Zeal for 'transformation of society' is certainly no bad thing. Indeed, Sergius Bulgakov said that Christians are placed in this world not merely to know but to transform. But there is also a Western tendency to assume that everything depends on us, and this is a sure recipe for burn-out.

The clear aim of Orthodox theology encompasses the transformation of the person through communion with God: *theosis*. This is the ultimate goal of the divine–human synergy mentioned above. But *theosis* is not a vague goal with an uncertain path. The Orthodox conviction is that the centuries-long church experience of prayer and inner life can be learned (this was touched on in John Chryssavgis's chapter). This is of great importance, because it shows how the Christian tradition can provide what so many people are seeking in New Age spiritualities and oriental religions.[11] Christianity too has a spiritual ascetic discipline as an integral part of life and an openness to the supra-rational: and this dimension of Christian spirituality is usually better preserved in the East than in the West.

THE PROBLEM OF ECUMENISM

Despite all that we have said, it remains true that ecumenical relations remain a touchy subject for a Church which in most official statements still regards itself as the true Christian Church, to which all others must return if they desire to enter the fullness of the one, holy catholic and apostolic Church. Interfaith relations remain even more problematic.

Most of the twentieth-century theologians mentioned in this book had active roles in, or were founders of, the modern ecumenical movement. Some were also leaders in interfaith dialogue (Lev Gillet and Archbishop Anastasios of Albania for example). And almost all the autocephalous Orthodox Churches are involved officially in ecumenical dialogue. But how involved they are, to what extent this activity is pursued at various levels of church life (international, national, local) and the degree of enthusiasm for Ecumenism vary tremendously from Church to Church, diocese to diocese and parish to parish.

There is vocal criticism of Ecumenism from self-styled 'traditionalists' who view ecumenical contacts and conversations as dangerous because they could lead to erosion of the Orthodox faith. Traditionalists apply the anathemas of the past with little or no modification to other Christians today and especially to 'ecumenists', as the most dangerous enemies of the Church. For example, the celebrated lifting of the anathemas of 1054 by Pope Paul VI and Patriarch Athenagoras in 1965 was condemned by Orthodox traditionalists as capitulation to the Papists. According to this view, dialogue is dangerous, and the truly Orthodox must simply avoid dialogue with persistent heretics. This includes both those who hold a form of Christianity outside Orthodoxy and those who falsely claim to be Orthodox. Their teaching is spiritually damaging, says Constantine Cavarnos, for example. It is poison, the venom of snakes, and there is 'clearly the danger of being infected spiritually by heretical ideas' followed by 'spiritual death'.[12]

An anti-ecumenical tract by Alexander Kalomiros says that the ecumenical movement is an especially pernicious pan-heresy because its goals of unity and brotherly love seem so admirable. Those who are involved 'while wearing the mask of the friends of God, are actually his enemies'. In fact, 'they are the Church's most dangerous enemies, the false prophets of the Gospel'.[13] It would be a mistake to dismiss this outlook too quickly, although one might disagree profoundly. There are people of intelligence, sincerity and deep Orthodox faith who hold these views and are opposed to ecumenical contacts of any kind. It should also be added than many of these anti-ecumenists are also remarkably full of love. I encountered one such Greek Old Calendarist working in a Protestant summer camp for disabled children outside Ottawa. He told me, 'We must love the truth but not be blinded by the truth. Love excludes fanaticism.' One of the noteworthy things about the rigorists (at least some of them) is that they simply do not fit into the Western stereotype of 'intolerance'. They consider Ecumenism to be 'hypocritical love' in much the same way that it would be 'hypocritical love' to give someone a hot toddy when what they needed was to have a tumour excised.

ECUMENISM: THE OFFICIAL VIEW AND THE QUESTIONS IT RAISES

The Orthodox rigorists take an extreme view. Yet even the official statements of Orthodox churches that participate in ecumenical dialogue raise questions that have not yet been fully debated, let alone resolved, regarding the ecclesial status of other Christians.

One of the most articulate policy statements is found in the *Encyclical On Christian Unity and Ecumenism* issued in 1973 by the bishops of the Orthodox Church in America (OCA).[14] The document is worth reading because it gives the full theological rationale for its position, and because this is still the policy in force in the Orthodox world. Keeping in mind that the OCA, like almost all Orthodox churches, has been actively involved in the ecumenical movement and has encouraged ecumenical dialogue and collaboration, the statement still clearly proclaims that, despite the confessed weakness and sins of its leaders and members, 'The Orthodox Church is the True Church', and 'there can be only one Church, for Christ founded but one Church. It is into this one Church that all must enter to live in perfect communion with God, with each other, and with all of creation.' Because the Orthodox Church is the True Church, according to this view, Orthodox participants in the ecumenical movement must guard against all relativism and secularism that would water down this conviction, and must remember that the ultimate aim of their participation is to draw others into the fullness of the Orthodox Church. This alone is the true fulfilment of Christ's prayer that 'all may be one' (Jn 17:11, 21, 22).

The Basic Principles of the Attitude of the Russian Orthodox Church Toward the Other Christian Confessions, officially promulgated in 2000, takes the identical view but also includes further statements about the ecclesial status of others: '1.16. The ecclesial status of those who have separated themselves from the Church does not lend itself to simple definition. In a divided Christendom, there are still certain characteristics which make it one: the Word of God, faith in Christ as God and Saviour come in the flesh (1 Jn 1:1–2; 4, 2, 9), and sincere devotion.' The fact that there are various rites of reception for converts to the Orthodox Church (through baptism, through chrismation, through repentance) 'shows that the Orthodox Church relates to the different non-Orthodox confessions in different ways. The criterion is the degree to which the faith and order of the Church, as well as the norms of Christian spiritual life, are pre-served in a particular confession.' But in spite of these distinctions, the Orthodox Church 'does not assess the extent to which grace-filled life has either been preserved intact or distorted in a non-Orthodox confession, considering this to be a mystery of God's providence and judgement'. This statement also explicitly rejects any notion of an 'invisible church' that exists across denominational barriers.

While this still may seem fairly hard-line to many non-Orthodox readers, it is remarkably refreshing in its emphasis on listening to and working with ecumenical partners.

> 4.5. Witness cannot be a monologue, since it assumes the existence of listeners and therefore of communication. Dialogue implies two sides, a mutual openness to communication, a willingness to understand, not only an 'open mouth', but also a 'heart enlarged' (cf. 2 Cor 6:11). That is why the problem of theological language, comprehension and interpretation should become one of the most important issues in the dialogue of Orthodox theology with other confessions.

The Russian Orthodox Church urges collaborating with non-Orthodox Churches in forming joint study centres, groups and programmes, theolo-gical conferences, seminars, scholarly meetings, exchanges of delegations, exchanges of publications and information as well as joint publishing pro-jects. It especially calls for exchanges of experts, teachers, students and theologians and specifically advocates training Orthodox students in 'major centres of non-Orthodox theological scholarship'. Beyond edu-cational programmes, the document calls on Orthodox and non-Orthodox to undertake 'joint work in the service of society'. And, in some situations, even 'joint programs of religious education and catechism should be developed'.

These are fair, even broad-minded and progressive expressions of mainstream Orthodox thought on Ecumenism. But the ecclesiological assumption throughout is that Orthodox participation with non-Orthodox Christians in ecumenical settings is ultimately for the purpose of making an effective witness that could eventually lead to the incorporation of the other into the true Church, i.e., the Orthodox Church.

Not all Orthodox theologians are satisfied with this. A few voices, since at least the 1930s, have been suggesting that, on this issue at least, the Orthodox have become stuck in an ideological time warp. John Zizioulas, for example, wonders whether such a closed model, with its closed Eucharist, is really adequate today:

> The concept of the Church as a confessional entity (Orthodox, Anglican, Lutheran etc.) is historically a late phenomenon and has come to complicate the situation to an alarming degree . . . Can we say that as the Eucharist brings together Jew and Greek, male and female, black and white, it should also bring together Anglican and Lutheran and Orthodox etc. in a certain local area?[15]

He acknowledges the well-known Orthodox objections to this, but insists on asking whether a confessional body (which he says is what the Orthodox have become today) can be legitimately regarded as a Church. His answer is 'no': 'A Church must incarnate people, not ideas or beliefs. A confessional Church is the most disincarnate entity there is.'[16] He argues that the local Church, to be truly the Church, must embrace all cultures of the locality, including, he implies, the ecclesial cultures. This is precisely what a confessional Church is unable to do, by definition.

Zizioulas admits that this is difficult to think about, but insists that 'we must begin to question the ecclesial status of *confessional churches* as such, and begin to work on the basis of the nature of the local Church'. This would leave all Churches re-examining their ecclesial status. This will not be easy because 'confessionalism is rooted deeply in our history'. But if we truly desire the unity of the local Church, 'we must be ready to admit that as long as confessionalism prevails no real progress towards ecclesial unity can be made'. This is a radical suggestion that, in my opinion, has not yet been taken up by the Orthodox Churches, but may prove, as he concludes, 'to be of extreme importance in the ecumenical movement'.[17]

RETHINKING RELATIONS WITH OTHER CHRISTIANS

Zizioulas is one of a number of respected Orthodox voices today and from the recent past calling for a re-thinking of Orthodox ecclesiology and relations with other Christians. This is not the place for a full exposition of this trend in modern Orthodox thought, but I would like to give some sense of the depth of views represented by this 'cloud of witnesses'.

Some of those who expressed themselves most sharply on this question in the twentieth century included Nicolas Afanasiev, Paul Evdokimov and the recently canonised Mother Maria Skobtsova.[18]

Fr Nicolas Afanasiev (1893–1966), in his essay *Una Sancta*,[19] proposed a model of autonomous Churches, each gathered around a bishop and self-organised, who share a unity that is not imposed, but emerges from mutual recognition or 'reception' of the faith and life of the others. With this model he accepts that it is possible to have disagreements and still be in communion. But this is not new, because 'history knows no period in which there was absolute dogmatic harmony' (p. 28). Similarly, it is also possible to have a break in communion, but still recognise that this is a break *within* the one Church. A break in communion therefore 'does not involve the deepest part of ecclesial life'. All who continue to participate in the Eucharist, in both Churches, are still partaking of one Eucharist, since there can only be one Eucharist eternally offered in Christ: 'There are not different Eucharists.'

What happened in 1054 was a break in communion, but not a break in ecclesial unity. The Orthodox and Catholics remained as part of the one Church of Christ. The sacraments of each remain of the Church, but they are not received by the other. Unfortunately, the polemics after 1054 were used to legitimate the separation rather than to heal it. This, in Afanasiev's view, is proof that the break in communion was not a pastoral decision inspired by devotion to the will of God and motivated by desire for ultimate healing. Instead, it was on both sides 'the sinful will of human beings acting out of consideration of ecclesiastical politics' (p. 25). It is no surprise that the long centuries of mutual isolation and acrimony that festered from this lack of love produced further deformities in both Churches. The fruit of this separation was not healing, but 'isolation of one church from the other and the impoverishment, and later the total end to the bonds of Love that ought to unite the churches'. Some lost their doctrinal truth, but others lost the truth of love. The reunion of the Churches in love will lead to their reunion in dogma (exactly the reverse of the current Orthodox position).

Despite post-1054 divergences, Afanasiev believes that an effort in love could produce renewed communion between the Roman Catholic and Orthodox Churches. But this would mean accepting each other *as is*, without placing demands on the other. Doctrinal disagreements (over papal authority for instance) would remain for the time being, and debate would continue, but these disagreements, as in the ancient Church, would cease to be Church-dividing. Afanasiev recognised the difficulties this poses, but everything should be secondary to following the commandment of love: 'In the face of the intransigence in which we live, Love ought to be the strongest feeling, for only love can conquer such hardness of heart' (p. 27).

Paul Evdokimov (1900–70) was also deeply involved in ecumenical settings, especially with Protestants. As director of a hostel for refugees, students, immigrants and troubled youth after the Second World War, he believed that the broken condition of the world demanded a 'social ecclesiology'. He called for a unified Christian witness to an 'ecumenical epiclesis', a common calling down of the Spirit of God. He insisted that Orthodox Christians should define themselves less by their differences from others than by what they have in common. The human person is not decisively defined by differences from others but mostly by the ability to identify with them, to create an 'intersubjectivity' in Christ which is communal and ecclesial.

> Society (or the world) is more desired by God than the Church for it is the ethical task of a social ecclesiology to transform the world into its proper reality . . . The world's destiny depends on the Church's creativity, her ability to welcome, her charism of being a servant and poor in the service of the poor and little ones of this world.[20]

Evdokimov recognises other Christian bodies as Churches, but also recognises the need of the Orthodox Church to stand up for historical, incarnational Christianity in the face of efforts to 'sterilize the Gospel'. The world finds much in Christianity repulsive, and this is in part the fault of Christianity's alignment with the structures and powers and comforts of this world, its self-preoccupation and pointless internal debates. Churches need to accept the reality that 'the Body of Christ overflows the limits of history' and that our vocation as Christians 'transcends the sociological cemeteries' of our particular Churches. Today, what Christians *do* is of overriding importance for the mission of Christ in a world which has no patience with mere Christian talk: 'The only message which is powerful any longer is not the one which simply repeats the words of Christ, the Word, but the one which makes him present. Only his presence will make the message, as the Gospel says, *light* and *salt* for the world.'[21] To do this, the Church will need to see itself as the Body of the *crucified* Christ, give itself and its own glories up for the love, care and sanctification of the world: 'The Church must proclaim a *social koinonia* but this demands sacrifices and sufferings for there can be no authentic communication without identification with the suffering of others' (p. 90).

This, said Evdokimov, will take the Churches well beyond polite ecumenical conversations that reinforce the impression that Christianity is interested primarily in its own issues. It will require nothing less than a new infusion of the Spirit, 'an ecumenical epiclesis', to transform the gifts of each Church into something life-giving for the world (p. 94). Such an 'epiclesis' begins with recognition that errors and sins cannot obliterate the presence of the Holy Spirit among those who confess Christ, and our schisms have not invalidated the life of Christ that flows in the life of the separated Churches: 'The Holy Spirit is not fenced out by canons.' Our internal Christian schisms – Orthodox, Roman Catholic, Reformation Churches – will be healed when we admit that we are incomplete, that we need each other's gifts to be whole, and we freely accept each other.

The supremacy of Christ is the key to relating with other Christians in the thought of St Mother Maria (Skobtsova, 1891–1945). Many others in the 'Paris School' spoke of 'churching' the world, but Mother Maria preferred to focus on Christ and to speak of 'christifying' the world. She felt that an emphasis on 'churching' all too often obscures the heart of commitment to Christ. By this she meant the desire to take every thought captive in order to obey Christ, to be able to say with St Paul, 'It is no longer I who live but Christ who lives in me' (Gal 2:20):

> If I am faced with two paths and I am in doubt, then even if all human wisdom, experience and tradition point to one of these, but I feel Christ would have followed the other – then all my doubts should immediately disappear and I should choose to follow Christ in spite of all the experience, tradition and wisdom that are opposed to it.[22]

Generous, self-emptying, kenotic love is what it means to follow Christ. This self-emptying extends as far as surrendering one's comfortable inner world:

> One need only pay attention to what Christ taught us. He said, 'if any man would come after me, let him deny himself, and take up his cross'. Self-denial is of the essence, and without it no one can follow him, without it there is no Christianity. Keep nothing for yourself. Lay aside not only material wealth but spiritual wealth as well, changing everything into Christ's love, taking it up as your cross.[23]

Christ's self-emptying sacrifice in no way diminishes his divinity or his love, just as in the Eucharist the Lamb is 'ever divided, yet never disunited, ever eaten yet never consumed'. Sacrificial generosity never diminishes the giver, but, on the contrary, according to the law of the gospel, if you give away your life you will find it returned to you with even greater richness. But if this is true, then it raises a question about the limits of the Church: 'If at the centre of the Church's life there is this sacrificial, self-giving eucharistic love, then where are the church's boundaries, where is the periphery of this centre? Here it is possible to speak of the whole of Christianity as an eternal offering of the Divine Liturgy beyond the church walls.'

Mother Maria did not judge others who continued to espouse a conventional Orthodox understanding of ecclesial limits, but she was no longer prepared to be silent about what she saw as an evangelical priority. She felt that the condition of the world (she was writing in 1937) no longer permitted Christians the luxury of letting their church life be deformed by peripheral issues. 'Perhaps in the past it was possible, but not today.'[24] Christ must be the sole focus: 'We must not allow Christ to be overshadowed by any regulations, any customs, any traditions, any aesthetic considerations, or even piety. Ultimately Christ gave us two commandments: on love for God and love for people. There is no need to complicate them, and at times supplant them, by pedantic rules.'[25] This approach could be called *kenotic ecclesiology*. But the ecclesiological implications of this self-emptying have yet to be widely discussed (although Metropolitan Georges Khodr has taken this up in relation to mission and other religions).[26] Indeed, for many Orthodox these views from seventy years ago still represent extremely radical Ecumenism. But even today there are some voices suggesting that the Orthodox should begin to reconsider their position.

Christos Yannaras, a veteran of many ecumenical dialogues, speaks of the need for an encounter willing to go outside the walls of ecclesial self-sufficiency:

> an ecumenism which will manifest a new 'coming together' through the encounter of people of any and every tradition and confession. It would be the ecumenism of concrete encounter between those who share a thirst for the life which can conquer death, people who are looking for real answers to the 'dead ends' of the civilization in which we live today . . .
>
> . . . We are full of faults, full of weaknesses which distort our human nature. But Saint Paul says that from our weakness can be born a life which will triumph over death. I dream of an ecumenism that begins with the voluntary acceptance of that weakness.[27]

Here we have a challenging vision of what Orthodox theology might bring to the wider world in the twenty-first century.

Further reading

Anglican–Orthodox Joint Doctrinal Commission, *Anglican–Orthodox Dialogue, The Dublin Agreed Statement (1984)*, London: SPCK, 1984, repr. Crestwood, NY: SVS Press, 1997.

Behr, J., Louth, A. and Conomos, D. (eds.), *Abba: The Tradition of Orthodoxy in the West. Festschrift for Bishop Kallistos (Ware) of Diokleia*, Crestwood, NY: SVS Press, 2003.

Erickson, J. and Borelli, J. *The Quest for Unity: Orthodox and Catholics in Dialogue*, Crestwood, NY: SVS Press, 1996.

Garvey, J., *Seeds of the Word: Orthodox Thinking on Other Religions*, Crestwood, NY: SVS Press, 2005.

Hilborn, D. (ed.), *Evangelicalism and the Orthodox Church*, London: Acute/Paternoster, 2001.

Hopko, T., *Speaking the Truth in Love*, Crestwood, NY: SVS Press, 2004.

Kimbrough, S. T., Jr (ed.), *Orthodox and Wesleyan Ecclesiology*, Crestwood, NY: SVS Press, 2007.

Limouris, G. (ed.), *Orthodox Visions of Ecumenism: Statements, Messages and Reports on the Ecumenical Movement 1902–1992*, Geneva: WCC, 1994.

Yannoulatos, Archbishop Anastasios, *Facing the World: Orthodox Christian Essays on Global Concerns*, Crestwood, NY: SVS Press, 2003.

Notes

1. K. Ware (Bishop of Diokleia), *The Inner Kingdom* (Crestwood, NY: SVS Press, 2000), p. 8.
2. V. Clark, *Why Angels Fall: A Journey Through Orthodox Europe from Byzantium to Kosovo* (New York: St Martin's Press, 2000), p. 414. Similar observations are found in W. Dalrymple, *From the Holy Mountain: A Journey in the Shadow of Byzantium* (London: Flamingo, 1998).
3. 'The Orthodox Church and the third millennium' (Balamand Monastery, 9 Dec. 1999), www.balamand.edu.lb/theology/ZizioulasLecture.htm.
4. www.wocati.org/COTSCongress.htm.
5. J. Byassee, 'Looking East: the impact of Orthodox theology', *Christian Century* (28 Dec. 2004).
6. T. C. Oden, *The Rebirth of Orthodoxy: Signs of New Life in Christianity* (San Francisco: Harper, 2003).
7. D. Hilborn (ed.), *Evangelicalism and the Orthodox Church* (London: Acute/Paternoster, 2001); B. McLaren, *A Generous Orthodoxy* (Grand Rapids, MI: Zondervan, 2004).
8. Zizioulas, 'The Orthodox Church and the third millennium'.
9. Byassee, 'Looking East'.
10. See, for example, P. Clayton and A. Peacocke (eds.), *In Whom We Live and Move and Have Our Being: Panentheistic Reflections on God's Presence in a Scientific World* (Grand Rapids, MI: Eerdmans, 2004); A. B. Nesteruk, *Light From the East: Theology, Science and the Eastern Orthodox Tradition* (Minneapolis, MN: Fortress Press, 2003).

11. See, further, K. C. Markides, *The Mountain of Silence* (New York: Doubleday, 2002).
12. C. Cavarnos, *Ecumenism Examined: A Concise Analytical Discussion of the Contemporary Ecumenical Movement* (Belmont, MA: Institute for Byzantine and Modern Greek Studies, 1996), p. 52.
13. A. Kalomiros, *Against False Union: Humble Thoughts of an Orthodox Christian Concerning the Attempts for Union of the One, Holy, Catholic and Apostolic Church with the So-called Churches of the West*, trans. George Gabriel (Boston, MA: Holy Transfiguration Monastery, 1967), p. 28.
14. The Holy Synod of the Orthodox Church in America, *Encyclical On Christian Unity and Ecumenism*, 1973: www.oca.org.
15. J. D. Zizioulas, *Being as Communion: Studies in Personhood and the Church* (Crestwood, NY: SVS Press, 1985), pp. 259–60. See also his 'Orthodox ecclesiology and the ecumenical movement', *Sourozh* 21 (1985), 16–27. For more on the Orthodox debate on the boundaries of the Church, see E. Clapsis, *Orthodoxy in Conversation* (Geneva and Brookline, MA: WCC / Holy Cross Orthodox Press), pp. 114–26.
16. *Being as Communion*, p. 260.
17. *Being as Communion*, p. 260.
18. See M. Plekon, 'The Russian religious revival and its theological legacy', above.
19. In M. Plekon (ed.), *Tradition Alive: On the Church and the Christian Life in Our Time. Readings From the Eastern Church* (Lanham, MD: Sheed and Ward, 2003), pp. 3–30. First published in *Irénikon* 36 (1963), 436–75.
20. 'The social dimension of Orthodox ecclesiology' in M. Plekon and A. Vinogradov (eds. and trans.), *In the World, Of the Church: A Paul Evdokimov Reader* (Crestwood, NY: SVS Press, 2001), p. 78.
21. P. Evdokimov, 'To the Churches of Christ (a message)' in Plekon and Vinogradov (eds. and trans.), *In the World, Of the Church*, p. 55.
22. Mother Maria Skobtsova, 'Types of religious lives', trans. Alvian Smirensky and Elisabeth Obolensky, *Sourozh* 76 (1999), 23.
23. Mother Maria Skobtsova, 'Types', 26.
24. Mother Maria Skobtsova, 'Types', 30.
25. In S. Hackel, *Pearl of Great Price: The Life of Mother Maria Skobtsova, 1891–1945* (Crestwood, NY: SVS Press, 1982), p. 73.
26. Abou Mrad, 'The witness of the Church in a pluralistic world: theological renaissance in the Church of Antioch', above.
27. C. Yannaras, 'Towards a new ecumenism', *Sourozh* 70 (November 1997), 1–4; www.orthodoxytoday.org/articlesprint/YannarasEcumenismP.shtml.

Glossary

Anaphora, lit. 'offering up': The central part of the eucharistic liturgy, including the recounting of all God's benefactions (*anamnesis*) and the invocation of the Holy Spirit upon the eucharistic gifts (*epiclesis*).

Antidoron, lit. 'instead of the gift': Blessed (not consecrated) bread offered to the whole congregation at the end of the eucharistic liturgy. It consists of the remainder of the loaf or loaves from which a portion has been taken to be consecrated.

Athonite: Of Mt Athos, also known as the Holy Mountain, the principal monastic centre in the Orthodox world.

Autocephaly: A Church is designated *autocephalous* (lit. 'with its own head') when it is not under the jurisdiction of any other Church and elects its own chief hierarch.

Dhimmi: (From *dhimma* ('covenant' or 'agreement')) under Islam, peoples of protected but subordinate status.

Dogmatikon: A hymn to the Mother of God on Psalm 140 [141] at Vespers, with detailed christological content.

Economy (Greek oikonomia, lit. 'household management'): The totality of God's activity towards his creation and its salvation.

Ecstasis, lit. 'being outside oneself': In contemporary Orthodox theology, a constitutive aspect of personhood that involves the state of being free from the finitude inherent in created nature, and is realised in communion with God.

Ecumenical: *See* Oikoumene.

Epiclesis: *See* Anaphora.

Filioque: The Western addition to the Nicene–Constantinopolitan Creed stating that the Holy Spirit proceeds from the Father *and the Son*.

Hesychasm: A monastic movement practising prayer in stillness (*hesychia*). Associated particularly with use of the Jesus Prayer ('Lord Jesus Christ, Son of God, have mercy on me') and with the vision of uncreated light which can be experienced in prayer.

Hypostasis: In contemporary Orthodox theology, a constitutive aspect of personhood indicating uniqueness and irreplaceability.

Kanon, lit. 'rule': (1) A regulation concerning church organisation or discipline; (2) a hymn of nine odes, each connected to a scriptural ode.

Kenotic: Related to God's 'self-emptying' (Greek *kenosis*) in the Incarnation, cf. Phil 2:7.

Millet: In the Ottoman empire, a subject 'nation' defined by religion.

Mystagogy: Introduction into a holy mystery. The term may be applied to an explanation of the significance of a mystery of the Church (St Maximus's *Mystagogy* is an exposition of the Divine Liturgy) or to the sacrament itself.

Oikoumene, lit. 'inhabited earth': Originally applied to the 'known' or 'civilised' world of the Eastern Roman, or Byzantine, period. In the present day, the term often refers to the whole Christian world. The derivative 'oe/ecumenical' indicates councils representing the Churches from the whole known world, rather than from just one region, and to the Patriarch of Constantinople as bishop of the imperial city.

Oriental Orthodox: The Syrian, Coptic, Armenian, Ethiopian and Malankara (Indian) Orthodox Churches, which reject the Council of Chalcedon. These Churches were formerly known as 'non-Chalcedonian' or 'Monophysite'.

Pentarchy, lit. 'rule of five': The theory of church structure adopted in the fifth century, ascribing particular honour to five patriarchal sees: Rome, Constantinople, Alexandria, Antioch and Jerusalem. Jurisdiction over the known world (apart from the self-governing Church of Cyprus) was divided among these patriarchates.

Romios/Rum: 'Roman', i.e. 'of the Eastern Roman Empire'. The Turkish form *Rum* referred to the Christian 'nation' in the Ottoman empire, and is still in use. In Greek, *Romios* and the abstract noun *Romiosyni* refer to a modern Greek culture rooted in Christian Byzantium rather than in classical antiquity.

Synergy: 'Cooperation' between humans and God (cf. 1 Cor.3:9). The term describes the relationship between God's grace and human freedom.

'Theotokos', lit. 'Birth-giver of God': Title of the Virgin Mary rejected by Nestorius but affirmed by the Council of Ephesus. The title underlines that God himself was conceived and born of a woman; he was not subsequently united to 'the man Jesus'.

Uniate: Churches of Eastern rite that have entered into union with Rome. Also known as 'Greek Catholic' or 'Byzantine Catholic'.

Bibliography

Primary sources

Acts of the Council of Chalcedon (AD 451)

Trans. R. Price and M. Gaddis, vols. I–III, Translated Texts for Historians, 45, Liverpool: Liverpool University Press, 2005.

Acts of the Quinisext Council 'In Trullo' (AD 692)

Trans. NPNF, series 2, vol. 14, pp. 359–408.

Apostolic canons

Trans. ANF, vol. 7, pp. 500–5.

Apostolic constitutions

Trans. ANF, vol. 7, pp. 391–505.

Athanasius of Alexandria

Against the Arians, trans. NPNF, series 2, vol. 4, pp. 306–447.
Against the Pagans ('Contra gentes'), trans. NPNF, series 2, vol. 4, pp. 4–30.
Epistle to the Africans, trans. NPNF, series 2, vol. 4, pp. 488–94.
Letter to Marcellinus in The Life of Antony and the Letter to Marcellinus, trans. R. C. Gregg, New York: Paulist Press, 1980.
The Life of St Antony, trans. C. White in *Early Christian Lives*, London: Penguin Books, 1998, pp. 7–70; *The Life of Antony and the Letter to Marcellinus*, trans. R. C. Gregg, New York: Paulist Press, 1980.
On the Decrees, trans. NPNF, series 2, vol. 4, pp. 150–72.
On the Incarnation, trans. a religious of CSMV (Community of St Mary the Virgin, Wantage, Oxon.); *St Athanasius on the Incarnation*, London and Oxford: Mowbray, 1982.
To Serapion, trans. NPNF, series 2, vol. 4, pp. 564–6.

Augustine of Hippo

Confessions, trans. R. S. Pine-Coffin, Middlesex: Penguin Books Ltd, 1961, reprinted.

Barsanuphios and John of Gaza

Barsanuphius and John, Questions and Answers, ed. and trans. D. J. Chitty, Paris: Firmin-Didot, 1966; *Barsanuphe et Jean de Gaza. Correspondance: recueil complet*, trans. L. Regnault, P. Lemaire and B. Outtier, Sablé-sur-Sarthe: Abbaye Saint-Pierre de Solesmes, 1972.
Letters, vols. I–II, ed. John Chryssavgis, Washington, DC: CUA Press, 2006–7.

Basil of Caesarea

Commentary on the Prophet Isaiah, trans. N. Lipatov, Texts and Studies in the History of Theology, 7, Mandelbachtal, Germany and Cambridge: Edition Cicero, 2001.
Divine Liturgy, trans Archimandrite Ephrem Lash, www.anastasis.org.uk/basil_liturgy.htm.
Epistle 38, To his Brother Gregory, trans. NPNF, series 2, vol. 8, pp. 137–41. On authenticity, see A. Casiday, 'Church Fathers and the shaping of Orthodox theology ' above, n. 21.
Hexaemeron, trans. NPNF, series 2, vol. 8, pp. 52–107.
Homily Against Anger, trans. Nonna Verna Harrison in *St Basil the Great: On the Human Condition*, Crestwood, NY: SVS Press, 2005, pp. 81–92.
Letters, trans. Sr Agnes Clare Way, CDP, *St Basil, Letters*, vols. I–II, Washington, DC: CUA Press, 1951–5.
On the Holy Spirit, trans. D. Anderson, Crestwood, NY: SVS Press, 1997; NPNF, series 2, vol. 8, pp. 1–50.
On the Origin of Humanity, trans. Nonna Verna Harrison in *St Basil the Great: On the Human Condition*, Crestwood, NY: SVS Press, 2005, pp. 49–64.
On the Words, 'Be Attentive to Yourself', trans. Nonna Verna Harrison in *St Basil the Great: On the Human Condition*, Crestwood, NY: SVS Press, 2005, pp. 93–105.

Clement of Alexandria

The Instructor (Paedagogus), trans. ANF, vol. 2, pp. 209–98.

Clement of Rome

First Epistle to the Corinthians, trans. K. Lake in *The Apostolic Fathers*, vol. v, Cambridge, MA, and London: William Heinemann Ltd, 1912; repr. 1959, pp. 9–121.

Diadochus of Photike

One Hundred Practical Texts of Perception and Spiritual Discernment from Diadochos of Photike, trans. and ed. J. E. Rutherford, Belfast: Belfast Byzantine Enterprises, 2000.

Didache

Staniforth, M. (trans.), *Early Christian Writings*, London: Penguin Books, 1968; rev. edn 1987, pp. 191–9.

(Ps-)Dionysius the Areopagite

On the Divine Names, trans. C. Luibheid in *Pseudo-Dionysius. The Complete Works*, New York and Mahwah: Paulist Press, 1987, pp. 49–131.

Dorotheus of Gaza

Discourses and Sayings, trans. E. Wheeler, Kalamazoo, MI: Cistercian Publications, 1977.

Eusebius of Caesarea

Oration on the Tricennalia of Constantine, trans. NPNF, series 2, vol. 1, pp. 581–610.

Evagrius Ponticus

Chapters on Prayer, trans. G. E. H. Palmer, P. Sherrard and K. Ware, *The Philokalia*, I, pp. 55–71; cf. *The Praktikos*, below.
The Praktikos and Chapters on Prayer, trans. J. E. Bamberger OCSO, Kalamazoo, MI: Cistercian Publications, 1981.

Evagrius Scholasticus

Ecclesiastical History, trans. M. Whitby, Translated Texts for Historians, 33, Liverpool: Liverpool University Press, 2000.

Gregory Akindynos

Discourse before Patriarch John XIV, trans. (Spanish) J. N. Cañellas in C. G. and V. Conticello (eds.), *La théologie byzantine et sa tradition*, vol. II, Turnhout: Brepols, 2002.

Gregory of Nazianzus

Epistle 101, trans. L. Wickham in *St Gregory of Nazianzus, On God and Christ*, Crestwood, NY: SVS Press, 2002, pp. 155–66.
Oration 2, In Defence of His Flight To Pontus, trans. NPNF, series 2, vol. 7, pp. 204–27.
Oration 14, On the Love of the Poor, trans. B. E. Daley, SJ, *Gregory of Nazianzus*, London and New York: Routledge, 2006, pp. 75–97; also trans. M. Vinson, *St Gregory of Nazianzus. Select Orations*, Washington, DC: CUA Press, 2003, pp. 39–71.
Oration 21, On the Great Athanasius, trans. NPNF, series 2, vol. 7, pp. 269–80.
Oration 31, The Fifth Theological Oration, On the Holy Spirit, trans. L. Wickham in *St Gregory of Nazianzus, On God and Christ*, Crestwood, NY: SVS Press, 2002, pp. 117–47; NPNF, series 2, vol. 7, pp. 318–28.
Oration 38, On Theophany, trans. NPNF, series 2, vol. 7, pp. 345–52.
Oration 40, On Holy Baptism, trans. NPNF, series 2, vol. 7, pp. 360–77.
Oration 42, The Last Farewell, trans. NPNF, series 2, vol. 7, pp. 385–95.
Oration 43, Panegyric on St Basil, trans. NPNF, series 2, vol. 7, pp. 395–422.
Oration 45, The Second Oration on Easter, NPNF, series 2, vol. 7, pp. 422–34.

Gregory of Nyssa

Against Eunomius, trans. NPNF, series 2, vol. 5, pp. 33–248.
Great Catechism, trans. NPNF, series 2, vol. 5, pp. 473–509.
Homilies on Ecclesiastes, ed. and trans. P. Alexandre in *Grégoire de Nysse, Homélies sur l'Écclésiaste*, SC 416, Paris: Éditions du Cerf, 1996.
Homily on the Beatitudes, trans. A. Meredith in *Gregory of Nyssa*, London and New York: Routledge, 1999, pp. 91–9; see also H. R. Drobner and A. Viciano (eds.), *Gregory of Nyssa: Homilies on the Beatitudes. An English Version with Commentary and Supporting Studies. Proceedings of the 8th Intl. Colloquium on Gregory of Nyssa*, Leiden, Boston and Cologne: Brill, 2000.
On the Creation of Humanity, trans. NPNF, series 2, vol. 5, pp. 387–427.
On the Love of the Poor, trans. S. Holman in *The Hungry are Dying*, Oxford: Oxford University Press, 2001, pp. 193–9.
On the Soul and Resurrection, trans. C. P. Roth, Crestwood, NY: SVS Press, 1993.

Gregory Palamas

Declaration of the Holy Mountain, trans. G. E. H. Palmer, P. Sherrard and K. Ware in *The Philokalia*, IV, pp. 418–25.
Homilies on the Transfiguration, trans. C. Veniamin, *The Homilies of St Gregory Palamas*, South Canaan, PA: St. Tikhon's Seminary Press, 2002.
The Triads, trans. N. Gendle, Classics of Western Spirituality, Mahwah, NJ: Paulist Press, 1983.
One Hundred and Fifty Chapters, trans. G. E. H. Palmer, P. Sherrard and K. Ware in *The Philokalia*, IV, pp. 346–417; see also R. E. Sinkewicz, CSB, *St Gregory Palamas, The One Hundred and Fifty Chapters*, Studies and Texts 83, Toronto: Pontifical Institute of Mediaeval Studies, 1988.

Irenaeus of Lyons

Against Heresies, trans. ANF, vol. 1, pp. 315–567.

Isaac of Nineveh (the Syrian)

Ascetical Homilies, trans. The Holy Transfiguration Monastery, Boston, MA: Holy Transfiguration Monastery, 1984.
Ascetical Homilies, 'The Second Part', chaps. IV–XLI, ed. and trans. S. Brock, CSCO, 224–5, Leuven: Peeters, 1995.
Mystic Treatises, trans. M. Hansbury, Crestwood, NY: SVS Press, 1989; trans. A. J. Wensinck, Amsterdam: Koninklijke Akademie van Wetenschappen, 1923; repr. Wiesbaden, 1969.

Isaiah of Scetis, Abba

Ascetic Discourses, ed. J. Chryssavgis and P. R. Penkett, Kalamazoo, MI: Cistercian Publications, 2002.

John Chrysostom

The Divine Liturgy According to St John Chrysostom, with appendices, South Canaan, PA: St Tikhon's Seminary Press, 1977.
Homilies on Genesis, trans. R. C. Hill in *St John Chrysostom. Homilies on Genesis 1–67*, 3 vols., Washington, DC: CUA Press, 1985–92.
Homilies on John, trans. NPNF, series 1, vol. 14, pp. 1–334.
Homilies on Romans, trans. NPNF, series 1, vol. 11, pp. 335–564.
Homilies on Wealth and Poverty, trans. C. P. Roth, Crestwood, NY: SVS Press, 1984.
Homily on the Enjoyment of Future Goods, PG 51, cols. 352–3.

John Climacus

Ladder of Divine Ascent, trans. C. Luibheid and N. Russell, CWS, London: SPCK, 1982.

John of Damascus (or Damascene)

Exposition of the Orthodox Faith or *Fountainhead of Knowledge*, trans. NPNF, series 2, vol. 9, pp. 1bis–101bis; ed. B. Kotter, OSB, *Die Schriften des Johannes von Damaskos*, vol. II, Berlin and New York: Walter de Gruyter, 1969, pp. 7–239.
On the Divine Images: Three Treatises Against Those Who Attack the Icons, trans. D. Anderson, Crestwood, NY: SVS Press, 1980.

John Moschos

The Spiritual Meadow, trans. J. Wortley, Kalamazoo, MI: Cistercian Publications, 1992.

Lenten Triodion

Trans. Mother Mary and K. Ware, London and Boston: Faber and Faber, 1978.

Ps-Macarius

Pseudo Macarius. The Fifty Spiritual Homilies and the Great Letter, trans. G. A. Maloney, SJ, New York and Mahwah: Paulist Press, 1992.

Maximus the Confessor

Ambigua, ed. PG 91, cols. 1032–417. 'Difficulties' 1, 5, 10, 41 and 71, trans. A. Louth, *Maximus the Confessor*, London: Routledge, 1996.
The Church's Mystagogy, trans. G. C. Berthold in *Maximus Confessor: Selected Writings*, New York and Mahwah: Paulist Press, 1985, pp. 183–225.
Opusculum 11, ed. PG 91, cols. 137–40.
Questions to Thalassius, trans. P. M. Blowers and R. L. Wilken in *On the Cosmic Mystery of Jesus Christ. Selected Writings from St Maximus the Confessor*, Crestwood, NY: SVS Press, 2003, pp. 131–43.
Record of the Trial, ed. and trans. P. Allen and B. Neil in *Maximus the Confessor and His Companions*, Oxford: Oxford University Press, 2002, pp. 49–73.

Methodius of Olympus

On the Resurrection, trans. (partially) ANF, vol. 6, pp. 364–77; ed. G. N. Bonwetsch, *Methodius*, GCS 27, Leipzig: J. C. Hinrichs, 1917, pp. 219–424.

Nicene Creed

Trans. NPNF, series 2, vol. 14, p. 3.

Nicephorus

Three Refutations against Constantine, ed. PG 100, cols. 205–534; French trans., M.-J. Mondzain-Baudinet, *Nicéphore: contre les iconoclastes*, Paris: Klincksieck, 1989.

Nicolas Cabasilas

The Life in Christ, trans. C. J. deCatanzaro, Crestwood, NY: SVS Press, 1974.

Nikodimos of the Holy Mountain (Mt Athos), with St Makarios of Corinth

A Handbook of Spiritual Counsel, trans. P. A. Chamberas, New York: Paulist Press, 1989.
The Philokalia, 5 vols. (see below for vols. I–IV in translation).
The Rudder (Pedalion), trans. D. Cummings, Chicago: Orthodox Christian Educational Society, 1957.

Origen

Commentary on the Epistle to the Romans, trans. T. P. Scheck, Washington, DC: CUA Press, 2001.
Commentary on the Gospel According to John, trans. R. E. Heine, Washington, DC: CUA Press, 1989–93.
'Commentary on the Gospel according to Matthew', ed. E. Klostermann and E. Berg, *Origenes Werke*, vol. XI: *Origenes Matthäuserklärung*, GCS 38, Leipzig: J. C. Hinrichs 1933; rev. edn U. Treu, Berlin: Akademie Verlag, 1976.
Homilies on Jeremiah, trans. J. Clark Smith, Washington, DC: CUA Press, 1998.
Homilies on Joshua, trans. B. J. Bruce, Washington, DC: CUA Press, 2002.
On First Principles, trans. G. W. Butterworth, Gloucester, MA: Peter Smith, 1973.

Peter Damascene

Treasury of Divine Knowledge, trans. G. E. H. Palmer, P. Sherrard and K. Ware in *The Philokalia*, III, pp. 74–281.

Philokalia

The Complete Text, compiled by St Nikodimos of the Holy Mountain and St Makarios of Corinth, vols. I–IV, trans. G. E. H. Palmer, P. Sherrard and K. Ware, London: Faber and Faber, 1979–95.

Photius

Letters, ed. B. Laourdas and L. G. Westerink in *Epistulae et Amphilochia*, Leipzig: B. G. Teubner, 1983–8.
The Mystagogy of the Holy Spirit, trans. J. P. Farrell, Brookline, MA: Holy Cross Orthodox Press, 1987.

Romanos the Melode

Kontakia on the Life of Christ, trans. Archimandrite Ephrem Lash, San Francisco, London and Pymble: HarperCollins, 1995.

Sayings

The Sayings of the Desert Fathers. The Alphabetical Collection, trans. B. Ward, London and Oxford: Mowbray, 1975; rev. edn 1981.

Symeon the New Theologian

Hymns of Divine Love, trans. G. A. Maloney, Denville, NJ: Dimension Books, 1978.

Theodore of Stoudios

On the Holy Icons, trans. C. P. Roth, Crestwood, NY: SVS Press, 1981.

Theodulf of Orléans

On the Holy Spirit, ed. PL 105, cols. 239–76.

Secondary reading (a select bibliography)

Afanasiev, N., *The Church of the Holy Spirit*, trans. Vitaly Permiakov, ed. M. Plekon, Notre Dame, IN: University of Notre Dame Press, 2007.
Alfeyev, Bishop Hilarion, *The Mystery of Faith. An Introduction to the Teaching and Spirituality of the Orthodox Church*, ed. Jessica Rose, London: Darton, Longman and Todd, 2002.
   'Orthodox theology on the threshold of the 21st century: will there be a renaissance of Russian theological scholarship?' *Ecumenical Review* 52.3 (July 2000), 309–25.
   Orthodox Witness Today, Geneva: WCC Publications, 2006.
   The Spiritual World of St Isaac the Syrian, Kalamazoo, MI: Cistercian Publications, 2000.
Andreopoulos, A., *Metamorphosis. The Transfiguration in Byzantine Theology and Iconography*, Crestwood, NY: SVS Press, 2005.
Anglican–Orthodox Joint Doctrinal Commission, *Anglican–Orthodox Dialogue: The Dublin Agreed Statement (1984)*, London: SPCK, 1984; repr. Crestwood, NY: SVS Press, 1997.
Arseniev, N., *Mysticism and the Eastern Church*, trans. A. Chambers, Crestwood, NY: SVS Press, 1979.
Ayres, L., *Nicaea and Its Legacy: An Approach to Fourth Century Trinitarian Theology*, Oxford: Oxford University Press, 2004.

Baggley, J., *Doors of Perception. Icons and Their Spiritual Significance*, Crestwood, NY: SVS Press, 1988.

Barrois, G., *The Fathers Speak. St Basil the Great, St Gregory Nazianzus, St Gregory of Nyssa*, Crestwood, NY: SVS Press, 1986.

Scripture Readings in Orthodox Worship, Crestwood, NY: SVS Press, 1977.

Baum, W. and Winkler, D., *The Church of the East*, London: Routledge, 2003.

Behr, J., *Formation of Christian Theology*, vol. I: *The Way to Nicaea*, Crestwood, NY: SVS Press, 2001.

Formation of Christian Theology, vol. II: *The Nicene Faith*, Pts 1–2, Crestwood, NY: SVS Press, 2004.

The Mystery of Christ: Life in Death, Crestwood, NY: SVS Press, 2006.

Behr, J., Louth, A. and Conomos, D. (eds.), *Abba. The Tradition of Orthodoxy in the West. Festschrift for Bishop Kallistos (Ware) of Diokleia*, Crestwood, NY: SVS Press, 2003.

Behr-Sigel, E., *The Ministry of Women in the Church*, trans. S. Bigham, Torrance, CA: Oakwood Publications, 1991.

The Place of the Heart. An Introduction to Orthodox Spirituality, trans. S. Bigham, Torrance, CA: Oakwood Publications, 1992.

Behr-Sigel, E. and Ware, K., *The Ordination of Women in the Orthodox Church*, Geneva: WCC, 2003.

Bigham, S., *Early Christian Attitudes Towards Images*, Rollinsford, NH: Orthodox Research Institute, 2004.

Binns, J., *An Introduction to the Christian Orthodox Churches*, Cambridge: Cambridge University Press, 2002.

Blane, A. (ed.), *Georges Florovsky: Russian Intellectual, Orthodox Churchman*, Crestwood, NY: SVS Press, 1993.

Bobrinskoy, B., *The Compassion of the Father*, trans. A. P. Gythiel, Crestwood, NY: SVS Press, 2003.

'The Church and the Holy Spirit in twentieth-century Russia', *Ecumenical Review* 52.3 (July 2000), 326–42.

The Mystery of the Trinity. Trinitarian Experience and Vision in the Biblical and Patristic Tradition, trans. A. P. Gythiel, Crestwood, NY: SVS Press, 1999.

Bouteneff, P., 'The mystery of union: elements in an Orthodox sacramental theology', in G. Rowell and C. Hall (eds.), *Gestures of God: Explorations in Sacramental Theology*, London and New York: Continuum, 2004, pp. 91–107.

Sweeter Than Honey: Orthodox Thinking on Dogma and Truth, Crestwood, NY: SVS Press, 2006.

Breck, J., *God With Us. Critical Issues in Christian Life and Faith*, Crestwood, NY: SVS Press, 2003.

The Power of the Word in the Worshiping Church, Crestwood, NY: SVS Press, 1986.

Scripture in Tradition: The Bible and Its Interpretation in the Orthodox Church, Crestwood, NY: SVS Press, 2001.

Bulgakov, S., *The Orthodox Church*, Maitland, FL: Three Hierarchs Seminary Press, 1935.

Burton-Christie, D., *The Word in the Desert: Scripture and the Quest for Holiness in Early Christian Monasticism*, Oxford and New York: Oxford University Press, 1993.

Casiday, A., *Evagrius Ponticus*, London: Routledge, 2006.

Cavarnos, C., *Ecumenism Examined: A Concise Analytical Discussion of the Contemporary Ecumenical Movement*, Belmont, MA: Institute for Byzantine and Modern Greek Studies, 1996.

St Nikodemos the Hagiorite (Modern Orthodox Saints, 5), Belmont, MA: Institute for Byzantine and Modern Greek Studies, 1974.

Chadwick, H., *East and West: The Making of a Rift in the Church*, Oxford: Oxford University Press, 2003.

Chryssavgis, J., *Beyond the Shattered Image*, Minneapolis, MN: Light and Life Publishing, 1999.

Light through Darkness: The Orthodox Tradition, London: Darton, Longman and Todd, 2004.

Soul Mending: The Art of Spiritual Direction, Brookline, MA: Holy Cross Orthodox Press, 2000.

Clapsis, E., *Orthodoxy in Conversation: Orthodox Ecumenical Engagements*, Geneva and Brookline, MA: WCC / Holy Cross Orthodox Press, 2000.

Clayton, P. and Peacocke, A. (eds.), *In Whom We Live and Move and Have Our Being: Panentheistic Reflections on God's Presence in a Scientific World*, Grand Rapids, MI, and Cambridge: Eerdmans, 2004.

Clément, O., 'Martyrs and confessors', *Ecumenical Review* 52.3 (July 2000), 343–50.

On Human Being: A Spiritual Anthropology, London: New City, 2000.

The Roots of Christian Mysticism, London: New City, 1993.

Constas, N. P., 'Commentary on the patriarchal message on the Day of the Protection of the Environment', *GOTR* 35.3 (1990), 179–94.

Cross, L., *Eastern Christianity. The Byzantine Tradition*, Sydney and Philadelphia: E. J. Dwyer, 1988.

Cunningham, M. B., *Faith in the Byzantine World*, Oxford: Lion Hudson, 2002.

'The meeting of the old and the new: the typology of Mary the Theotokos in Byzantine homilies and hymns', in R. N. Swanson (ed.), *The Church and Mary*, Studies in Church History 39, Woodbridge and Rochester: Boydell Press, 2004, pp. 52–62.

David, S. T., Kendall, P., SJ, and O'Collins, G., SJ (eds.), *The Trinity: An Interdisciplinary Symposium on the Trinity*, Oxford: Oxford University Press, 1999.

Davis, N., *A Long Walk to Church: A Contemporary History of Russian Orthodoxy*, 2nd edn, Boulder, CO: Westview Press, 2003.

Demacopoulos, G., *Five Models of Spiritual Direction in the Early Church*, Notre Dame, IN: Notre Dame University Press, 2007.

Driscoll, J., *Steps to Spiritual Perfection: Studies on Spiritual Progress in Evagrius Ponticus*, Mahwah, NJ: Paulist Press, 2003.

Dvornik, F. *The Photian Schism*, Cambridge: Cambridge University Press, 1948.

Ellis, J., *The Russian Orthodox Church: A Contemporary History*, Bloomington and Indianapolis, IN: Indiana University Press, 1986.

Erickson, J. and Borelli, J., *The Quest for Unity: Orthodox and Catholics in Dialogue*, Crestwood, NY: SVS Press, 1996.

Evdokimov, P., *Ages of the Spiritual Life*, Crestwood, NY: SVS Press, 1998.

The Art of the Icon: A Theology of Beauty, trans. Fr Steven Bigham, Redondo Beach, CA: Oakwood Publications, 1990.

Woman and the Salvation of the World: A Christian Anthropology on the Charisms of Woman, trans. A. P. Gythiel, Crestwood, NY: SVS Press, 1994.

Florensky, P., *The Pillar and Ground of the Truth*, trans. B. Jakim, Princeton: Princeton University Press, 1997.

Florovsky, G., *Collected Works of Church History*, 14 vols., vols. I–IV, Belmont, MA: Nordland Publishing Co., 1972– ; vols. VI–XIV, Vaduz: Büchervertriebsanstalt, 1987–9.

Fortounatto, M., 'The veneration of the Mother of God and her icon', *Priests and People* 2.4 (May 1988), 140–5.

Garvey, J., *Seeds of the Word: Orthodox Thinking on Other Religions*, Crestwood, NY: SVS Press, 2005.

Gavrilyuk, P., 'The kenotic theology of Sergius Bulgakov', *Scottish Journal of Theology* 58 (2005), 251–69.

'Universal salvation in the eschatology of Sergius Bulgakov', *JTS*. n.s. 57.1 (2006), 110–32.

Gillet, L. (Archimandrite), *Orthodox Spirituality: An Outline of the Orthodox Ascetical and Mystical Tradition*, Crestwood, NY: SVS Press, 1996.

Golitzin, A., *The Living Witness of the Holy Mountain*, South Canaan, PA: St Tikhon's Press, 1996.

'Spirituality: Eastern Christian' in *Encyclopedia of Monasticism*, vol. II, Chicago: Fitzroy Dearborn, 2000.

Hackel, S., *Pearl of Great Price: The Life of Mother Maria Skobtsova, 1891–1945*, Crestwood, NY: SVS Press, 1981.

Hadjinicolaou, J. (ed.), *Synaxis: An Anthology of the Most Significant Orthodox Theology in Greece Appearing in the Journal Synaxi from 1982 to 2002*, 3 vols., Montreal: Alexander Press, 2006.

Hamant, Y., *Alexander Men: A Witness for Contemporary Russia (A Man for Our Times)*, Torrance, CA: Oakwood Publications, 1995.

Hanson, R. P. C., *The Search for the Christian Doctrine of God. The Arian Controversy, 318–381*, Edinburgh: T. & T. Clark, 1988.

Harrison, Verna E. F., 'Gregory of Nyssa on human unity and diversity', *Studia Patristica* 41 (2006), 333–44.

'Male and female in Cappadocian theology', *JTS*, n.s. 41 (1990), 441–71.

'Women, human identity and the image of God: Antiochene interpretations', *Journal of Early Christian Studies* 9 (2001), 205–49.

Hausherr, I., *Penthos: The Doctrine of Compunction in the Christian East*, Kalamazoo, MI: Cistercian Publications, 1982.

Hilborn, D. (ed.), *Evangelicalism and the Orthodox Church: A Report by the Evangelical Alliance Commission on Unity and Truth Among Evangelicals (ACUTE)*, London: Acute/Paternoster, 2001.

Hopko, T., 'The Bible in the Orthodox Church', *SVTQ* 14 (1970), 66–99.

Speaking the Truth in Love, Crestwood, NY: SVS Press, 2004.

'The Transfiguration Liturgy in the Orthodox Church' in S. T. Kimbrough Jr (ed.), *Orthodox and Wesleyan Scriptural Understanding and Practice*, Crestwood, NY: SVS Press, 2005, pp. 305–20.

Hussey, J. M., *The Orthodox Church in the Byzantine Empire*, Oxford: Clarendon Press, 1986.

Ignatius IV, Patriarch of Antioch, *Orthodoxy and Other Issues*, Balamand, Lebanon: Balamand University Press, 2006.

Jakim, B. and Bird, R. (trans. and eds.), *On Spiritual Unity. A Slavophile Reader*, Hudson, NY: Lindisfarne Books, 1998.

Jevtić, A., Bishop of Herzegovina, 'The eschatological dimension of the Church', *GOTR* 38.1–4 (1993), 91–102.

Kalaitzidis, P., 'The temptation of Judas: Church and national identities', *GOTR* 47 (2002), 357–79.

Karras, Valerie A., 'Eschatology', in S. F. Parsons (ed.), *The Cambridge Companion to Feminist Theology*, Cambridge: Cambridge University Press, 2002, pp. 243–60.

'Orthodox theologies of women and ordained ministry', in A. Papanikolaou and E. Prodromou (eds.), *Thinking Through Faith*, Crestwood, NY: SVS Press, 2008.

Kelly, J. N. D., *Early Christian Creeds*, 3rd edn, Harlow, Essex: Longman, 1972.

Early Christian Doctrines, 5th edn, London: A. and C. Black, 1977.

Khodr, Metropolitan Georges, 'Christianity in a pluralistic world', *Ecumenical Review* 23 (1971), 118–28.

'The Orthodox in the Lebanon: to be witnesses to the meekness of the Gospel', *Sourozh* 2 (1980), 42–9.

Kimbrough, S. T., Jr (ed.), *Orthodox and Wesleyan Ecclesiology*, Crestwood, NY: SVS Press, 2007.

Orthodox and Wesleyan Spirituality, Crestwood, NY: SVS Press, 2002.

Orthodox and Wesleyan Scriptural Understanding and Practice, Crestwood, NY: SVS Press, 2005.

Kitzinger, E., 'The cult of images before the age of Iconoclasm', *Dumbarton Oaks Papers* 8 (1954), 83–150.

Kontoglou, F., *Byzantine Sacred Art: Selected Writings*, Belmont, MA: Institute for Byzantine and Modern Greek Studies, 1985.

Krivocheine, B. (Archbishop), *In the Light of Christ: Saint Symeon the New Theologian. Life, Spirituality, Doctrine*, Crestwood, NY: SVS Press, 1986.

Larchet, J., *The Theology of Illness*, Crestwood, NY: SVS Press, 2002.

Lash, Archimandrite Ephrem, 'Mary in Eastern Church literature', in A. Stacpoole, OSB (ed.), *Mary in Doctrine and Devotion*, Dublin: Columba Press, 1990, pp. 58–80.

'Search the scriptures: a sermon preached before the University of Cambridge', *Sourozh* 64 (May 1996), 1–11.

www.anastasis.org.uk (contains English translations of many Orthodox liturgical texts).

Limouris, G., *Icons. Windows on Eternity. Theology and Spirituality in Colour*, Geneva: WCC Publications, 1990.

(ed.), *Orthodox Visions of Ecumenism: Statements, Messages and Reports on the Ecumenical Movement 1902–1992*, Geneva: WCC, 1994.

Lossky, V., *In the Image and Likeness of God*, ed. J. H. Erickson and T. E. Bird, Crestwood, NY: SVS Press, 1974.

The Mystical Theology of the Eastern Church, London: James Clarke & Co., 1957; repr. Crestwood, NY: SVS Press, 1998.

Orthodox Theology: An Introduction, trans. I. and I. Kesarcodi-Watson, Crestwood, NY: SVS Press, 1978.

The Vision of God, trans. A. Morehouse, London: Faith Press, 1963.

Louth, A., *Maximus the Confessor*, London and New York: Routledge, 1996.

The Origins of the Christian Mystical Tradition From Plato to Denys, Oxford: Clarendon Press, 1981.

Louth, A. and Casiday, A. (eds.), *Byzantine Orthodoxies*, Aldershot: Ashgate, 2006.

Markides, K. C., *The Mountain of Silence*, New York: Doubleday, 2002.

McGuckin, J., *The Orthodox Church*, Oxford: Blackwell Publishing, 2008.

'Patterns of biblical exegesis in the Cappadocian Fathers: Basil the Great, Gregory the Theologian, and Gregory of Nyssa' in Kimbrough (ed.), *Orthodox and Wesleyan Scriptural Understanding and Practice*, pp. 37–54.

'Recent biblical hermeneutics in patristic perspective: the tradition of Orthodoxy', in Stylianopoulos (ed.), *Sacred Text and Interpretation*, pp. 293–324.

Meerson, M. A., *Modern Russian Theology: Bukharev, Soloviev, Bulgakov*, Grand Rapids, MI: Eerdmans, 2000.

The Trinity of Love in Modern Russian Theology, Quincy, IL: Franciscan Press, 1998.

Men, A., *Christianity for the Twenty-first Century: The Prophetic Writings of Alexander Men*, ed. and trans. Elizabeth Roberts and Ann Shukman, New York: Continuum, 1996.

Meyendorff, J., *Byzantine Theology. Historical Trends and Doctrinal Themes*, London and Oxford: Mowbrays, 1974.

Christ in Eastern Christian Thought, Crestwood, NY: SVS Press, 1975.

'Creation in the history of Orthodox theology', *SVTQ* 27 (1983), 27–37.

Living Tradition, Crestwood, NY: SVS Press, 1978.

The Orthodox Church: Its Past and Its Role in the World Today, London: Darton, Longman and Todd, 1962.

Rome, Constantinople, Moscow: Historical and Theological Studies, Crestwood, NY: SVS Press, 1996.

St Gregory Palamas and Orthodox Spirituality, Crestwood, NY: SVS Press, 1974.

A Study of Gregory Palamas, Crestwood, NY: SVS Press, 1998.

Mitri, T. (ed.), *Religion and Human Rights: A Christian–Muslim Discussion*, Geneva: WCC, 1996.

Murray, Sister M. C., 'Art and the early Church', *JTS*, n.s., 28 (1977), 303–44.

Nellas, P., *Deification in Christ: Orthodox Perspectives on the Nature of the Human Person*, Crestwood, NY: SVS Press, 1987.

'Redemption or deification? Nicholas Kavasilas and Anselm's question "Why did God become Man?"' in J. Hadjinicolaou (ed.), *Synaxis: An Anthology of the Most Significant Orthodox Theology in Greece Appearing in the Journal Synaxi from 1982 to 2002*, vol. 1 (Montreal: Alexander Press, 2006), pp. 79–98.

Nesteruk, A., *Light from the East: Theology, Science and the Eastern Orthodox Tradition*, Minneapolis, MN: Fortress Press, 2003.

Nichols, A., *Light from the East: Authors and Themes in Orthodox Theology*, London: Sheed and Ward, 1995.

Theology in the Russian Diaspora: Church, Fathers, Eucharist in Nikolai Afanas'ev 1893–1966, Cambridge: Cambridge University Press, 1989.

Osborne, B., Bishop of Sergievo, 'Beauty in the Divine and in nature', *Sourozh* 70 (November 1997), 28–37.

Ouspensky, L., *Theology of the Icon*, 2 vols., trans. A. Gythiel with E. Meyendorff, Crestwood, NY: SVS Press, 1992.

Ouspensky, L. and Lossky, V., *The Meaning of Icons*, Crestwood, NY: SVS Press, 1983.

Papadakis, A., with Meyendorff, J., *The Christian East and the Rise of the Papacy*, Crestwood, NY: SVS Press, 1994.

Papanikolaou, A., *Being with God: Trinity, Apophaticism, and Divine–Human Communion*, Notre Dame, IN: University of Notre Dame Press, 2006.

'Byzantium, Orthodoxy and democracy', *Journal of the American Academy of Religion* 71.1 (March 2003), 75–98.

Papathanasiou, A. N., *Future, the Background of History: Essays on Church Mission in an Age of Globalization*, Montreal: Alexander Press, 2005.

'Reconciliation: the major conflict in post-modernity. An Orthodox contribution to a missiological dialogue', *Sobornost* 28.1 (2006), 8–20.

'Theological challenges facing the Church of Greece', *Koinonia, The Journal of the Anglican and Eastern Churches Association*, n.s. 49 (Summer 2004), 11–20.

Parry, K., *Depicting the Word. Byzantine Iconophile Thought of the Eighth and Ninth Centuries*, Leiden, New York and Cologne: Brill, 1996.

(ed.), *The Blackwell Companion to Eastern Christianity*, Oxford: Blackwell Publishing, 2007.

Parry, K., Melling, D. J., Brady, D., Griffith, S. H. and Healey, J. F., *The Blackwell Dictionary of Eastern Christianity*, Oxford: Blackwell Publishing, 1999.

Patton, K. C. and Hawley, J. S. (eds.), *Holy Tears: Weeping in the Religious Imagination*, Princeton and Oxford: Princeton University Press, 2005.

Pelikan, J., *The Christian Tradition. A History of the Development of Doctrine*, vol. II: *The Spirit of Eastern Christendom (600–1700)*, Chicago and London: University of Chicago Press, 1974.

Christianity and Classical Culture: The Metamorphosis of Natural Theology in the Christian Encounter with Hellenism, New Haven and London: Yale University Press, 1993.

Imago Dei. The Byzantine Apologia for Icons, New Haven and London: Yale University Press, 1990.

The Vindication of Tradition, New Haven: Yale University Press, 1984.

Peters, G., 'Peter of Damascus and early Christian spiritual theology', *Patristica et medievalia* 26 (2005), 89–109.

'Recovering a lost spiritual theologian: Peter of Damascus and the Philokalia', *SVTQ* 49 (2005), 437–59.

Pevear, R. and Volokhonsky, L. (trans.), *Mother Maria Skobtsova: Essential Writings*, Maryknoll, NY: Orbis, 2003.

Plekon, M., *Living Icons: Persons of Faith in the Eastern Church*, Notre Dame, IN: University of Notre Dame Press, 2002.

(ed.), *Tradition Alive: On the Church and the Christian Life in Our Time. Readings from the Eastern Church*, Lanham, MD: Rowman and Littlefield / Sheed and Ward, 2003.

Plekon, M. and Vinogradov, A. (trans. and eds.), *In the World, Of the Church. A Paul Evdokimov Reader*, Crestwood, NY: SVS Press, 2001.

Plested, M., *The Macarian Legacy: The Place of Macarius-Symeon in the Eastern Christian Tradition*, Oxford: Oxford University Press, 2004.

Pospielovsky, D. V., *A History of Soviet Atheism in Theory and Practice, and the Believer*, 3 vols., New York: St Martin's Press, 1987–8.

Prestige, G. L., *God in Patristic Thought*, London: Heinemann, 1936; repr. SPCK, 1952.

Ramfos, S., *Like a Pelican in the Wilderness*, Brookline, MA: Holy Cross Orthodox Press, 2000.

Ramsey, B., *Beginning to Read the Fathers*, New York: Paulist Press, 1985.

Romanides, J. S., *An Outline of Orthodox Patristic Dogmatics*, Rollinsford: Orthodox Research Institute, 2004.

Romanides, J. S., *The Ancestral Sin*, Ridgewood, NJ: Zephyr Press, 2002.

Runciman, Sir S., *The Great Church in Captivity*, Cambridge: Cambridge University Press, 1968.

Russell, N., *The Doctrine of Deification in the Greek Patristic Tradition*, Oxford: Oxford University Press, 2004.

'Theosis and Gregory Palamas: continuity or doctrinal change?' *SVTQ* 50 (2006), 357–79.

Sakharov, N. V., *I Love Therefore I Am: The Theological Legacy of Archimandrite Sophrony*, Crestwood, NY: SVS Press, 2002.

Schmemann, A., *The Eucharist*, Crestwood, NY: SVS Press, 1987.

For the Life of the World: Sacraments and Orthodoxy, Crestwood, NY: SVS Press, 1973.

Introduction to Liturgical Theology, Leighton Buzzard: The Faith Press, and Crestwood, NY: SVS Press, 1966; 2nd edn 1975.

The Journals of Father Alexander Schmemann, trans. J. Schmemann, Crestwood, NY: SVS Press, 2000.

'Liturgy and eschatology', *Sobornost* 7.1 (1985), 9–10.

Liturgy and Tradition. Theological Reflections of Alexander Schmemann, ed. T. Fisch, Crestwood, NY: SVS Press, 1990.

Sophrony, Archimandrite, *His Life is Mine*, London: Mowbrays, 1977.

St Silouan the Athonite, trans. R. Edmonds, Tolleshunt Knights: Stavropegic Monastery of St John the Baptist, 1991.

Speake, G., *Mount Athos. Renewal in Paradise*, New Haven and London: Yale University Press, 2002.

Stăniloae, D., *The Experience of God. Orthodox Dogmatic Theology*, 2 vols., trans. I. Ionita and R. Barringer, Brookline, MA: Holy Cross Orthodox Press, 1994–2000.

Orthodox Spirituality. A Practical Guide for the Faithful and a Definitive Manual for the Scholar, South Canaan, PA: St Tikhon's Seminary Press, 2002.

Stylianopoulos, T. G., *The New Testament: An Orthodox Perspective, Scripture, Tradition, Hermeneutics* Brookline, MA: Holy Cross Orthodox Press, 1997.

'Orthodox biblical interpretation', in John H. Hayes (ed.), *Dictionary of Biblical Interpretation*, Nashville, TN: Abingdon Press, 1999, pp. 227–30.

The Spirit of Truth: Ecumenical Perspectives on the Holy Spirit, Brookline, MA: Holy Cross Orthodox Press, 1985.

(ed.), *Sacred Text and Interpretation: Perspectives in Orthodox Biblical Studies, Essays in Honor of Professor Savas Agourides*, Brookline, MA: Holy Cross Orthodox Press, 2006.

Tarazi, P., *Historical Trends*, Crestwood, NY: SVS Press, 1991.

The New Testament: Introduction, vols. I–IV, Crestwood, NY: SVS Press, 1999–2004.

The Old Testament: Introduction, vols. I–III, Crestwood, NY: SVS Press, 1991–6.

Theokritoff, E., 'The poet as expositor in the golden age of Byzantine hymnography and in the experience of the Church', in Kimbrough, Jr (ed.), *Orthodoxy and Wesleyan Scriptural Understanding and Practice*, pp. 259–75.

'Praying the scriptures in Orthodox worship' and 'The poet as expositor in the golden age of Byzantine hymnography and in the experience of the Church', in Kimbrough, Jr (ed.), *Orthodoxy and Wesleyan Scriptural Understanding and Practice*, pp. 73–87, 259–75.

Torrance, T. F. (ed.), *Theological Dialogues Between Orthodox and Reformed Churches*, Edinburgh and London: Scottish Academic Press, 1985.

Turcescu, L. (ed.), *Dumitru Staniloae. Tradition and Modernity in Theology*, Iasi: Center for Romanian Studies, 2002.

Vallière, P., *Modern Russian Theology: Bukharev, Soloviev, Bulgakov – Orthodox Theology in a New Key*, Grand Rapids, MI: Eerdmans, 2000.

Vasileos of Stavronikita, Archimandrite, *Hymn of Entry. Liturgy and Life in the Orthodox Church*, Crestwood, NY: St Vladimir's Seminary Press, 1984.

Vassiliadis, P., 'Canon and authority of scripture: an Orthodox hermeneutical perspective', in Kimbrough, Jr (ed.), *Orthodox and Wesleyan Scriptural Understanding and Practice*, pp. 21–35.

Eucharist and Witness: Orthodox Perspectives on the Unity and Mission of the Church, Brookline, MA: Holy Cross Orthodox Press, 1998.

'Greek theology in the making. Trends and facts in the 80s – vision for the 90s', *SVTQ* 35.1 (1991), 33–52.

Vischer, L. (ed.), *Spirit of God, Spirit of Christ. Ecumenical Reflections on the Filioque Controversy*, Geneva: WCC, 1981.

Walker, A. and Carras, C. (eds.), *Living Orthodoxy in the Modern World: Orthodox Christianity and Society*, London: SPCK, 1996; repr. Crestwood, NY: SVS Press, 2000.

Ware, K. T. (now Metropolitan of Diokleia), 'Orthodox and Catholics in the seventeenth century: schism or intercommunion?' in D. Baker (ed.), *Schism, Heresy and Religious Protest*, Cambridge: Cambridge University Press, 1972, pp. 259–76.

The Orthodox Way, Oxford: Mowbray, 1979.

Ware, K. T. (Bishop of Diokleia), *How Are We Saved? The Understanding of Salvation in the Orthodox Tradition*, Minneapolis, MN: Light and Life, 1996.

The Inner Kingdom, Collected Works, vol. I, Crestwood, NY: SVS Press, 2000.

Through the Creation to the Creator, London: Friends of the Centre, 1997.

'The unity of the human person according to the Greek Fathers', in A. Peacocke and G. Gillett (eds.), *Persons and Personality: A Contemporary Enquiry*, Oxford: Basil Blackwell, 1987, pp. 197–206.

Ware, T. (now Kallistos, Metropolitan of Diokleia), *The Orthodox Church, New Edition*, London: Penguin Books, 1993.

Williams, R., *Sergii Bulgakov: Toward a Russian Political Theology*, Edinburgh: T. & T. Clark, 1999.

Wimbush, V. and Valantasis, R. (eds.), *Asceticism*, Oxford and New York: Oxford University Press, 1995.

Yannaras, C., *Elements of Faith: An Introduction to Orthodox Theology*, trans. Keith Schram, Edinburgh: T. & T. Clark, 1991.

The Freedom of Morality, trans. E. Briere, Crestwood, NY: SVS Press, 1984.

On the Absence and Unknowability of God: Heidegger and the Areopagite, trans. H. Ventis, ed. A. Louth, Edinburgh: T. & T. Clark, 2005.

Orthodoxy and the West, trans. P. Chamberas and N. Russell, Brookline, MA: Holy Cross Orthodox Press, 2006.

Person and Eros, trans. N. Russell, Brookline, MA: Holy Cross Orthodox Press, forthcoming.

'Theology in present-day Greece', *SVTQ* 16.4 (1972), 195–214.

Yannoulatos, Archbishop Anastasios, *Facing the World: Orthodox Christian Essays on Global Concerns*, Crestwood, NY: SVS Press, 2003.

'The purpose and motive of mission from an Orthodox point of view', *International Review of Mission* 54 (1965), 298–307.

Young, F. M., *Biblical Exegesis and the Formation of Christian Culture*, Cambridge: Cambridge University Press, 1997.

Zander, V., *St Seraphim of Sarov*, London: SPCK, 1975.

Zernov, N., *Eastern Christendom. A Study of the Origin and Development of the Eastern Orthodox Church*, London: Weidenfeld and Nicolson, 1961.

The Russian Religious Renaissance of the Twentieth Century, New York: Harper & Row, 1963.

The Russians and Their Church, Crestwood, NY: SVS Press, 3rd edn, 1978.

Zizioulas, J. D., Metropolitan of Pergamon, 'Apostolic continuity and Orthodox theology: towards a synthesis of two perspectives', *SVTQ* 19.2 (1975), 75–108.

Being as Communion. Studies in Personhood and the Church, Crestwood, NY: SVS Press, 1985.

Communion and Otherness. Further Studies in Personhood and the Church, ed. P. McPartlan, London and New York: T. & T. Clark, 2006.

'The Eucharist and the Kingdom', *Sourozh* 58 (November 1994), 1–12; 59 (January 1995), 22–38; 60 (May 1995), 32–46.

Eucharist, Bishop, Church: The Unity of the Church in the Divine Eucharist and the Bishop During the First Three Centuries, trans. E. Theokritoff, Brookline, MA: Holy Cross Orthodox Press, 2001.

'Preserving God's creation: three lectures on theology and ecology', *King's Theological Review* 12 (1989), 1–5, 41–5; 13 (1990), 1–5.

Index